Using

Skilled

Dialogue

to Transform
Challenging Interactions

Using
Skilled
Dialogue
to Transform
Challenging Interactions

Honoring Identity,
Voice, & Connection

by

Isaura Barrera, Ph.D.
The University of New Mexico
Albuquerque

and

Lucinda Kramer, Ph.D.
National University
Costa Mesa, California

·P A U L·H·
BROOKES
PUBLISHING CO. ®

Baltimore • London • Sydney

Paul H. Brookes Publishing Co.
Post Office Box 10624
Baltimore, Maryland 21285-0624
USA

www.brookespublishing.com

Typeset by Integrated Publishing Solutions, Grand Rapids, Michigan.
Manufactured in the United States of America by
Sheridan Books, Inc., Chelsea, Michigan.

Permission to use the Trust Bridge Exercise information on pages 91–92 is gratefully
acknowledged; from Bryner, A., & Markova, D. (1996). *An unused intelligence: Physical
thinking for 21st century leadership* (Chapter 3, Practice 5). San Francisco: Conari Press.

The case stories in this book are composites based on the authors' experiences. These
composite accounts do not represent the lives or experiences of specific individuals, and
no implications should be inferred.

Library of Congress Cataloging-in-Publication Data
Barrera, Isaura.
    Using skilled dialogue to transform challenging interactions: honoring identity, voice,
and connection / by Isaura Barrera and Lucinda Kramer.
        p.   cm.
    Includes bibliographical references and index.
    ISBN-13: 978-1-55766-955-1 (pbk.)
    ISBN-10: 1-55766-955-4 (pbk.)
    1. Social interaction—Study and teaching (Early childhood).   2. Social learning.
3. Early childhood special education.   4. Multicultural education.   5. Problem
children—Behavior modification.   I. Kramer, Lucinda.   II. Title.
LB1139.S6B36 2009
371.9'04393—dc22   2009008677

British Library Cataloguing in Publication data are available from the British Library.

2012   2011   2010   2009
10   9   8   7   6   5   4   3   2   1

Contents

About the Authors vii
Foreword   *Lynn Andrews and Charlotte M. Brantley* ix
Preface xiii
Acknowledgments xvi
Introduction: Beyond Understanding Cultural Linguistic Diversity xvii
Glossary xxv

Part I	Honoring Identity, Voice, and Connection 1
Chapter 1	Nurturing Children's Spirits and Sense of Self 5
Chapter 2	Seeing Different Behaviors Differently 15

Part II	Skilled Dialogue Framework 33
Chapter 3	Respect, Reciprocity, and Responsiveness 37
Chapter 4	Choosing Relationship over Control 51
Chapter 5	Setting the Stage for Miracles 71
Chapter 6	Between Dispositions and Outcomes: Skilled Dialogue in Action 93

Part III	Skilled Dialogue Strategies 107
Chapter 7	Differences Do Not Make People Wrong: *Welcoming* and *Allowing* 113
Chapter 8	Diversity Is Always Life Enhancing: *Sense-Making* and *Appreciating* 131
Chapter 9	There Is Always a Third Choice: *Joining* and *Harmonizing* 149

Part IV	Skilled Dialogue Applications: Weaving Dispositions and Strategies 167
Chapter 10	Challenging Adult–Adult Interactions 177
Chapter 11	Challenging Adult–Child Interactions 195
Chapter 12	Practice Cases 227

References 235

Appendix A	Overview of Behavioral Approaches to Challenging Behavior 241
Appendix B	Frequently Asked Questions 249
Appendix C	Blank Forms 253

Index 263

About the Authors

Isaura Barrera, Ph.D., grew up on the Texas–Mexico border speaking only Spanish until the age of 6. The challenges and gifts of this bilingual and bicultural environment sparked her interest in communication across diverse perspectives, languages, and cultures. Skilled Dialogue was born out of her experiences with those challenges and gifts. She holds a master's degree in speech pathology and received her doctoral degree in educational evaluation from the University at Buffalo, The State University of New York, with concentrations in special education, early childhood, and bilingual education. Her professional interests are in early childhood, bilingual education, and special education. Dr. Barrera is currently a faculty member in special education in the College of Education at The University of New Mexico in Albuquerque.

Lucinda Kramer, Ph.D., earned her doctoral degree in special education with a concentration in early childhood special education from The University of New Mexico. As an associate professor in the Department of Special Education at National University in Costa Mesa, California, she coordinates the credential and graduate programs in special education. Dr. Kramer has served as Chair of the Multicultural Committee for the Council for Exceptional Children's Division for Early Childhood and has worked with teachers, families, schools, and agencies in Texas, Arizona, and California.

Foreword

Clayton Early Learning, a nonprofit organization in Colorado, focuses on improving early childhood education through direct services to young children in the Clayton Educare program and through research and direct services to professionals provided by the Clayton Institute. Our goal is that all children, especially those with limited opportunities, are prepared for success in school and society. We partner with families, educators, communities, and policy makers in achieving this goal. We find that the Skilled Dialogue framework outlined in this book contributes substantially to the success of our own programs as well as to our work with other early childhood education providers.

The Clayton Early Learning Institute provides coaching, technical assistance, and training to early childhood education teachers, family educators, and administrators who have varied backgrounds and are working in varied settings—family child care homes, Head Start programs, faith-based and school-based preschool programs, and teen parenting programs. Our objective is to create a collaboration with each program that will lead to systematic, sustainable program operations to support each child's learning and development.

Needless to say, we encounter diverse ideas about what that means and what it looks like, including different theories and beliefs about child development, classroom management, instructional methods, employee relations, the role of parents, and just about any other aspect of running an education program for young children.

Recently, one of our coaches was experiencing frustration with how meals were being provided to children in a small child care center. The staff member who was responsible for how meals were served was resisting the coach's recommendations for children to eat family style and be allowed to serve themselves. She was concerned that given this degree of independence, children might not make nutritional choices and that food would be wasted. On one visit, while waiting to begin an unrelated meeting, the coach happened to ask the staff member how long she had been working at the center. The staff member explained that prior to working there, she had worked at a residential facility for youthful offenders, where she had started a training program in food services for the adolescent residents. She saw that these teens needed to feel that they could succeed at something, needed a sense of direction and some skills that would help them be independent when they left the system. This opened a whole new dialogue between the coach and the staff member about what young children can learn at mealtime, and it led to a change in the mealtime routine for children in the program that both the coach and the staff member felt comfortable with. Although this conversation was not planned to address the conflict, it demonstrated the power of using Skilled Dialogue to achieve collaboration in challenging interactions.

In education and human services, collaboration is the gold standard to which many professionals aspire as a process for decision making and problem solving. We believe that effective strategies for meeting the educational and human needs of children, families, those living in poverty, and other groups who are at the receiving end of our services require their full and equal participation. So, for example, we want parents to participate in decision making for their child's educational program, particularly if that child has special needs. We look for parent and other consumer representatives to sit on advisory and governing boards of our schools and organizations.

Implicit in models of collaboration is the premise that diversity adds value to the problem-solving process and outcome—that when different resources, perspectives, and ideas are brought to the table, more creative, effective solutions to problems can emerge than would be possible if the collaborators were working independently or competing with each other. This is all wonderful in theory. Any of us who holds collaboration as a value has likely had the experience of sitting at the table with a colleague or a parent whose perspective is so different from ours that it appears contradictory—one of us has to be right and the other has to be wrong!

For example, those of us trained as early childhood educators in the past 20 years have learned that responding to crying infants by holding them and trying to soothe them is best practice. This is one way that infants learn to trust that their needs will be met—an important developmental task. How then, do we collaborate with a parent who believes that this does a child a disservice? A parent whose very real experience—perhaps based on discrimination or family background—has taught her that expecting to have one's needs met will only lead to disappointment or will even be dangerous. In the face of such differences, we may feel defeated in our efforts to collaborate. We may conclude that all we can do is agree to disagree. When this occurs, we not only risk failing to find the best solution to the problem, we also risk a breech in the relationship with our intended partner.

"Celebrating diversity" has become a catch phrase, especially in the field of education. Yet, in today's world, we sometimes feel increasingly divided by our differences. Differences in language, political ideology, educational philosophy, and so forth hamper our efforts to solve complex, entrenched problems such as closing the academic achievement gap. These differences are not trivial. In the arena of language differences, a 2005 study of state-funded preschool programs in five states found that 32% of teachers spoke Spanish in the classroom and 5% spoke another language other than English (Early et al., 2005) Still, we have not reached agreement about the most effective approaches to or even the need for bilingual education. Despite these realities, we seem to be entering an era of openness to new approaches to these difficult problems. We are eager to find a bridge across the divide.

In *Using Skilled Dialogue to Transform Challenging Interactions: Honoring Identity, Voice, and Connection*, Barrera and Kramer have given us some tools to build that bridge. Skilled Dialogue is not just a matter of "skill," however. It is a way of *being* in relationship. It requires approaching an interaction made challenging by differences with the recognition that diversity cuts both ways. That is, if your ideas or beliefs are different from mine, then it is also true that my ideas and beliefs are different from yours. Bringing this understanding to an exchange in which differences are creating conflict helps us to suspend judgment about those differences. Skilled Dialogue requires a willingness to suspend one's own agenda in the moment. It requires being open to learning from the other person and to letting go of expectations about the resolution of the problem to create a 3rd Space in which new solutions may take shape. Barrera and Kramer refer to these *dispositions* as "Choosing Relationship over Control" and "Setting the Stage for Miracles." These are the foundation for specific strategies that the authors provide to facilitate collaborative problem solving when entering challenging interactions. Because they are grounded in these dispositions, the strategies are deeper and broader than those which many of us have learned as active listening communication techniques. They are strategies for communicating respect, reciprocity, and responsiveness, which the authors define as honoring identity, honoring voice, and honoring connection. These are not easy lessons to learn, but they are critical to our effectiveness as educators.

Here at the Clayton Early Learning Institute, we are learning to use Skilled Dialogue with early care and education programs to help them create high-quality learning environments for children from birth to age 5. We have learned that to create sustainable change, the people whom we coach must have ownership of the goals, processes, and outcomes that are the focus of our coaching "contract." Early on, we recognized that this depends on developing authentic relationships with the people we coach. We arrive on their doorstep as outside "experts," whether or not that is how we wish to be perceived. Defining the Skilled Dialogue outcomes of respect, reciprocity, and responsiveness has increased our awareness of the need to be sensitive to this perceived difference in authority. It has helped us to be more intentional about these relationships and has provided a compass for navigating the chasms that can open when differences cause conflict. In this and similar contexts, in which a coach is working with a teacher, an administrator is working with a parent, or a teacher is working with a child, we have seen greater willingness to take ownership of change when both parties feel honored for who they are, when their beliefs and actions—their "voice"—is valued and when they are co-constructing the solutions or decisions needed.

In our work with Skilled Dialogue, we have learned what can happen when we let go of our assumptions and preconceived answers and are open to the other person's experience and wisdom, as well as the possibilities he or she has to offer. This is what this book is truly about: possibilities—possibilities that can emerge for children, for families, and for us, as professionals, out of true collaboration that embraces, and in fact benefits from, our differences.

Lynn Andrews, M.S.
Senior Director
Professional Development Services
Clayton Early Learning Institute
Denver, Colorado

Charlotte M. Brantley, M.A.
President and CEO
Clayton Early Learning
Denver, Colorado

REFERENCE

Early, D.M., Barbarin, O., Bryant, D., Burchinal, M.R., Chang, F., Clifford, R.M., et al. (2005). *Pre-kindergarten in eleven states: NCEDL's multi-state study of pre-kindergarten & Study of state-wide early education programs (SWEEP), preliminary descriptive report.* In L. Kagan, K. Kauerz, & K. Tarrant (2008) *The early care and education teaching workforce at the fulcrum: An agenda for reform* (pp. 24–25). New York: Teachers College Press.

Preface

This book is the outgrowth of the authors' continuing adventures with Skilled Dialogue. Its purpose is to share new ideas and materials garnered from our reflective practice and teaching of Skilled Dialogue as well as from the rich pool of practitioner feedback received in the years since the publication of the first Skilled Dialogue book (Barrera, Corso, & Macpherson, 2003). Through these experiences and feedback, we (Barrera and Kramer) have come to realize that it is diversity itself, regardless of its source, which confronts us with the greatest challenges. Somehow, in a country that celebrates individuality, we have forgotten how to celebrate the differences that distinguish one individual from another. Our fear of such differences has gained ground while our appreciation of them has lessened. As the strengths of biodiversity and its contribution to sustaining life are receiving increasing recognition (Chivian & Bernstein, 2008), the strengths of cultural, linguistic, psychological, gender, and other diversity are still often overlooked. As leaders in human relations and corporations focus on an expanded understanding of relationships and learning (Isaacs, 1999; Jaworski, 1996; Kahane, 2004; Senge, Scharmer, Jaworski, & Flowers, 2005; Wheatley, 2005), education is increasingly focusing on a narrowed understanding of learning and evidence for effective teaching. In sharing this book with you, it is our hope to promote both an increased recognition of diversity's strengths and an expanded focus on the relationships and learning that make for great teaching.

Like the first book on Skilled Dialogue, this book has a style and organization that tends to vary from that common to academic texts. Figure 2 in the Introduction depicts the spiral organization of the book's material. This organization reflects both the principles of spiral learning and my (Barrera) own cultural perspective, which privileges a less linear style than that typically used in U.S. academic texts. Figures and tables are used throughout to balance this lack of linearity, thus capitalizing on the strengths of linearity while retaining the strengths of a nonlinear organization in the narrative. This integration of styles reflects a 3rd Space option similar to those discussed in Chapter 5 and several of the case studies in Part III.

In addition, the use of both nonlinear organization and a more personal writing style mirrors two of the evidence-based beliefs discussed in Chapter 1:

1. *I–Thou Trumps I–It Every Time:* We have used a first-person perspective (*we, our, us*) as much as possible in place of the third-person perspective typical to Euro-American Normative Culture (ENC) academic texts. A third-person perspective (e.g., *the authors*) was unfortunately necessary in places in order to avoid confusion. We do want to convey, however, that we are not speaking from an impersonal authoritative perspective but as practitioners speaking to practitioners.

2. *Inspiration Is More Powerful Than Motivation:* By describing the elements of respectful, reciprocal, and responsive interactions and providing examples of what

these might look like, we hope to inspire readers to set Skilled Dialogue dispositions and use Skilled Dialogue strategies in their interactions with the children and adults around them. In not providing all of the answers, we emphasize the open-endedness of inspiration as compared with the tight control of motivation.

These beliefs are further reinforced in the two Skilled Dialogue dispositions described in Chapters 4 and 5: Choosing Relationship over Control and Setting the Stage for Miracles. Through these dispositions, Skilled Dialogue invites practitioners to examine not just what they do with children, families, and other practitioners, but also *how* they do what they do. The importance of relationship as a means for and support to learning is being increasingly documented in the literature (Goleman, 1995, 2006; Langer, 1997, 2005). Other literature attests to the fact that no interaction can truly be disengaged or truly objective (Wheatley, 2005). One writer refers to the prevalence of the language of fight and conflict (i.e., control) as compared with the language of music (i.e., relationship) (Childs, 1998). What if we were to switch from the first to the second? Would we then talk about children as strongly expressive rather than aggressive? Could we perceive then as moving to their own music rather than as hyperactive? And, if we did so, how might our responses to them change? Skilled Dialogue's first disposition invites us to explore such a shift.

Its second disposition—Setting the Stage for Miracles—is a corollary one. Though we have received only one comment regarding our use of the word *miracle*, perhaps we should explain our choice, which was a deliberate one. Miracles, as defined in this book, refer to events, behaviors, and/or outcomes that cannot be imagined or predicted based on existing facts. They are neither linear nor logical (i.e., cannot be controlled). They invite an expansion of our vision for and of others rather than the mere implementation of a set procedure or activity. Though such implementation need not be necessarily abandoned, it should not be allowed to limit individuals, including young children with delays and/or disabilities. This disposition invites us to see children first, not "as a problem faced with a complex of problems" but "as a mystery surrounded by mystery" (Marty, 2007, p. 1)—for it is in what we do not know that the greatest potential for growth exists rather than in what we do know (e.g., developmental level, ability limitations, absent skills).

No written text can do justice to live interactions, of course, and it is in live interactions that the essence of Skilled Dialogue can be found. We invite readers to participate in such interactions by contacting us via our web site (http://www .skilleddialogue.com) and/or attending our presentations and workshops. We gratefully acknowledge all those who have already done so and, as a consequence, provided us with the inspiration for this book.

REFERENCES

Barrera, I., Corso, R.M., & Macpherson, D. (2003). *Skilled Dialogue: Strategies for responding to cultural diversity in early childhood.* Baltimore: Paul H. Brookes Publishing Co.
Childs, C. (1998). *The spirit's terrain.* Boston: Beacon Press.

Chivian, E. & Berstein, A. (Eds.). (2008). *Sustaining life*. New York: Oxford University Press.

Goleman, D. (1995). *Emotional intelligence*. New York: Bantam.

Goleman, D. (2006). *Social intelligence: The new science of human relationships*. New York: Bantam.

Isaacs, W. (1999). *Dialogue and the art of thinking together*. New York: Doubleday.

Jaworski, J. (1996). *Synchronicity: The inner path of leadership*. San Francisco: Berrett-Koehler.

Kahane, A. (2004). *Solving tough problems: An open way of talking, listening, and creating new realities*. San Francisco: Berrett-Koehler.

Langer, E.J. (1997). *The power of mindful learning*. New York: Perseus Books.

Langer, E.J. (2005). *On becoming an artist: Reinventing yourself through mindful creativity*. New York: Ballantine Books.

Marty, M.E. (2007). *The mystery of the child*. Grand Rapids, MI: Eerdmans.

Senge, P.M., Scharmer, C.O., Jaworski, J., & Flowers, B.S. (2005). *Presence: Human purpose and the field of the future*. New York: Currency/Doubleday.

Wheatley, M.J. (2005). *Finding our way: Leadership for an uncertain time*. San Francisco: Berrett-Koehler.

Acknowledgments

No book is an individual effort and that is certainly true for this book. Many individuals have supported both the development of Skilled Dialogue and the writing of this second book. First of all, I want to acknowledge my coauthor and good friend, Lucinda Kramer. Her support and contributions make this book so much more than it could otherwise be. Lucinda has worked with me and supported the development of Skilled Dialogue since our first discussion of diversity's challenges. I truly appreciate her continued support and collaboration.

Second, I'd like to acknowledge all of the editorial staff at Brookes who have given so unstintingly of their support. I especially want to acknowledge Heather Shrestha. Heather's belief in Skilled Dialogue and her support throughout the writing of the first book and the conceptualization of this one gave me not only invaluable guidance, but also the courage to continue writing when I otherwise might have stopped. I also want to acknowledge Johanna Cantler and Julie Chavez, with whom I worked more directly while finishing this book. Their editing and patient responses to all my questions made my writing much easier than it might otherwise have been.

Finally, I want to acknowledge all of my students at The University of New Mexico—especially those in my diversity seminar—and the practitioners I have met through our workshops and presentations for their valuable and stimulating ideas, feedback, and questions. I especially want to thank Lynn Andrews of the Clayton Early Learning Institute, who has so willingly supported our most recent field research.

Isaura Barrera

Introduction

Beyond Understanding
Cultural Linguistic Diversity

In the first Skilled Dialogue book (Barrera, Corso, & Macpherson, 2003), the primary focus was communication and interaction with others who are significantly culturally linguistically diverse from ourselves. A great deal of emphasis was placed on knowing about and understanding how cultural dynamics operate in general as well as on how various cultural perspectives understand the world. Although this information continues to be important, our work since the publication of that book has revealed that the primary challenge to interactions between adults and between adults and children whose values and perspectives differ is not limited understanding of the content or dynamics of particular cultural communities. Rather, what people report finding the most challenging is the fact that the person —adult or child—with whom they wish to interact or communicate does not agree with them and, in fact, sees the situation in question totally differently. Knowing the source of another's distinct perspective can legitimize why he or she holds that perspective, yet it often leaves those who hold different beliefs and behaviors no closer to authentic collaboration and just as desirous of changing the other's behavior! Knowing that someone's consistent lateness for scheduled meetings, for example, may be because of his or her culturally based values and frame of reference can be helpful. In all probability, however, it will not decrease either the frustration of the person waiting or the need to start meetings at a particular time because it is the only available time. One person will continue to feel the need for the other to share his or her value of punctuality ("After all, how else can we get things done?" he or she may ask. "Am I just supposed to accept and indeed respect consistent lateness?") Simple understanding that another's behavior stems from cultural or other diversity fails to address how to establish respectful, reciprocal, and responsive interactions with others whether consistent lateness is associated with cultural frameworks or only with other factors. Similarly, it is useful to know that a child may consistently speak out of turn or resist working "independently" because of cultural influences. As in the previous case, however, knowing this will not change the fact that these behaviors are not considered appropriate in certain settings and will carry the consequences thereof.

So, an underlying question addressed by this book is "Well, it's a culturally diverse response; now what do we do?" Or, "Cultural diversity doesn't explain this behavior; now what do we do?" In the current early childhood context, it seems that two choices have become salient: 1) honor differences when they are ascertained to be rooted in culture or 2) treat differences as idiosyncratic behaviors that when, deemed inappropriate, should be given neither respect nor voice. This book takes a wider perspective that can be summarized in the three statements attached to the discussion of Skilled Dialogue strategies in Chapters 7, 8, and 9:

1. Differences do not make people wrong (no matter their source).

2. Diversity is always life enhancing (i.e., all differences have something positive to offer).

3. There is always a third choice (i.e., the best response lies outside a dualistic perspective).

The discussions in this second book therefore shift from examining the source and type of diversity to transforming our understanding of and relationship to differences expressed by others with whom we interact, whether children or adults. The use of Skilled Dialogue to access and leverage these differences, regardless of their source, is its main focus.

Undergirding this focus is an understanding of diversity as a single indivisible phenomenon that reflects both individual and social dimensions. All behavior is, at some level, expressive of cultural perspectives, even when these are not part of an identified ethnic community. All culture is behaviorally expressed both idiosyncratically and socially. The following sections summarize and extend this point.

CULTURAL DIVERSITY

Culture is a pervasive reality that shapes and affects all behavior, whether explicitly recognized as culturally rooted or not. Several people may exhibit the same behavior—for example, arriving "late" for appointments. For one, this behavior may be rooted in a communal culture that conceptualizes time differently than the professional majority in the United States. For another, it may be rooted in patterns of behavior idiosyncratic to his or her familial culture—no one in his or her family ever arrived at a set time! For still another, it may be rooted in a less culturally tied variable such as an anxiety disorder or attention-deficit disorder or simply lifestyle —though the conceptualization and expression of these variables are culturally embedded. That is, what an anxiety disorder is and how it is expected to manifest are culturally constructed and vary across communities.

A full discussion of the scope and complexity of cultural diversity is beyond both the purpose and the scope of this text. Nevertheless, behavior cannot be discussed without reference to culture at some level. To ignore culture is to quite literally take behavior out of context. The previous Skilled Dialogue book (Barrera et al., 2003) discussed culture in more depth. The following statements taken from pages 24–28 of that book summarize that discussion, which readers are encouraged to review along with other sources referenced in that text.

1. "All human beings are entirely the same, entirely different, and somewhat the same and somewhat different at the same time" (Malina, 2001, p. 7). [See Figure 1 for a schematic of this statement.]

$$\bullet \ \bullet \ \bullet$$

2. There is a distinction between *culture* and *cultures*, just as there is a distinction between *language* and *languages*.

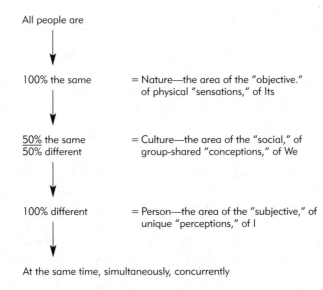

All people are

100% the same   = Nature—the area of the "objective."
                            of physical "sensations," of Its

50% the same   = Culture—the area of the "social," of
50% different   group-shared "conceptions," of We

100% different   = Person—the area of the "subjective," of
                            unique "perceptions," of I

At the same time, simultaneously, concurrently

Figure 1. Similarities and differences spectrum. (Reproduced from *The New Testament World* © 2001 Bruce J. Malina. Used by permission of Westminster John Knox Press.)

• • •

3. Cultures are mental models or paradigms developed by communities over time to make sense of their physical, emotional, and social environments and to determine how best to operate within them.

• • •

4. [People] learn and internalize "sets of cultural cues that lead [them] to perceive, feel, act, believe, admire, and strive in ways that make sense to [them] as well as to others" [within their given community] who share those cues (Malina, 2001, p.16). [*This statement is of particular relevance to Chapter 2's discussion in this book.*]

• • •

5. There are both levels of culture and levels of participation in cultures.

• • •

6. Culture functions to connect groups as well as to distinguish them.

• • •

7. Personal and group histories simultaneously enhance and limit the degree to which children and families can gain access to and express [the] cultural values [of the communities with which they affiliate].

In short, whether culture is overtly acknowledged or not, it is the "sea" (i.e., social context) within which all behavior occurs.

BEHAVIORAL DIVERSITY

All behaviors are culturally embedded. No behavior is ever independent of social or environmental contexts, even when these contexts are not easily identified. Some contexts may be formally named (e.g., Italian, Asian, Indian). There are, in fact, many books to help us make these associations (e.g., Lynch & Hanson, 2004). The cultural contexts of other behaviors, however, may be much less visible as generations pass and original contexts change.

This became clear to me (Barrera) many years ago at a workshop I gave on cultural diversity. One of the participants, whose family had emigrated from Yemen to Western New York, told the story of a "game" that she and her siblings played at the dinner table with their mother. The family rule was that only the right hand could be used on the table; the left must always stay below table level. The children quickly learned that they could get their mother's attention by slowly raising their left hand and seeing how long it would take for their mother to notice and scold them. For many years, they all believed that this was a peculiar familial idiosyncrasy. They did not see it in the homes of nonfamily members because theirs was the only one in their neighborhood that was rooted in Middle Eastern culture. It was not until a visit to Yemen much later that they discovered that it was, in fact, a culturally rooted behavioral expectation. In Yemen, as in other parts of the Middle East, it is culturally inappropriate to use the left hand at the table as it is culturally understood to be the hand reserved for personal hygiene. Without that visit, however, they might never have learned the cultural context of that particular behavior.

In another case, a person told of her need to always ascertain the placement of the salt shakers on the table before sitting down. Again, it was not until a visit to the Scandinavian country of her family's origin that she discovered her ancestors had paid careful attention to sitting "above" or "below" the salt since salt, necessary for preserving fish over long winters, was a highly valued and valuable commodity.

Specific behaviors such as these become diverse and/or challenging depending on the social context(s) in which they are exhibited. Within the context of origin they may be neither diverse nor challenging. Used in a different context, though, they would certainly be diverse—and perhaps also challenging, depending on the expectations and values of the new context. The term *challenging behaviors* has come to be used primarily in relation to children's behaviors that are considered inappropriate (e.g., aggressive, resistive). For that reason, the term *challenging interactions* is used throughout the majority of this book. When the term *challenging behaviors* is used in the book, it denotes any behavior, whether exhibited by a child or an adult, considered challenging by the other person(s) in the interaction.

The authors' premise in writing the current text is that the meanings and interpretations attached to behaviors (i.e., appropriate, inappropriate, positive, negative) are actually rooted in the context in which a behavior is exhibited rather than in the behavior itself. Paying attention to every single sound and sight, for example, is a perfectly acceptable and positive behavior when one believes oneself to be threatened or when entering a novel environment. It would not, however, be perceived as either acceptable or positive in an early childhood classroom, where such attention would distract from giving priority to the teacher's instructions. Similarly, speaking a language other than English is deemed acceptable in certain contexts and not in others.

It is, therefore, not the source of a behavior (i.e., culture, personal history, gender, temperament) that determines the degree to which it is perceived as challenging but rather our perception and interpretation of its meaning. That is, the perception and meaning we have learned to attribute to it within our own particular context(s) determines whether we judge it as inappropriate or appropriate, respectful or disrespectful, and so on. A behavior may, for example, be deemed appropriate or inappropriate in its "home" context (e.g., speaking Spanish in Mexico or with other Spanish speakers). It may, however, be perceived differently when used to interact with monolingual English speakers. It might be perceived as 1) acceptable but not functional (e.g., speaking Spanish to a non-Spanish speaker is okay but does not serve communication goals very well), 2) unacceptable within the new context but acceptable within the original context (e.g. speaking Spanish is okay in Mexico but not in the United States), or 3) unacceptable in both the original and the new context (e.g., speaking Spanish to interrupt someone).

SKILLED DIALOGUE

Skilled Dialogue is an approach to diverse behaviors that are found to be challenging, whether culturally, socially, individually, or otherwise rooted. It is designed to increase the probability of interactions that honor diverse identities, voices, and connections and thus respond to behavioral diversity in ways that leverage strengths and perspectives across multiple contexts without denying contradictory perceptions. Such a response emphasizes the expansion rather than the constriction of available behavioral options.

All too often, there is the tendency to perceive certain behaviors as contradictory to other behaviors—that is, to see one behavior (e.g., speaking Spanish) as somehow inhibiting the development of another behavior (e.g., speaking English) or, conversely, to believe that honoring an existing behavior (e.g., speaking Spanish) somehow diminishes another behavior (e.g., speaking English). Although the argument is most commonly expressed in relation to languages, it remains valid even when the focus of attention is behavior rather than words. Skilled Dialogue challenges this tendency. It proposes that what appear to be contradictory behaviors are, in fact, complementary and essential components of desired outcomes.

ORGANIZATION OF MATERIAL

Figure 2 depicts the overall organization of this book. In Part I, the authors set a conceptual base for the use of Skilled Dialogue in relation to collaboration and behavioral support by discussing two topics that have yet to receive their fair share of attention yet are essential to honoring connections across diverse identities and voices. The first—nurturing children's spirits and sense of self—is addressed in

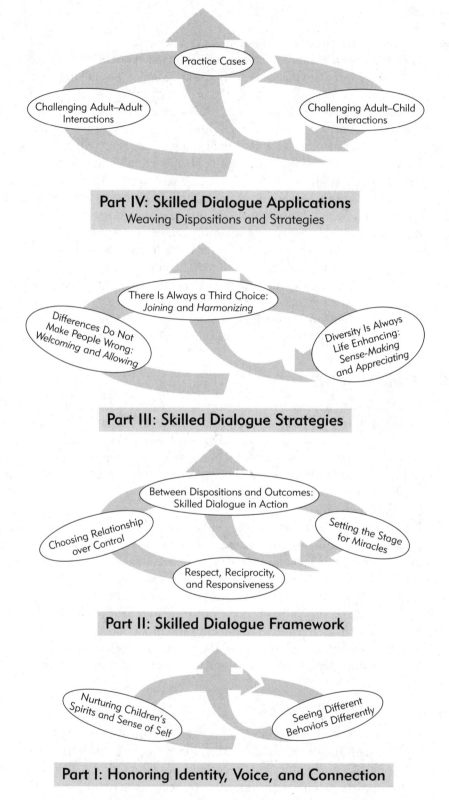

Practice Cases

Challenging Adult–Adult Interactions

Challenging Adult–Child Interactions

Part IV: Skilled Dialogue Applications
Weaving Dispositions and Strategies

There Is Always a Third Choice: *Joining* and *Harmonizing*

Differences Do Not Make People Wrong: *Welcoming and Allowing*

Diversity Is Always Life Enhancing: *Sense-Making and Appreciating*

Part III: Skilled Dialogue Strategies

Between Dispositions and Outcomes: Skilled Dialogue in Action

Choosing Relationship over Control

Setting the Stage for Miracles

Respect, Reciprocity, and Responsiveness

Part II: Skilled Dialogue Framework

Nurturing Children's Spirits and Sense of Self

Seeing Different Behaviors Differently

Part I: Honoring Identity, Voice, and Connection

Figure 2. Spiral organization of the book.

Chapter 1. This chapter discusses culturally influenced perspectives underlying current approaches to challenging behaviors in relation to the need to honor children's behaviors and identities in ways that nurture their spirits and sense of self, even while recognizing the need for children to understand and abide by necessary behavioral boundaries.

Chapter 2 discusses the challenge of becoming "behaviorally literate"—that is, of becoming familiar with multiple behavioral "languages" in order to break out of prevalent dualistic frameworks that necessarily limit one perspective in order to privilege another. It explores varying perceptions of differences, including behavioral differences, and invites the reader to recognize the multiplicity of meanings and intentions that can be associated with identical behaviors. This is in no way meant to negate one set of meanings or intentions for another—quite the opposite in fact. It is intended to communicate that just as there are distinct spoken languages, there are also diverse behavioral languages, which must be understood if optimum communication is to occur.

Part II introduces the Skilled Dialogue framework, discussing what it is and what it is not. This discussion updates information from the previous book and introduces new information developed as a result of field-based research into the use of Skilled Dialogue by early childhood practitioners. It describes the basic elements of Skilled Dialogue as these relate to communication across diverse behavioral languages. A table at the beginning of each chapter in Part II highlights the particular elements addressed in that chapter.

Chapter 3, the first chapter in Part II, focuses on the foundation of Skilled Dialogue: the targeted outcomes of respect, reciprocity, and responsiveness, which honor identity, voice, and connection respectfully. Chapter 4 describes Choosing Relationship over Control, one of two key dispositions that drive Skilled Dialogue's application and act as the bridge across its outcomes and specific strategies. This disposition is associated with both the specific outcomes it supports and the specific strategies through which it is concretized. Finally, Chapter 5 discusses Setting the Stage for Miracles, Skilled Dialogue's second disposition. It too is discussed in relation to the outcomes and the specific strategies with which it is concretized. Chapter 6 briefly introduces Skilled Dialogue in action by describing the concrete strategies that are detailed in Part III. The discussion in Chapter 6 puts both outcomes and dispositions together to show how the strategies are generated at the interface between the two. This last chapter in Part II is intended to highlight Skilled Dialogue's integrative and synergistic nature within which all its various components work in interrelationship with each other.

Part III then examines Skilled Dialogue's strategies in more depth and detail as the most concrete aspect of its application. Each chapter presents an opening table highlighting the specific strategies addressed in that chapter. The six strategies are organized according to their primary focus on either identity, voice, or connection. This organization is one that works well for initial learning. Chapter 7 discusses the two strategies used to generate and sustain respect, focusing on the fact that differences do not make people wrong. Chapter 8 describes the strategies that establish and maintain reciprocity, grounded in the fact that diversity is always life enhancing.

Finally, Chapter 9 examines the strategies associated with developing and sustaining responsiveness. These are grounded in the belief that there is always a third choice.

Parts II and III are designed to provide basic information on the elements of Skilled Dialogue. Though containing many examples, their purpose is not to demonstrate how Skilled Dialogue is learned and used. That is the aim of Part IV, which focuses directly on weaving dispositions and strategies so as to craft respectful, reciprocal, and responsive interactions with adults and children whose behavior presents particular challenges to collaboration and/or to development of positive behavior. In this final part, the strategies are first discussed and illustrated with anecdotes and examples of interactions between practitioners as well as interactions between practitioners and families. Chapter 10 provides examples related to challenging interactions between adults—that is, among practitioners and between practitioners and families. Chapter 11 parallels this initial discussion but focuses on interactions between practitioners and children and between family members and children. Chapter 12, the final chapter, provides a variety of practice cases for readers wishing to practice applying Skilled Dialogue.

NOTE: The material presented in this book, like the material in the previous Skilled Dialogue book, is organized in a reiterative spiral fashion rather than a strictly linear one (see Figure 2). Starting with Part II, the concepts and elements of Skilled Dialogue are presented. These are revisited in Part III as new material is introduced. To facilitate linkages between related ideas, material is cross-referenced to either previous or subsequent discussions and sometimes to the previous Skilled Dialogue book. The specific aspects of Skilled Dialogue discussed in Chapters 3–9 are depicted using the figure of the Skilled Dialogue framework to show how they are always embedded in the overall framework even when discussed separately.

Finally, this book uses a number of terms that may be unfamiliar to the reader. See the following glossary for information on key terms.

REFERENCES

Barrera, I., Corso, R.M., & Macpherson, D. (2003). *Skilled Dialogue: Strategies for responding to cultural diversity in early childhood*. Baltimore: Paul H. Brookes Publishing Co.

Haviland, W.A. (1993). *Cultural anthropology*. New York: Harcourt Brace.

Kramer, K. (2003). *Martin Buber's I and Thou: Practicing the living dialogue*. Mahwah, NJ: Paulist Press.

Lynch, E.W., & Hanson, M.J. (Eds.). (2004). *Developing cross-cultural competence: A guide for working with children and their families* (3rd ed.). Baltimore: Paul H. Brookes Publishing Co.

Malina, B.L. (2001). *The New Testament world: Insights from cultural anthropology*. Louisville, KY: Westminster John Knox Press.

Vygotsky, L. (1978). *Mind in society*. Cambridge, MA: Harvard University Press.

Glossary

Allowing: This term refers to the first strategy associated with Setting the Stage for Miracles. It is introduced in Chapter 6 and discussed more fully in Chapter 7.

Anchored Understanding of Diversity: This term refers to *knowing*, an understanding of diversity that can only be gained from actual experience as contrasted with *knowing about*, which can be gained through reading or other public information sources. The term Anchored Understanding of Diversity was used in original Skilled Dialogue work (Barrera et al., 2003). It is now subsumed under the disposition of Choosing Relationship over Control.

Appreciating: This term refers to the second strategy associated with Setting the Stage for Miracles. It is introduced in Chapter 6 and discussed more fully in Chapter 8.

challenging behaviors: This term is, typically, used in early childhood to refer to children's behaviors that are deemed as impediments to learning, as disruptive to learning situations, and/or as socially unacceptable.

challenging interactions: This term refers to just what it says: interactions that challenge us in some way—cognitively, emotionally, linguistically, or behaviorally. They may involve behaviors we cannot understand, a language we cannot speak, behaviors we do not value or desire, behaviors that stir up negative emotions, feelings of confusion or incompetence, or other such factors.

Choosing Relationship over Control: This term refers to the first of two dispositions necessary for Skilled Dialogue. This disposition is introduced and discussed in Chapter 4.

culture: Per Haviland, culture is "The abstract values, beliefs and perceptions of the world that lie behind people's behavior, and which are reflected in their behavior" (1993, p. 29).

EuroAmerican Normative Culture (ENC): This term was first introduced and discussed in Barrera et al. (2003). It refers to the institutionalized cultural norms against which cultural diversity is defined. This term is used by the authors instead of more common terms, such as *White* or *European*.

evidence-based beliefs: Beliefs that are supported by professional literature and research as well as field-based work with early childhood practitioners.

Harmonizing: This term refers to the third strategy associated with Setting the Stage for Miracles. It is introduced in Chapter 6 and discussed more fully in Chapter 9.

I–Thou and I–It: These terms were first used by Martin Buber (Kramer, 2003). I–Thou interactions are interactions of genuine connection and authenticity between two people. Each treats the other as someone worthy of respect, reciprocity, and responsiveness. I–It interactions are more superficial interactions within which my agenda, rather than the other, is primary.

Joining: This term refers to the second strategy associated with Choosing Relationship over Control. It is introduced in Chapter 6 and discussed more fully in Chapter 9.

miracle: This term refers to positive and desired outcomes that, given existing data, we believe cannot or will not happen but that do happen.

models of agency: As used in this text, the term *models of agency* refers to the different ways in which communities think about how and why people take action in particular ways. Three different models are discussed in Chapter 2.

Sense-Making: This term refers to the second strategy associated with Choosing Relationship over Control. It is introduced in Chapter 6 and discussed more fully in Chapter 8.

Setting the Stage for Miracles: This term refers to the second of two dispositions necessary for Skilled Dialogue. This disposition is introduced and discussed in Chapter 5.

3rd Space: This term is used in reference to both a mindset and a skill. As a mindset, 3rd Space refers to a conceptual perspective defined by the following three characteristics: 1) thinking of reality as multidimensional rather than dichotomous, 2) believing that there are always three choices rather than only two (i.e., this or that), and 3) understanding differences as complementary rather than divisive. As a skill, 3rd Space refers to the ability to create multiple choices and leverage the complementary aspects of apparently contradictory choices.

Welcoming: This term refers to the first strategy associated with Choosing Relationship over Control. It is introduced in Chapter 6 and discussed more fully in Chapter 7.

zone of proximal development: First used by Vygotsky (1978), this term refers to the "zone" just beyond what one already knows or can do without assistance; it is the next possible step, beyond what is already learned but not so far above it that it cannot be readily learned.

To my parents, who lived Skilled Dialogue long before I could put it into words
To J and S, who nurture my spirit and sense of self in more ways than I can say
(IB)

To my parents and sons,
Elliotte Clifton, Francis Clifton, Ben Kramer, Adam Kramer, and Sam Kramer,
for making it all worthwhile
(LK)

Honoring Identity, Voice, and Connection

Our understanding and acceptance of other people's behaviors is typically grounded in our familiarity with and understanding of the meaning(s) that behavior is intended to convey. When our perceived understanding differs from another person's intended meaning, both the efficacy and quality of the communication and/or interaction can be significantly compromised. For that reason, diversity is often seen as more of a challenge than an opportunity or strength. This book focuses on Skilled Dialogue as a tool for working with diversity from the latter perspective. The authors address the following two questions in particular:

1. How can we respond to behaviors that we do not understand, do not value, and/or do not find acceptable in ways that help us access and mine their strengths and, in so doing, honor rather than diminish their expression of identity, voice, and connection?

2. When these behaviors are exhibited by young children acting in ways perceived as inappropriate or less than competent, how can we respond in ways that nurture their spirits and sense of self while simultaneously supporting appropriate and competent participation in social interactions and situations?

The first question is critical as we increase our focus on inclusion and collaboration between and among early childhood practitioners, families, children, and others involved in providing quality services for young children. All too often, differences trigger exclusion rather than inclusion and limit our efforts toward the collaboration we wish to develop. Subtle and not so subtle dynamics of power undermine authentic collaboration and inclusion by sending a message of "this way, not that way" rather than "two perspectives are better than one."

The second question is one that has consistently, although only sporadically, received attention in literature on early education and parenting. Gurian (2007) noted it as one that needs more consistent recognition. He said,

> Although setting high goals for our kids is crucial to their thriving, what is problematic is the lack of attention to understanding and nurturing who our specific children really are—so that we can help them set the *right* high goals for themselves. (2007, pp. 36–37)

This statement is an important reminder that, as we figure out how to respond to a child's challenging behaviors, we also need to remember to listen to their whispered request for recognition, "Look, here is the person I am. Look into my eyes! Pay attention to *me*" (Gurian, 2007, p. 37). However inexpertly children with challenging behaviors express themselves, they are nevertheless expressing their unique nature and asking us to help them do it more skillfully.

In a way, collaboration with adults and behavioral support for children are but different sides of the same coin. Both require alignment between points of view rooted in diverse cultural, social, personal, economic, or other perspectives. In this book, we propose the use of Skilled Dialogue as a tool for crafting authentic collaboration between adults as well as for developing responses that nurture both the spirit and sense of self that underlie children's behavior. Chapter 1 discusses four evidence-based beliefs that support the use of Skilled Dialogue for these purposes:

1. I–Thou relationships trump I–It interactions every time.

2. Adults' nurturing of spirits and sense of self is a key contributor to children's primary happiness, which, in turn, motivates their collaboration with adult requests and expectations.

3. Inspiration is a much more effective, efficient, and powerful initiative for change than motivation.

4. All children (and families) are behaviorally literate within their cultural context(s) according to their ages and developmental skills.

Chapter 2 lays further groundwork for the use of Skilled Dialogue by discussing common perceptions of differences, especially those that we believe reflect beliefs and values that do not meet personal or social expectations and demands. It is important to discuss our perceptions of differences before discussing differences themselves because our understanding of the idea of differences is a critical aspect of working with children and families from diverse backgrounds. Whether adult behaviors or child behaviors, the particular behaviors that challenge us in home and early childhood (EC) settings are simply that—differences. Our perception of differences in general is, therefore, a key aspect that determines whether or not our responses to these behaviors engender collaboration and nurture children's spirits and sense of self. The underlying premise of the second chapter is that our interpretation of and response to challenging behaviors, particularly those stemming from diverse cultural contexts, is shaped by implicit and unexamined perceptions of individual, social, and cultural differences. Three different ways of constructing and perceiving actions are presented to illustrate the variation of meanings that can be attached to behaviors.

The second chapter also addresses another key aspect of our responses to challenging behaviors—the degree to which we balance our focus on the problematic aspects of differences with a complementary focus on their positive aspects. It is, unfortunately, all too common to perceive the "challenge" in challenging behaviors as primarily negative. When properly balanced, however, negative "bumps" can act as triggers that open us to previously unseen options outside our familiar paradigms. Together, these first two chapters set a conceptual context for the need to respond to children's challenging behaviors in ways that honor their identities and voices as well as our connection with them (i.e., nurture their spirits and sense of self).

Nurturing Children's Spirits and Sense of Self

A large part of the early childhood literature on working with diversity focuses on honoring families' diverse identities and voices as well as building connections across these diverse identities and voices. A smaller part focuses on honoring the diverse identities and voices of children, which is the focal point of this first chapter. Children's social and emotional development is vulnerable to the types of interpersonal responses that adults make to their behaviors. Their cognitive and linguistic development is equally vulnerable to the instructional responses of these same adults.

How can we respond to children's diverse behaviors, especially challenging ones, in ways that nurture their spirits and sense of self while simultaneously supporting appropriate and competent participation in social settings and situations? All too often, it seems that these two goals cannot be simultaneously addressed, especially with children whose behavior is perceived to be particularly difficult.

There is a story about a gifted 5-year-old child that, whether true or not, conveys great truth about nurturing a child's spirits and sense of self (Yaconelli, 1998). According to the story, in a moment when his mother was distracted, a child climbed onto the stage where the famous pianist Paderewski was about to give a concert. Once on stage, he sat on the piano bench and began to play "Chopsticks" with all of the concentration and enthusiasm that only a 5-year-old child can muster. What happened next was quite predictable. Startled ushers rushed on stage amid cries of both concern and outrage from the audience. They reached for the child to remove him from the stage. Behind the scenes, Paderewski, who had heard both the playing and the subsequent commotion

> Quickly grabbed his tuxedo jacket . . . and then stepped in the full view of the audience. The boy, oblivious to what was happening, continued to play. Paderewski came up behind him, went down on his knees, and whispered in the little boy's ear, "Don't stop. Keep on playing. You're doing great." While the boy continued to play, the great pianist put his arms around the boy and began playing a concerto based on the tune of "Chopsticks." While the two played, Paderewski kept on saying to the boy, "Don't stop. Keep on playing." (Yaconelli, 1998, pp. 144–145)

The two goals of nurturing children's spirits and sense of self and teaching appropriate social skills are, unfortunately, seldom integrated so masterfully. How did Paderewski's response teach appropriate skills when the seemingly inappropriate skill of jumping on stage was not addressed? The answer is one that can be easily overlooked: At the root of all learning, especially social learning, is the development of trusting relationships with adults. By affirming this child's impetuous expression of a desire to make music, Paderewski set the stage for subsequent trust in adult expectations and demands. To have responded otherwise might have achieved behavioral compliance, but only at the expense of the connection of the compliance with the child's authentic self! The message sent through Paderewski's response was that expression of one's needs and/or desires need not be in opposition to adults' acceptance, expectations, and goals. The importance of this message cannot be overemphasized. It is when children see their needs and/or desires as being in opposition to adults' acceptance, expectations, and goals that they learn to violate one in favor of the other (e.g., violate adults' acceptance, expectations, and goals in favor of meeting their own needs).

It is all too common to perceive the goals of nurturing children's spirits and sense of self and teaching appropriate social skills as contradictory, especially in instances such as the child taking the stage. The tension between social *shoulds* and the unique nature of individual children is eloquently acknowledged by Gurian (2007). According to Gurian,

> In the last decades especially, our social trends parenting advisors have moved us far toward focusing mainly on socialization as the most powerful cause of how our children are—and should be. We've moved so far this way in four decades that we neglect, at times, to look deeply into each child's eye. (p. 48)

That is, we do not honor their uniqueness.

Watson (2003) made the point that the responses to children's behavior in this country are too often rooted in learning and Freudian theory, which are embedded in ENC contexts. "Both theories begin with the premise that children are isolated individuals focused on seeking personal pleasure and avoiding pain" (Watson, 2003, p. 8). Given this premise, she went on to state that "when children behave in antisocial ways [even when these are perfectly appropriate in other diverse contexts], it is assumed that they are succumbing to their selfish desires and failing to control themselves" (p. 8). Such an assumption, unfortunately, leaves little room for the type of spirit-sustaining response illustrated by Paderewski's response to the 5-year-old child.

Many might ask whether such a spirit-sustaining response might just encourage inappropriate behavior and disregard for adult convention. Wouldn't this response just teach a child that he or she can get away with following his impulses without regard for social settings?

These questions are both common and legitimate topics of discussion. Behaviors inappropriate to particular contexts, even when less public than the example in the story, pose some of the greatest challenges to adults who care for and about children's spirits and sense of self. It is relatively easy to engage in positive and spirit-nurturing interactions when children are behaving in ways deemed to be appropriate by the observer(s). It is, however, much more difficult to do so when these behaviors challenge our sense of what is right and trigger both our negative emotions and our need to change the situation.

Statements such as "It's just the terrible twos," "She's just doing it for attention," "I don't know what to do with him," "She just doesn't understand," "He's strong willed," "I wish she'd just pay attention," "She just won't listen," "She insists on not speaking English," and "He is always looking to me for help rather than figuring it out himself," are testimony to the frustration families and practitioners face when dealing with young children's difficult behaviors. That is, those behaviors—regardless of their source—are behaviors that in some way challenge adults' values, beliefs, or expectations about what is appropriate or necessary.

The material in this book addresses the use of Skilled Dialogue as a framework not only for use with adults but also for responding to children's diverse and challenging behaviors in ways that help us nurture children's spirits and sense of self while simultaneously supporting their learning of appropriate social skills and behaviors. How this works is illustrated in detail, starting with this chapter's discussion of the beliefs that provide the broader evidence-based context for Skilled Dialogue and its strategy sets. This discussion, along with the ideas presented in the next chapters, provide essential foundational information to help readers understand and adapt Skilled Dialogue to their specific needs. Subsequent chapters provide examples of applications to specific scenarios. Chapter 11 focuses specifically on challenging adult–child interactions.

APPROACHES TO CHILDREN'S CHALLENGING BEHAVIORS

Skilled Dialogue strategies are grounded in two dispositions: *Choosing Relationship over Control* and *Setting the Stage for Miracles* (Jaworski, 1996). (See Chapters 4 and 5 for more details about Skilled Dialogue strategies.) These dispositions emphasize relationship and creative collaboration while simultaneously supporting the development of interactional and communicative skills necessary for appropriate participation in social settings and situations.

There are, of course, many other approaches to behaviorally challenging situations with children. Many of these approaches tend to focus on external management and/or control. Typically, approaches involve an analysis of external factors, such as rewards and reinforcers, that can then be manipulated to either maintain a behavior or reduce its presence in favor of a more socially appropriate behavior. A brief overview of some of these approaches is provided in Appendix A in the back of this book. Skilled Dialogue strategies are not designed to be substituted for these approaches; rather, they create a more respectful, reciprocal, and responsive context for their use when appropriate.

The behavioral approaches reviewed have been shown to be effective in changing behavior and can serve as valuable resources. Nevertheless, it is important to recognize that they can also be used in ways that are not developmentally, psychologically, culturally, or emotionally responsive to young children's spirits or sense of self. Several sources address this point both descriptively and empirically (see Noddings, 2005; Pieper & Pieper, 1999; Roberts, 2001).

Two statements illustrate the need to place behavioral approaches more deeply within the context of relationship and creative collaboration. The first statement comes from Margaret Watson, whose research into this area led her to say, "If we try to teach these children to want to be cooperative and prosocial by rewarding their good behavior, we only succeed in confirming their view of relationships as coercive and encourage their tendency to be self-focused [at the expense of a broader social focus]" (2003, p. 12).

The second statement comes from Alfie Kohn's book, *Unconditional Parenting: Moving from Rewards and Punishments to Love and Reason* (2006). Kohn said,

> Nearly half a century ago, the pioneering psychologist Carl Rogers offered an answer to the question "What happens when a parent's [or other significant adult's] love depends on what children do?" He explained that those on the receiving end of such love come to disown the parts of their selves that aren't valued. Eventually they regard themselves as worthy only when they act (or think or feel) in specific ways. (p. 20)

These statements highlight the tension between choosing relationship (power with) and choosing control (power over) and the contrast between setting the stage for miracles and following a prescribed agenda to achieve a preset outcome. The tension between choosing relationship and choosing control is triggered every time a child acts in ways contrary to the social norms and expectations of a given community or context. This tension is evident in the anecdote at the beginning of this chapter about the boy on Paderewski's stage. In such a situation, some adults would choose control (i.e., remove the child from the stage or tell him to stop and return to his mother). Paderewski, however, chose relationship, because he was confident that the benefits would outweigh the risks in the long run. The tension between control and relationship is a tension that, at first glance, asks us to choose between discipline and permissiveness. Perhaps, though, it is the dichotomization of choices—placing them at odds with each other—rather than the choices themselves that reduces our ability to truly nurture children's spirits and sense of self. The contrast between setting the stage for miracles and orchestrating a prescriptive outcome, however, is the difference between leading and managing. The phrase "setting the stage for miracles" (Jaworski, 1996) highlights the contrast between responses that seek to draw out with those that strive to shape from the outside.

Evidence-Based Beliefs

There are two levels of evidence that support the use of Skilled Dialogue strategies with children as well as adults. The first level, discussed in this chapter, is a broad conceptual level characterized by four evidence-based beliefs: 1) I–Thou trumps I–It every time, 2) primary happiness is the greatest motivation for becoming and remaining a competent and compassionate participant in social communities,

3) inspiration is more powerful than motivation, and 4) all children are behaviorally literate within their cultural contexts. The second level of evidence is more specific to the authors' field-based research on Skilled Dialogue and is referred to in subsequent chapters.

These beliefs at this first level are supported by evidence from general early childhood, developmental intervention, special education, and brain-based research (see discussions of each belief in the following sections). This evidence, in turn, provides support for the need to respond to young children's challenging behaviors in respectful, reciprocal, and responsive ways and underlie the specific strategies associated with Skilled Dialogue.

I–Thou Trumps I–It Every Time Relationship implies two subjects (I–Thou), rather than a subject and an object (I–It). Paradoxically, one of the strongest and clearest illustrations of this premise comes from the area of working with horses. Roberts (2001) and Wood (2005) both speak to the difference between approaching horses as subjects with whom to relate rather than as objects to be coerced or manipulated.

While the role of relationship in learning has been positively recognized for a longer period of time (e.g., Anne Sullivan's work with Helen Keller), it is only recently that its legitimacy is gaining more widespread recognition. Research on emotional intelligence (Goleman, 1995), "heartmath" (Childre & Rozman, 2005), "caring schools" (Koplow, 2007; Noddings, 2005), and responsive education (Bowers & Flinders, 1990) highlights the delicate yet significant role of choosing to be in relationship with the children we teach over merely being in control of their behavior. More recent research into social intelligence (Goleman, 2006) supports and extends these earlier findings. "Children learn not only to calm down or resist emotional impulses [through observing and participating in relationships] but also to strengthen their repertoire of ways to affect others" (Goleman, 2006, p. 174).

When responses to challenging behaviors are placed within a relational framework, such as Skilled Dialogue, the recognition that children are "predisposed to acquire the desire to be cooperative and prosocial as a result of experiencing sensitive and responsive care" (Watson, 2003, p. 11) is brought front and center, along with the acknowledgment that, whereas the strongest foundation for such care is laid in the home by a child's significant caregivers, the process of socialization does not stop there. According to Bowers and Flinders, "The procedure of teaching is embedded in a complex ecology of relationships, and . . . within those relationships the teacher plays a critically important gatekeeper role" (1990, p. 91).

I–Thou relationships are characterized by this type of reciprocity. In her book *The Dancing Dialogue: Using the Communicative Power of Movement with Young Children,* Suzi Tortora used a highly descriptive metaphor. In discussing what she termed a "dancing duet," she stated, "To dance with another, both dancing members must be aware of their own and their partner's individual styles of moving, as well as the overall feeling tone created as they move together and their individual qualities combine" (2005, p. 7). Similarly, I–Thou relationships honor the identity and voice of those involved. Even when one person may have more knowledge and authority than the other, I–Thou relationships recognize both as equal participants (see Chapter 8 for more information on establishing this type of reciprocity).

Primary Happiness Is the Greatest Motivation

Primary Happiness Is the Greatest Motivation   The recognition of the role of early attachment in later development and learning is one that has yet to receive full attention in relationship to challenging behaviors. Watson (2003) is one of this concept's clearest voices through her articulation of what she termed "developmental discipline." Pieper and Pieper's (1999) earlier work provided a rich context for such discipline. These authors presented the concept of primary happiness, which lies at the heart of that sense of well-being that yields the greatest motivation for becoming and remaining a competent and compassionate participant in social communities. "Primary happiness originates in the conviction that all infants bring into the world that they are causing their parents [caregivers], whom they adore more than life itself, to pay loving attention to their developmental needs" (Pieper & Pieper, 1999, p. 2).

According to Pieper and Pieper, when children lose their primary happiness—the conviction that they can cause significant others to pay loving attention to their developmental needs—they shift from authentic and respectful behaviors to contrived and power-focused behaviors. As children observe responses and consequences to behaviors that do not pay loving attention to their developmental needs, they form subconscious conclusions about which behaviors are safe and which ones are not (e.g., this behavior worked, this one is bad, this one pleases others). Even when original responses and contexts are no longer present, it is these conditioned beliefs—or premature cognitive commitments, as Langer (1997) termed them—rather than their deeper needs that continue as the basis for children's subsequent actions and reactions. Changing these actions and reactions remains ineffective or inconsistent as long as these precognitive commitments remain the substitutes of the experience of primary happiness.

Inspiration Is More Powerful than Motivation

Inspiration Is More Powerful than Motivation   Inspiration is a much more effective, efficient, and powerful initiative for change than motivation. Although the terms *motivation* and *inspiration* have similar meanings, they have quite distinct connotations. Motivation connotes an externally imposed influence or push that moves us toward a particular outcome. It is the stereotypical carrot approach, or the idea that a person must receive an external reward or reinforcer to perform a desired behavior (i.e., do this to get that), that is being increasingly questioned (Roberts, 2001; Wood, 2005). Inspiration, however, connotes a more subtle inner pull or vision that draws us toward something (i.e., do this as an expression of your identity or as an end in itself). Motivation tends to be predictable and controllable. Inspiration tends to be much less so, and it seems to come to us on its own timeline and conditions.

Many current approaches to challenging behaviors reflect a perspective that values motivation over inspiration; that is, other approaches focus on using motivation to enforce and control change. There are two aspects of this perspective that can negatively affect children's spirits and sense of self. First, motivational perspectives focus on doing or giving to get; that is, children are motivated to perform desired behaviors through the offering of external rewards and reinforcers, whether externally imposed or self-chosen. Their sense of self thus becomes contingent on others' perceptions and interpretations. They learn to read others at the expense of staying in tune with themselves. Second, many current motivational approaches tend to model exactly what the approach is intended to change—reactivity rather than responsiveness. It is common to hear teachers of young children ask, "How did that make you feel?" The implicit message of these words is one that decreases our sense of control. Such messages, albeit often unintentionally, emphasize external control (i.e., you are made to feel something by someone else). These messages reinforce the belief that circumstances and/or others' behaviors make us do particular things. Being hit, for example, is linked to hitting back, or, at the very least, to *wanting* to hit back! The latter is a slippery slope for young children and children with exceptionalities that delay or inhibit their impulse controls.

Inspirational perspectives, however, focus on inviting change not through the extinction of undesired behavior but through the modeling of behaviors deemed critical to the development of qualities, such as empathy, which lead to appropriate choices in the face of negative external conditions. These perspectives emphasize desired behavior as rewarding because of its impact on a person's sense of well-being and competence, regardless of external reward or response. Inspirationally based behaviors thus carry their own reward and can continue even in the absence of scheduled rewards or reinforcers.

All Children Are Behaviorally Literate within Their Cultural Contexts   All children are behaviorally literate within their cultural contexts, according to their ages and developmental skills. That is, all children—to the level of their age and developmental skills—learn the behaviors necessary for participation in their primary environments. Current research reveals the extent to which all children desire to participate competently in the social and physical environments in which they find themselves and will learn to do so to the limits of their developmental abilities (Goleman, 2006). The research on children's acculturation (i.e., the learning of their first culture) also affirms children's development of the skills and knowledge valued within the cultural context of their home environment (see Figure 1.1) (Hanson & Lynch, 2003; Moll, Amanti, Neff, & Gonzalez, 1992).

Children's sense of competent participation in their home environment is strongly shaped by 1) the behavior of significant adults in their lives and 2) the concrete responses to and consequences of their behavior and the behaviors of others around them. Children develop and strengthen behavior that allows them to survive and obtain what they need; that is, behavior that works for them in their primary environment. It is behavior selected because experiential evidence precludes other perceivable choices. All behavior, therefore, makes sense (i.e., is literate) within its original context.

Thus, when presented with a behavior that seems negative or destructive to us, we need to ask, "What is it that makes this behavior seem both positive and constructive to this child?" Or, conversely, "What is it that makes the behavior I believe to be positive and constructive seem negative or destructive to this child?"

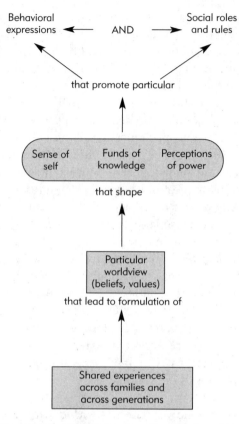

Figure 1.1.   The layers of culture. (From Barrera, I., Corso, R.M., & Macpherson, D. [2003]. Skilled Dialogue: Strategies for responding to cultural diversity in early childhood [p. 26]. Baltimore: Paul H. Brookes Publishing Co.; reprinted by permission.)

A physical therapist once told me (Barrera) that the smooth hand-to-mouth behavior I was teaching a child who had cerebral palsy probably felt as "abnormal" to that child as the child's wavering and jerky motion would feel to me. That statement is one that I have never forgotten.

The unfamiliar never feels as smooth or "normal" as the familiar. What a child knows and has practiced will always feel more normal than what is unknown and disconnected from his or her daily experience. Even when the new behavior may objectively be more desirable, the old behavior carries the weight of both familiarity and experiential data.

Skilled Dialogue Applications to Challenging Behaviors

Although the overall use of Skilled Dialogue with children is discussed in much more detail in Part II of this book, it is important at this point to provide an overview of how it aligns with the four premises just discussed and why the application of its strategy sets to challenging behaviors can generate responses that nurture children's spirits and sense of self.

First, Skilled Dialogue is a relational approach for crafting respectful, reciprocal, and responsive interactions in situations where there is a significant degree of disagreement or contradiction. One of its primary dispositions is Choosing Relationship over Control, which acts as a means of honoring diverse identities, voices, and connections. Three strategies are associated with this disposition: *Welcoming, Sense-Making,* and *Joining.* These strategies are designed to promote I–Thou connections through the use of behaviors that emphasize the validity of another person's perspectives (see Chapters 7–9 for more information on these strategies).

Second, Skilled Dialogue places a strong emphasis on being responsive rather than reactive (i.e., staying open to diverse perspectives rather than merely adhering to existing perspectives and agendas). This emphasis is embodied in a second disposition: Setting the Stage for Miracles. The strategies associated with this second disposition—*Allowing, Appreciating,* and *Harmonizing*—are designed to stimulate shifts in familiar paradigms and transform learning, thus serving as effective tools for understanding and inviting change in precognitive commitments developed when primary happiness is weakened or lost (see Chapter 8). In addition, these strategies are specifically designed to transform, include, and integrate what seem to be contradictory perspectives, thus communicating a true responsiveness to them (see Chapter 5).

Third, the Skilled Dialogue approach is designed to inspire rather than motivate change. It does so through its advocacy of modeling respect (i.e., understanding that differences do not make people wrong); reciprocity (i.e., understanding that diversity is life enhancing rather than life threatening); and responsiveness (i.e., understanding that there is no need for a power struggle because there is always a third choice; see Chapter 3). Its strategies are designed to provoke thoughtful collaboration along with the transformation of contradictions that are exclusive into paradoxes that are inclusive (see Chapters 7–9).

Finally, Skilled Dialogue invites practitioners to identify children's existing behavioral repertoires (i.e., cultural literacies) and seek their strengths (see Chapters 8 and 9). Skilled Dialogue advocates the understanding that these strengths are children's most powerful resources for learning new behaviors that expand their skill repertoires. These same strengths can expand our own behavioral repertoires and provide us with previously unimagined options to nurture not only children's spirits but our own spirits as well. All children, if we can but observe and appreciate their cultural literacies, "are informants with a wealth of cultural and linguistic knowledge" (Murray, 1992, p. 260) from whom we can all learn.

Part II of this book discusses these points in greater detail as it presents the framework underlying the specific strategies discussed in Part III. Skilled Dialogue's three characteristic qualities and its two primary dispositions are described in detail, along with the evidence and conceptual bases that have informed them.

DISCUSSION QUESTIONS AND ACTIVITIES

1. Discuss the four evidence-based beliefs presented in this chapter: I–Thou trumps I–It every time, primary happiness is the greatest motivation for becoming

and remaining a competent and compassionate participant in social communities, inspiration is more powerful than motivation, and all children are behaviorally literate within their cultural contexts. What are your thoughts about each belief? How similar or dissimilar is your own perspective in relation to each belief?

2. What are your thoughts on the opening anecdote about Paderewski and the young child? Would you endorse such a response? Or, would you fear that it might just reinforce similar behavior from the child in the future?

3. Read Chapter 2 and then come back to these questions. Have any of your views shifted or become stronger?

Seeing Different Behaviors Differently

Skilled Dialogue was originally developed to address differences associated with groups and individuals considered to be culturally and/or linguistically diverse as compared with EuroAmerican Normative Culture (ENC). (ENC refers to the institutionalized cultural norms against which cultural linguistic diversity is defined [Barrera, Corso, & Macpherson, 2003]. It is chosen over more common terms, such as *white* or *European,* to highlight the fact that it refers to institutionalized cultural norms rather than the personalized cultural framework of particular individuals.) As we developed and worked with it within this context, we realized that, for many people, differences classified as culturally linguistically diverse were somehow seen as distinct from differences not so classified. Differences with no clear ethnic associations (e.g., differences associated with purely individual variations or with certain groups, such as gangs; differences associated with religion, gender, and familial cultures) tended not to be considered diverse. When we talked about differences at various workshops without clearly relating them to cultural diversity there seemed to be a perception that we were not talking about culture at all.

Therefore, the first point it is necessary to make in this chapter is that all discussions of behavior are discussions of culture. Culture is not something that only some people "have" and others do not. It is the perceptual and conceptual web of beliefs and understandings that undergirds all that people see and think, regardless of whether it can be given an ethnic label (e.g., Hispanic, American Indian) or not (e.g., ENC, white). Barrera et al. (2003) present a more detailed discussion of culture and cultural diversity (see Chapters 1–3).

There is a tendency to perceive culturally sanctioned behaviors (i.e., those shared and valued by a cultural group) as somehow more valid and more worthy of respect than those associated primarily or exclusively with the family or other source, such as religion. Carrying infants older than 2 years of age, for example, tends to be considered more valid when it is a common practice shared by an entire cultural community. When the community practice is to stop carrying infants past that age, however, and only certain individuals do so, it is more likely to be perceived as less valid (i.e., more diverse or deviant).

All behaviors, however, are equally embedded in a social context and deserve no more or no less respect than any other behavior. *Typically, it is not the source of a particular difference that presents the strongest challenge but rather the perception of that difference itself as valuable or not, appropriate or not, amenable to change or not, and competent or not.*

Although knowing the source of a difference can provide invaluable information that can assist people to make sense of it (see discussion of *Sense-Making* strategy in Chapter 8), it will not necessarily make it easier to work with or to accept. For example, knowing that a parent's consistent lateness stems from her culturally based understanding of time may prompt practitioners to refrain from trying to change the practice yet may not necessarily diminish their frustration with it or change their basic response to it as problematic or unacceptable. Therein lies the greatest challenge posed by diversity: how to honor other's diverse beliefs and practices while simultaneously honoring our own. Addressing this challenge is a key focus of Skilled Dialogue.

PERCEIVED BEHAVIORAL DIFFERENCES

Knowing how we perceive and sort differences is a necessary prerequisite for understanding and using the strategies associated with Skilled Dialogue. This chapter provides initial information on this topic with the caveat that the subject of perception is much more complex and extensive than can be addressed within the scope of a single chapter. It is nevertheless essential that in our efforts to honor diversity and nurture children's spirits and sense of self, we first look at our perceptions of behavioral differences.

An underlying theme of Skilled Dialogue is the need to see different behaviors differently. To be able to see chair-throwing not only as a negative and difficult behavior that needs to be changed but also as an expression of a positive intent based on an entirely different perceptual framework is as important as being able to see speaking Spanish as an equally valid alternative to speaking English, although one is clearly less effective in some contexts than in others. In both cases (i.e., chair throwing in an early childhood settings and speaking Spanish in a monolingual English context), there is a clear need to introduce another choice. However, whether the stated need to change will honor another's diverse expression of self will depend on what perception of the initial behavior is communicated. Being told one needs to change because an existing behavior is wrong or not as valuable as another is quite different from being invited to add to one's behavioral repertoire in order to function effectively in more than one context (i.e., to have more choices).

Individuals' responses to all behaviors, whether challenging or not, are unavoidably grounded in how differences in general are perceived both personally and within particular sociocultural contexts. If a person perceives difference as deviation from what is acceptable or desirable, he or she will respond to it negatively. If a person perceives difference as simply an alternative way to do something, he or she will respond positively. Although differences may come from a variety of sources (e.g., gender, culture, ability), their greatest challenge is simply their nature as *differences*. Are they perceived as positive or negative? Are they systematically sorted into acceptable and unacceptable differences? Are they welcomed? Feared? Ignored? Controlled?

Thomas (1996) summarized a range of common responses to differences that range from inclusion or exclusion to suppression, isolation, and tolerance. Watson made a succinct reference to the root of these response choices. She said

> All of us have powerful belief systems that shape the way we see the world. We build these belief systems out of the experiences of our daily lives, the content of our formal educations and reading, and the general beliefs that are part of the culture in which we live. (2003, p. 8)

Control over Relationship

Watson's (2003) discussion references two distinct views of the belief systems held in regard to children's behaviors. The first view emphasizes control and is perhaps the most common one in child care and educational settings. According to Watson (2003), this view is founded on both ENC-based learning theory and Freudian theory. From the perspective of this view, "It is necessary to tame children's pleasure seeking in order to socialize them to become productive members of society" (p. 8). This view is one that tends to choose control over relationship. For example, a child's choice to gaze out the window rather than participate in a small group activity will typically be met with displeasure and censure or at least strong encouragement to stop gazing out the window. Meeting one's needs and following one's inclination tend to be perceived as contradictory to becoming a productive member of society.

Relationship over Control

The second view, which is the focus of Watson's (2003) research, is embedded within a very different belief system based on attachment theory. This view tends to be less common in educational settings for children past the age of 3 years or so. It assumes "that children are socially oriented from birth" and that socialization is consequently a "collaborative process between child and adult rather than a coercive one" (Watson, 2003, p. 9). This view is one that lends itself most easily to choosing relationship rather than control (see Chapter 4 for a discussion of this choice as one of Skilled Dialogue's key dispositions).

These two views of children's behaviors illustrate how cultural perspectives influence quite distinct responses to behavior. They highlight the degree to which responses to challenging behaviors (i.e., behavioral differences perceived as negative) are grounded in larger culturally influenced perceptions rather than in absolute reality. Acknowledging this fact opens the door to the possibility of expanding the perceptual frameworks to more competently nurture children's spirits and sense of self.

EXPANDING PERCEPTUAL
FRAMEWORKS WITH SKILLED DIALOGUE

This expansion of perceptual frameworks is supported by the Skilled Dialogue approach, which proposes that both children's and adult's challenging behaviors be seen as more than just obstacles or "rocks" that hinder appropriate socialization and need to be changed. Diverse behaviors that challenge our sense of what should be also need to be perceived as potential resources or "diamonds" to be leveraged in the service of expanding behavioral repertoires.

When only one side (i.e., rocks or diamonds) is emphasized, the ability to communicate with and learn from (as well as teach) those whose beliefs and behaviors are different from our own is decreased, whether they are the behaviors of adults from other cultures or of children acting differently than desired by the adults around them. A one-sided view undermines the probability that our response to these adults and children will be perceived as respectful and responsive and achieve desired goals.

Within Skilled Dialogue, the obstacle or rock aspect is recognized not as a negative element but as a wake-up call alerting us to the fact that we need to turn off our autopilot approach to others and examine what is happening more closely. At the same time, the diamond or resource aspect is recognized as an invitation to the possibility of accessing previously unimagined options that enhance our own perspective as well as that of others. The following discussions of common ENC perceptions of differences and of varying models of agency across cultures provide clues as to how our perceptions of differences might become more flexible.

Common EuroAmerican Normative
Culture Perceptions of Differences

Balancing and integrating the rock and diamond aspects of behaviors diverse from our own is a key goal of the Skilled Dialogue approach. Examining common perceptions and understandings of differences within ENC contexts is a necessary first step to achieving this goal. These perceptions and understandings are not necessarily held consciously, nor are they necessarily true to any single cultural community. They are, however, discussed here as they are most often reflected in the larger ENC institutionalized cultural milieu that surrounds early childhood practices and settings in the United States.

Although seldom identified explicitly, current literature and rhetoric on diversity reflects three distinct perceptions of differences that may contribute to the prevalent one-sided tendency to focus on differences as problematic. These perceptions, which limit our ability to appreciate the gifts and strengths inherent in differences (i.e., their diamond aspect), stem from culturally embedded patterns of perception and thinking, as stated earlier (see also Stewart & Bennett, 1991).

Perception of Differences Based on What Is Not   The first of these patterns is the perception of differences as something based on what something or someone is *not*. That is, the tendency to first identify a referent reality—typically ENC in this case—and then identify what is *not* like that reality (i.e., we are deemed different when we are different from that reality). Stewart and Bennett presented an extensive discussion on the role of "negative thinking and null logic in American thought" (1991, p. 36). More specifically, they referenced "the existence in English of extreme dichotomies" that influence "how Americans manage their relations with others" (1991, p. 52).

Nuclear families, for example, are often understood only in contrast to extended families. Because I (Barrera) was familiar only with extended families for a long time as a child, my first understanding of nuclear families was simply "families that were not extended." It was the dichotomy of extended family–nuclear family that set the reference point.

Similarly, extended families, typically the less familiar reality in ENC, tend to be understood only as being what nuclear families, the more familiar configuration, are *not*. This pattern is reflected in what Stewart and Bennett termed "the negative precision of English qualifiers" (1991, p. 54). This pattern, in turn, facilitates the management of others and differences by focusing on what is *not* present. We may, in fact, not even be able to perceive what *is* present because it does not look like anything we have seen before; that is, we have no perceptual box for it.

As an example of this latter nonperception, behaviors different from those associated with independence in one culture (e.g., ENC) are almost always automatically perceived and classified as *not* independent (i.e., dependent), when in fact they may fit an entirely different third category, such as interdependence, that we may be unable to perceive. Whereas this bias toward contrast is a natural and useful tendency, it nevertheless obscures the actual nature of less familiar behaviors.

Focusing primarily on what is *not*, subtly, yet insistently, attaches differences only to those who are *not* like those who exhibit ENC values, beliefs, and behaviors (i.e., *they* are different, *we* are not). In effect, one reality (i.e., one culture, one behavior, one experience) becomes normative and all others are perceived as diverse. When this happens, the culture designated as normative is also assumed to be the "normal" nondiverse culture—the one that does not need to be examined or changed. If certain behaviors, values, and beliefs are different from the referent culture, then those who exhibit them are obviously the ones who are diverse and, by implication, the ones who need to change.

Perception of Differences as Contradictory   A second related perception is the perception of differences as contradictory. That is, if something is not like A, it must contradict, disagree with, or somehow diminish A. This perception is undergirded by an either-or perspective that places one reality at one end of a continuum and the contrasting reality at the other end. To get to one, the other must be somehow left behind or accessed only by invalidating the first. "Modern consciousness . . . is conditioned to think in either-or terms" (Sewall, 1999, p. 17).

According to Stewart and Bennett, "English demands that a continuum be represented by its extreme poles rather than by concepts drawn from the middle ground between opposites" (1991, p. 53). This tendency is apparent in efforts to compare ENC to other cultures. Many of these comparisons are conceptualized in two-column formats that emphasize the contrast between the two. In their classical work on cultural analysis, for example, Hall and Hall (1990) discussed underlying structures of culture with several either-or continua: fast and slow messages, high and low contexts, and monochromic and polychromic time.

The resulting tension between "this or that" sets up the perception of different behaviors and practices as contradictory, even though that may not be the initial intent. A common example is the perception of "living in two [hyphenated] worlds" (i.e., Mexican-American, Polish-American, and so on) that has been described in the literature by those who are bi- or multicultural (Lahiri, 2006). Another example is the prevailing discussion about the use of a language other than English in academic settings. Embedded in one side of this discussion—the side that advocates English only—there seems to be the message that using another language is contradictory to the use of English and will diminish it in some way, even when research clearly shows that the opposite can be true (i.e., that the use of an already existing language can strengthen and promote the learning and use of English) (see http://www.iteachilearn.com for more information).

When differences are perceived as contradictory, however, it is only a small step to perceive those who hold diverse views as being in disagreement or conflict with those who do not. Diversity is thus subtly, yet powerfully, silenced within a social code that responds negatively to disagreement (e.g., makes it not nice, perceives it as insubordinate or disrespectful, seeks to control it through the use of power, marginalizes it). Even when perceived only as making conversations difficult, diverse perspectives can be silenced (Copenhaver-Johnson, 2006).

Perception of Differences as Divisive   The perception of differences as contradictory is linked to a third perception—the perception that differences divide or separate rather than connect. After all, if one end of a continuum can be chosen only at the expense of the other, how can the two ends connect? This perception reflects cognitive confusion between being distinct and being separate.

The more recent perception that two apparently contradictory realities can be true at the same time (e.g., light can be both a particle and a wave) has yet to be fully integrated into general perceptions of differences to any significant degree (Wheatley, 2005). Within ENC contexts, differences between people are still commonly perceived as disagreements that separate or disconnect rather than as distinctions that can connect and offer rich alternatives. The efforts to keep languages other than English out of the schools bear witness to the underlying belief and subsequent perception of differences as divisive. The resulting tendency is to be threatened rather than intrigued by diverse lifestyles and cultural mores. Cummins (1989) termed this perception and its resulting responses to children as "subtractive" rather than "additive." In an earlier work, Cummins (1984) likened it to being forced to create a unicycle when a bicycle would be as or more useful.

Similarly, rivers between two countries are most often seen as dividing rather than connecting. Having grown up by such a river, however, I (Barrera) have seen how rivers can also serve as points of contact and meeting places between communities. Sewall discussed an interesting understanding of boundaries as unitive: "It [the edge] marks what is on the *other side* of our attention, of our current reality, signifying that the world is more" (1999, p. 135).

All three perceptions just discussed are simply variations on a theme of differences as contradictory polarities. It is not important to tease out where one perception stops and another begins. What is important is to acknowledge and explore the degree to which these perceptions, when taken for granted, undermine the very goal we so sincerely and persistently work to achieve, which is to honor and respect differences, whether linguistic, cultural, behavioral, or of another sort. Unacknowledged perceptions, such as the three just described, unfortunately perpetuate a misunderstanding of diversity that resists being truly responsive to it.

Differences cannot be truly honored when they are perceived as contradictory and divisive or at least mutually exclusive rather than complementary and unitive. In addition, when differences cannot be truly honored, unique identities and voices are lost and the ability to nurture children's spirits and sense of self is stunted. More specifically to challenging behaviors and interactions, we cannot honor, much less nurture children's spirits and sense of self, when we perceive these behaviors as contradictory and divisive—and, thus, behaviors to be eliminated—rather than as potentially complementary and unitive—and, thus, behaviors to be valued and leveraged.

Perceiving differences as complementary and unitive does not, however, mean that all behaviors—whether reflective of legitimate cultural perspectives or "only" of individual values and beliefs—should be allowed to continue without question. Such a response does not honor differences, it merely tolerates them and leaves both ourselves and the children with whom we work without the tools to participate successfully in multiple environments. Skilled Dialogue is an alternative way of perceiving differences, one that mines and leverages their strengths without requiring their denial or erasure (e.g., as illustrated in the opening anecdote in Chapter 1).

THE SKILLED DIALOGUE APPROACH

The Skilled Dialogue approach provides a practical framework for framing realities along an inclusive spectrum that supports both individual uniqueness and communal realities rather than an exclusive continuum that forces a choice between the two. Within this Skilled Dialogue framework, differences, whether cultural or "merely" personal, are perceived not only as potential obstacles, but also as diamonds—treasures to be mined in their own right rather than solely in reference to arbitrary norms. They are acknowledged as complementary rather than contradictory and as connective rather than divisive. The more detailed description of Skilled Dialogue's characteristic qualities and dynamics in the following chapters illustrates just how diversity can be reperceived in a way that supports our own development and learning as well as the development and learning of children, families, and colleagues from backgrounds, values, and behaviors diverse from are own.

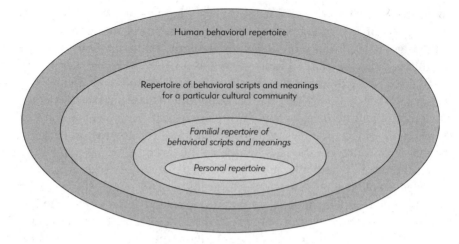

Figure 2.1.   Behavioral repertoires.

VARYING MODELS OF AGENCY

Beyond understanding common ways of perceiving diversity, there is also a need to understand the variety of ways in which people conceptualize and understand how and why they act (i.e., their agency). A discussion of the specific ways in which behavior can be structured and understood concretizes the preceding discussion and provides an extended backdrop to the discussion of Skilled Dialogue strategies in Part III of this book.

It is first important to recognize that all behavioral repertoires in which we may consider ourselves literate are nested in a larger human behavioral repertoire and, for that reason, have many similarities as well as dissimilarities (see Figure 2.1). It is the dissimilarities that are the focus of the following discussion, with the caveat that no single set of behaviors is ever exclusive to a single community (see Barrera et al., 2003, for a more detailed discussion of this aspect of culture).

Access to the larger repertoire of human behaviors is filtered through the lenses of culturally distinct communities, which select certain sections of that larger repertoire and then adapt them according to their experiences and geographic setting. These smaller repertoires do not limit an individual's access to the larger repertoire, but they do define the meaning(s) associated with individual behaviors and, consequently, the degree to which these behaviors are valued (i.e., considered good or appropriate). For example, everyone has access to the behavior of shouting in public. The value attached to that behavior, though, can vary significantly, either encouraging or discouraging its use.

Similarly, families adopt and adapt scripts and meanings from the larger cultural repertoires they experience. Out of the possible ways to greet strangers sanctioned by their culture, for instance, families will tend to prefer one to the others. Individual children are then acculturated and become "literate" in the preferred behaviors (i.e., behavioral "language") of their home community according to the level of their ability to learn and communicate.

Table 2.1. Models of agency overview

	Contractual–structural conjoint model	Relational–interpersonal conjoint model	Disjoint model
Definition of good actions	Script focused	Relationship focused	Self-focused
Consequences of actions	Affirm social order and social position	Affirm the interdependent self	Express and affirm the independent self
Style of action	Actively promoting social contracts	Actively referencing	Actively controlling
Sources of action	Actions are responsive to social structures, obligations, and roles	Actions are responsive to the nature of relationship with others	Actions are freely chosen

Reprinted from *Cross-Cultural Difference in Perspectives on the Self*, volume 49 of the Nebraska Symposium on Motivation, by permission of the University of Nebraska Press. © 2003 by the University of Nebraska Press.

The ways in which cultures structure the definition, consequences, style, and source of actions can differ significantly. Markus and Kitayama (2003) presented one useful framework for exploring these differences. They identified two models of agency (i.e., models about "the self in action," p. 1) that are particularly relevant to making sense of diverse behaviors (see also Chapter 8). They called the first a conjoint model and the second a disjoint model. Each model may be thought of as a behavioral language distinct from the others in at least the following four aspects:

1. How "good" actions are defined

2. Desired consequences of good actions

3. Action styles

4. The sources of actions

We have split Markus and Kitayama's conjoint model into two parts to distinguish between more formal conjoint models, such as those found in Asian and Middle Eastern cultures, and similar but less formal models, such as those found in Mexican and South American cultures, thus ending up with the three distinct models shown in Table 2.1.

The first of these models, which we have termed a *contractual–structural conjoint model,* privileges set social contracts and obligations. The second, which we have termed a *relational–interpersonal conjoint model,* privileges interdependence and more personally determined relationships. Finally, the third, termed a *disjoint model* by Markus and Kitayama, emphasizes a more self-focused and controlling perspective.

There is an important caveat to the discussion that follows. Discussions of group characteristics—whether characteristics of culture or gender or any other socially defined group—involve a certain level of generalization out of necessity. It can be said, for example, that men *generally* have greater upper body strength than women. Although this statement is true at a general group level, it may not be true of any particular man. It is simply more *probable* that if you are a man, you will have greater upper body strength than your sister. The following discussion of models of agency involves this same level of generality. Its statements cannot and should not be interpreted as prescriptive of any particular group or culture. They simply state probabilities associated with certain communities. It is when they are taken as predictions that stereotyping occurs. As Skilled Dialogue strategies are discussed more specifically in Part III of this book, the importance of staying open to exceptions is reemphasized.

Given this caveat, it can be said that each model of agency shown in Table 2.1 sets a distinct context for becoming literate in a community's behavioral repertoire(s). That is, it sets the parameters for reading and understanding the behavioral norms, expectations, and meanings associated with particular situations and environments. A young child wanting to exhibit compliant behavior, for example, might ask multiple questions during adult conversations in one cultural context, whereas in another context that very same behavior could communicate radical noncompliance or even disrespect (see the following discussion on disjoint model of agency). However, even though no one style absolutely defines any single community, it is almost always the case that one or another is valued more or less within one context or environment than in another context or environment.

Disjoint Model of Agency

Table 2.2 details the core elements of the disjoint model of agency. Communities that privilege a disjoint model of agency tend to define *good action* as action rooted in an individual's preferences, intentions, and goals (i.e., action that is self-referenced or self-focused). Such actions are valued to the degree that they lead to the expression and affirmation of an independent self. Individuals are consequently seen as responsible for their actions whose outcomes are believed to be largely personally controllable. A common proverb that reflects this emphasis says, "There are three kinds of people: those who make things happen, those who watch things happen, and those who don't know what is happening."

The disjoint model fosters an actively controlling style of action, which is a style that acts on others in a proactive fashion (i.e., makes things happen). In addition, individuals operating within a disjoint model perceive their actions to be freely chosen, contingent only on their own preferences, goals, intentions, and motives.

Although there are always exceptions, ENC culture tends to reflect the beliefs associated with the disjoint model of agency. According to Markus and Kitayama, "Normatively good actions originate in an *independent,* autonomous self, and the actions of this self are disjoint, that is, in some ways separate or distinct from the actions of others" (2003, p. 2). Because this type of model is prevalent in ENC, these statements may seem self-evident; however, they reflect only one way of perceiving and judging action.

Similar to speaking more than one language, it is possible that more than one model may be adopted within a single community. A disjoint model of agency, for example, may surround children acculturated into ENC. Such a model will encourage and reward autonomy and independent thinking. When they enter school, however, they may be expected to exhibit a degree of compliance to social expec-

Table 2.2. Disjoint model of agency

	Core perspective	Description
Definition of good actions	Self-focused	Inside-out perspective is dominant. Perceive self as independent from others; good action is action that follows from expression of individual's preferences, intentions, and goals.
Consequences of actions	Express and affirm the independent self	Actions are diagnostic of the self, and individuals are perceived to be responsible for the consequences of their actions. Agentic feelings may include esteem, efficacy, and power.
Style of action	Actively controlling	Influencing others, the world; fosters a proactive stance.
Sources of action	Actions are freely chosen	Contingent on one's own preferences, goals, intentions, and motives. Outcomes of actions are perceived to be largely personally controllable.

Reprinted from *Cross-Cultural Difference in Perspectives on the Self*, volume 49 of the Nebraska Symposium on Motivation, by permission of the University of Nebraska Press. © 2003 by the University of Nebraska Press.

tations and obligations that is more in keeping with the contractual–structural conjoint model (see Table 2.3). This shift to an entirely different behavioral language may be an implicit one that is not explicitly acknowledged. In most cases, in fact, the inconsistency will be denied.

Contractual–Structural Conjoint Model of Agency

Table 2.3 describes the contractual–structural conjoint model of agency, which is characteristic of diverse cultures, such as Asian and Middle Eastern, as well as of many institutionalized systems in the United States, such as schools and corporations. This second model focuses on social relationships, but it does so more impersonally than the relational–interpersonal conjoint model discussed later. The behavioral language of the contractual–structural model of agency defines good action as more than self-referenced. In contrast to the disjoint model, this model

Table 2.3. Contractual–structural conjoint model of agency

	Core perspective	Description
Definition of good actions	Script focused	Take into account contractual and/or procedural constraints; social and/or communal perspective is primary. Interdependent with others; good action is based on adherence to social contracts and/or scripts.
Consequences of actions	Affirm social order and social position	Agentic feelings may include sense of correctness, community support, and maintaining order. Actions are diagnostic of degree of socialization and social competence.
Style of action	Actively promoting social contracts	Adjusting to social mores; fosters an expressive enforcing stance.
Sources of action	Actions are responsive to social structures, obligations, and roles	Intentions are externally anchored in social expectations and/or contracts. Outcomes are contractually determined and controlled.

Reprinted from *Cross-Cultural Difference in Perspectives on the Self*, volume 49 of the Nebraska Symposium on Motivation, by permission of the University of Nebraska Press. © 2003 by the University of Nebraska Press.

bases its determination of goodness on contractual and procedural constraints rather than purely individual or interpersonal relational ones. Whereas recognizing the interdependence of people, it perceives actions as good based on the degree to which they affirm social order and position rather than particular relationships. Within this model, "'Authentic' or preferred action is often depicted as meeting expectations, being part of a group, or resulting from some process of mutual accommodation among people in a socially significant group" (Markus & Kitayama, 2003, p. 10).

Similar to the disjoint model, the contractual–structural conjoint model tends to privilege action that enforces a particular stance, although it defines such a stance by social contract or script rather than personal self-reference. Within this framework, outcomes are contractually determined and controlled. A proverb attributed to Saudi Arabian origin mirrors this perspective: "Know each other as if you were brothers; negotiate deals as if you were strangers to each other." In other words, do not rely on relationship to ensure desired outcome.

This proverb points out a distinction between formal objective and less formal subjective conjoint models. This latter type, discussed in the next section, is perhaps less well recognized. The distinctions between the two are significant.

Relational–Interpersonal Conjoint Model of Agency

Although also focused on social relationships, the relational–interpersonal conjoint model affirms the interdependent self rather than formalized social order and social position. The relational–interpersonal conjoint model tends to perceive relationships between people as the glue that holds communities together and, consequently, ensures adherence to social contracts (see Table 2.4).

In contrast to the disjoint model or the more formal contractual–structural conjoint model, some communities adhere to a relational–interpersonal conjoint model. Within this framework, actions are relationship focused rather than self-focused or contractually focused. This is not, however, the type of casual, informal, and totally personal relationship focus common to friends within ENC contexts (Stewart & Bennett, 1991). It is a relationship focus embedded in a network of "relational obligation" (Stewart & Bennett, 1991, p. 95).

> They [Americans operating with a disjoint model of agency] accept and express gratitude for a social act such as an invitation or gift, but the recipient is under no obligation to reciprocate. There does exist the vague propriety of a return gesture, but it does not have the binding and formal quality evident in other cultures. (Stewart & Bennett, 1991, p. 94)

Whereas both relational–interpersonal and contractual–structural models place an emphasis on social roles, those roles within a relational–interpersonal model tend to be embedded within and defined by social and kinship networks rather than formalized contracts.

> This entails making a fundamental shift in perspective. It means taking into account not only what things may look like from one's own perspective, but how they look

Table 2.4.   Relational–interpersonal conjoint model of agency[a]

	Core perspective	Description
Definition of good actions	Relationship focused	Take into account the perspective of others—mutual perspective is relevant. Interdependent with others, "good actions" arise in interaction with others, are responsive to others.
Consequences of actions	Affirm the inter-dependent self	Agentic feelings may include relatedness, connectedness, and sympathy. Actions are diagnostic of the nature of relationship, and consequences for actions are shared among those in the relationship.
Style of action	Actively referencing	Actively adjusts to others, the world; fosters a receptive stance.
Sources of action	Actions are responsive to the nature of relation-ship with others	Intentions are interpersonally anchored. Outcomes are largely jointly determined and controlled.

From *Cross-Cultural Difference in Perspectives on the Self*, volume 49 of the Nebraska Symposium on Motivation, by permission of the University of Nebraska Press. © 2003 by the University of Nebraska Press.

[a]Adapted from original conjoint model.

and feel from the perspective of the whole web of relationships among the people concerned. (Isaacs, 1999, p. 103)

From a relational–interpersonal conjoint perspective, the degree of goodness of an action is defined by the degree to which a person takes others' perspectives into account and is responsive to those perspectives. "Good" actions are designed to affirm the interdependent, rather than the independent self. Their outcome is "diagnostic of the nature of relationships, and the consequences for actions are shared among those in the relationships" (Markus & Kitayama, 2003, p. 7). Adjusting to, rather than influencing or controlling, is the valued style of action, and "outcomes are largely jointly determined and controlled" (Markus & Kitayama, p. 7). In this type of model, "individuals experience themselves as interdependent selves—as in-relation-to-others, as belonging to social groups, and/or as significantly and reciprocally enmeshed in families, communities, or work groups" (Markus & Kitayama, p. 10). The relational–interpersonal conjoint model emphasizes interdependence at a social and person–person level rather than a contractual one. A Mexican proverb (Foster, 1970) reflects this emphasis: "Dime con quien andas y te dire quien eres," which literally translates as "Tell who you spend time with and I will tell you who you are." I (Barrera) encountered the contrast between this perspective and the perspective espoused by the disjoint model in one of my seminar classes. I had asked students to identify personal "definers" (e.g., wife, student, artist). The difference between two particular students was striking. One student, a Navajo woman, defined herself entirely in relationship terms (e.g., aunt, mother, daughter, clan member); the other, a student who claimed no distinct cultural affiliation typified the disjoint perspective, although I did not know it as such then. This latter student, also a woman, used only self-referenced terms (e.g., artist, loner, writer, student).

BEHAVIORAL LANGUAGES

Each of the three models of agency can be thought of as a distinct behavioral language in which children gain proficiency (i.e., literacy) as they develop words and concepts. While verbal languages are both more explicit and more visible, behavioral languages are for the most part implicit and assumed. When someone speaks a verbal language that we do not understand, for example, it is easy to perceive him or her as simply using a different language, perhaps even one we have heard before or know about. When someone "speaks" a different behavior language, however, the tendency is to perceive him or her as doing something wrong or inappropriate. If a person's behavioral language reflects a relational–interpersonal conjoint perspective, he or she may, for example, always look to his or her friends before volunteering an answer in class or before going somewhere. A constant refrain in my (Barrera) years as a primary school student was "Miss, can I go get a drink of water?" followed by "Can Jane go with me?" Without an understanding of the relational–interpersonal conjoint model of agency, such behavior can easily be read as codependent or lacking in sufficient autonomy, which leads practitioners to want to change it. Another example comes to mind. When I (Barrera) directed a preschool program in an area with an approximately 98% Hispanic population, the practitioners in the program who were not Hispanic would often come in talking about the personal questions parents asked them on home visits (e.g., Are you married? Where do you live?). From the disjoint perspective in which the practitioners operated, such questions were either inappropriate or attempts to initiate personal friendships. From the parents' relational–interpersonal conjoint perspectives, however, they were attempts to situate the practitioners within a relational network so that they could assess their trustworthiness and credibility.

There are, of course, other models than the three just discussed, and, in all probability, few people operate totally in only one model. This discussion is meant only to illustrate the degree and kind of variation in cultural literacy that must be understood for differences to be perceived differently. This understanding is important to accurately assess and read the behavioral knowledge and skills—the behavioral language—that young children bring into service environments. Such assessment and reading is, in turn, critical because it is within the context of each child's behavioral language vis-à-vis the behavioral language desired in a particular setting that challenging behaviors arise and require a response. Similar to a verbal language, it is critical to differentiate between what is challenging or inappropriate within a given context but appropriate in another and what would be unintelligible or inappropriate in even the home context.

Table 2.5 illustrates how a challenging behavior—noncompliance to adult direction—could have dramatically distinct meanings depending on the model of agency within which the child and adult in question learned to operate.

Within a disjoint model, for example, noncompliance is typically understood as the assertion of one's own will and interests. This is, in fact, a common understanding in the face of young children's challenging behaviors (Watson, 2003), as

Table 2.5. Sample worksheet showing diverse behavioral perspectives based on model of agency

Sample behavior: Noncompliance with adult direction

	Contractual–structural conjoint model	Relational–interpersonal conjoint model	Disjoint model
Definition of action as "good"	*Script focused:* It's my responsibility as older brother to go see why my little brother is crying.	*Relationship focused:* I want to stay with my friend or brother.	*Self focused:* I want to follow my own interests and preferences.
Expected outcomes/consequences	*Affirm social order and social position:* To carry out my role as older brother; to merit my community's respect	*Affirm the interdependent self:* To strengthen my friendship and model what I'd like my friend or brother to do for me	*Express and affirm the independent self:* To feel powerful rather than subservient
Style of action	*Actively promoting social contracts:* I am true to social expectations and obligations.	*Actively referencing:* I am responsive to others who are significant to me.	*Actively controlling:* I can direct my own life.
Sources of action	*Actions are responsive to social structures, obligations, and roles:* My decisions affirm my participation in a social structure. It's about social propriety and obligations.	*Actions are responsive to the nature of relationship with others:* My decisions are based on others' needs as well as my own. It's about us.	*Actions are freely chosen:* I make my own decisions. It's about me.

well as the behaviors of those who disagree with us. Could such behavior be per-ceived differently? Could it reflect entirely different motivations and intentions? These questions are critical to the ultimate outcome of challenging adult–child and adult–adult interactions. The example would be a similar one if talking about a family's seeming resistance to suggested changes.

From the perspective of the relational–interpersonal conjoint model, however, a child's noncompliance might be understood as a gesture of loyalty and solidarity with a friend (e.g., I won't do it if my friend can't also do it.). How then might one respond? Similarly, a contractual–structural conjoint perspective might frame the behavior as one rooted in the child's understanding of his or her responsibility as an older brother (e.g., I won't do it because I have to go get my brother.). How could this perception affect one's choice of a response?

Understanding the models of agency within which both adults and children function is as important as understanding the verbal languages they use. If the child cannot understand the language of the adult—be it a verbal or a behavioral language—then using that language to remedy the interaction is both ineffective and self-defeating. Compliance may still be achieved, but only as a result of sheer power and at the cost of children's conviction in their ability to elicit "loving at-tention to their developmental needs" (Pieper & Pieper, 1999, p. 5)—that is, at the cost of undermining their spirits and sense of self.

With an adult, the push to achieve compliance without understanding the model of agency underlying the behavior in question can easily lead to disengage-ment or anger. An example of this occurred in relation to a young African Amer-ican woman being trained as a coach of early childhood care providers. The coach-ing model being used was embedded in the disjoint model of agency. The young woman's behavioral language with the providers, however, tended to reflect more of the relational–interpersonal conjoint model with which she was most familiar. As a consequence, her behavior tended to be perceived by her supervisors as more personal and less professional. At least that was her understanding of the feedback she received given her prior professional and personal contexts. The actual mes-sages being given to her were not truly heard except as a call to become like the other coaches. Each person was, quite literally, speaking a different language. Note that this is *not* to say that one party was more correct than the other or that either deliberately misunderstood or ignored the other. It is to say that, without under-standing the differences in the models of agency being used, the opportunity to leverage and integrate the strengths of both disjoint and conjoint models was missed. Reciprocity was not established, and neither party felt the other was re-sponsive to their perspective (see Part IV of this book for additional examples). For reciprocity and responsiveness to be established and sustained as complements to respect, the goal must be twofold, at least as understood from a Skilled Dialogue perspective. The first part is to understand and respect the model of agency from which the child or adult with whom a practitioner is interacting is operating; it is both that person's language and a reflection of his or her identity. The second part is equally critical: for the professional to expand his or her own, as well as the child's or adult's, behavioral options (i.e., to promote "behavioral bilingualism"). This latter part requires respectful teaching of alternative models of agency that *add* to the child's or adult's skills while recognizing that the existing model is still of value (i.e., has strengths that can bear on the interaction in question). When a bully insists on compliance with his demands, for example, noncompliance is a perfectly valid response. Even in a situation such as that of the young African American coach, noncompliance can be a strength. In refusing to comply with the request to shift models, this particular coach could bring to the forefront issues that the providers themselves might not feel confident enough to voice but that are critical to achieving the goals of all the coaches.

This need to recognize and honor diverse models of agency is revisited as the discussion of Skilled Dialogue continues later in this book. The content in the next three chapters, although more specific to Skilled Dialogue itself, is embedded within this need as well as with the network of ideas discussed in the first chapter. Chapter 3, for example, starts with the presentation of Skilled Dialogue's three essential qualities or outcomes: respect, reciprocity, and responsiveness. These qualities are necessary to nurturing children's spirits and sense of self yet can be interpreted differently depending on the model of agency being used. The two chapters that follow explore key dispositions that underlie and shape the concrete strategies.

DISCUSSION QUESTIONS AND ACTIVITIES

1. Review the three models of agency in Tables 2.2, 2.3, and 2.4. Discuss various behaviors you have encountered and see if you can determine the model in which they might have been embedded.

2. Which model(s) of agency do you think best characterizes your response to children's challenging behaviors? Do you ever use more than one? Can you determine what shifts you from one to another?

3. Think of your own early environment. Which model(s) of agency seemed to be the most prevalent? Is this the same as the one you now use?

4. Discuss the relative strengths and limitations of each model in relation to expected behavior in early childhood settings. Are these the same or different in relation to social-emotional intelligence? To character development?

5. Identify a challenging behavior you have experienced (or shown yourself). Use the worksheet in Table 2.6 to reflect on the model of agency underlying that behavior, as you understood it. Brainstorm different ways in which persons using a different model of agency might perceive that behavior.

6. Search for proverbs from different cultures. Discuss which model(s) of agency they reflect.

7. How do you perceive differences? Make a list of differences you consider very positive (e.g., speaking three languages), differences that you consider quite negative (e.g., stealing), and those that you consider relatively neutral (e.g., handedness). Compare your list with those of your peers and discuss similarities and differences.

Table 2.6. Worksheet for exploring diverse behavioral perspectives

Sample behavior: _____

	Contractual–structural conjoint model	Relational–interpersonal conjoint model	Disjoint model
Definition of action as "good"	*Script focused:*	*Relationship focused:*	*Self focused:*
Expected outcomes/consequences	*Affirm social order and social position:*	*Affirm the interdependent self:*	*Express and affirm the independent self:*
Style of action	*Actively promoting social contracts:*	*Actively referencing:*	*Actively controlling:*
Sources of action	*Actions are responsive to social structures, obligations, and roles:*	*Actions are responsive to the nature of relationship with others:*	*Actions are freely chosen:*

Skilled
Dialogue Framework

Caveat: Our apologies to readers who may be tempted to race ahead to Chapters 7 and 8 in Part III, or who may already have done so. Please bear with us and give equal attention to Chapters 3–6 in this part of the book. Skilled Dialogue is an organic rather than a linear process. Every element is a critical and inextricable part of every other element. To focus only on one (e.g., the strategies) is to quite literally take that element out of context and, ultimately, distort its true nature. The material discussed in these chapters will add both depth and substance to the material specific to the strategies. It is, in some ways, the most critical material. If the dispositions discussed in these chapters are in place, it is more likely that any strategies used will promote and sustain respect, reciprocity, and responsiveness. If they are not in place, even using the exact strategies proposed in this book cannot reliably promote or sustain these qualities.

Part I of this book set a context for the challenges posed by diverse perspectives. This second part focuses more specifically on the Skilled Dialogue framework. Isaacs described dialogue as "a process by which we can create containers that are capable of holding our own experience [and those of others] in ever more rich and complex ways, making legitimate many approaches and styles" (1999, p. 256). This description captures the essence and primary goal of the Skilled Dialogue well: to create interactional and conceptual containers for interactions with diverse people and, in doing so, transform the contradictions of contrasting perspectives, which reinforce either-or perspectives and choices, into paradoxes, which promote inclusive and integrative perspectives. It is this goal that provides both meaning and context to the use of its specific strategies. (Note: As used here, *contradictions* refers to differences in values, beliefs, perspectives, and behaviors; it is not synonymous with *disagreements*, though these may also be present)

As shown in Table II.1, the Skilled Dialogue framework is composed of three elements: qualities (or outcomes), dispositions, and strategies. The first two elements are addressed individually in Chapters 3, 4, and 5. Strategies, the third

Table II.1. Skilled Dialogue framework

Qualities	Dispositions		
	Choosing Relationship over Control		Setting the Stage for Miracles
	Strategies		
Respect (Honoring identity)	*Welcoming*		*Allowing*
		Differences do not make people wrong	
Reciprocity (Honoring voice)	*Sense-Making*		*Appreciating*
		Diversity is always life enhancing	
Responsiveness (Honoring connection)	*Joining*		*Harmonizing*
		There is always a third choice	

element, are introduced in Chapter 6, which details their relationship with both dispositions and qualities. They are then discussed in more detail in Part III, and, finally, illustrated through a variety of examples in Part IV.

Chapter 3 introduces the qualities that characterize Skilled Dialogue: respect, reciprocity, and responsiveness. These qualities are both the foundation and the desired outcomes of Skilled Dialogue. It is the degree of their presence—rather than individual behavioral outcomes—that ultimately determines the success of the interactional container (Isaacs, 1999) created as Skilled Dialogue strategies are applied to concrete situations and interactions.

This initial discussion of qualities in Chapter 3 is followed in Chapters 4 and 5 by a discussion of Skilled Dialogue's dispositions. These dispositions replace the two skills referred to in earlier work (Barrera et al., 2003). The decision to change this aspect of the Skilled Dialogue framework from skills to dispositions was made based on participant feedback over several years of fieldwork. Two aspects of the earlier use of skills that did not work as well as intended became salient through this feedback. The first was the use of the term *skills*. This term connoted an ability that could be mastered. It soon became clear that the understanding of these skills as an ongoing process that could be deepened and enriched, but never fully mastered, was often lost. The second aspect involved the names given to the skills themselves. After experimenting with several different terms, the term *disposition* was chosen as a better descriptor. Schulte, Edick, Edwards, and Mackiel (2004) cited Katz's (1993) definition of a disposition as "a pattern of behavior exhibited frequently and in the absence of coercion, and constituting a habit of mind under some conscious and voluntary control, and that is intentional and oriented to broad goals" (p. 10). This definition fits the use of the term in relation to Skilled Dialogue. Its dispositions are designed to act as the driving force behind the choice and application of specific strategies. Although less concrete than these strategies, the dispositions are nevertheless a critical element. In effect, the dispositions determine *how* we enter into an interaction, whereas the strategies determine *what* we do within those interactions.

Participant feedback also indicated that the original terms—Anchored Understanding of Diversity and 3rd Space—had significant drawbacks. Anchored Understanding of Diversity tended to be understood as only an increased cognitive understanding of differences rather than as an experiential grounding of existing understandings. Even when it was pointed out that this was not the case, the idea that this skill referred to the development of a deepened understanding anchored in relational and experiential contexts rather than in objective information continued to be less than clear.

The newer term—Choosing Relationship over Control—more clearly expresses the original intended meaning of Anchored Understanding of Diversity. It emphasizes working with differences from a subjective and relational perspective as a dynamic disposition rather than a static skill. Although subsuming all that was addressed through the original term (e.g., understanding diverse values and behaviors), the newer term now also addresses the intention behind the acquiring of such understanding. Of particular importance is the focus of this disposition on the primacy of seeking an experiential relational context with the goal of coming to *know* another, rather than merely the acquisition of objective information with the goal of knowing more *about* and, thus, feeling more in control and less vulnerable.

The disposition of Choosing Relationship over Control helps to generate and sustain respect, reciprocity, and responsiveness through its emphasis on both the intent and the practice of developing a contextualized and relational understanding of differences. By itself, however, this disposition can neither generate nor sustain inclusive and integrative options beyond those already present. The corollary disposition of Setting the Stage for Miracles is required for that.

Similar to Choosing Relationship over Control, Setting the Stage for Miracles also replaces an earlier term—3rd Space. As with Anchored Understanding of Diversity, participant feedback reflected a need to clarify this earlier term because of its unfamiliarity to many people, as well as because it tended to be understood as merely a type of mental gymnastics. For that reason, this element has also been renamed with a phrase that both makes its nature as a disposition clear and hints at its power: Setting the Stage for Miracles. "I have come to see this as the most subtle territory of leadership, creating the conditions for 'predictable miracles'" (Jaworski, 1996, p. ix).

The disposition of Setting the Stage for Miracles captures the original sense of 3rd Space as an energetic intent rather than merely a skill. It focuses on opening up perceptual and conceptual space so that exclusive contradictions can be transformed into inclusive paradoxes. It emphasizes a focus on outcomes beyond those that could be predicted or expected from existing data, as well as on outcomes not based on the actions or decisions of a single person. Although a single person can set the stage and increase the probability of a desired outcome, he or she cannot determine with any certainty what subsequently emerges.

Chapter 6 concludes the discussion of qualities and dispositions by briefly overviewing the strategies that are the concrete expression of Skilled Dialogue. This chapter integrates both qualities and dispositions and shows how these generate distinct strategies. Part III then moves on to provide detailed information on each strategy.

Chapter 3

Respect, Reciprocity, and Responsiveness

Skilled Dialogue is a process rooted in the literature on dialogue that conceives of interactions as relational and reciprocal rather than purely linguistic or behavioral (Isaacs, 1999; Yankelovich, 1999; Zaiss, 2002). Major proponents of the dialogic approach state the following: "Dialogue is a process by which we can create containers that are capable of holding our experience in ever more rich and complex ways . . ." (Isaacs, 1999, p. 256). More specifically, Skilled Dialogue stems from research into the qualities necessary to competently navigate and negotiate across interpersonal differences. Three qualities have been found to be particularly critical: respect, reciprocity, and responsiveness. These qualities are, therefore, the focal outcomes that now define Skilled Dialogue as a tool for the generation of optimal responses to diverse behaviors and perspectives. (See Barrera et al., 2003, for more information on the development of Skilled Dialogue.)

Recent research into perception and behavioral interactions indicates that people can read the intent of one another's actions even before the actions themselves are fully initiated. In a recent article, Rizzolatti, Fogassi, and Gallese (2006) concluded that the acts of discriminating a goal and discerning intention prior to completion of an act were carried out or mirrored in an observer's brain through the activation of similar motor pathways in that observer's brain. Although in its initial stages, this research seems to support the intuitive and experiential data underlying Skilled Dialogue.

Skilled Dialogue posits that a different message is communicated and different outcomes are achieved when interacting or communicating in the absence, as compared to the presence, of respectful, reciprocal, and responsive contexts. There is, in fact, additional research that bears this out. Langer's research showed that adults who were mindful (i.e., attentive, curious, interested, and respectful) in their interactions with children affected the children's level of self-esteem.

Some of the material in this chapter reprises the material in Chapter 4 of Barrera et al. (2003). Readers may want to refer to that material as well.

Interacting with a mindless adult pretending to be positive led to a drop in the children's self-esteem. They felt less competent, were less willing to help other [children], and had some negative feelings toward the adult when the adult was mindless. (2005, p. 31)

Given these and other similar data, it may be assumed that a perfectly appropriate behavior, such as switching to a person's home language, can either convey a message of welcome and appreciation or one of condescension or lack of any real interest, depending on whether or not it occurs within a respectful, reciprocal, and responsive context.

I (Barrera) still remember a situation that took place in a part of Texas that at that time had a large number of adults who spoke little or no English. My mother was an elderly gray-haired woman who did not present a "professional" appearance (as defined in ENC) and whose name identified her as Hispanic. During a medical appointment, the technician, with whom she had not had any previous interactions, addressed her in Spanish. She was not asked if she preferred that language, and, because she had not spoken yet, the technician had no information on her English fluency. Speaking in Spanish in that situation, although most likely intended to be respectful, carried another message to anyone familiar with common perceptions of elderly Hispanic women in that geographic area, which was that they were not expected to speak or understand English very well. My mother held a master's degree and had been a high school history teacher for more than 20 years; yet, in that particular environment, there was no acknowledgment or even curiosity about her as a person—acknowledgment and curiosity that would have sent a message of respect rather than of stereotypical perceptions.

Langer commented on this type of situation: "Whenever we work from scripts and not from our experience, we are mindlessly approaching the situation, taking our cues from fixed beliefs [i.e., stereotypes] about what is right, oblivious to alternatives and ignoring the variation of the situation" (2005, p. 25). The three qualities that characterize Skilled Dialogue—respect, reciprocity, and responsiveness—are intended to avoid such scripted interactions. They are intended to establish interactions that honor identity rather than presume it, that honor voice rather than silence it, and that honor connection rather than assume its absence or force its presence.

The following scenario is used to illustrate each of the three qualities more concretely. Within this scenario, issues of communicating skillfully and effectively are addressed at two distinct levels: adult–adult (i.e., practitioner–parent) and adult–child (i.e., practitioner–child or parent–child). The challenges inherent in any behavioral interaction can lie in any or all of these levels. (So that readers focus solely on the interaction, the source of differences in caregiver and parental perspectives is purposely omitted in this scenario. See Discussion Question 3.)

JOEY AND CAMILLA

Camilla, an early childhood practitioner, posed the following question: "How can I develop positive behavioral supports that nurture children's spirits and sense of self while also communicating the need to change particular behaviors? There are times when I am frustrated by the behaviors of the family and other practitioners who work with that same child as by the child's behaviors.

"Take 3-year-old Joey, for example. He resists direction and exhibits behaviors that are highly disruptive in teaching and learning environments. His Head Start teachers find themselves needing to pay a lot of attention to his behaviors, whereas they spend less time paying attention to those children who are participating as desired in ongoing activities. Some parents have noticed and commented on this. One of his teachers was instrumental in referring him for services.

"Joey's mother, JoAnne, is a single parent holding two jobs. She believes that there is nothing she can do about Joey's behavior and that he just needs 'more room.' When I talk with her about the need for more structured home routines and behavioral consequences, she tells me that Joey is a spirited child and, while she can see the problems he is having in our program and at home, she thinks that the recommended structured routines and behavioral consequences are both time consuming and impractical. 'And besides,' she said, 'Joey is a bright, creative child. He'll settle down as he gets a bit older. My brother had much the same problems as a child and he is just fine now.'"

• • •

This scenario represents a typical problem reported to us in our work. The behavior of concern often, although not always, involves some kind of noncompliance and disruption. In this scenario, the focus is on both the parent and the child, although that does not always need to be the case. Sometimes the parent(s) agrees with the practitioners, and the focus is only on the child. At other times, it is the behavior, beliefs, or values of the parent or caregiver that are most troubling to a practitioner, not the behavior, beliefs, or values of the child. Occasionally it is the practitioners, rather than family members, who diverge in their opinions as to what needs to be done.

In all cases, the important and common factor is a difference in beliefs or perspectives as to what should happen, but is not happening, or as to what is happening and should not be happening. For the purposes of this discussion, Camilla, Joey, and his mother, JoAnne, are followed throughout this chapter. The focus of this scenario is primarily on the qualities of respect, reciprocity, and responsiveness. In subsequent chapters and in other scenarios, the focus switches to the Skilled Dialogue predispositions that sustain and promote these qualities (i.e., Choosing Relationship over Control and Setting the Stage for Miracles).

RESPECT: DIFFERENCES DO NOT MAKE PEOPLE WRONG

Respect is the hallmark quality of Skilled Dialogue. It can be defined as the quality of honoring another's behavior as a legitimate and evidenced-based expression of their identity at a particular point in time. Table 3.1 shows an example and a non-example of underlying attitudes and comments that reflect the presence of respect.

Table 3.1.   Example and nonexample of respect

Example[a]	Nonexample[b]
"I welcomed the opportunity to hear what she had to say. I sat relaxed as I listened to her, leaning towards her with my arms open."	"One could easily see that the teachers had already decided that a father with an IQ of 70 was not capable of raising a daughter."
Underlying attitude: I don't really know who this person is.	Underlying attitude: I know who this person is.

[a]Both the example and the nonexample are taken from comments of workshop participants describing specific situations. We thank all workshop participants who gave permission for their comments to be used as part of our research data.

[b]The nonexample is not necessarily incorrect or inappropriate; however, it does not reflect the quality of respect.

The example in Table 3.1 comes from a workshop participant who clearly communicates that she is welcoming of the other person and willing to learn from her. This openness reflects an attitude that acknowledges that she does not have all the answers, which is a critical aspect of respect. When we respect someone we perceive him or her as a competent problem solver and creator in one or more dimensions of his or her life; that is, he or she is approached with an underlying attitude that acknowledges the fact that we—the relative newcomers to the situation—do not necessarily have the best answers, and that the other person has crafted competent answers given personal values and perceived choices.

When we disrespect someone, however, we tend to perceive him or her as somehow incompetent or not as competent as ourselves in solving his or her problems and creating his or her life. We perceive that person as having it wrong in some way, and believe that we, who have not lived his or her life, know better.

Respect encompasses behaviors and attitudes toward others that honor another's identity (i.e., acknowledge and honor a person's boundaries and the behaviors that manifest them as integral and legitimate expressions of self). We communicate respect when we believe that the behaviors others exhibit are the result of competent problem solving given their knowledge and life experience within a particular situation, rather than the result of faulty or incompetent problem solving or of not knowing what we know. Believing this, *we can respectfully acknowledge that, however differently we think we would choose or want them to choose, we would in all probability be exhibiting the same or similar behaviors, given their specific knowledge and life experience.*

There are many different things in the world, but dissimilarities do not make one wrong and another right. For example, roses are different from tulips and cars are different from horses. Respect starts with the premise that *differences do not make people wrong—they just make them different.* This is not to say that we cannot or should not invite change or that all behaviors are equally life supporting and fully adaptive to a given environment. It is to say that to be respectful, we must first acknowledge the other person's resources, strengths, and ability to learn. Many families and children, after all, manage to adapt to situations and challenges that would almost certainly overwhelm those who have never faced them.

Respect neither requires nor communicates agreement. It must simply communicate acknowledgment of the legitimacy of the ways others have crafted their lives in response to perceived and learned choices within particular circumstances. Isaacs defined respect indirectly, but powerfully, through his statements regarding its absence:

> The loss of respect manifests in a simple way: My assessment that what you are doing should not be happening. [This assessment] causes me to immediately look for a way to change you, to help you see the error of your ways. . . . People on the receiving end of this attitude experience violence—the imposition of a point of view with little or no understanding. (1999, p. 132)

Respect acknowledges differences without being judgmental. Individual boundaries mark individual differences (e.g., height, world views, values). They identify the parameters of the spaces we choose to occupy based on our circumstances and perceived choices. Physical boundaries delineate the physical space around us. When entered without our permission, we feel disturbed, perhaps even violated. When acknowledged and entered with our permission, however, we feel supported and connected. Similarly, emotional boundaries identify parameters of relatedness. They define when words and actions convey insult, praise, or disinterest, for example. Cognitive boundaries determine what we believe to be true and we believe to be false or not true. When these are crossed, we may not understand what is said, or we may feel confused, angry, or powerless. When validated, however, there is a greater sense of confidence and competence. Spiritual boundaries define our connection with those aspects of the universe bigger than us (e.g., God, Spirit, Energy, Self). When these boundaries are crossed, we may feel lost or somehow less well defined.

In short, the boundaries that we hold and the behaviors we use to express and maintain them reflect our basic assumptions about others, the surrounding world, and ourselves. These assumptions, most often learned early and unconsciously, are at the core of the actions and words we use and the meanings we attach to others' actions and our words (i.e., behavioral literacy).

Awareness and acknowledgment of different boundaries, especially when these seem to contradict our own, can challenge our assumptions. As a result, working with those who are diverse can pose particular challenges. Once differences are perceived, it may seem that to welcome those beliefs or values is to no longer be able to maintain connections with or control over our own sense of the world.

It is so often believed that what divides us are these very distinctions and that the only things that can connect us are our similarities. But is that true? Or is it instead the *meanings* attached to distinctions rather than the distinctions themselves that divide or connect? Wheatley alludes to this when she states that when connectedness is acknowledged, "rather than being a self-protective wall, boundaries become the place of meeting and exchange" (2005, p. 48).

How then can diverse boundaries become such a place in situations similar to that of Camilla, Joey, and JoAnne? Would respecting them just lead to undesired outcomes (i.e., letting things go on as they are)? Would it just "reinforce" the current behavior(s) that the practitioner wishes to change? These questions arise fairly easily. It is not as easy to recognize that not acknowledging diverse boundaries can also lead to undesired outcomes. Not having our boundaries recognized can generate thoughts that we are somehow not quite up to par or fully acceptable as a person and can increase child or parent resistance to our efforts.

In the sample scenario, Camilla can communicate respect through her explicit awareness and acknowledgment of JoAnne's and Joey's boundaries. She can choose to connect with them as they present themselves and as she wants them to connect with her. Doing this first requires remembering that there are many aspects to individuals and to the roles they choose to play in relation to each other. No one is ever fully defined by the behaviors they exhibit. To respect differences does not mean that individuals agree but that they acknowledge one another as more than just this or that "unacceptable" or "inappropriate" behavior. Ultimately, it also means releasing those labels.

Respecting a mother who refuses to adopt a practice a practitioner believes is necessary means first acknowledging that her perceptions and experiences are as legitimate within her context as the practitioner's are within his or her context. Later, the practitioner can seek to communicate alternatives that the mother may want to consider. Even then, however, the mother has the same right to her original perspective as the practitioner does to his or her own.

When I (Barrera) worked in an early intervention program in South Texas, it was not uncommon to hear practitioners trying to encourage mothers to stop carrying their toddlers given the "fact" that the children, who had physical disabilities, would have greater difficulty learning to walk if they were not allowed to walk more on their own. Their perspective was valid, given their perceptions and experiences (as well as their education and training). What they often failed to recognize, however, was that the mothers also had a valid, evidence-based set of perceptions and beliefs. These mothers had themselves been carried past the age when they could walk and had nevertheless become fully ambulatory, as had their extended family and friends. Their experiences and perceptions supported the "fact" that being carried had no correlation with how soon or how well one learned to walk, even when physical impairments were present. There is, by the way, no research data that support a detrimental effect to carrying children—unless, of course, they are never allowed to set their feet on the ground.

This recognition—that others see the world differently from us not because they are somehow wrong or less capable to learn about it than we are, but because their experience and perceptions support different "facts"—is a critical aspect of respectful communication for Camilla to acknowledge. Similarly, Joey's boundaries, even when so aggressively set, are creative and evidence-based expressions of his identity and need to be recognized as such. Somewhere, he too has amassed data that support these boundaries.

The recognition of a valid experiential database does not, however, mean that either Camilla or JoAnne needs to accept the status quo and seek no further change. It only reflects a willingness to 1) acknowledge differing perceptions and boundaries as legitimate evidence-based expressions of learning and 2) suspend the need to immediately change them to match someone else's perceptions and boundaries. (This does not mean condoning the use of abuse; see Barrera et al.,

Table 3.2. Example and nonexample of reciprocity

Example[a]	Nonexample[b]
"I asked both [parents] to describe what they want for their child. I asked them to describe specific situations which they have tried and been frustrated with."	"One person kept saying, 'I understand what you are saying, but you're wrong in that . . . .' The other man kept saying that he wished he could debate as well as his friend."
Underlying attitude: I need to ask you about what you know. I do not yet have enough information to know the best options and/or answers.	Underlying attitude: I already know what is wrong (with what they are doing and/or how they are doing it). There is no need to get any additional information from you.

[a]Both the example and the nonexample are taken from comments of workshop participants describing specific situations. We thank all workshop participants who gave permission for their comments to be used as part of our research data.

[b]The nonexample is not necessarily incorrect or inappropriate; however, it does not reflect the quality of reciprocity.

2003, for more detail.) The quality of respect thus opens the door to interactions within which Camilla, Joey, and JoAnne can all feel valued and remain open to each other. The specific Skilled Dialogue strategies for promoting such interactions are discussed and exemplified in Chapter 7.

RECIPROCITY: DIVERSITY IS ALWAYS LIFE ENHANCING

Reciprocity, a second quality necessary to navigating and negotiating across differences, builds on respect. It rests on the premise that diversity is always life enhancing (i.e., it adds to, rather than detracts from, available resources). This is a growing understanding in current environmental and other research (Chivian & Berstein, 2008).

Reciprocity seeks to honor another's "voice" or power as a life-enhancing resource that brings as much to an interaction as one's own voice. At its core is the recognition that the behavior of each person in an interaction is an expression of his or her competence and ability to learn rather than of an inability or refusal to learn. To understand reciprocity in this sense is to distinguish the common ENC understanding of power as expertise, authority, or ability to exert force from a less common understanding of power as capacity or capability. This latter understanding is reflected in the Spanish word *poder,* which is both a noun meaning power and a verb meaning to be able, as in "yo puedo" ("I can").

Table 3.2 presents illustrative comments that reflect the presence as well as the absence of reciprocity. These comments capture the essence of reciprocity—an attitude of openness to another's diverse perspectives (i.e., an attitude of "I don't have all the answers."). Such an attitude leaves room for another's voice (i.e., perspective and values) even when it disagrees with one's own. In contrast, the nonexample in Table 3.2 reflects an attitude that privileges one perspective, typically that of the "expert," over that of the child and/or family. Reciprocity does not require denying that one person has more expertise or knowledge than another in particular areas (e.g., adult compared with a child) or that one person has more institutionalized authority (e.g., a social worker with the authority to remove children from their home compared with a parent). What reciprocity does require is acknowledging and trusting that another's behavior is an expression of *different* learning rather than *deficient* learning, and, thus, is of equal value to one's own.

Unfortunately, it can be all too easy to fall into the roles of expert or helper and believe that one needs only to teach and/or give and that there is nothing to learn and/or receive.

In reciprocal relationships everyone is perceived as having something to offer that enriches not only the potential outcome of their interactions but also the persons involved. The recognition that one point of view need not dominate or exclude a diverse point of view, and the consequent support of free choice over forced (either-or) choice are two important aspects of reciprocal interactions.

When differences are acknowledged as reciprocal, no sense of debt is incurred by any of the persons involved; no one is solely giver or receiver (Dunst et al., 1988). *Entering into interactions only to give—whether knowledge, support, direction, or something else—with no acknowledgement of what others, even children, can contribute inhibits not only what we might receive, but also the full potential of what we seek to give.* Ultimately, the lack of reciprocity erases respect because it reflects the perception that one person or one viewpoint is of more value than others, which are perceived as needing to be changed (see previous quotation on lack of respect from Isaacs, 1999).

Regarding the vignette of Camilla, the early childhood practitioner who seeks JoAnne's agreement on how to manage Joey's behavior, how might reciprocity be established? Respect yields a simple nonjudgmental acknowledgment that legitimate, albeit diverse, perspectives are present. This acknowledgment suspends the need to impose one experience of reality on another (e.g., push JoAnne to become engaged with Joey in the ways that Camilla values, or conversely, to acquiesce and offer no options for change). Reciprocity takes this a step further by encouraging the expression of diverse perspectives as a means of mining their strengths. Examples of reciprocity would include concrete expressions of the following three beliefs:

1. The belief that JoAnne's beliefs and behaviors are the result of competent learning, based on her experiences and abilities, rather than the result of learning that is somehow faulty or less capable than that of Camilla—the "expert" or "helper."

2. The belief that JoAnne's behaviors have, at their core, something of value. It is only when exaggerated that the expression of that core value leads to inappropriate use of those behaviors. Asserting boundaries is a highly valuable skill. It is only when it is exaggerated (i.e., done forcefully and at the expense of others' boundaries) that it becomes inappropriate.

3. The belief that JoAnne and Camilla are both teacher and learner (i.e., reciprocally engaged with each other). They are each experts with something to teach each other. They are also learners who can learn from each other.

More specifically, supporting reciprocity in relation to Camilla's interactions with JoAnne would require two things at a minimum: 1) acknowledgment of what resources and insights JoAnne brings to this particular situation and 2) curiosity about how JoAnne's current behavior is contributing something of value to the desired outcome (e.g., trusting Joey's own developmental wisdom, listening to Joey's needs). This acknowledgment and recognition can then lead to affirming JoAnne's capacity to competently craft interactions with her child at other times and in other settings. It is this capacity, after all, that Camilla must tap in order to initiate desired change. There is, however, a significant difference between perceiving it as an existing capacity that can be tapped and perceiving it as a capacity that needs to be taught. The former supports authentic learning, and the latter supports only one-way transmission of information.

Eventually, to fully establish reciprocity, Camilla must understand that JoAnne is already involved with Joey in a variety of ways, albeit perhaps not in the ways Camilla would want. This realization shifts the focus from trying to increase JoAnne's involvement, which is currently perceived as nonexistent, to expanding her repertoire of involvement behaviors (i.e., from replacing to adding to). This is similar to recognizing that children in the United States who are proficient in languages other than English do not need to learn language. They already have a language; they merely need to learn English, which is an entirely different task and one to which they bring rich cognitive and linguistic resources (see Barrera et al., 2003).

Reciprocity is more effectively established when the interactional focus shifts from changing behavior to finding ways to expand existing behavioral repertoires. Because power is, at its root, about the number of options available in any given situation, a focus on eliminating one behavior in order to develop another diminishes power (i.e., removes an existing option). Active curiosity about how a person's current behavior contributes something of value to the desired outcome, however, adds a second option and thus increases power.

In a parallel fashion, supporting reciprocity in Camilla's and JoAnne's interactions with Joey would invite acknowledgment that Joey is already exercising competent learning (although perhaps not performance appropriate to a given context) given his experiences and interpretation of those experiences.

An example of a different child may illustrate this point more clearly. A mother came to me (Barrera) and asked about toilet training her child—a boy who was almost 4 years old and still not using a potty. He just refused, she explained. Her husband, who had experienced late toilet training as a child himself, saw no problem. The childcare facility they were using, however, did see it as a problem. They refused to move her son out of the 2-year-old room until he could consistently use toileting facilities. Establishing reciprocity (i.e., honoring voice) in this situation required 1) acknowledging her son as a competent learner who, for some as yet undetermined reason, saw not using the potty as a more appropriate and right behavior than using it and 2) becoming curious as to what data might support that fact. Eventually the mother realized that her son was, in fact, learning— and mirroring back—exactly what she and her husband were teaching as he understood it. She realized that it was not that he was not learning. He was actually learning quite competently, just not what she believed she was teaching. He was, in fact, very accurately mirroring back her perception that learning to use the potty was a difficult task and one that his father did not think very important at this point. In addition, the more the mother tried various methods to teach him, the more he learned that he must not be a very good learner.

As she realized this, she began to trust that that her son was a competent learner. At last report, the child had learned the appropriate behaviors with no further difficulty. (It is important to note that in this case there was no true learning delay or disability. When a delay or disability is present, the messages between parent and child can become even more complicated and misunderstood.)

Similarly, establishing reciprocity in interactions with Joey invited both Camilla and JoAnne to acknowledge his competence and learn from him. In doing so, they modeled for him how he could learn from them. They could, for example, learn from him how to more consistently and clearly structure their own messages about his behavior (e.g., Camilla's message that Joey's behavior is "uncontrollable" and JoAnne's message that it is "creative") so that he could better distinguish creative behavior from uncontrollable behavior.

Perhaps they might also learn about being willing to express boundaries, even when such expression is perceived by others as inappropriate. That is not to say that Joey's violation of others' boundaries should become something to be praised. Rather, it is to recognize the value that is at the core of his behavior so that it is not lost as he is asked to honor others' voices. This is not an easy balance. (See Part III, especially Chapter 8, for more on this topic and on how to interact in such a way as to support the positive core of a behavior without simultaneously reinforcing its exaggerated expression.)

RESPONSIVENESS: THERE IS ALWAYS A THIRD CHOICE

If respect is about recognizing different boundaries and reciprocity is about acknowledging that every person has something of value to contribute, then responsiveness is about honoring connections rather than divisions. At the core of responsiveness is the recognition that there are always more than two choices. This recognition requires a willingness to allow others "to uncover who they are rather than shaping them into who we want or need them to be" (Freedman & Combs, 1996, p. 281). To be responsive is to acknowledge the need to step outside of an either-or framework, which disconnects and ultimately distorts both perspectives in question.

Table 3.3 defines the quality of responsiveness and gives an example and a nonexample of its presence. As with respect and reciprocity, responsiveness is characterized by an attitude of openness. It reflects a "we" perspective rather than a "you" perspective and acknowledges that the identified problem occurs within the context of particular relationships and not in isolation (e.g., Joey's behavior is not solely his problem).

To be responsive to another is to entertain the possibility of connection rather than follow the certainty of separation. It is to be willing to look beyond obvious contradictions and shift focus from what divides to what connects. When we see a behavior or an interaction and it seems quite incompatible with what we would like to see, or when we experience things that seem contradictory to our perspec-

Table 3.3. Example and nonexample of responsiveness

Example[a]	Nonexample[b]
"With this parent it is important that I remember to listen and pay attention or I might miss important detail. I also need to remember that what works for me may not work for her and that I am just part of her process. Sometimes just repeating back to her what she said is enough to give her new insight."	"I have taken all of her stories into consideration and come up with a plan to make sure the children are safe and well cared for. In so doing, these modifications in her own [sic] will also improve the quality of her life by fixing the things in her home which she desperately needs."
Underlying attitude: It is about us and the connection between us.	Underlying attitude: It is all about her; it has nothing to do with me.

[a]Both the example and the nonexample are taken from comments of workshop participants describing specific situations. We thank all workshop participants who gave permission for their comments to be used as part of our research data.

[b]The nonexample is not necessarily incorrect or inappropriate; however, it does not reflect the quality of responsiveness.

tives, being responsive calls us to ask "Where are the connections between our perspective and what we see? What is it about the diverse perspective that complements, encourages, evokes, or somehow keeps it connected with our own?" "Mistakes," for example, are always connected with what is "correct," otherwise they could not be judged as mistakes.

All differences have something in common. Efficiency and laziness, for instance, have in common the goal of conserving energy. At that level, there is no contradiction. Responsiveness seeks to affirm how differences are joined (i.e., how there are similarities in the differences to the same degree as there are differences in the similarities) by shifting perceptions from a "you and I" perspective to a "we" perspective.

Responsiveness entertains mystery. Entertaining mystery requires that practitioners attend to children and families "with focused attention, patience and curiosity" (Freedman & Combs, 1996, p. 44) in order to interact with who they truly are, not who the practitioners think they are. If we seek only certainty and forget mystery, children and families become frozen within our own categories and labels. They are reduced to a singular generic identity (e.g., the child with attention-deficit/hyperactivity disorder [ADHD], the resistant mother). Practitioners are no longer in interaction with *them*—only with their own *ideas* about them.

Remen (2000) wrote about how individuals get stuck in images and become reactive rather than responsive. She noted that "Knowing where we are going encourages us to stop seeing and hearing and allows us to fall asleep . . . [such knowing allows] a part of [us] to rush ahead to [our destination] the moment [we] see it" (2000, p. 289). This is, unfortunately, all too apt a description of what can happen as practitioners confront diversity with all of their certainties and recommendations. It is all too easy to rush ahead to conclusions about what a behavior means and what needs to be done without taking the time to discover underlying patterns of connections that can motivate and support change.

Responding and responsiveness are not necessarily the same. Responding merely replies. It gives an answer, but not necessarily one that connects to the other person's true concern or question. The following scenario illustrates this point. Mary, a supervisor, asked Judy, an EC teacher, "How are you today?" Judy answered, "Well, I'm really worried about those things that you told me I needed to do to stay in compliance." Mary then replied, "I'm sorry. Here are the toys I mentioned I'd be bringing by today. Where would you like me to put them?" This type of immediate shift back to one's original agenda always acts against communicating true responsiveness.

Responsiveness addresses not only the question but also the context that frames that question (e.g., "I'm so sorry that you're worried. Would you like to talk about it before we talk about what I brought for you?") It requires leaving room for the unexpected and the unpredictable (i.e., taking the time to talk off topic). Furthermore, it may not be as off topic as one thinks. Perhaps attending to Mary's worry will lead to greater responsiveness on her part in the future. Maybe she will change via routes not yet explored as a result of the response to her concerns. Maybe she will become much more resourceful than was foreseen. Responsiveness, however, should not be used only as a means to an end. It should be sought as an end in itself.

The quality of responsiveness is particularly important in situations where practitioners and children and/or families hold radically different perspectives or beliefs. Through their diversity, these situations challenge practitioners to recognize that a person is always more than, perhaps even radically different from, the ideas about whom they are or what they can do. While it is not always possible to eliminate preconceived ideas and judgments (i.e., the "boxes" in which people and experiences are placed), it is possible to remain open to what might lie outside of them. (see Chapter 9 for exercises that can facilitate this openness.)

With regard to the vignette about Camilla and JoAnne, how might Camilla be responsive to JoAnne and Joey as well as to her own needs? Remember that responsiveness builds on reciprocity and, thus, is not about one perspective being given more voice than another. The answer will naturally vary according to the specifics of a given situation, but here are some possibilities. Camilla might be responsive through one or more of the following:

1. She can appreciate Joey's ability to learn and not "freeze" her idea of him as a child with ADHD or a child who is unwilling or unable to change. She can seek aspects of his behavior and personality that are outside of those perceptions (e.g., Are there times when he seeks change? Can part of his behavior be seen as a need for change? Are there times when he listens well, perhaps when he is listening to music or a DVD?).

2. She can seek similarities in their behaviors—how might Joey's ADHD mirror a facet of Camilla's behavior, as she pushes her agenda and/or ideas at the expense of Joey's? How is JoAnne's noninvolvement mirrored by Camilla's behavior? Is she also staying uninvolved at some level, perhaps by trying too hard to remain objective? Finding these similarities can dissolve the "us–them" dichotomies that are keeping her from fully understanding Joey's and JoAnne's perspectives.

3. She can understand that she is making sense of the situation through the lens of a disjoint model of agency and recognize that approaching the situation

from a different model might be more effective (see Chapter 2). This might mean shifting to a different lens and understanding Joey's "problem" as more than just *Joey's* problem, thus shifting from an independent disjoint model perspective (e.g., outcomes of actions are largely personally controlled) to an interdependent or script-focused conjoint perspective (e.g., outcomes are largely jointly determined and controlled). From this latter perspective, she can ask herself how she might be unconsciously and unintentionally supporting Joey's behavior.

4. She can ask JoAnne what changing Joey's behavior means to her. Perhaps she fears crushing Joey's or even her own creativity and intelligence that she is currently affirming indirectly through his behavior. Perhaps it means that he would be labeled as needing special education and would not be considered "okay." Perhaps it would mean expending more energy than she believes she has. Perhaps it would mean having to face her sense of being overwhelmed.

5. She can value JoAnne's perception of the situation as much as her own and explore what value it might be contributing to the situation, rather than just seeing it as an obstacle to desired goals. Does JoAnne truly believe that there is no room for change? Or, does she not feel that she has the ability to carry out the proposed program, which might open her to being shamed if she tried? What specific responsibilities is she assigning JoAnne with her proposed program? Has she studied JoAnne's daily schedule to determine just how it could be done? Has she considered how it might affect JoAnne's current acceptance of Joey?

6. She can share with JoAnne all that she has to offer in this situation and structure sessions so that JoAnne also can contribute her knowledge (e.g., having her share what she believes about discipline and how she supports autonomy with Camilla).

These possibilities (and other similar ones) may not necessarily "solve the problem." Skilled Dialogue is not designed to do that. They will, however, gradually redefine existing perceptions and options, changing the tenor of interactions among Camilla, JoAnne, and Joey and increasing the possibility of arriving at more satisfactory and competent interactions and options. That is the purpose and goal of Skilled Dialogue.

The three qualities of respect, reciprocity, and responsiveness provide the defining context for Skilled Dialogue. Establishing and supporting these qualities is the focus of the dispositions discussed in the next two chapters. Chapter 6 then puts it all together and illustrates how dispositions and qualities generate distinct strategies.

DISCUSSION QUESTIONS AND ACTIVITIES

1. Think of someone you respect highly. How do your interactions with him or her reflect respect, reciprocity, and responsiveness as discussed in this chapter?

2. Think of someone you would like to change in some way. In what ways might his or her present behavior reflect a competent choice given their particular circumstances and experiential knowledge?

3. Reread the sample scenario in this chapter. If you knew that Camilla's behavior reflected her cultural affiliation, would that make a difference in how you interpreted and responded to it? Would you think differently if you knew that her neighbors and extended family members agreed with you? Why do you think this information would make a difference?

4. Think of a challenging interaction in which you have recently been involved. How did you respond? Place your responses in either the example or non-example columns of Tables 3.1, 3.2, and 3.3. If you have nonexamples for any quality, brainstorm responses that would have more fully reflected that quality.

5. Think of a "negative" behavior exhibited by someone you know. Brainstorm how your own behavior(s) might be supporting or enabling it even though that is not your intention. For example, are you someone who is always well organized, and is there someone you know who is chronically disorganized? Can you picture that person becoming organized? If not, how are you communicating your lack of belief in his or her ability to organize?

Choosing Relationship over Control

The disposition of Choosing Relationship over Control acts as an energetic intention that focuses on creating a relational space where disparate identities can be welcomed, disparate voices can be placed in contexts that make sense, and connections between disparate perspectives can be acknowledged. It contrasts with a disposition toward choosing control, which emphasizes certainty and predictability, and implicitly or explicitly communicates a hierarchy of identity and voice that disconnects rather than connects.

Although the word *relationship* is common, it is not always easy to define (Josselson, 1996). The *Merriam-Webster Online Dictionary* (2008)[1] gives the following definition for *relationship:* "the state of being related or interrelated." A search for the definition of *related* yielded "connected by reason of an established or discoverable relation." Finally, *relation* is defined as "an aspect or quality (or resemblance) that connects two or more things or parts as being or belonging or working together or being of the same kind." These definitions contrast with the one given for *control,* which is "to exercise restraining or directing influence over," "to have power over." Furthermore, *controlling* is defined as "inclined to control others' behavior."

The meaning of choosing relationship over control can be inferred from these descriptions and definitions. It may best be captured, though, in a quote from Josselson who talked about "the space between us" and said that it involved "actually or metaphorically . . . reaching through space (or being reached) and being in contact with each other" (1996, p. 6). Whereas control emphasizes a unidirectional act, relationship focuses on a two-way connection.

Choosing Relationship over Control does not refer to establishing personal relationships. Rather it refers to the willingness to craft interactions within which identity and voice are honored as being of value in their own right, not just through desired outcomes; diverse identities and voices are acknowledged as complementary (i.e., connected) rather than as separate; and subjective knowledge is valued (see discussion on relational knowledge later in this chapter).

The choice between relationship and control is not an either-or choice, however. Both have something of value to offer depending on the degree to which

---

[1]Definitions used by permission. From the *Merriam-Webster Online Dictionary* © 2009 by Merriam-Webster Incorporated (www.Merriam-Webster.com).

dialogue, which is "a process of successful relationship building" (Yankelovich, 1999, p.15), is desired as well as on the specific context in which either relationship or control is chosen. Although dialogue is always a valid choice, theoretically speaking, it may not always be a wise choice in contexts where our own limitations leave us vulnerable to its abuse (e.g., with a physically violent person about to attack us).

Skilled Dialogue calls for a disposition toward choosing relationship for several additional reasons. These include the following: 1) as a counterbalance to the tendency to choose control; 2) as a direct expression of another's dignity and worth as equal to one's own; 3) as a more effective means of establishing truly collaborative partnerships; and, perhaps most important, 4) as a reflection of the growing recognition that reality is composed of relationships between things, not of the things themselves. This latter recognition has its roots in science as it investigates the interdependence of all things (e.g., Shelton, 1999; Wheatley, 1992, 2005), as well in the most recent conceptualizations of social intelligence (Goleman, 2006).

Wheatley said,

> It is impossible to look into the natural world and find a separated individual. As an African proverb states, "Alone, I have seen many marvelous things, none of which were true." Biologist Lynn Margulis expresses a similar sentiment when she comments that independence is a political concept, not a biological concept. "Everywhere life displays itself as complex, tangled, messy webs of relationships. . . . Organisms shape themselves in response to their neighbors and their environments. All respond to one another, coevolving and cocreating the complex systems we see in nature." (as cited in Wheatley, 2005, p. 25)

Diversity is but the visible manifestation of these co-evolved and co-created complex systems.

Similarly, a disposition toward choosing relationship places an implicit and explicit focus on mutual understanding and acknowledgement of another's unique perspective as connected with one's own. In contrast, a disposition toward choosing control instead places an emphasis on nonmutuality and the certainty and predictability of one's own perspective independent of anyone else's. Interactional strategies selected based on choosing control communicate a hierarchy of identity and voice (e.g., indicate what or who is "right" or has more power) and place connection into that hierarchy.

Table 4.1 summarizes information on disposition of Choosing Relationship over Control. Its examples illustrate giving priority to the person(s) with whom we are interacting rather than to our agenda or targeted outcomes. In other words, the other person's perspective, feelings, and concerns are recognized and acknowledged prior to emphasizing our own agenda.

ANCHORED UNDERSTANDING OF DIVERSITY

The disposition of Choosing Relationship over Control is closely tied to the skill of Anchored Understanding of Diversity, discussed in Barrera et al. (2003). Anchoring one's understanding of others experientially as well as cognitively facilitates

Table 4.1. Definition and description of Choosing Relationship over Control, including examples and nonexamples

Description	Underlying purpose and key question	Associated strategies
The intent to enter into respectful, reciprocal, and responsive I–Thou relationships rather than to merely engage in agenda-driven I–It interactions	*Purpose:* To understand and relate with another in ways that honor their identity, their voice, and establish a mutual connection across differences *Key question:* Am I willing to acknowledge the legitimacy of another's perspective and the connection between our views and behaviors?	Choosing Relationship over Control involves the strategies of *Welcoming, Sense-Making,* and *Joining,* discussed in Chapter 6 and Part III.

Examples[a]	Nonexamples[b]
"Mary is someone I have gotten to know in the last 6 years. I have discovered through conversation with her what a different understanding of the world she has . . . she is very lonely."	"This partner had very quick answers to all questions, was not focused on what was being said, and obviously appeared like he knew everything already and didn't need anything from me."
"It was during my next visit that I discovered that Sam did not understand supervision and scheduling of staff requirements . . . I approached the appointed director about these issues and tried to understand her thinking. I gave her correct information and expectations. She in turn told me about the small town situation she was dealing with."	"I could tell from [his] tone and responses that he was not very happy. At first I interpreted this 'tone' to mean that he was angry with me. This interpretation did not make me want to offer much to the conversation."

[a]Both the examples and the nonexamples are taken from comments of workshop participants describing specific situations. We thank all workshop participants who gave permission for their comments to be used as part of our research data.

[b]The nonexamples are not necessarily incorrect or inappropriate; however, they do not reflect the disposition of Choosing Relationship over Control.

subjective relational knowledge (i.e., knowledge that unfolds with the context of engagement with a specific unique person in concrete situations) in contrast to "objective" unanchored knowledge. Relational knowledge yields information on the meaning of *this* behavior exhibited by *this* person in *this* situation. It is such knowledge that moves the other from object (i.e., It) to subject (i.e., Thou) (see Chapter 1 for discussion of this distinction).

In contrast, unanchored understanding is generic, abstract, and divorced from the specific aspects of concrete situations. It comes "prepackaged" (e.g., discussions of typical behaviors for particular cultural or ethnic communities, such as Hispanic or African American). These discussions are true at a general level and useful in gaining a broad overview of possible behaviors, as is all such knowledge. It is "true," for example, that most men have greater upper body strength than women. It is similarly "true" that most Hispanics speak Spanish and value interdependence over independence. These statements are "true," but only as generalities; that is, until they are applied to individual men or individual Hispanics. When anchored experientially, they may or may not be true. What is typical or "average" is never 100% true.

Relationally anchored knowledge tells us what is true in *this* situation for *this* person and is derived from direct experience in that situation with that person. If we remain at the abstract unanchored level, however, we can choose relationship only with a generic reality (e.g., a generic male or a generic Hispanic) and will overlook or try to control the specifics that do not match the generic depiction. For example, when interacting with a Southeast Asian family, we may overlook skills or knowledge that have not been identified in generic descriptions simply because we do not know to look for them or think that they cannot be there.

Although certainly valuable, such knowledge subtly warps perceptions and interpretations by disconnecting them from particular personal and experiential contexts. It can lead us to fit families and children into preexisting labels (e.g., ADHD, Hispanic, resistant) and, consequently, to focus primarily, if not solely, on the data that conform to those labels rather than on the specific person who stands before us. As noted by a comment from a 1930 report to the White House Conference on Children and Youth (as cited in *The Learning Compact Redefined;* Association for Supervision and Curriculum Development, 2007, p. 10), "To the doctor, the child is a typhoid patient; to the playground supervisor, a first baseman; to the teacher, a learner of arithmetic. . . ."

From this unanchored generic perspective, behaviors that reflect curiosity in one child, for example, may instead be perceived as distractible once that child is identified as having ADHD. Similarly, persistent questioning can be perceived as negative (something to be eliminated) or positive (something to be encouraged) depending on the abstract category or categories through which we filter our perceptions. A tolerance for such questioning can, for example, be quite expansive if we believe it to be an expression of giftedness. If, however, we are already convinced that this child is stubborn, our tolerance will in all probability diminish considerably.

Without the disposition of Choosing Relationship over Control, we may thus fail to step back and consider multiple perspectives and instead fall back on a single meaning. From a perspective that primarily values abstract "knowing *about,*" the answer lies in objective information independent of the practitioner's relationship with the person being questioned. (It is interesting to note that people often rely on such "objective" information primarily with people with whom they do not have or do not wish to have a relationship outside of narrowly defined roles.) From an anchored experiential perspective, however, the answer lies embedded in the relationship itself.

Choosing Relationship over Control focuses on establishing an understanding of differences that is anchored experientially and relationally in face-to-face and hands-on experience with particular children and families in order to concretize and contextualize more abstract information and thus make it truly comprehensible.

It is relational experience, for example, that changes generic understanding of *snow* to a concrete understanding of its weight, appearance, and feel under specific circumstances. When I (Barrera) first heard of *wet snow,* I had only objective knowledge of snow, so I thought the phrase was nonsensical. Wasn't all snow wet by definition, objectively speaking? It was not until I moved to Buffalo, New York, and had to shovel snow that I learned the difference between *wet snow* and *dry snow.* (For those readers who have had this experience, it is okay to laugh. For those who have not, it should be noted that *wet snow* not only feels radically different but also weighs significantly more than *dry snow,* similar to a bag of wet sand as compared to a bag of dry sand. Even that, however, remains only an abstract understanding until one has had to shovel both types!)

A similar shift in understanding is illustrated in the following story. Imagine that you have stopped at the grocery store on your way home after a long and frustrating day at work. You want to just run in and out and so, once you have your groceries, you choose a checkout line that has only one person ahead of you. As that person reaches the cashier, though, she places a baby carrier with an infant on the counter. She and the cashier then proceed to have a 15-minute conversation about the baby. *How would you interpret their behavior at this point, without knowing either person?*

Finally, their conversation ends, and it is your turn. As you place your groceries on the counter, the cashier turns to you and says, "Thank you so much for your patience. That was my babysitter and my child. My husband died suddenly several months ago, and I had to take a job. This is the only time I get to see my baby because I have to leave in the morning before she wakes up and can't return home until evening, after she has gone to sleep." *How would you interpret the two women's behavior now that one of them is no longer just a generic cashier?*

If you exercised the disposition of Choosing Relationship over Control during this interaction, you would search for ways to relate with the situation as created by these particular people in this particular context so that you could better ascertain its meaning for them. You would reject objective (i.e., out of context) judgments as inappropriate and inconsiderate, knowing that they are limited by being based only on your preexisting knowledge, values, and/or beliefs. Being disposed to choose to enter into relationship with the person chatting with the cashier, even at a minimal level, would at least open the possibility of taking his or her values and beliefs into account in addition to your own. Choosing relationship invites respect *for* what happened rather than control (e.g., attending only to its violation of your expectations and to set social norms for cashiers' behaviors) *over* what happened.

The disposition of Choosing Relationship over Control is both particular and reciprocal. It generates knowledge in context; that is, knowledge that "arises not from standing back in order to look at [and control], but by active and intentional engagement in lived experience" (Groome, 1980, p. 141). Talking generally about a behavior exhibited by a family, for example, is quite different from carrying out that discussion over time directly with a particular family—seeing their faces and hearing their stories. Extended face-to-face interactions create two types of contexts that facilitate Choosing Relationship over Control.

First, they create an interpersonal context. Within such a context, knowledge becomes about someone whom we actually know and with whom we are in relationship. For example, it becomes about Cathy, a unique child with particular characteristics and talents who happens to have autism, and not just about Cathy, the child with autism.

Second, face-to-face interactions—unlike less personal ones—stimulate inclusive conceptual contexts that increase one's ability to make sense of, rather than merely judge, others' behaviors and perspectives. For example, knowledge about parenting children with Down syndrome that is gained objectively (e.g., from reading about mothers with children with Down syndrome, from attending a panel presentation given by these mothers) shifts powerfully when your best friend gives birth to a child with Down syndrome and you see her daily experiences as she seeks to learn her child's needs and talents. Only then can you particularize the more general knowledge you possess and see how it really plays out in concrete circumstances and contexts. Granted, not every mother's experience with a child with Down syndrome will be the same; however, your understanding of those other mothers' experiences would no longer be what it had been before.

Within concrete and specific contexts, previously held categories and assumptions are challenged (e.g., "It's not all about struggle and grief," "Just where does time to simply be a parent and spouse come in as we recommend all those services and home activities?"). Practitioners learn that there is more to a situation than they may have once believed. When they bring their understanding of something that they have not experienced face-to-face with a relationship with those who have lived it, it acquires depth and specificity that, although not generalizable to all situations, nevertheless expands and enriches their understanding of the various ways in which that "something" manifests in concrete situations.

Remen (2000) told a cautionary tale that further illustrates the distinction between knowing what is experientially and relationally anchored (i.e., rooted in the disposition of Choosing Relationship over Control) and knowing that remains generic and objective (i.e., rooted in choosing control over relationship). (This story was shared in Barrera et al., 2003; it is included here as well because it is such a striking illustration of whether we choose relationship or control.) She told of a young physician who had an elderly Navajo woman as her patient. She had seen this woman regularly for years, treating her for a variety of diseases. After the Navajo woman died at the age of 96, the physician received a call from a researcher writing a book about American Indian medicine traditions. This researcher told the physician that he had been told about a great medicine woman. When he contacted her family to learn more of her, he was told that their mother had been cared for by this physician who "would have the answers he needed" (Remen, 2000, p. 69). Remen recounted her own experience with this physician, who sadly told her that he had remained unaware that his patient had been a renowned medicine woman. The physician told her, "'I had been so busy with my numbers and my tests [trying to control the situation instead of relating with her]. What I would give for even one hour with her now, to ask her any of my unanswered questions . . . Or simply to ask for her blessing'" (2000, p. 69).

As EC practitioners, we are the recipients and generators of a large volume of information *about* the young children and families with whom we work. Yet, how often do we remain like that physician, unaware of what lies beyond our objective information? Can we, for example, talk about the family's hopes and dreams, frustrations and anxieties from their perspective? Can we describe a particular child without reference to developmental status or disability conditions? Can we define what success or family mean to that particular child and family? The ability to answer these questions reflects the degree to which we have chosen relationship over control in our work.

Face-to-face interactions provide direct and experiential anchors, as well as cognitive anchors (i.e., the recognition that the individual behaviors encountered in face-to-face interactions have a larger context than just the ones defined by the characteristics on which practitioners are focused). The interpretation of behaviors needs to be anchored not only in one's knowledge of a particular child or adult, but also in a pool of evidenced-based information about these larger contexts.

It is through cognitive anchoring that we, as practitioners, come to affirm that all behaviors make sense once their intent and the particular conditions under which they are operating is identified. In addition to everything discussed to this point, the disposition of Choosing Relationship over Control rests on this broader recognition and acknowledgment of diverse behavioral contexts as legitimate evidence-based expressions of identity and competence.

DIVERSE BEHAVIORAL CONTEXTS

Markus and Kitayama (2003, p. 5) noted, "Most of human behavior . . . is realized through culture-specific language, schemas, practices, and tools and thus unfolds in culture-specific ways." These culturally specific ways of behaving have evolved over time in response to specific experiential evidence. Understanding this fact allows people to anchor their knowledge not only in particular face-to-face experiences, but also in broader cultural perspectives within which others' diverse behaviors are more than just idiosyncratic choices. From this double perspective, all behaviors, no matter how different from one's own, both make sense and invite respect. (See the discussion of models of agency in Chapter 2. Also, see Barrera et al., 2003, for more detail on the various aspects of cultural beliefs and values.)

To believe that behavior can be interpreted or modified without first understanding its subjective and cultural context is to ignore the multiplicity of the very real networks of beliefs and values within which human activity occurs and, consequently, to privilege one such network over others. Asking a mother, for instance, to change her feeding routines or disciplinary practices without first seeking to anchor our understanding of those practices risks communicating deep disrespect at best and diminished care and nurturing at worst. A teacher in one of my (Barrera) classes shared a striking example of what can happen when practitioners intervene without experiential and relational knowledge. She had a young child in her class that consistently bit other children. Understandably, she initiated strategies to eliminate this behavior and was successful. The child did stop biting other children— only to start biting herself. The teacher realized that she had not taken the time to truly enter into relationship with this child and uncover the context that fueled the biting.

Of course, biting other children was a behavior that could not be allowed to continue. The issue was not whether or not it should have been eliminated. The core issue was *how* it could best be eliminated: within a context of relationship? Or one of control? The first would communicate support and responsiveness; the second would only throw the child back on her own resources.

Acquiring the disposition of Choosing Relationship over Control in interactions with others whose identities and voices are diverse from our own does not require that we admire the behaviors they exhibit, only that that we understand how that behavior makes sense from their cultural as well as their personal and experiential perspectives. (See the Guide to Identifying Cultural Data in Appendix C at the end of the book. See also Barrera et al., 2003, for a more detailed discussion of culture and its associated variables.) Without such understanding, it becomes all too easy to simply believe that they have nothing of relevance to contribute and, therefore, withhold our respect.

When someone's behavior does not make sense to the person observing it—or only makes sense as something negative—respect is subtly yet powerfully undermined, as are reciprocity and responsiveness. Nothing undermines these qualities as strongly as the perception that our behavior is somehow judged to be of less value or as having less legitimacy than another's. This does not necessarily mean that we overtly disrespect the other person, merely that we may not accord the appropriate degree of attention and interest.

A practitioner may not admire the behavior of a caregiver that sets no firm bedtime for his or her 4-year-old child, for example. Nevertheless, that practitioner can communicate his or her understanding that such behavior makes sense from that caregiver's experiential evidence and culturally based perspective. The disposition of Choosing Relationship over Control invites all of us working with children and families to become curious as to just how the experiential, emotional, and cultural framework within which the family operates brings sense to that behavior. Why does this caregiver in this family perceive this behavioral option as more appropriate than the option preferred or seen as more appropriate by the practitioner (e.g., a set and consistent bedtime)? What understanding of how the world works underlies this behavior, which is believed to be inappropriate and which, in fact, may even be inappropriate in contexts outside those familiar to this caregiver and this family?

The disposition of Choosing Relationship over Control requires the ability to anchor the general understanding brought to particular contexts according to the concrete aspects of these contexts, instead of remaining tied to abstract understandings of that reality. Without that ability, we end up relating only to our *idea* and *image* of the specific person with whom we are interacting. We will, for example, tend to relate with Mrs. Miller only as the "Overwhelmed and Disrespected Teacher" or with Mrs. Taylor only as the "Disrespectful Parent Unwilling to Discipline Her Child." Although it is useful to acquire general information, it is critical to anchor that information in the particular and subjective aspects of concrete contexts. Relationship cannot be chosen at a generalized abstract level; it can only be chosen with a specific context with particular people and concrete circumstances.

Without Choosing Relationship over Control, our primary orientation in interactions with others remains instrumental and tactical (i.e., focused on changing X, accomplishing Y, or controlling Z). In his foreword to Kahane (2004), Peter Senge talked about such an orientation. He said,

> Our typical patterns of [interacting with others] in difficult situations are tactical not relational. . . . We sift through others' views for what we can make use of to make our own points. We measure success by how effective we have been in gaining advantage for our favored positions. (2004, p. x)

In other words, control is chosen over relationship, albeit perhaps unintentionally. Practitioners at Skilled Dialogue workshops echo this same point when they ask, "How can we take the time to get to really know our families when we have to show measurable progress toward our stated objectives in a specified amount of time [sometimes only a few weeks after meeting the family]?" They repeatedly express frustration at the tension between taking the time to establish sufficient rapport with a family and changing their behavior to meet stated objectives. Choosing Relationship over Control, however, means intentionally connecting with families and others in ways that make the accomplishment of preset goals and objectives secondary to honoring their (and the practitioner's) identity and voice.

The distinction between relationship and control is a critical one, especially in professions such as early childhood where so often progress is measured based solely on movement toward targeted goals and objectives rather than on the quality of relationships with families and the families' own perceptions of respect, reciprocity, and responsiveness. In ignoring the latter, it is easy to miss nontargeted outcomes, such as increased self-competence or expanded problem-solving skills. Even more significantly, an exclusive focus on preset outcomes fails to honor others' diverse experiences and perceptions as legitimate (i.e., fails to truly respect them and draw from them) and can, in fact, inhibit the emergence of the very outcomes sought.

CRITICAL ASPECTS OF CHOOSING RELATIONSHIP OVER CONTROL

Dispositions may be thought of as being composed of two levels of inclinations: internal (e.g., Are you disposed to choose relationship?) and external (e.g., Are you willing to act in accordance with that disposition?) (Tishman, Jay, & Perkins, 1992). Within Skilled Dialogue, each disposition is associated with certain critical aspects that are reflective of the external level of its inclinations. These critical aspects shape and guide the specific behavioral indicators associated with the strategies discussed in Part III of this book. That is, the strategies work best when their respective behavioral indicators spring from the inclinations associated with choosing relationship rather than from inclinations reflective of a desire to control outcomes (e.g., being polite as a means to achieve an outcome of choice rather than pushing a personal agenda at the cost of someone else's). More specifically, three sets of critical aspects define Choosing Relationship over Control (see Table 4.2). Each one is discussed in the following sections.

Table 4.2. Critical aspects of Choosing Relationship over Control

- Assumption of equal competency to craft a behavioral repertoire adaptive to the given contexts
- Acceptance of diverse behavior(s) as evidence based
- Willingness to communicate unconditional respect

- Sense of curiosity about other people's stories and interpretations of reality
- A learner's attitude and mindset
- Nonjudgmental information gathering
- Perspective taking

- Explicit recognition of the messages sent
- Recognition that contradictory behaviors can be complementary
- Willingness to change verbal and nonverbal messages

First Set of Critical Aspects

The first set of critical aspects associated with Choosing Relationship over Control focuses on establishing an initial context of respect. Each aspect addresses the need to welcome the other as a peer who can make valuable contributions to the interaction.

Assumption of Equal Competency The assumption that everyone (i.e., this child, this family, or this person) is competent (i.e., has the ability to craft behavioral repertoires adaptive to their given environments) negates the power imbalance that defines control. That is, it keeps one person from believing that he or she knows more or better and can, therefore, dictate to another. Although one person may, in fact, have more authority, status, or expertise than another, the capacity of the other craft to competent behavioral repertoires adaptive to a given environment can still be recognized and acknowledged.

To gain insight into the degree to which there is equal competency between individuals in an interaction, it is important to ask the following: What thoughts, beliefs, and/or feelings do we bring to our interactions with this other person? Are we, for example, convinced that a child is incapable of managing his or her behavioral impulses or that our coteacher just cannot control this child? Or, are we convinced, or do we at least suspect, that we could do better in their shoes? It is one thing to have a deeper range of expertise; it is another to assume that, because of that, the other person is incapable of acquiring a similar expertise or at least of changing his or her behavior in the desired direction.

Acceptance of Diverse Behaviors as Evidence Based Accepting diverse behaviors as evidence based (i.e., stemming from direct experiential or other evidence) affirms our recognition of another's competence. This affirmation reflects an underlying belief that the other's behavior, however diverse and/or unacceptable from our perspective, is based on evidence that grounds the other's choices rather than being the outcome of ignorance or incapacity. When diverse behaviors are accepted as evidence-based, there is a recognition of their validity as well as of the other's competence.

Willingness to Communicate Unconditional Respect There is no authentic relationship without unconditional respect. When one person withholds such respect from another, the balance of power between them shifts toward control rather than relationship. One person is placed in the position of either having to earn the other's respect or being deemed as powerless to do so. In both scenarios, the innate capacities (i.e., power) of one of the participants remain unrecognized or devalued, which makes reciprocity untenable (see Chapter 3 for further discussion on respect).

Second Set of Critical Aspects

The next set of critical aspects that define Choosing Relationship over Control focuses on making sense of another's behavior(s) in order to be able to relate more fully to who that person is and what that person believes.

Sense of Curiosity About Other People's Stories and Interpretations of Reality Having a sense of curiosity about others' stories and interpretations of reality involves acknowledging that we do not have enough information about them and asking questions such as the following: What do they tell themselves about their behaviors and/or beliefs and what they mean? Do they, for example, believe that yelling at their children is an expression of concern? Or, do they believe that yelling is the only way to get their children to really listen? How do their stories and interpretations differ from our own? It is typically the behaviors that contrast with our own stories and interpretations that make the least sense to us or can make sense only in a negative way (e.g., behavior X indicates that the parent is not really concerned about his or her child).

Learner's Attitude and Mindset Having a learner's attitude and mindset is a corollary to maintaining a sense of curiosity. When we take on a learner's attitude and mindset, we acknowledge a lack of answers and release the certainty that we know what is right or better, which so often drives our need to control. With this acknowledgment, it is then possible to relate to differences—and the people who exhibit them—as realities we have yet to make sense of, rather than as realities that do not make any sense.

Nonjudgmental Information Gathering A learner's attitude and mindset supports nonjudgmental information gathering—a third critical aspect associated with Choosing Relationship over Control. As we become curious about others' stories and interpretations and begin to gather information about those stories and interpretations, it is important to listen nonjudgmentally (i.e., without attaching our own stories and interpretations). Rather than thinking, "Oh, I know what that means," we need to think, "Hmm, I know what that would mean from my perspective, but I wonder if it doesn't mean something entirely different from the other person's perspective."

Upon finding that a parent has failed to show up for one more appointment, for example, we can think, "I know what that means (from my perspective); it means that parent is being disrespectful and doesn't really care about working with me on Justin's behavior." Nonjudgmental listening, however, would result in thinking something such as "Even though I know that from my perspective not showing up for an appointment and not calling to say one can't show up means disrespect and disruption of relationship, I wonder what it means from the parent's perspective." This would then lead to increased curiosity and a learner's attitude and mindset once again, and the cycle would continue until we could ascertain the meaning of that behavior from the parent's viewpoint. If we find that, in fact, it does mean an intentional message of disrespect, then we would start to wonder what story supports the parent's decision to send such a message at this time.

Perspective Taking   Perspective taking is the "see the world through their eyes" aspect of choosing relationship (see discussion of reciprocity in Chapter 7). Perspective taking does not mean that we need to abandon our own perspective in favor of the other person's perspective. In fact, to do that would violate the reciprocity necessary to the relationship we are seeking to establish. It instead means seeing the situation and/or behavior through both our personal perspective and the other person's perspective simultaneously. Doing this will, similar to seeing with two eyes, shift our vision from a flat image with no depth perception to a 3-dimensional image that will facilitate authentic relationship.

Third Set of Critical Aspects

The last set of critical aspects focuses on how the various behaviors being exhibited are connected within the particular context(s) within which they are occurring. It reflects the recognition that no behavior exists independent of its social context.

Explicit Recognition of the Messages Sent   The first critical aspect of this last set of aspects involves the explicit recognition of the messages we send, which others may pick up as strong or nonnegotiable invitations. It is these messages that connect one person's behaviors with another's even when the message received may not be the message that was intended.

The choice of how to behave with another person is significantly influenced by the messages we perceive in a particular situation, as well those we have internalized from previous similar situations. Whereas a family member's choice to consistently arrive at meetings after their set time, for example, may be a reflection of their personality, the use of that choice in a particular situation with a particular person is also elicited in part by the concrete characteristics of that situation and that person. This means that choosing relationship requires looking at our own behavior in relationship to the other's behavior. There is, as a colleague said, a difference between having a button and having that button pushed. Her specific comment was "They may push your buttons, but they didn't install them!" (D. Macpherson, personal communication).

Recent literature is beginning to pay attention to just how one person's behavior can affect another's (Goleman, 2006). This is something not easily accepted from the perspective of a disjoint model of agency, which insists that our behavioral choices are strictly our own. In some ways this is true—these choices are not forced upon us. We can, however, be issued strong "invitations" to do something through peer pressure, direct commands, and so forth, and have limited abilities to refuse those invitations. As my (Barrera) first boss was fond of saying, "This is just a suggestion, but don't forget who is making it!"

When we perceive and, thus, receive a "suggestion" from a significant person, be it a parent, dear friend, or authority figure (and all adults are authority figures to children), we may lack the cognitive and/or social-emotional abilities to resist that invitation. A common and unfortunate message given by practitioners is transmitted through the phrase, "How did that make you feel?" Children can read this question as a statement that affirms that external circumstances can *make* us feel one way or another (i.e., that we are at their mercy). There is, thus, a fine line between making a suggestion and hearing a directive. When this is not clarified, children (as well as adults) can easily receive mixed messages about how much influence other's have on their behavior and how much freedom they have to choose their own behaviors.

A teacher repeatedly telling a child to sit still, for example, may well be perceived by that child to be saying "You can't sit still." Those very words may even be used at times. The child may then perceive that as a concrete definition of who he or she is and accept the invitation to be "the child who can't be still" and behave accordingly. There is no simple equation, however; a different child may perceive the same message in an entirely different manner.

Similarly, a teacher asking for a meeting with a parent and setting the day and time without consulting that parent might be perceived as disrespectful or uncaring of the stress and difficulties in that parent's daily life. That parent might then turn the invitation around and send the same message back to the teacher, effectively disrupting any positive communication between them.

The recognition that all behavior is jointly constructed and maintained can help to disentangle these situations. This aspect of Choosing Relationship over Control helps to reclaim our power to change situations without requiring that someone else change first.

Recognition that Contradictory Behaviors Can Be Complementary   Once the shared nature of all behavior is recognized, another aspect of choosing relationship can be more easily accessed—the recognition that even apparently contradictory behaviors can be complementary (i.e., that they support and fuel each other). Some things are related through their similarities. Others, however, are related through their contrasts. The concept of *light*, for example, exists only in contrast to *darkness*. Similarly, the idea of *empty* would have no meaning if there was no concept of *full*. Making the choice toward relationship invites exploration into how behaviors that are uncomfortable or undesirable may, in fact, be supported and fueled by our own more comfortable and desired behaviors. Does insistence on timeliness, for example, somehow support and fuel the tardiness that we continually find and dislike in others? The answer to this question might be found by asking the following questions: How could we define and identify timeliness if

there were no tardiness? How could we pride ourselves on our own timeliness if there was no tardiness? What are we keeping out of our experience when we refuse to allow for alternative conceptions of time? (See the discussion about *Harmonizing* in Chapter 9 for further discussion of this point.)

Willingness to Change Verbal and Nonverbal Messages   The critical aspect of being willing to change verbal and nonverbal messages is about being able to change the messages we send that contribute to and sustain the identified problem. Sometimes the simple recognition of these messages is sufficient to initiate change. Sometimes more may be required (e.g., receiving confirmation of the messages from a trusted person, role-playing sending different messages). (See the Selected Resources at the end of this chapter for additional insight into this aspect.)

CAMILLA AND JOANNE

This section uses the vignette about Camilla and JoAnne from Chapter 3 to show how Camilla, the EC practitioner, might behave if it was her intention to choose relationship with JoAnne over control of her behaviors. Some possibilities include the following:

1. Camilla can remind herself that, although she has certain information about JoAnne, she is still missing critical experiential knowledge necessary to correctly interpret that information. For example, she may know that JoAnne has a history of being slow to accept practitioners' recommendations. She cannot, however, interpret that as resistance or lack of caring without getting to know the experiential base and cultural understanding that shape what "changing" really means to JoAnne. Does it mean a rejection of whom she believes herself to be? Does it mean a loss of security? Does it mean cognitive disorganization? To answer those questions appropriately, as well as respectfully, Camilla must look to her relationship with JoAnne, not just to the objective information in the case files.

2. Camilla can listen and ask questions to help her better understand JoAnne's child-rearing choices within the context of JoAnne's particular experiences and culturally based learning. She can seek to discover how these choices make sense (i.e., reflect problem-solving competence) given those experiences and learning.

3. Camilla can verbally affirm JoAnne's competence—what she is doing well with Joey—and identify how JoAnne's behavior can complement the desired outcomes targeted by Camilla. That is, she can choose to find a way to bring those strengths and complementary behaviors into the relationship along with her current understanding and perspective rather than trying to control Camilla through exclusion and/or demands for change.

4. Camilla can ask herself, "What can I learn from JoAnne (e.g., about making decisions under difficult circumstances, about unconditional parenting)?

5. She can *join* with JoAnne (see Chapter 9 for a detailed description of the *Joining* strategy) by attending to her with focused attention, patience, and curiosity (i.e., modeling how she would like JoAnne to attend to her).

After spending time with JoAnne and following some of these suggestions, the degree to which Camilla successfully chooses relationship over control will be evident in the degree to which she can honestly believe that, given JoAnne's experiences and cultural perspectives, she, too, might behave as JoAnne did and refuse to implement a behavioral support plan given to her by a practitioner.

• • •

As long as we can say, "I would never do that" or "I can't believe someone would do that," in reference to behavior deemed unacceptable, we have not yet truly chosen relationship over control (i.e., we have been unable to relate their perspective to our own). In that case, at some level, we have remained unable to anchor our understanding of another's diverse behavior experientially or cognitively. To that degree, we continue to carry and communicate, explicitly or implicitly, a judgment of ourselves as better or more competent than the other person.

CHOOSING RELATIONSHIP OVER CONTROL AND SKILLED DIALOGUE'S THREE QUALITIES

The disposition of Choosing Relationship over Control supports Skilled Dialogue's three qualities—respect, reciprocity, and responsiveness—through its focus on establishing rapport and anchoring understanding of differences experientially (i.e., in relational interactions) and cognitively (i.e., in the new understandings generated by those interactions). This disposition promotes respect (i.e., honors identity) as it encourages us to first get to know someone's identity as a person of value and dignity before seeking to change a targeted behavior. It establishes reciprocity (i.e., honors voice) as it urges us to relate to others as competent individuals who have crafted legitimate sets of behavior given their particular circumstances and perspectives. Finally, it stimulates the generation of multiple options that are truly responsive (i.e., reflect others' unique perspectives and beliefs, as well as the needs of a given situation without requiring either the elimination of one perspective or the privileging of another).

To exercise the disposition of Choosing Relationship over Control, we must examine the perceptions, beliefs, and thoughts that shape our interactions with others. It is important to ask ourselves if the goal is to change the other person. Or, is it to first get to know the person so as to better understand his or her perceptions and perspectives? To what degree are we truly disposed to connect with him or her in ways that can lead to mutual growth rather than only to the achievement of our preset objectives? Is there a perception of a problem or need as something that belongs only to that person?

Being more disposed to achieving the goal of change rather than to establishing rapport and relationship can, unfortunately, lead to the exclusion of respect, reciprocity, and responsiveness in its reflection of a conviction that all the relevant information is already at hand. In contrast, choosing to connect (i.e., choosing relationship) leads to change that exceeds our goals, precisely because it is not bound by those goals.

LOOKING AHEAD

Choosing Relationship over Control is linked with a second complementary disposition that increases the probability of change that exceeds our expectations: Setting the Stage for Miracles. This latter disposition, which is discussed in Chapter 5, supports and extends Choosing Relationship over Control. Without it, aspects of control will always seep into even the best-intentioned interactions, undermining the very qualities that we seek to promote. Similarly, without Choosing Relationship over Control, the challenge of integrating diverse perspectives, which is the essence of Setting the Stage for Miracles, can easily become an overwhelming one.

The link between the two dispositions is more clearly illustrated as the individual strategies are discussed in Chapters 7–9. These chapters show how the dispositions of Choosing Relationship over Control and Setting the Stage for Miracles generate the individual strategies that concretize the qualities of respect, reciprocity, and responsiveness.

DISCUSSION QUESTIONS AND ACTIVITIES

1. Can you think back to how your initial impressions of someone changed as you got to know that person? What did you learn that triggered those changes?

2. The following list identify some behaviors that are significantly influenced by culturally based differences: a) rules related to how to enter into a group that is already working together, b) behaviors to communicate pleasure or displeasure in social settings, c) behaviors considered appropriate for listeners and speakers, d) ways of asking for help, e) ways of communicating welcome, and f) behaviors associated with initiating a conversation. Identify your beliefs and/or behaviors related to these areas (you may add others). Can you explain to another why your beliefs make sense other than because they simply seem right? Find someone with different beliefs and/or behaviors. Discuss the differences between his or her beliefs and/or behaviors and your own. Can you arrive at a point where the others' beliefs and/or behaviors make sense to you?

3. Examine Table 4.3, which shows dramatically different perceptions of the same behavior. Can you fill in the blank opposites? Can you come up with other examples?

Table 4.3. Contrasting behavioral perceptions

Gold nuggets (Positive interpretation)		Diamond in the rough (Negative interpretation)
Curious about information; inquisitive; does not accept information at first glance; questions and pushes for more information (very bright)	◄──────►	Obnoxious with questions; likes to "stump" people with hard questions (thinks he or she knows more than anyone else)
Learns at a faster rate than his or her peer group; absorbs more with less practice; able to accelerate his or her learning; displays eagerness to do work (excellent student)	◄──────►	Finds it hard to wait for others; unwilling to do detail work; shows reluctance to do some assignments because he or she already "knows" content or skill (likes to get away with as little work as possible)
Deeply interested in many things; good at many things; loves to learn new things (attentive, eager to learn)	◄──────►	Finds it difficult to make decisions or makes decisions quickly without regard for consequence; appears random (jumps from one to another without thought)
Sees patterns in things; can transfer learning to new situations; sees big picture; discovers new information (creative, always thinking of something new)	◄──────►	Reluctant or unwilling to learn details and/or facts to support generalizations; may have difficulty producing because work lacks substance (talks a good game)
	◄──────►	Starts a task but rarely finishes; when faced with a new task, direction, or request, he or she balks or procrastinates. (If asked to do something he or she does not want to do, refuses to comply)
	◄──────►	Is defensive and reacts physically to perceived intrusions (looks for trouble)
	◄──────►	Likes to do things in own way and time; challenges directions and/or authority
Shows unique or unusual responses to questions and/or problems; can see more than one answer to everything	◄──────►	
Makes connections; sees relationships between or among diverse ideas or events	◄──────►	
Uses language in powerful ways; able to use language to connect with others and build personal relationships	◄──────►	

From Slocumb, P.D., & Payne, R.K. (2000). Removing the mask: Giftedness in poverty, from *Slocumb-Payne Teacher Perception Inventory: A Rating Scale for Students from Diverse Backgrounds*; Highlands, TX: aha! Process; adapted by permission.

4. Can you think of a time when you interpreted someone's behavior in one way and later discovered that it had an entirely different meaning?

5. What are your beliefs about objective and subjective information? Do you tend to value one over the other? Why or why not?

SELECTED RESOURCES FOR LEARNING MORE ABOUT CHOOSING RELATIONSHIP OVER CONTROL

The critical aspects associated with Choosing Relationship over Control are based on the authors' experiences as well as on a variety of sources outside the discipline of early childhood special education. This section reviews several of these key sources for readers who wish to deepen their understanding of the critical aspects of Choosing Relationship over Control.

Goleman, D. (2006). *Social intelligence: The new science of human relationships.* New York: Bantam Dell.

Much of the material in Goleman's text remains abstract as the study of social intelligence is only newly emerging as a hard science. Nevertheless, this resource provides solid support for the disposition of Choosing Relationship over Control. As stated previously, this disposition taps into social and emotional intelligence. In this book, Goleman identifies four relevant skills and/or abilities: self-awareness; self-management; social awareness, which includes primal empathy, empathic accuracy, listening, and social cognition; and social facility or relationship management, which includes synchrony, self-presentation, influence, and concern. "The most powerful force in the brain's architecture," he asserted, "is arguably the need to navigate the social world, not the need to get A's" (p. 334). Choosing Relationship over Control is, ultimately, about learning to access and harness this force in support of children's spirits and sense of self.

Langer, E. (1997). *The power of mindful learning.* New York: Addison Wesley.

Langer's book on mindful learning is a powerful testament to the need for and nature of curiosity as a learning tool. The similarities between Skilled Dialogue and her definition of mindful learning are easily discerned. She noted, "A mindful approach to any activity has three characteristics: the continuous creation of new categories; openness to new information; and an implicit awareness of more than one perspective" (p. 4). She also asks several intriguing questions that are particularly relevant to *Sense-Making:* "How can we know if we don't ask? Why should we ask if we are certain we know?" (p. 139).

Langer, E. (2005). *On becoming an artist: Reinventing yourself through mindful creativity.* New York: Ballantine Books.

This book is in several respects a sequel to Langer's *The Power of Mindful Learning* (1997). One statement in particular captures her message, "To draw a tree, we shouldn't just imagine touching a tree, we ought to imagine being a tree" (p. 175). This statement could easily be paraphrased to capture the essence of perspective taking, which is one of the critical aspects of *Sense-Making*—to truly meet someone, we should not just imagine what his or her life must be like, we should imagine being that person. The author also presents evidence to support the importance of underlying intentions and inclinations (i.e., dispositions). "When we are mindful, do others know?" (p. 31). She then presents empirical evidence that the answer is yes.

Marcum, D. & Smith, S. (2007). *Egonomics: What makes ego our greatest asset (or most expensive liability).* **New York: Fireside/Simon & Shuster.**

This book focuses on how our sense of importance (i.e., our ego) can work both for us and against us in interactions with others. With the focus on self-esteem at the forefront of much of education, it offers some important insights. Although the authors' focus is the business world, their message is equally applicable to the world of early childhood and education. The authors' early warning signs that ego is becoming a liability can easily be recognized as saboteurs of the critical aspects of Choosing Relationship over Control. The first of these warning signs is being too comparative. By comparing ourselves to others—and others to ourselves—we give up our potential to recognize our own unique strengths, as well as those of others. Being defensive is the second warning sign they list. "When we can't 'lose,' we defend our positions as if we're defending who we are, and the debate shifts from a we-centered battle of ideas to a me-centered war of will" (p. 23). A third sign is showcasing ourselves, wanting or expecting others to "recognize, appreciate or be dazzled by how smart we are" (p. 23). The fourth sign is similar and is common to many people working with families or children—seeking acceptance and then equating acceptance or rejection of our help and/or ideas as acceptance or rejection of ourselves. Three corrective principles are then offered. The first two—humility and curiosity—are interrelated. "Once humility creates an open mind and a deep commitment to progress, curiosity is the active ingredient that drives the exploration of ideas [and perspectives]" (p. 29). The third—veracity— addresses the "habitual pursuit of, and adherence to, truth" (p. 31) even when it may reveal what we do not wish to see (e.g., that it is our own behavior that is triggering the behavior we reject in another).

Rosenberg, M. (1999). *Nonviolent communication: A language of compassion.* **Encinitas, CA: PuddleDancer Press.**

"NVC [Nonviolent communication] fosters deep listening, respect, and empathy and engenders a mutual desire to give from the heart" (p. 12). This book is especially valuable in teaching the use of nonjudgmental vocabulary in situations that trigger difficult feelings and reactions. It shows how to express anger within a context of empathy, for example. Its wealth of examples can be extremely helpful in formulating responses that express the critical aspects of Choosing Relationship over Control. There are also references to NVC materials for use with children. (Note: There are also more recent audio materials available through http://www .soundstrue.com).

Shafir, R.Z. (2000). *The Zen of listening: Mindful communication in the age of distraction.* **Wheaton, IL: Quest Books.**

This book contains a wealth of practical and valuable information on listening. "Our goal in becoming mindful listeners is to quiet the internal noise to allow the whole message and the messenger to be understood. In addition, when we listen mindfully to others, we help quiet down *their* internal noise" (p. 13). A useful tool included in this book is a questionnaire to help assess how well we listen. Some of the items on this questionnaire include the following (pp. 28–31): "[Do you] Think about what *you* are going to say while the speaker is talking?", "[Do you] Allow the speaker to vent negative feelings towards you without becoming defensive or phys-ically tense?", and "[Do you] Assume that you know what the speaker is going to say and stop listening?" Shafir also provides concrete examples and suggestions.

Winslade, J., & Monk, G. (2000). *Narrative mediation: A new approach to conflict resolution.* **San Francisco: Jossey-Bass.**

This book provides an overview of various strategies to "loosen" participants' ad-herence to the stories they tell themselves in conflict situations about each other and the situation itself. These include strategies such as "building relationship in mediation," "externalizing conversations," and "constructing solution-bound narratives." Of particular interest is the focus of a narrative approach to mediation: "co-constructing a context in which a change in the set of alternatives from which choice is made becomes possible" (Fruggeri, as cited on p. 46). Curiosity is again a major element discussed. The authors provide rich examples of how a problematic situation can be shifted toward a solution-focused one even when all involved have strong and contradictory perspectives.

Chapter 5

Setting the Stage for Miracles

Setting the Stage for Miracles complements and extends Choosing Relationship over Control by capitalizing on the potential of the diverse identities, voices, and connections to enrich and expand available response options. Choosing Relationship over Control focuses on perceiving the resources offered by these diverse identities, voices and connections. It leads us to discover the legitimacy of diverse perspectives but cannot take us beyond those perspectives. It is the disposition of Setting the Stage for Miracles, however, that moves us beyond that simple recognition to appreciate and mine the identified resources.

The title of this disposition—Setting the Stage for Miracles—comes from Jaworski's (1996) thoughts on miracles, which have particular relevance to sustaining and promoting respect, reciprocity, and responsiveness across diverse beliefs, values, and perspectives. As defined within Skilled Dialogue, a miracle is a happening or outcome that could not have been predicted given the data present prior to its occurrence. Functioning at or near age level would be considered a miracle if 3 years prior to functioning at that level a child showed signs of severe cortical blindness and did little more than scream continuously. At or near age level functioning could not have been predicted within that time span and therefore qualifies as a miracle. Some miracles may be less striking. One person learning Skilled Dialogue reported that her 21-year-old son, with whom she had not been able to have conversations of any length, told her after a lengthy conversation, "Mom, this is the best conversation we've ever had." She could not have predicted that outcome given their history.

The word *miracle*, according to Jaworski, involves "listening to what is wanting to emerge" (1996, p. 182) rather than to what is apparent. "What is 'miraculous,'" he stated, "might be just what is beyond our current understanding" (1996, p. 14) and, we would add, what cannot be predicted given present data and familiar ways of thinking and perceiving.

Jaworski's words allude to the necessity for both paradigmatic and perceptual shifts in our approach to identified challenges. It is these shifts that the disposition of Setting the Stage for Miracles seeks to stimulate. Its focus is, in fact, just this: the willingness to participate with another in the creation of unimagined and

Table 5.1. Definition and description of Setting the Stage for Miracles, including examples and non-examples

Description	Underlying purpose and key question	Associated strategies
The intent to stimulate transformative change by identifying and leveraging the complementary aspects of contradictory beliefs, behaviors, or perspectives	*Purpose:* To create 3rd space: conceptual and emotional space within which exclusive contradictions can be transformed into inclusive, albeit paradoxical, options *Key Question:* What is the third choice (i.e., the option generated by acknowledging and integrating the strengths of diverse perspectives)?	Setting the Stage for Miracles involves the strategies of allowing, appreciating, and harmonizing. (See Chapter 6 and Part III.)

Examples[a]	*Nonexamples*[b]
"At first we both wanted our own way. After initially clashing over this topic we realized that what we both wanted was the best for our own daughter. So we stayed with the tension [generated by our diverse views] and kept working."	"I hope that through our discussions she has learned other methods of guiding the children and may indeed take some classes. I believe that she is interested in doing a good job and staying in compliance and that she is willing to change what she did during licensed hours."
"Finally, we came up with a solution. I wanted him to take the quiz (everyone else expected him to take it), but he did not want to because it would affect his grade. Since this is not a common occurrence we came up with a third solution."	"I suggested many possibilities, such as putting a fence around the trampoline so they could keep it up. She said her husband was not willing, and he was very angry about this whole situation. I knew that I would not be able to get an exception passed with the state to have the trampoline accessible to the children."

[a]Both the examples and the nonexamples are taken from comments of workshop participants describing specific situations. We thank all workshop participants who gave permission for their comments to be used as part of our research data.

[b]The nonexamples are not necessarily incorrect or inappropriate; however, they do not reflect the disposition of Setting the Stage for Miracles.

seemingly impossible options by reframing diverse behaviors or perspectives as complementary rather than polarized.

The disposition of Setting the Stage for Miracles taps into one's creativity. It focuses on creating a cognitive space within which disparate identities can be allowed to exist side by side, disparate voices can be simultaneously appreciated, and disparate perspectives can be integrated and harmonized (see Table 5.1). For there to be Skilled Dialogue, it is not enough to choose relationship, it is also necessary to consciously and creatively open a space where its diverse strengths and resources can flourish. In reference to such space, Isaacs said, "Perhaps one of the most important dimensions of dialogue concerns the atmosphere or energetic 'field,' in which it occurs. . . . We cannot manufacture a 'field.' *But we can create the conditions* [italics added] [i.e., set the stage]. . . . These conditions make up what we have called the *container* for dialogue, *in which deep and transformative . . . [options] become possible* [italics added] (1999, p. 242).

To set the stage for miracles, diverse and disparate perspectives must not only be welcomed, they must also be allowed to stand beside one's own perspectives while searching for how they might make sense. Once the sense to other perspectives is discovered, it becomes possible to focus on intentionally identifying the particular contributions of each perspective. This, in turn, makes finding the similarities in the differences much easier. Setting the Stage for Miracles, however, remains incomplete without also integrating the positive and complementary aspects that have been identified between perspectives so that miracles—previously unimagined options—can emerge.

Just what does it mean to set the stage for miracles in this fashion? It means being disposed to create what does not yet exist. Rather than looking only at how predetermined solutions may be implemented, the disposition of Setting the Stage for Miracles focuses on creating the conditions within which optimum options— options that are inclusive, collaborative, and responsive to multiple perspectives— can emerge.

Setting the Stage for Miracles both extends and complements Choosing Relationship over Control. With this added disposition, connections between disparate perspectives become deeper and more capable of being sustained even in difficult circumstances. Without it, choosing relationship remains subtly biased toward control: one's actions remain controlled by the specific "hows" believed to be necessary to achieve the desired outcome(s). We follow our predetermined map without being open to other maps and other paths.

It is the disposition of Setting the Stage for Miracles that releases the fixation on the idea that there is only one particular way of achieving an outcome (e.g., this parent must implement this plan or behave this way if this problem is ever to be resolved). In doing so, it opens us to the possibility of multiple ways of reaching a desired outcome, some of which may not or cannot be known until they occur. Wheatley referred to Joel Barker, the first person to popularize the concept of paradigm shifts for the corporate world, in reference to this point: "[Baker] stated that when something is impossible to achieve with one worldview, it can be surprisingly easy to accomplish with a new one" (2005, p. 75). Wheatley went on to state the following:

> Life relies on diversity to give it the possibility of adapting to changing conditions. When one form [or perspective] is dominant, and that form [or perspective] no longer works . . . the entire system can collapse. Where there is diversity [of perspectives] . . . innovative solutions are created all the time, just because different people do things differently. (2005, p. 78)

Setting the Stage for Miracles is a disposition that capitalizes on this reality. Skilled Dialogue emphasizes this disposition for that very reason: as a direct expression of the value and worth of diverse perspectives. Setting the Stage for Miracles is also emphasized as a direct expression of the value of and need for creative collaboration across diverse perspectives.

The disposition of Setting the Stage for Miracles works with what Childs called the "juxtaposition of what is and a clarified, deeply poetic vision of what can be" (1998, p. 29). What is required to achieve this juxtaposition is to remain "grounded in existing realities while insistently acknowledging the *possibility* of achieving a goal" (Childs, 1998, p. 30) that honors two or more apparently contradictory perspectives or beliefs. Examples include a practitioner's knowing that child has minimal impulse control and frequently acts without thinking while simultaneously remaining open to the *possibility* that things can be different: that the child will be able to exhibit desired social skills. Or a practitioner's knowing that a mother has never agreed with him or her and does not like the options presented while simultaneously being willing to entertain the *possibility* that today they can come closer to agreement. Without this juxtaposition, it is all too easy to become boxed in by identified polarities and push to reduce or eliminate one thing in order to bring a second into prominence.

3rd SPACE

As stated in the introduction to Part II of this book, Setting the Stage for Miracles replaces the skill and mindset of 3rd Space discussed in earlier work. Although 3rd Space still continues to constitute a significant part of this disposition, it is now subsumed under the broader focus that was always at its core—stimulating "breakthrough thinking" (Perkins, 2000, p. 9) that dissolves the stalemate of exclusive either-or scenarios and opens the way for inclusive and unanticipated scenarios. An essential component of developing and expressing the disposition of Setting the Stage for Miracles, therefore, is an understanding of paradox (i.e., inclusive and integrative space within which two or more apparently contradictory perspectives and/or actions can both be true).

For purposes of clarity, it needs to be noted that 3rd Space should not be confused with the term *Third Space* that is used in a wide range of literature (e.g., King & Browitt, 2004). In much of this literature, *third space* refers to a kind of in-between or hybrid space. Although there is some overlap between the two perspectives, 3rd *Space* within Skilled Dialogue is defined specifically as a conceptual, relational, and emotional space within which complementary aspects of diverse views and/or behaviors (i.e., contradictions) are identified and integrated to generate a sum greater than those aspects individually (e.g., the perceptual space where blue and yellow combine to become green, the conceptual space where light is both particle and wave; the relational space where diverse perspectives are connected in support of one another) (see also Barrera et al., 2003).

As a mindset, 3rd Space refers to a conceptual and interactional space within which complementary aspects of contradictions can be identified and integrated without needing to blur their differences. 3rd Space is the space of paradox where two apparently contradictory views and/or perspectives can be simultaneously true (e.g., a parent can be resistant and cooperative at the same time, a child can be attentive and distracted at the same time). As shown by the small circles in the well-known yin-yang symbol (see Figure 5.1), each "side" contains an aspect of the other.

A parent's resistance to a practitioner's suggestions, for example, can also simultaneously reflect, albeit perhaps unconsciously, cooperation with the practitioner's expectations for resistance or with members of his or her family who urge caution. A child's distractibility may in fact reflect attention, but to multiple things or to something other than what a practitioner believes is pertinent. To totally exclude the complementarity of seeming opposites is to void the possibility of connecting with and leveraging the diverse strengths each brings to the table.

Figure 5.1. Yin-yang symbol. (From Barrera, I., Corso, R.M., & Macpherson, D. [2003]. *Skilled Dialogue: Strategies for responding to cultural diversity in early childhood* [p. 36]. Baltimore: Paul H. Brookes Publishing Co.; reprinted by permission.)

As a skill, 3rd Space starts with this ability to hold two or more divergent and seemingly contradictory truths in mind at the same time without forcing a choice or compromise (e.g., to suspend one's need to hold opposites apart). Only with this ability in place, does it become possible to join and harmonize (i.e., leverage) the strengths and resources offered by views and behaviors that seem to contradict one's own. Adopting the mindset and developing the skill of 3rd Space is what allows opposites to be integrated in ways that yield previously unimagined and inclusive options responsive to the needs of all involved.

3rd Space contrasts with dualistic space. In dualistic space, the choice of one option most typically necessitates the exclusion of all others (i.e., either-or). It is sometimes possible to maintain two options (i.e., both this and that), but only as separate but equal and side by side, which excludes the possibility of integration without compromising, merging, or diluting the options involved (Zaiss, 2002). (See also the discussion of 3rd Space in Barrera et al., 2003.)

"Either-or" space tends to be the norm in ENC, although there is a growing recognition of "both-and" space. Realities and perceptions tend to be split into two (e.g., "abled" or "disabled," "competent" or "incompetent," "tall" or "short"). A vivid example of this dualistic splitting can be found in materials that compare and contrast some aspect of reality (e.g., cultures). These comparisons and contrasts are almost always set up in tables with two columns. One interesting exception is Ruby Payne's work (2005), which compares and contrasts three socioeconomic levels rather than just two.

Although everyone understands that the two sides of most comparisons are only the ends of an extreme, what is between those ends nevertheless tends to be minimized or ignored altogether. There is, as well, an implicit understanding that moving toward one end necessitates distancing from the other. There is only this or that. At best, dualistic space allows for both-and or side-by-side comparisons in which diverse options can co-exist but cannot be integrated or transformed (e.g., both blue and yellow, but not green). In contrast, by opening the possibility of integration, 3rd Space eliminates the need to defend one option at the expense of another because of a fear that one will be lost if the other is chosen. Conversely, in 3rd Space there is no need to eliminate one choice (e.g., speaking Spanish) in order to support or strengthen another (e.g., speaking English). There is instead the understanding that one can complement and perhaps even strengthen the other (e.g., see Cummins's research on bilingualism at http://www.iteachilearn.com/cummins).

More specifically, the following characteristics of 3rd Space give some indication of how this complementarity works:

1. Reality in 3rd Space is nondichotomous; it is perceived more as a spectrum than a continuum. In relation to Camilla, JoAnne, and Joey, who were introduced in Chapter 3, this aspect of 3rd Space introduces the possibility of conceptualizing each one's perspectives as complementary with the others (i.e., in nonpolarized ways where one choice is not exclusive of the other) rather than contradictory.

2. There are always at least three or more choices in 3rd Space. This aspect of 3rd Space requires creatively generating alternatives beyond the obvious (e.g., implement the recommended program or give up on implementing it). As discussed in Chapter 2, dualistic thinking tends to be predominant in ENC. For that reason learning to entertain the possibility of third (and fourth or fifth) choices can be quite challenging at first.

3. The whole is more than the sum of the parts. The idea that two or more perspectives, no matter how seemingly contradictory, can be combined or integrated into a larger whole is a core aspect of 3rd Space. In 3rd Space, differences are understood to be complementary rather than divisive. Boundaries are understood to serve both as distinctions and as points of contact. Like the poles of a battery, boundaries are understood to generate constructive rather than destructive tension when connected.

The following analogy illustrates how 3rd Space can set the stage for miracles (i.e., previously unimagined options) by shifting one's perspective. Imagine actual rooms in physical space. These can be perceived in at least three ways (there is always a third choice!).

From a *singular space* perspective, the perception is that there is, literally, only one room: the one occupied by the perceiver. This individual believes that his or her room (i.e., view or perspective) is the only one that exists and can neither see nor imagine other views. If told about other rooms, this person would not accept them as real. Events and interactions can only take place in the one room they occupy. Other rooms are either nonexistent or totally discounted. This, fortunately, is not a perspective that is encountered frequently. It is most clearly illustrated by children who exhibit certain behaviors associated with the autism spectrum.

From a *dualistic space* perspective, a much more common perspective, one realizes that his or her room is not the only room that exists. Other views are accepted as real but placed outside, or excluded from the individual's own room. From this perspective the perceiver holds that he or she is in one room and people who are different from him or her are in other rooms. There is no shared space. There is only either one room or the other. Events and interactions can only take place in one *or* the other room (e.g., my way or your way, either this or that, right or wrong). From this dualistic perspective, it is not possible to meet on common ground unless one or both people move. That is, *A* must leave *A*'s room (i.e., comfortable space) *or* *B* must leave *B*'s room *or* both must leave their rooms and go to another neutral room. At best, if there is a both-and perspective, each person can remain in his or her separate room, side by side, and able to acknowledge the right to be in separate rooms—yet unable to create common shared space (i.e., perspectives).

In contrast, there also exists a 3rd Space perspective. This perspective invites people to consider the possibility that diverse perspectives do have aspects in common no matter what their apparent differences, and that they are, in fact, complementary. This is a relatively rare perspective in ENC (see discussion in Chapter 2); it tends to be somewhat more common in cultures that function with conjoint models of agency.

When we see things from a 3rd Space perspective we routinely ask the following question: How can we both end up in the same space without moving? This question shifts the attention from the differences in rooms to the wall(s) that define them. It challenges us to realize that it is the wall and not our individual perspectives that keep us from occupying common space.

A 3rd Space perspective recognizes that walls are different from boundaries. Boundaries are markers of space and identity. They may generate diversity "bumps" (see Barrera et al., 2003), but they do not obstruct the view, and are permeable when so desired. Walls, however, are opaque and impenetrable. Depending on their size and thickness, walls exclude and separate, resulting in diversity clashes and even outright crashes.

Nevertheless, walls serve a legitimate function and should not be taken lightly. They almost always represent a boundary that has fossilized over time, becoming hard and dense in response to repeated assaults on it. It is this aspect of walls that makes them resistant to change and worthy of respect. To disrespect them is only to affirm and confirm the assaults that established them in the first place. From a 3rd Space perspective, therefore, we are invited to honor walls and to recognize their function and their strengths in ways that are respectful, reciprocal, and responsive. (See Chapter 10 for further discussion and exercises to practice recognizing and honoring walls.)

Understanding walls and responding respectfully to them opens possibilities for creating a perspective greater than our individual and separate perspectives. (See Part III for further discussion and examples of how to do this.) This larger more inclusive perspective (i.e., 3rd Space) sets the stage for miracles, and in so doing promotes and sustains Skilled Dialogue's three qualities—respect, reciprocity, and responsiveness—within given interactions with children, families, colleagues, and other persons.

CRITICAL ASPECTS OF SETTING THE STAGE FOR MIRACLES

The critical aspects of Setting the Stage for Miracles, similar to those for Choosing Relationship over Control, represent internal inclinations that guide and shape the behaviors associated with concretely expressing the disposition. Table 5.2 lists these aspects. Each aspect in some way reflects an inclination toward acknowledging and creating 3rd Space as a means of setting the stage for previously

Table 5.2. Critical aspects of Setting the Stage for Miracles

- Willingness to stay with the tension (i.e., acknowledge another's perspective without needing to explain or defend one's own
- Willingness to release stories and fixed interpretations about others' behaviors and/or beliefs
- Perception of diverse perspectives as potentially complementary rather than divisive or polarized

- Willingness to identify *gold nuggets* in others' behaviors and/or beliefs
- Recognition that every negative behavior is a positive behavior exaggerated
- Willingness to learn from others' behaviors and/or beliefs

- Willingness to reframe perceptions
- Openness to brainstorming
- "Thinking in threes" (i.e., 3rd Space thinking)

unimagined and unexpected options that include and are responsive to all of the perspectives involved (i.e., miracles). These aspects can be grouped into sets of three. The first set of critical aspects reflects a willingness to allow diverse perspectives to stand side by side. Aspects in the second set focus on identifying and affirming the potential or actual value of others' perspectives in relation to the current situation. Finally, those in the third set focus on the direct creation of 3rd Space by integrating and harmonizing differences in order to generate response and action options that leverage the strengths and resources of those very differences.

First Set of Critical Aspects

This section describes how willingness to stay with the tension and the perception of diverse perspectives as complementary are essential components of Setting the Stage for Miracles.

Willingness to Stay with the Tension The first critical aspect of this first set is the willingness to stay with the unease or discomfort generated by diverse perspectives, especially when these seem to contradict each other. More specifically this aspect addresses the willingness to suspend our agenda and acknowledge another's perspective without immediately needing to explain or defend our own.

Staying with the tension encompasses the inclination to refrain from acting to dissolve or resolve what seems inappropriate, incomplete, or contradictory. It involves a willingness to listen to another without jumping in to correct or defend against statements with which we disagree. This aspect of Setting the Stage for Miracles requires that we be willing to 1) accept a certain degree of unease or discomfort without immediately moving to change things, 2) permit others to be as they are, and 3) recognize another's behavior as an expression of his or her identity in relation to us.

However, staying with the resulting tension does not and should not communicate agreement or even tolerance. Rather, it should communicate respect and the willingness to wait for more information even as we act to protect and maintain boundaries. If a child hits another child, it is possible to respond to contain that behavior while simultaneously allowing the child time and space to express his or her version of events. Or, if a child says, "But he hit me," we might simply say "I see," or "Tell me more," rather than "He did not," or "What did you do first?" or "I don't think that's what happened." Similarly, if a parent consistently does not show for meetings and does not call, we can "allow" him or her to make that choice while also allowing ourselves to state our need to stop scheduling meetings, not because the parent needs to give up their behavior but simply because we value a commitment to communication and punctuality. (See Rosenberg, 1999 for suggestions on how to accomplish this.)

Willingness to Release Stories and Fixed Interpretations   The second aspect goes hand in hand with the one just discussed: the release of stories and fixed interpretations about others' behaviors and/or beliefs. The willingness to suspend the interpretations and stories we assign to what others say involves letting go of thoughts such as "He means this or that" or "She always behaves this way" in order to listen to what the other person might actually be expressing.

In the example of the child hitting another child, this aspect invites those interacting with that child to release their version of what may have happened and wait to get the child's version. This is not to confirm it as preferable to their own but to examine it as the raw data necessary for subsequent responses. In the example of the parent who neither comes to appointments nor calls to cancel (e.g., possibly meaning that he or she does not care or is being disrespectful), the practitioner's version of the story and his or her fixed interpretations also need to be released.

Stories attached to what another person says are composed of the thoughts held about that person that are brought to interactions with them (e.g., "She won't show up, she never does," "He just refuses to listen," "There's no discipline in that home"). They reflect fixed interpretations about specific behaviors (e.g., not doing what we tell others to do means they are not listening, no set bedtime means no discipline).

Releasing these stories and interpretations, however, does not mean believing they are wrong. It means loosening our hold on them so as to allow new information and new meanings to stand side by side with our initial stories and fixed interpretations. This loosening dissolves the need to defend and/or explain because one view is not juxtaposed with the other in such a way that it invalidates it. In the end, the truest interpretation may be neither the listeners' or the speakers', but something completely different.

Remaining certain of what we believe, see, and hear inhibits moving on to subsequent aspects of Setting the Stage for Miracles. We are, in effect, stuck only part way to a possible miracle! The release of stories and fixed interpretation not only opens up our ability to listen, it also moves us from certainty into uncertainty.

Perception of Diverse Perspectives as Complementary   As diverse perspectives are allowed to stand side by side, the challenge is to simultaneously see both how they are different and how they are similar. This is the third critical aspect in this first set: perceiving others' perspectives as diverse yet at the same time complementary to our own. Langer (2005) called this type of perception seeing the similarities in the differences and the differences in the similarities.

Seeing the similarities in the differences keeps them from being polarized (i.e., put into dualistic space), and seeing the differences in the similarities keeps distinctive strengths and resources from being merged and made indistinguishable (i.e., put into singular space). This balance of retaining differences while simultaneously identifying commonalities can be challenging. When social, cultural, and educational contexts privilege dualistic space, it is not only individual concepts that are polarized, it is also our overall perception of reality that is polarized. In work around cultural linguistic diversity, for example, it is common to see this polarization. The distinctive aspects of cultural communities are either emphasized (e.g., they are so different that we cannot connect or communicate; we are so different that we cannot be ourselves outside of our community) or they are erased (e.g., we are not so different from each other; there are people who believe or do the same thing who are not members of that community).

The first response (i.e., polarizing differences) prevents empathy and blocks respect. It also wastes valuable resources. One can say, for example "There's no way I can relate with this person." By saying that, whether the person is a parent, child, colleague, administrator, or other individual, one not only restricts oneself to unanchored understanding but also wastes that person's potential contributions to the situation.

For example, a parent's deep knowledge of his or her child will be missed because of our assumption that the parent does not really know his or her child; for example, "he thinks she is an angel and overlooks all of the child's faults." Or a child's potential to voluntarily and joyfully channel his or her energy into positive behaviors is missed because one is unable to relate with him or her as he or she is.

Ironically, the second response to diversity—emphasizing similarities—does the same thing. In both cases, it is connection that is sacrificed and resources that are excluded. Both responses privilege one worldview at the expense of all others. There can be no dialogue when that happens, only monologues.

When both similarities and differences are held in tension and diversity is allowed to be, a powerful paradox emerges. Wheatley said, "If we are willing to listen for diverse interpretations [without splitting them], we discover that our differing perceptions most often share a unifying center. . . . We recognize that *through our diversity* [italics added], we share a dream, or we share a sense of injustice" (2005, p. 80). A practitioner and a parent may discover, for example, that at the core of their different perceptions of a child lies the same dream for that child as a competent learner and participant.

Second Set of Critical Aspects

The second set of aspects focuses on contributions to a shared purpose. The first of these aspects is the willingness to identify the *gold nuggets* in others' behaviors and beliefs and the positive contributions these can make (see Table 4.3 for more

information). Wheatley said, "Problems of diversity disappear as we focus on contribution to a shared purpose rather than the legislation of correct behavior"
(2005, p. 51).

In a similar vein, Zaiss explained that

> Dialogue is not about trying to change anyone's opinions but is about understanding
> that people's opinions, their truths, [and] can actually be a contribution to a collective
> truth. That is perhaps the fundamental purpose of dialogue—to create shared under-
> standing beyond our individual points of view. (2002, p. 88)

All of us structure our world through a complex framework of values, beliefs,
and behaviors. When we encounter values, beliefs, and behaviors consonant with
our own, we tend to value them and easily see how they bring positive contributions. When we encounter diverse values, beliefs, and behaviors that are dissonant
with our own, however, it can be much more challenging to discover their positive contributions.

Willingness to Identify Gold Nuggets in Others' Behaviors and/or Beliefs
The inclination to perceive the value (i.e., *gold nuggets;* see also Table 4.3) that underlies all behaviors is the first critical aspect in the second set. This is an important statement. It does not mean that we need to see value in one child hitting
another; it does mean, however, that we can come to see value in that child's
attempt, however unskillful, to define and protect his or her boundaries. It does
not mean that we need to see value in a parent's limited responses to his or her
children's needs; it does mean, however, that we can see the value of seeking self-
survival (similar to pre-flight instructions given on airplanes to put on your oxy-
gen mask first).

The level of skill with which a behavior is expressed can easily obscure its underlying value. It is too easy to "throw the baby out with the bathwater" when behaviors are expressed at low levels of skill. I (Barrera) often tell my students that
I am more hopeful for a child who bites or screams than for a child who sits pas-
sively. The first is still trying, however unskillfully, to communicate; the second
has lost that motivation.

The value of behaviors that we deem to be positive (e.g., timeliness, appropriate attention to adults) is typically easy to identify. Behaviors that we deem to
be negative (e.g., tardiness, inattention to adults) are more challenging to value.
Setting the Stage for Miracles, however, requires that we find the value even in
those behaviors, perhaps especially in those behaviors. The *gold nugget* of a child's
inattention to adults, for example, may be that child's ability to concentrate on
something else or it may be the refusal to choose a behavior that makes no sense
to him or her. Concentration and refusing to do something merely because someone with more authority demands it are both valuable skills.

Tardiness might also reflect similar skills. Again, this is not to say that refusal
to comply and tardiness should simply be left unchanged, but it is to say that their
inherent value can be leveraged in the service of higher levels of skill.

In reference to cultural differences specifically, Rosinki stated that

> Leveraging cultural differences is a proactive attitude. You look for gems [i.e., *gold nuggets*] in your own culture(s) and mine for treasures in other culture(s). . . . The riches appear in the form of useful insights, alternative perspectives on issues, and can be collected from human wisdom accumulated through space and time. (2003, p. 40)

Similarly, Murray said, "In the anthropological sense, our students [or any other person] are informants with a wealth of cultural and linguistic knowledge [whether tied to specific ethnic communities or not]; however this knowledge is rarely conscious and rarely articulated in . . . classrooms" (1992, p. 260).

Recognition that Every Negative Behavior Is a Positive Behavior Exaggerated

The recognition that behaviors perceived as negative are, in fact, positive behaviors in exaggerated form is the second aspect of this second set of critical aspects of Setting the Stage for Miracles. It relates closely to the first aspect of being able to identify *gold nuggets* and can, in fact, be a way of finding the *gold nuggets*. One way of meeting this challenge is to recognize that, amazingly, all behaviors considered negative are, typically, exaggerations of the very behaviors we already value. Tardiness, for example, may be an exaggerated version of attention to others (e.g., "I'm always late because I'll take every phone call even when it comes as I'm leaving.") or of attention to self (e.g., "I can't deal with one more demand on my time."). When this critical aspect is recognized, Setting the Stage for Miracles becomes not about eliminating behaviors but about expanding behavioral repertoires and bringing complementary behaviors into balance. Laziness, for example, can be an exaggerated form of efficiency (i.e., the desire to use the lowest amount of energy possible) when not balanced by a focus on desired outcomes, which characterizes efficiency. Order, when exaggerated, can become rigidity if it is not balanced with the flexibility of some chaos.

Willingness to Learn from Others' Behaviors and/or Beliefs

Encountering what we consider to be negative behaviors can be an opportunity to learn about our own behaviors. Being willing to ask questions such as "How am I dealing with self-care?" upon meeting someone who is inordinately self-focused or, conversely, totally inattentive to self allows us to learn from others. "How much attention am I paying to others' demands?" might also be a good question when meeting someone whose attention we desire but are not receiving. In some instances, over-attention is unsettling. In those instances, the key question to ask is "What about this person's exaggerated behavior might be a call to examine my own?"

Another way to learn from others is to be willing to ask "What specific skill or information can I learn about how to deal with X or Y? Can I learn how to be more of a risk taker or, conversely, less of one?" In the case of a parent who refused to comply with the request from Head Start staff to implement a home behavioral support plan for example, the Head Start staff could perhaps learn about trusting the child's decision-making and self-help skills as a balance to direct control of external behavior so that neither is exaggerated at the expense of the other. This would not mean that inappropriate behavior should be allowed but rather that the intervention might be examined from a different, more balanced perspective.

Third Set of Critical Aspects

The last set of critical aspects for Setting the Stage for Miracles focuses on inclinations related to integrating the respective contributions of others' differences with our own. Allowing and appreciating diversity is a strong first step. It opens endless opportunities. But it is not enough; attention also needs to be paid to what happens next. 3rd Space cannot be fully created until we can also leverage the strengths and resources inherent to the diverse perspectives, behaviors, and beliefs we encounter (i.e., access their strengths and apply them to the interactions in question).

Willingness to Reframe Perceptions   The first aspect in this third set of critical aspects of Setting the Stage for Miracles is addressing the reframing of perceptions (i.e., thinking of things in novel ways). One particularly illustrative example of this is found in Zander and Zander : "The lesson I learned is that *the player who looks the least engaged may be the most committed member of the group.* A cynic, after all, is a passionate person who does not want to be disappointed again" (2000, p. 39). In this example, disengagement is reframed into passionate engagement, and cynicism and commitment are integrated in one fell swoop! (See the Selected Resources list at the end of this chapter for other sources that contain similar examples.)

Openness to Brainstorming   Openness to brainstorming is the second critical aspect of the third set. To set the stage for miracles, it is important not to censure or devalue options merely because they seem to be impossible. Being willing to brainstorm how a child who, for example, has been running around, yelling, and challenging everyone who gets near her may in fact be a child who cares desperately about relationships is one example of this type of brainstorming.

Thinking in Threes   It is important to go beyond dualistic binary thinking and "think in threes" if we are to truly craft 3rd Space options. This type of thinking challenges us to leave the dualities such as appropriate behavior and inappropriate behavior, respect and disrespect, and sitting still and running around to search for third (and fourth and fifth) options created by the integration of these contradictions. The stage for miracles cannot be completely set unless we are willing to ask, "What are the strengths of each end of the polarized continuum that we set up initially?" and "What can emerge if we integrate those strengths?" (See Selected Resources at the end of this chapter and the discussion in Chapter 9 for additional information and illustrations.)

Once all of these critical aspects of Setting the Stage for Miracles are in place, their concrete behavioral expression can be examined. The following section returns to the example of Camilla, JoAnne, and Joey in order to examine these aspects more concretely.

CAMILLA AND JOANNE

The term 3rd Space is used in relation to the space created as well as to the skill of creating such space. When used in this sense, 3rd Space refers to the ability to respectfully hold divergent and sometimes seemingly contradictory views at the same time without forcing a choice between them and, as a result, generate previously unimagined options that are responsive to the unique aspects of each view. It is in so doing, that the stage is set for both Camilla, the early childhood practitioner introduced in Chapter 3, and JoAnne, Joey's mother with whom Camilla is having difficulty relating, to move to "what is beyond [their] current understanding" (Jaworski, 1996, p. 14) and find options that acknowledge and integrate their diverse strengths and perspectives.

For example, JoAnne's present behavior (e.g., allowing Joey to run around and act impulsively) could be examined to identify what aspect(s) of it might complement Camilla's goal (e.g., decreasing Joey's intrusions into others' space). How could this be done? How could more than two choices to resolving this seeming contradiction be found?

Although Choosing Relationship over Control can lead Camilla to recognize the legitimacy of JoAnne's current behaviors, it is the complementary disposition of Setting the Stage for Miracles that allows the strengths of those behaviors to be accessed as tools for acquiring new behaviors. The disposition of Choosing Relationship over Control is, thus, not sufficient in and of itself. On its own, it still leaves us with equally undesirable choices; that is, to silence or at least turn down the volume of one perspective or remain stuck within an either-or frame that favors one behavior at the expense of another. At best it can lead to a separate but equal perspective that allows but does not leverage differences.

Camilla can be disposed to choose relationship over control, for example. She can certainly *intend* to respect JoAnne's existing behaviors. Yet, even so, Camilla might remain convinced that JoAnne needs to give up those behaviors in favor of the behaviors she deems more desirable and productive. Even if Camilla comes to agree with JoAnne but does so without also setting the stage for miracles, JoAnne's unique perspective, which would have enriched the ultimate outcome, will be lost. Only one perspective, Camilla's, would ultimately remain. Camilla and JoAnne would both remain trapped within an exclusive either-or paradigm that favors control over relationship.

Without exercising the disposition of Setting the Stage for Miracles, we are left with two contradictory perspectives: 1) Camilla's perspective that JoAnne needs to become more involved with implementing the recommended behavioral support program for Joey (i.e., change her current behavior); and 2) JoAnne's perspective that to do so would violate both Joey's creativity and her own sense of the right thing to do. Even if these contradictory perspectives were to be framed within a both-and perspective, this frame maintains the disconnection between diverse perspectives and creates only a separate but equal context (see previous discussion of 3rd Space). Similar to an either-or frame, both-and frames stop short of achieving the integration and resulting synergy of contradictory perspectives.

In Camilla's case, either of these frames would still leave her wanting one set of behaviors and JoAnne wanting another; both are perhaps recognized as equally valid, yet each is perceived as impossible to reconcile or integrate. The disposition of Setting the Stage for Miracles, however, prompts practitioners to ask: How can *both* implementing this behavioral support plan for Joey *and* JoAnne's current interactions with Joey be reconciled? (See Part III for strategies and examples that answer this question.) How can the strengths of each choice be leveraged in support of the other? Answering this question requires the willingness to create 3rd Space, within which contradictions (i.e., where the presence of one thing excludes the other) can be creatively reframed into paradoxes (i.e., where the presence of one thing is placed into a complementary relationship with the other).

How might Camilla act if she chose to express the disposition of Setting the Stage for Miracles?

1. She would approach the situation with the understanding that JoAnne's behavior stems from specific experiential data and that, given that data, her choices reflect competent rather than limited or incompetent problem-solving skills.

2. She would choose to wait before giving solutions and trying to change JoAnne's beliefs and/or behaviors, knowing that her desire for change can coexist with JoAnne's insistence on not changing without the need to erase one or the other. She would remember that JoAnne is not disagreeing with her or telling her that she is wrong; rather, she is simply being different.

3. Camilla would verbally affirm JoAnne's concerns and competence and state that she is interested in expanding that competence, not in eliminating current behavior.

4. She would reflect on JoAnne's behavior and seek to identify its strengths related to the change she desires to see. For example, she might gain insight into the fact that JoAnne's unconditional affirmation of Joey's current behavior might foster a sense of acceptance and fearlessness that could actually make it easier for Joey to try new behaviors.

    This was actually the case in a situation that I (Barrera) witnessed during a meeting of practitioners. Some of the practitioners were commenting on what they perceived as the extreme permissiveness of a family toward a child. "They do everything for her," they said. "She's not required or expected to do anything." These practitioners wanted to work with the family to help them set more defined expectations and behavioral demands for their child. After a while, however, the conversation shifted and began to focus on the family's cultural background. One practitioner remarked on how family members wanted to avoid causing the child pain, as their chief goal was her happiness. After this perspective was discussed for a while, the breakthrough happened. A therapist realized that the parent's current behavior might be why the child was trusting, rather than simply passive, during therapy work—an observation noticed by another therapist as well: "You know, perhaps that's why this child is so trusting. She allows me to move her and position her with little resistance, and it's clear that's not just passivity." Almost by accident, this team reached a point where they could see that the family's behaviors complemented rather than contradicted their work. At that point, the quality of both their statements and their feelings about that family changed.

5. Camilla might explore different ways of interpreting JoAnne's behavior (e.g., rather than seeing it only as resistant or neglectful, perhaps she could see it as a strong and courageous commitment to her child).

6. Camilla would seek to discover how to collaboratively generate options that honored JoAnne's current perspective without sacrificing Joey's need for more mature social skills.

7. She would remind herself that there is a positive core in every negative behavior. She might then start to recognize that JoAnne's allowing of Joey's choices is not, in and of itself, a negative behavior. It is, in fact, a skill that every parent must learn to use (e.g., unconditional acceptance). In JoAnne's case, however, that skill is exaggerated. That is, it is overused without balancing it with an equal respect for Joey's need for direction. Rather than trying to eliminate the behavior, therefore, Camilla might look for ways to balance it.

• • •

These ideas are meant to illustrate what being disposed to set the stage for miracles might look like. Its specific expressions are explored in more detail in Part III.

It is important to note, however, that this particular disposition is not one that yields a priori options. It is highly context embedded, and born of and responsive to the specific variables and personalities involved. To pre-identify 3rd Space options outside of a collaborative context negates the spirit of Setting the Stage for Miracles, which is to remain open to the unexpected and/or unanticipated synergy between specific perspectives. Even when a person has worked with this disposition for a long time and can envision possible options from past experience, it remains important to voice these in ways that are not perceived by other(s) as directives given the power dynamics that may be at play. There are times when suggestions carry an implicit message. For example, as my (Barrera) first boss once said, "This is only a suggestion, but don't forget who made it." Anything that unbalances reciprocity works contrary to Setting the Stage for Miracles.

LOOKING AHEAD

The foundational knowledge discussed in this chapter and the two preceding chapters is designed to provide what Nakkula and Ravitch (1998) term *forestructure*. Forestructure is composed of the learning and knowledge that assist with the "assimilation of anything new" (Nakkula & Ravitch, 1998, p. 5). The following chapter concludes the formation of this forestructure by introducing the six specific strategies that translate the dispositions of Choosing Relationship over Control and Setting the Stage for Miracles into concrete behavioral expressions that support and promote respect, reciprocity, and responsiveness. Part III starts the more specific illustrations of using Skilled Dialogue as it discusses each strategy in greater detail and provides exercises for practicing their application to various scenarios, such as that between Camilla and JoAnne.

DISCUSSION QUESTIONS AND ACTIVITIES

1. What is your understanding of *paradox?* Discuss this concept with others and identify at least three examples of a paradox. (See also Chapter 9 for more information on this concept.)

2. Read and discuss the following quotation:

   > We split paradoxes so reflexively that we do not understand the price we pay for our habit. The poles of a paradox are like the poles of a battery: hold them together, and they generate the energy of life; pull them apart, and the current stops flowing. When we separate any of the profound paired truths of our lives, both poles become lifeless as well. Dissecting a living paradox has the same impact on our intellectual, emotional, and spiritual well-being as the decision to breathe in without ever breathing in would have on our physical health. (Palmer, 1997, p. 64)

3. Think of a recent interaction with a parent or co-worker in which you wanted something to happen that was not currently happening or wanted something that was happening to stop happening. Describe your desired outcome as clearly and specifically as you can. Now think of and list all the obstacles to that outcome that immediately come to mind. They may be about you (e.g., "I don't know how to do that") or about the other person (e.g., "She would never do that"). Again, describe them as clearly as you can without censoring them or telling yourself that you should not believe them. Now, hold both the desired outcome and obstacles in your mind at the same time side by side. Reflect on your experience as you do this. Were you able to do it? Did one seem more real than the other? Were you able to allow the energy between the two to simply be? If you were able to do it, contrast your experience with times when you have not done that.

4. A good example of 3rd Space was provided by Southwest Airlines. When faced with two views—one that advocated assigned seating so that customers would no longer need to stand in line to ensure preferred seating and one that vastly preferred open seating—Southwest came up with a third option that honored

both sides of the issue. They now number boarding passes (e.g., A1, A2). The numbers effectively hold customers' places in line in groups of 10 (e.g., 1–10, 11–20) so that there is no longer a need to stand in place until just before boarding. Once boarded, however, seating remains open. Both views were honored without placing them on an exclusive either-or continuum that required eliminating one to achieve the other. Think of similar either-or scenarios. Brainstorm with other people to identify additional examples of 3rd Space.

SELECTED RESOURCES FOR SETTING THE STAGE FOR MIRACLES

Although literature on relational approaches to interactions is relatively common in educational and related disciplines, literature on generating creative options is, unfortunately, much more rare. Current literature, in fact, seems as though it is becoming more and more prescriptive. Learning to set the stage for miracles, however, has a contrasting emphasis—stretching the boundaries of one's thinking. The references listed here reflect this focus and may therefore seem somewhat unorthodox for a text of this type. Have fun stretching!

Childs, C. (1998). *The spirit's terrain: Creativity, activism and transformation.* **Boston: Beacon Press.**

This book explores creativity in both practical and visionary terms. It has some powerful examples of 3rd Space. In discussing how change is approached, Childs makes the following statement that captures the disposition of Setting the Stage for Miracles: "They start with a list of known techniques before clearly establishing the *goal* those techniques are meant to serve" (p. 116). When we start with a positive behavioral support program, for example, is the goal to eliminate an undesirable behavior? Is it to substitute a more desirable behavior? Or, is the goal to nurture a child's spirit and sense of self in such a way that he or she can learn to read social situations and select behaviors that meet his or her needs and the constraints of a particular situation?

Childs continued,

> But truly creative organizations [and individuals] begin with little or no interest in technique. They instead begin by . . . envisioning, usually in colorful detail, the genuinely desired result. . . . They agree to begin with *absolutely no assumed limitations:* they simply will not in the words of Cornel West, 'allow the present circumstances to dictate [their] conception of the future.' But they begin with an honest and accurate accounting of those present circumstances, good and ill, on both visible and invisible levels. (p. 116)

Dobson, T., & Miller, V. (1993). *Aikido in everyday life: Giving in to get your way* **(2nd ed.). Berkeley, CA: North Atlantic Books.**

This book describes what the authors term *"attack-tics,"* which is, according to them, "a wedding of martial arts and theater" (p. xiii). Through the use of visual shapes, it describes a number of options to give us a novel way of viewing our conflicts and creative way of responding to them. They provide a variety of concrete exercises for choosing how to respond to conflicts in ways that seek to achieve harmony.

Fletcher, J., & Olwyler, K. (1997). *Paradoxical thinking: How to profit from your contradictions*. San Francisco: Berrett-Koehler.

This book provides specific information and techniques for transforming contradictions into paradox, one of the core goals of Setting the Stage for Miracles. The authors discuss two aspects of this process that have particular relevance to learning to think in threes. The first of these is "finding your core personal paradox" (p. 3). In doing this, we learn to bring contradictions "home" and work with them before trying to address them in others. The second aspect is "perception-shifting . . . Breaking open your narrow judgments about the positive or negative value of your contradictory qualities" (p. 3). I (Barrera) have found that instructing teachers to do this helps also to break open their judgments about the positive or negative value of others' qualities that contradict their own.

Fritz, R. (1989). *The path of least resistance: Learning to become the creative force in your own life*. New York: Fawcett Columbine.

This book is one of the best I (Barrera) have found on the process of creative thinking, which is an essential part of *Harmonizing*. It makes an initial distinction related to how we frame the situations we want to change.

> When we think of them as problems, we try to solve them. When you are solving a problem, you are taking action to have something go away: the *problem*. When you are creating, you are taking action to have something come into being: the *creation* [i.e., the miracle]. (p. 11)

There is also a detailed discussion of how to work with opposites and contradictions.

Fritz, R. (1991). *Creating: A practical guide to the creative process and how to use it to create anything—a work of art, a relationship, a career or a better life*. New York: Fawcett Columbine.

This is a later book by Fritz in which he revisits and extends his discussion from *The Path of Least Resistance*. Learning and practicing the creative process as Fritz describes can be an invaluable support for strengthening both our inclination toward and our skills for Setting the Stage for Miracles.

Katie, B., & Mitchell, S. (2002). *Loving what is: Four questions that can change your life*. New York: Three Rivers Press.

The four questions addressed in the book as well as on the associated web site (http://www.thework.org) are very helpful in learning how to reframe perceptions and judgments about others.

Perkins, D. (2000). *The eureka effect: The art and logic of breakthrough thinking*. New York: W.W. Norton.

Perkins's book is another resource with a description of creative thinking and exercises for developing it. His focus is on the unpredictable apparently instantaneous "breakthrough" or "aha" moments as contrasted with "more incremental [linear and logical] thinking" (p. 9). At its best, *Harmonizing*, a strategy associated with Setting the Stage for Miracles, culminates in a "breakthrough" (e.g., an insight into an unimagined option, a shift in perception that reveals a new path to the desired goal)—an "aha" that changes everything. That is one reason why Skilled Dialogue can never be a prescriptive process with each step mapped out in detail. The "ahas" that we experience in solving puzzles of various sorts are breakthrough moments in miniature. The following is one such puzzle provided by Perkins:

> You are driving a jeep through the Sahara desert. You encounter someone lying face down in the sand, dead. There are no tracks anywhere around. There has been no wind for days to destroy tracks. You look in a pack on the person's back. What do you find? (pp. 28–29) The answer turns out to be an unopened parachute.

Wind, Y., & Cook, C. (2004). *The power of impossible thinking: Transform the business of your life and the life of your business*. Philadelphia: Wharton School Publishing.

This book is innovative in both its format and its content. It has much information on mental models and on how to identify and shift them. Of particular interest is its discussion of "zooming in" and "zooming out":

> The first step on how to identify and shift mental models is to make sure we pay attention to the relevant portion, so our perspective is not built on shifting sand or the wrong information. We do this by zooming in and examining interesting details closely. This helps us identify disconfirming information that should cause us to challenge our broader [mental] models [i.e., current understandings]. The second challenge is to make sure that we gain sufficient perspective to create a coherent picture. . . . We do this by zooming out and looking at the big picture. (p. 103)

This "big picture" is what we refer to when talking about harmonizing opposites into inclusive paradoxes in Chapter 9.

Zander, R.S. & Zander, B. (2000). *The art of possibility: Transforming professional and personal life*. Boston: Harvard Business School Publishing.

The authors of this book provide many short exercises for understanding and developing reframing. Their perspective is best described in the book's opening paragraph.

> This a how-to book of an unusual kind. . . . Our premise is that many of the circumstances that seem . . . [problematic] . . . may only appear so based on a framework of assumptions we carry with us. Draw a different frame around the same set of circumstances [i.e., reframe them] and new pathways come into view. Find the right framework and extraordinary accomplishment becomes an everyday experience. (p. 1)

The discussion of "downward spiral talk" (p.108) is particularly relevant to difficult situations and conversations practitioners may encounter. Downward spiral talk focuses "On the abstraction of scarcity, [it] creates an unassailable story about the limits to what is possible and tells us compellingly how things are going from bad to worse" (p. 108). Zander and Zander emphasize the importance of separating "our conclusions about events [and people] from our description of the events [and people] themselves" (p. 106). This latter practice is especially relevant to using the strategy of *Appreciating*.

OTHER RESOURCES

A sense of 3rd Space can also be gained from working with the following resources.

Magic Eye Books

These books illustrate a picture within a picture and capture the sense of 3rd Space as a reality that is always present but not readily discerned.

Photomosaic Puzzles

These puzzles are referred to in the earlier Skilled Dialogue book (Barrera et al., 2003). They are a fairly exact visual depiction of something in 3rd Space—in this case an image—created by the positioning of other smaller somethings—in this case smaller images—without in any way changing those smaller things.

Trust Bridge Exercise

This exercise is contained in *An Unused Intelligence: Physical Thinking for 21st Century Leadership* (Bryner & Markova, 1996). The exercise is a marvelous way of physically experiencing 3rd Space. I (Barrera) use it to illustrate 3rd Space as follows:

1. Ask two people (A and B) to come forward. "Person B forms an arched bridge by kneeling on hands and knees. Person A then bends over and uses elbows and forearms to lean on B" (A rests on B's back for support).

2. "Suddenly and without notice B collapses." Person A typically also collapses as B's support is lost. This is Option 1.

3. In the next step, B again forms a bridge and A leans over. This time, however, A is asked to resume the same position but not to rely on B's support, just in case B collapses again.

4. "Suddenly and without notice B collapses." In this case, A typically does not collapse. This is Option 2.

5. These two options now form the contradiction—dependence and independence.

6. Participants are then asked to think about a third option. After several minutes of discussion Person B is once more asked to form a bridge. A is then told that this time he or she must place his or her weight on B and also remain aware of his or her own balance and center.

7. As before, B collapses suddenly and without warning. This time, A typically moves somewhat but does not fall. This is Option 3, which might be described as interdependence. Option 3 integrates dependence and independence physically and gives A the physical experience of 3rd Space.

Between Dispositions and Outcomes

Skilled Dialogue in Action

The development of Skilled Dialogue started with a focus on how to best achieve and maintain the qualities of respect, reciprocity, and responsiveness as identified through the observation and analysis of two practitioners the authors judged to be exceptionally culturally responsive and competent (see Barrera et al., 2003, for further discussion). As our initial concept of Skilled Dialogue was field tested and analyzed, it quickly became clear that the success of these practitioners was not simply about the mechanical application of certain strategies. It was also about the *quality* of the attention and *intention* underlying their use of the strategies. This realization led to the crystallization of the two Skilled Dialogue dispositions of Choosing Relationship over Control and Setting the Stage for Miracles that were addressed in the previous two chapters. Further study and observation then led to the development of specific strategies as the integrated and integral link between the targeted qualities and the dispositions. This chapter discusses all three aspects of Skilled Dialogue—dispositions, qualities, and strategies—as an introduction to the detailed description of the individual strategies in Part III. These strategies, however, can only express the dispositions and achieve the qualities when the overall articulation among all elements is understood and maintained.

The dispositions promote and sustain the qualities through their focus on relationship and miracles. The qualities (i.e., targeted outcomes) give direction and focus to the dispositions. Both together give rise to and support specific behavioral strategies as their external and concrete expression. Without that concrete behavioral expression, neither disposition nor targeted outcome is enough. Similarly, the strategies without attention to the qualities and dispositions remain ultimately ineffective.

SKILLED DIALOGUE STRATEGIES

The six strategies introduced in this chapter—*Welcoming, Allowing, Sense-Making, Appreciating, Joining*, and *Harmonizing*—reflect the evolution of the original strategies.

Table 6.1.   Skilled Dialogue framework

Qualities	Dispositions		
	Choosing Relationship over Control		Setting the Stage for Miracles
	Strategies		
Respect (Honoring identity)	Welcoming		Allowing
		Differences do not make people wrong	
Reciprocity (Honoring voice)	Sense-Making		Appreciating
		Diversity is always life enhancing	
Responsiveness (Honoring connection)	Joining		Harmonizing
		There is always a third choice	

Although the original strategies (see Figures 9 and 10 in Barrera et al., 2003) can still be easily connected to the current ones, the latter are now both more precise and more comprehensive. Chapters 7–9 of this book discuss them in more depth, providing detailed examples of their application to challenging interactions with both children and adults.

As shown in Table 6.1, there are three strategies associated with the expression of each disposition. Each strategy targets a different quality or outcome. The three associated with Choosing Relationship over Control include *Welcoming*, which targets the development and maintenance of respect; *Sense-Making*, which targets establishing reciprocity; and *Joining*, which is designed to develop responsiveness. Three additional strategies are associated with the expression of Setting the Stage for Miracles. The first of these is *Allowing*, which extends *Welcoming* and, in similar fashion, targets the development and maintenance of respect. The second is *Appreciating*, which extends *Sense-Making* and, similarly, is designed to establish reciprocity. Finally, the third strategy is *Harmonizing*, which extends *Joining* and targets the development of truly responsive options. Each of these strategies is discussed in the following sections.

Strategies Associated with Choosing Relationship over Control

Welcoming, Sense-Making, and *Joining* are the strategies critical to setting the disposition of Choosing Relationship over Control. Each is described next.

Welcoming   The strategy of *Welcoming* focuses on expressing the disposition of Choosing Relationship over Control for the purpose of promoting and sustaining respect (i.e., honoring identity). It emphasizes the importance of communicating not only our welcoming of the opportunity to interact with another but also our welcoming of the other person him- or herself. How we first approach people is often the key to the nature and outcome of our subsequent interactions with them.

We may not agree or even like others' decisions or the resulting behaviors and/or perspectives. We may clearly see those behaviors and/or perspectives as inappropriate or limiting in relation to other contexts. Nevertheless, communicating our respect for another person cannot be fully accomplished without welcoming that other person not just as someone we can teach but also and more critically as someone from whom we can learn.

In other words, *Welcoming* helps to communicate our recognition of the other person as someone whom we can respect for his or her ability to adapt and survive within a given environment, even when he or she is doing so in ways that we cannot understand or value. This presumption of equal ability to craft a behavioral repertoire adaptive to a given context is a key characteristic of *Welcoming*. Two other characteristics expand on this one: acceptance of another's behavior and/or perspective as legitimate within a given context and a willingness to communicate unconditional respect (see Chapter 7 for examples and further discussion).

Sense-Making   The second strategy of *Sense-Making* further deepens the expression of Choosing Relationship over Control by seeking to establish reciprocity (i.e., honoring the expression of another's identity as equally valid as our own). It does so by inviting us to seek to understand others' beliefs, behaviors, and/or perspectives in such a way that they make as much sense within their given context as ours do within our own context.

It is difficult to appreciate that which makes no sense to us or, worse yet, only makes sense in the context of being wrong or inappropriate. The strategy of *Sense-Making* draws our attention to finding ways of, quite literally, making sense of another's behavior, beliefs, and/or values. It invites us to search for and find the meaning(s) that underlies and structures that behavior, belief, and/or value.

Welcoming affirms the fact that another's behaviors make sense in some way, although it may not be initially clear to us just how it does that. *Sense-Making* focuses on identifying what that meaning is (i.e., how a particular behavior, belief, and/or perspective makes sense). The first requisite characteristic of *Sense-Making* is an attitude of curiosity. Such an attitude helps us to interact with another as a learner who seeks information rather than as an expert who is there only to give information or promote change. A second requisite characteristic is attentive listening to the stories, experiences, and thoughts that support the other person's particular behaviors and perspectives. These are elicited and listened to nonjudgmentally until it becomes possible to see ourselves behaving similarly given the same circumstances. It is through honoring another person's voice that respect deepens into reciprocity (see Chapter 7 for examples and further discussion).

Joining   The strategy of *Joining* completes the expression of the disposition of Choosing Relationship over Control by inviting us to identify the larger shared context within which our beliefs and those of another person are connected as an expression of a single reality. *Joining* acknowledges the recognition that all interactions are constructed and enacted within a joint context (i.e., are connected) and that, consequently, the behaviors that compose them are not isolated and in-dependent but rather are linked in some way.

This strategy rests on the previous strategy of *Sense-Making* and helps achieve responsiveness by honoring connection. It seeks to establish a common space within which one person can connect with another. Connection cannot, however, be honored until we make sense of another's behavior. Until then, the person's behavior remains in the "not like me at all" and "I can't relate to it" category. It is relatively easy to resist joining (i.e., connecting) with what we cannot relate to or with what we perceive to be of little value.

Before interpersonal contexts can be shifted or expanded—the ultimate goal of Skilled Dialogue—it is necessary to relate to others' behaviors as somehow *inter*personal (i.e., connected and connective). Until then, it is, unfortunately, all too easy to situate the "problem" out there—in others and having nothing to do with us (e.g., "It is *their* behavior or perspective that is problematic and needs to change"). Senge, Scharmer, Jaworski, and Flowers captured the pitfalls of this tendency to disconnect the problematic from ourself in the following words:

> If you feel you've got a problem to solve that is "out there" and you don't see or want to see any possible relationship between the "you" who is trying to solve the problem and what the problem actually is, you may wind up not being able to see the prob-lem accurately. . . . (2005, p. 51)

The strategy of *Joining* presents the challenge of joining with another person by identifying how his or her behavior or perspective links with our own. It fo-cuses on identifying and acknowledging the joint "field" within which current interactions are taking place. As discussed in Chapter 5, *Joining* is about seeing beyond the walls of our personal space into the common room within which both people stand.

If, for example, a practitioner perceives a person's behavior as inattentive but that person perceives it as attentive, what is the context within which *both* per-ceptions exist? What is the "whole" reflected in each of the perceptions? One way of answering these questions is to realize that both people are standing in a single "room" called *attention*. One person perceives the absence of attention and the other perceives its presence; however, both perceive *attention*. Senge and colleagues called this "understanding the whole to be found in the parts" (2005, p. 46). They used the metaphor of individual leaves—each different from the others yet all within a single whole (p. 46) of the whole plant or tree. *Joining* challenges us to shift our focus from the parts to the whole, from half empty or half full to the con-tainer that holds both perspectives as one.

Joining asks us to affirm that a given solution is not about changing *them*, rather, it is about changing our perception of *them* and our behavior so that new possibil-ities can emerge. Its two requisite characteristics are 1) an acknowledgment that every interaction is mutually constructed and maintained, and 2) a willingness to identify specific aspects of how our own behavior and beliefs contribute to and sustain that interaction.

Block stated, "When we honestly ask ourselves about *our* [italics added] role in the creation of a particular situation that frustrates [or confuses or challenges] us, and set aside asking about *their* [italics added] role, then the world changes around us" (2002, p. 21). It is then possible to be participants in a mutual context within which the possibilities for change become both clearer and easier to access. The identification of this mutual context through *Joining* is key to the companion strategy of *Harmonizing* (discussed in the next section).

In summary, the disposition of Choosing Relationship over Control is expressed through the following:

- *Welcoming*—inviting others into relationship with me no matter how different they, their behaviors, or their perspectives may be from my own

- *Sense-Making*—learning as much as possible in order that I may make sense of others' diverse behaviors, beliefs, and/or perspectives before concluding that they are somehow less competent than my own and therefore need to be changed

- *Joining*—finding how others' behaviors, beliefs, and/or perspectives are connected with our own so that it is possible to relate with them from a shared "we/our" perspective rather than an exclusive "you/yours" perspective

Strategies Associated with Setting the Stage for Miracles

Three additional strategies are associated with the expression of Skilled Dialogue's second disposition of Setting the Stage for Miracles. They are *Allowing, Appreciating,* and *Harmonizing.* This disposition deepens and extends the disposition of Choosing Relationship over Control through its focus on literally setting the stage for transformational shifts in the conceptual and perceptual paradigms that inform and shape interactions between diverse individuals. Its three strategies, similar to the previous strategies, also address respect, reciprocity, and responsiveness, but they do so in a distinct fashion. Their aim is to reframe existing contexts and relationships rather than to only relate with them. Current understandings can then be moved into new integrative and inclusive frames within which novel, even miraculous, outcomes can be co-constructed (Jaworski, 1996).

Allowing Similar to *Welcoming, Allowing* promotes respect by honoring identity. It is distinct, however, in that its purpose is to set the stage for miracles by making space for what is diverse, not just so that it may be welcomed, but so that it may be allowed to remain diverse. It supports the establishment of respect by permitting others to be who they are without first requiring compromise or change. This does not, however, mean a simple passivity in the face of behaviors and/or beliefs that are less than optimal in a given environment. Rather, it means allowing what *is* to be as it *is* before determining how it needs to change.

Typically, *Welcoming* and *Allowing* strategies are used almost simultaneously, with one reinforcing the other. No matter how we approach someone, *Welcoming* cannot be fully articulated if we cannot at least momentarily suspend the promotion of our own agenda over the other person's agenda. That is the goal of *Allowing*—the suspension of the need to privilege our agenda (i.e., give it priority), however subtly, over someone else's. *Allowing* challenges our understanding and use of power. If someone listens to an interaction, for example, could they tell whose agenda was most important? Would it be ours? Do we perceive and communicate that we somehow have more power or competence than the others with whom we are interacting?

Perhaps the most challenging aspect of *Allowing* is what is known as "staying with the tension"; that is, allowing *both* multiple agendas on the table simultaneously without forcing a choice between them. It is this sort of suspension of the need to fix, resolve, or defend that begins to set the stage by creating conceptual and emotional space within which diverse identities can be honored without either needing to be erased or merged.

Our research and fieldwork on Skilled Dialogue has highlighted three characteristics that are necessary to creating this type of interpersonal context. The first is the one just discussed—the willingness to suspend judgment and simply remain present without fixing or judging others. Perhaps they appear careless of their responsibilities, yet there is always at least a 1% possibility that our judgment of this "fact" is based on insufficient or incorrect information. Even 60 seconds given to that consideration can set the stage for miracles!

Related to this characteristic is a second and similar characteristic: the willingness to release our stories and interpretations about another's behaviors and beliefs. Wilson's (2001) article "Looking Closer," which was reprinted with permission as Appendix B in *Skilled Dialogue: Strategies for Responding to Cultural Diversity in Early Childhood* (Barrera et al., 2003), provided an excellent illustration of how easy it is "to assume that quick judgments and first impressions tell us all we need to know about each other" (as cited in Barrera et al., 2003, p. 221). Wilson told the story of a mother who was arrested and sentenced for driving without a license. At first glance, she was judged by those trying to help her as a "typical" thoughtless person who was unwilling to do the necessary work to obtain a license; however, this was not the case. As the people involved obtained more information, they learned that their initial judgments were far from complete. Wilson concluded, "How easy it is, even for those of intelligence and heart, to preconceive and presuppose based on the apparent rather than the true" (as cited in Barrera et al., 2003, p. 222).

The strategy of *Allowing* focuses on loosening preconceptions and presuppositions in order to make room for unimagined and/or unexpected truths to emerge (see Chapter 7 for further discussion and examples).

Appreciating   *Appreciating*, the second strategy associated with Setting the Stage for Miracles, builds on *Allowing* by focusing on the value and worth present in what *is*, as it is, simply because it is acknowledged as an evidence-based expression of someone's competence, however limited or different from our own. Similar to *Sense-Making*, *Appreciating* thus seeks to establish reciprocity and honor voice, even when significantly diverse from our own. It does so by going beyond the understanding gained through *Sense-Making* and acknowledging the inherent value and potential contribution of what another brings to the table. *Appreciating* deepens interpersonal connection and space so that the worth of diverse identities can be brought to the stage that is being set. This strategy, similar to that of *Sense-Making,* focuses on establishing and maintaining reciprocity. Only after something makes sense can it truly be appreciated.

The strategy of *Appreciating* expresses the belief that everyone has something of value to contribute to a given interaction, even if that something is a wake-up call to the limitations of current behaviors. It includes not just recognizing the sense and value of a behavior and/or belief for the person exhibiting it, but also the value of that behavior and/or belief in relation to ourself and the goal(s) we wish to attain.

In Skilled Dialogue, this is referred to as finding the *gold nuggets* (see also Table 4.3). What unique example or lens (i.e., *gold nugget*) does someone bring to a situation that can enrich us and our view, not only of this particular interaction, but also of the larger world? For example, can someone's insistence on only his or her own perspective be a reminder of the value of our own perspective, which perhaps we tend to undervalue except when it is clothed in the guise of "expert advice?" Or, perhaps, might it bring with it an invitation to reflect on our own misuse of power? Until we can acknowledge the value of another's behaviors and/or perspectives in relation to ourself, it is difficult to truly honor another's voice.

Appreciating can be further defined through its critical aspects: The first is the willingness to explicitly communicate our perceptions of the value and worth of another person's behaviors and/or perspectives in relation to his or her experiences and needs. Doing this involves first identifying those aspects of another's behavior that have the potential to enrich our sense of who the other is. Statements may be as simple as "I see" or as detailed as "I understand how helpful this has been in coping with your child's situation."

A second aspect focuses on identifying what another's diverse behaviors and/or perspectives can teach us (i.e., identifying the value of another's behaviors and perspectives in relation to ourself). This aspect requires acknowledging that every behavior or perspective encountered may, in fact, mirror something within ourself (Hatfield, Cacioppo, & Rapson, 1993; Jaffe, 2007), although perhaps in an exaggerated form. Time and again in working with practitioners learning to use Skilled Dialogue, we find that the behaviors they identify as the most challenging are those that call attention to some aspect of themselves that they do not wish to acknowledge or that they have struggled with in the past. Sometimes the behaviors may reflect a hidden strength that they have yet to acknowledge in themselves, or something they always admired but have not felt able to express.

The third aspect facilitates our willingness to appreciate even those behaviors we may find unacceptable. It invites us to acknowledge that all negative behavior can, from one perspective, be understood as a good behavior exaggerated. What seems to be "indecisiveness," for example, may actually reflect the love of learning as much as possible and a reluctance to miss out on anything (see Table 4.3 in Chapter 4 for additional examples).

One person's "obnoxious" questioning can be another's positive "inquisitive-ness" (Payne, 2005). With the understanding that every negative behavior is a positive behavior exaggerated, we might learn from a parent who allows children to yell and argue the value of allowing children self-expression, even when they express themselves differently from what we prefer, though *not* the value of al-lowing the behavior to that extreme. Or, perhaps, we might learn the value of allowing ourselves to express disagreement or frustration, although perhaps in a more skillful manner. Through these aspects, *Appreciating* completes the honoring of voice first addressed through *Sense-Making* by promoting and not just under-standing the value of diverse perspectives or voices.

Harmonizing   The third strategy associated with Setting the Stage for Mir-acles—*Harmonizing*—complements *Joining*, which was discussed in relation to Choosing Relationship over Control. Like *Joining*, it builds responsiveness through honoring connection. Its goal, however, is not just to create contexts where all can have an equal voice. It is, rather, to shift the focus of interactional contexts from the noncomplementary aspects of diverse perspectives (i.e., the contradictions) to their complementary, albeit paradoxical, aspects. This shift allows for the trans-formation of the exclusive, either-or nature of contradictions into the inclusive, multidimensional nature of paradoxes within which third (and fourth or even fifth) option(s) responsive to initial differences as well as to desired circumstances can be generated.

Harmonizing thus redefines interpersonal contexts as complementary rather than oppositional so as to be able to leverage and integrate their strengths. The strategy of *Harmonizing* is, in some ways at least, the most challenging of Skilled Dialogue's six strategies. It requires going beyond what seems apparent on the surface and, "paradoxically . . . looking inside" (Senge et al., 2005, p. 113). It is related to the aptitude of "symphony" identified by Pink who said, "Symphonic thinking is a signature ability of composers and conductors, whose jobs involve corralling a diverse group of notes, instruments, and performers and producing a unified and pleasing sound" (2006, p. 130). Similar to integrating the color blue with the color yellow or integrating individual musical notes into a chord, *Harmo-nizing* integrates disparate perspectives into a larger and more inclusive reality where each can remain itself while simultaneously becoming part of a third as yet unrealized option(s). The use of this strategy transforms interactional contexts, finding and leveraging the complementary aspects of existing behaviors and/or perspectives. It resolves the tension between diverse perspectives that has been allowed to continue up to that point as the gifts and connections within contradic-tions have been explored.

In summary, the disposition of Setting the Stage for Miracles is expressed through the following:

- *Allowing*—suspending "stories" and understandings about a person and/or what is happening and remaining open to alternative "stories" and understandings

- *Appreciating*—finding the value of a person's behaviors and/or perspectives not only for him or her but for oneself as well

- *Harmonizing*—integrating the "poles" of the identified contradiction and lever-aging their complementary aspects in order to generate previously unimagined options

SKILLED DIALOGUE IN ACTION

Skilled Dialogue can be applied in any interaction where the intent is to be re-spectful, reciprocal, and responsive to and with another. It is especially useful for interactions within which different beliefs or values generate miscommunication, dissonance, or tension, regardless of whether these beliefs or values stem from cul-tural, personal, experiential, or other sources. The example used in the following sections is provided to broadly illustrate how it might work. (More detailed and specific examples are provided in Part III of this book.)

Welcoming

Before meeting with the person with whom she is having difficulty, the person using Skilled Dialogue (a practitioner hereafter referred to as Dale) focuses on her aware-ness that her viewpoint or perspective is not necessarily the only right or desirable one and examines any assumptions about this she may be bringing into the inter-actional context (e.g., "I'm the expert," "I know more about behavior management than this other person," "This other person obviously needs help"). As Dale meets with the other person, she makes every effort to communicate that she welcomes both the person and the opportunity to explore her perspective as legitimate. Both verbally and nonverbally she expresses respect based on recognition of the other's unique identity, not just on the level of agreement or similarity of perspectives.

Allowing

As Dale listens to what the other person is saying, she intentionally drops her story(ies) about the other person. These stories may include the following thoughts, for example, "This is a very angry person," and "This must mean that she really doesn't like what I am proposing." Or she may think, "I really like what she's say-ing," and "Wow, she's such a nice person." In using the strategy of *Allowing*, though, she would simply tell herself, "These are my thoughts, and I have to re-member that I don't really know this person. It is neither necessary nor desirable to express agreement or disagreement at this point. What is important is to listen without trying to change the other's mind, defend my own perspective, or move to conclusions and action before further interaction." (Allowing what *is* does not, however, mean delaying necessary actions in situations that require immediate change, such as one in which child abuse is present; see Chapter 7.) It is also okay to say things such as "I think very differently, but I really want to hear how you think about it." Or, "It sounds like we think in similar ways."

Sense-Making

Dale consciously remembers to be a learner, releasing her role as expert and listen-ing attentively and with curiosity to what the other says without making judgments about what it means at that point. She moves from "I know what that means" (e.g., this person believes that it is okay to let children yell and argue with adults) to "I wonder how that choice makes sense to her; I'll just ask more questions and listen more carefully so that I can understand it from her perspective." Or, conversely, she may think, "She sounds just like me; I wonder if she is making that choice for the same reasons I would." Dale realizes that to truly make sense of another's words and behaviors, no matter how similar or dissimilar to her own, she must drop her assumptions about what they mean and, instead, obtain direct information. Questions such as "What do you think and/or feel when I talk about doing X?" and "What do you think might happen if you didn't do Y?" can be helpful.

Appreciating

As she starts to understand the other person's perspective and see the situation through the other person's eyes, Dale begins to recognize how much the other person has to contribute to the situation at hand. She realizes, for example, that the other person believes in her child's ability to learn and become competent much more than she does, grounded as she is in assessment and developmental data. She also learns about herself. She learns that just as the other person insists on her own perspective and resists opening to new perspectives, she too has that same tendency. Dale then starts to communicate her appreciation for what the other has to offer (e.g., telling how much she appreciates her persistence in stating her perspective until Dale can really understand it because Dale really wants this to be a collaborative effort) and what she is learning (e.g., telling her how much she is learning about herself through this exchange of ideas). In expressing her appreciation in this manner, Dale honors the other person's voice and sets a tone of partnership rather than of merely helper and helpee or teacher and learner. She starts to listen as a learner herself.

Joining

At this point, having come to appreciate the other person's diverse understandings and behaviors, Dale would initiate the strategy of *Joining*. She looks for ways in which she and the other person share a common context by asking questions about her own behavior, such as "How am I contributing to the current miscommunication?" (e.g., Am I modeling the same inattentive or resistant behaviors that I am asking the other to change? Am I not really listening and not willing to change my mind, which is thus fueling the other person's need to advocate for unconfined expression?). Dale also looks for times when she has been where this mom seems to be, that is, times when she has been inattentive or resistant (i.e., has shared that same perspective that so frustrates her now). She thus moves from a "One of us has a problem, and it isn't me" view to a "We're in this together on this joint problem" view. This requires looking for similarities in the stated differences (e.g., "Oh, I see—we're both really frustrated with this situation").

Dale starts to see that, up to that point, they have both accepted their roles in a familiar script of "expert outsider coming in to help" and "unskilled parent needing to do it another's way," and begins to wonder if there might not be better scripts that are more responsive to their identities as well as to the child's needs.

Harmonizing

Once a collaborative, although perhaps not optimal, perspective has been acknowledged (i.e., once Dale and the parent have joined forces), Dale turns her attention to searching for an inclusive perspective within which the existing exclusive options that are in play can be harmonized (i.e., how compliance and resistance can be leveraged to create options that tap the strengths of both and form something richer and more stable than either one alone).

Starting with the similarities that she identifies through *Joining*, Dale brainstorms collaboratively with the other person to find options that integrate the strengths of their current perspectives. For example, she might ask what options could be created when her task-focused perspective is integrated with the other's less structured perspective without forcing a choice of one or the other? (See Chapter 9 for further information and exercises related to this strategy.)

It is important to note that Skilled Dialogue is a process over time. It is common to address only the first three strategies during initial interactions and then move to the latter three as the relationship is more firmly established.

SKILLED DIALOGUE IN ACTION: HORIZONTAL AND VERTICAL SEQUENCES

The strategies of *Allowing, Appreciating,* and *Harmonizing,* along with the strategies of *Welcoming, Sense-Making,* and *Joining,* are the external expressions of Skilled Dialogue in action. Although discussed sequentially so far, the strategies are in fact reiterative and nonsequential. For example, without the strategy of *Welcoming* it is difficult to establish a context of reciprocity within which practitioners, as well as those with whom they are interacting, can appreciate and make sense of each other's diverse perspectives. However, it is much more challenging to welcome that which we cannot understand and that which does not make sense to us. Similarly, as trust is established through the strategies of *Appreciating* and *Joining,* then *Welcoming,* and *Allowing* are facilitated. Each strategy thus supports and stimulates the others.

This discussion nevertheless requires some sort of structured sequencing. Skilled Dialogue strategies can be sequenced in two ways: by disposition, as discussed previously, or by quality (see Table 6.1). Whereas the vertical sequence is useful to gain an understanding of each disposition separate from the other, the horizontal sequence emphasizes their interweaving and has proven the most successful for initial learning and practice. Each type of organization has something distinct to offer. The authors' field research has shown that the horizontal sequence is most useful in deepening understanding of the dispositions as well as checking for their presence. This sequence has proven most useful in applying Skilled

Dialogue to particular situations. It is difficult, for example, to move from *Welcoming* to *Sense-Making* without moving through *Allowing*. These sequences are summarized in the next section.

Horizontal—by Quality—Sequence

This sequence starts with the two strategies associated with respect, then moves to the two associated with reciprocity, and, finally, addresses the two associated with responsiveness.

Respect is established and sustained through the following two strategies:

- *Welcoming*—extending unconditional respect as an expression of honoring another's identity as legitimate and evidence based

- *Allowing*—allowing differences to stand without trying to change them or defend one's "side"

Reciprocity is created and sustained through the following two strategies:

- *Sense-Making*—searching for how the other's stories, behaviors, and understandings make as much sense within their context as the practitioner's do within his or her context

- *Appreciating*—identifying the value and/or strengths of other's behaviors and/or beliefs for them as well as for oneself (e.g., asking "What I can learn?")

Responsiveness is developed and sustained through the following two strategies:

- *Joining*—identifying the specific manner in which the practitioner and another person share a single context and co-construct their behavior within that context

- *Harmonizing*—co-constructing previously unimagined and novel options that leverage the strengths of both "sides" of the identified contradictions

Vertical—by Disposition—Sequence

This sequence starts with the strategies associated with the disposition of Choosing Relationship over Control, starting with *Welcoming,* then *Sense-Making,* and, finally, *Joining.* It then moves on to the strategies associated with the disposition of Setting the Stage for Miracles, starting with *Allowing,* then *Appreciating,* and, finally, *Harmonizing.*

Choosing Relationship over Control is expressed concretely through the following strategies:

- *Welcoming*—relating with another as someone whose identity is as evidence based and valid as one's own

- *Sense-Making*—acknowledging that another person's behavior makes as much sense as one's own and seeking to find how that is so

- *Joining*—identifying shared context(s)

The disposition of Setting the Stage for Miracles is concretely expressed through the following strategies:

- *Allowing*—releasing preset judgments and stories about who the other person is or is not

- *Appreciating*—identifying how the lens through which the other person sees this situation can enrich one's understanding of it and oneself

- *Harmonizing*—brainstorming for ways of establishing 3rd Space within which diverse strengths and perspectives can be leveraged to reach desired outcomes

As readers become more familiar with the strategies, they are encouraged to explore and use them in whatever sequence seems easiest and most efficient. In some cases, one or two strategies may be easier to apply than others (e.g., it may be less problematic to first make sense of a parent's or child's diverse behaviors before trying to harmonize those behaviors with ones advocated by the practitioner). *What is ultimately important is to understand the interplay among qualities, dispositions, and strategies.*

LOOKING AHEAD

There is a critical caveat to the discussion in this chapter. Given the necessarily sequential discussion of the strategies, it is important to remember that Skilled Dialogue stems from the presence of and synergy among all six strategies. That is the rationale for the general overview in this chapter prior to the in-depth discussion of each strategy in Part III. Readers are encouraged to read information on all six strategies before seeking to apply any single one.

Any single strategy is insufficient and falls short of its intended purpose when used by itself. Just *Welcoming* or *Allowing*, for example, or even both *Welcoming* and *Allowing* together are insufficient to promote the conceptual and perceptual shift(s) necessary for the generation of desired outcomes. When used in isolation from the other strategies, these strategies can deteriorate into simple passive tolerance. When used as part of the whole set of strategies, however, they become what they are meant to be, that is, necessary prerequisites for honoring voice and, subsequently, harmonizing contradictions into truly responsive options. Similarly, attempts to harmonize contradictions without first honoring identity and voice become only a more subtle aspect of control. It is with this caveat, therefore, that the overview of Skilled Dialogue's strategies in Part III continues.

SUMMARY

The strategies associated with Choosing Relationship over Control and Setting the Stage for Miracles are not simply a series of techniques to achieve pre-identified goals. Rather, they are tools for collaboratively crafting interactions that honor diverse identities, voices, and the connections among them. It is in this sense that they become most truly about expressing the dispositions of Choosing Relationship over Control and Setting the Stage for Miracles.

Skilled Dialogue strategies should be used thoughtfully and never at the risk of our own identity or voice. There are times when it is not possible to engage with others to the degree required by Skilled Dialogue, as well as times when our own energy and boundaries may not be strong enough to allow such engagement safely. It is important to recognize those times (see further discussion of this point in Part III of this book). The goals of Skilled Dialogue cannot and should not be achieved at the cost of anyone's values and beliefs. (More will be discussed on this point in Parts III and IV.)

DISCUSSION QUESTIONS AND ACTIVITIES

1. Review the discussion of each of the six strategies—*Welcoming, Allowing, Sense-Making, Appreciating, Joining,* and *Harmonizing*—in this chapter. Discuss how they relate to and reflect the qualities and dispositions of Choosing Relationship over Control and Setting the Stage for Miracles.

2. Think of an interaction you have recently had. Discuss each of the Skilled Dialogue elements—dispositions, qualities, and strategies—in relation to that situation. Can you identify which ones were present as evidenced by the presence of particular aspects? Which ones were strongest? Are there any that you cannot yet identify? Discuss results with one or more person and see if you can brainstorm ways in which you might change the interaction if you could do it again. (This is a preliminary exercise; it will be revisited in Part IV.)

3. Which elements—dispositions, qualities, and strategies—are the easiest for you to understand? Which are the most difficult? Discuss these in a group. Are the same ones easy or difficult for others?

Skilled
Dialogue Strategies

It is through the use of its strategies that Skilled Dialogue moves from a relatively abstract understanding and philosophy to an applied practice. These strategies serve a twofold purpose. First, they express the dispositions of Choosing Relationship over Control and Setting the Stage for Miracles in concrete form. Second, they generate and sustain the desired qualities of respect, reciprocity, and responsiveness. In doing this, they honor and nurture both children's and adults' spirits and sense of self.

Part I of this book introduces the conceptual foundation of Skilled Dialogue. Part II overviews its components (i.e., qualities, dispositions, and strategies). This information sets the general context for the use of Skilled Dialogue strategies. Part III provides greater detail and more examples of each strategy in relation to a sample scenario provided at the end of this Part III introduction. The purpose of Part III is to deepen and extend previous information on these strategies, which are the most visible aspects of Skilled Dialogue.

The chapters in this part of the book address each strategy and then examine its application in relation to the sample scenario. This examination is designed not to provide answers, but to stimulate questions and further thought as to the nature of the strategies, especially as understood within particular interactions. In large part, therefore, the strategies are still discussed separately as they have been in previous chapters. It is not until Part IV (Chapters 10–12) that all Skilled Dialogue elements are fully linked together through concrete illustrations using a variety of case studies, vignettes, and anecdotes.

Each chapter in Part III addresses two strategies using a horizontal sequence, according to the quality they are designed to promote and sustain—respect, reciprocity, or responsiveness. The first strategy in each pair expresses the disposition of Choosing Relationship over Control and the second expresses the disposition of Setting the Stage for Miracles. This organization *across* dispositions has proven most successful in initial learning and practice. (See Chapter 6 for discussion of horizontal and vertical organizations.)

CONNECTION AMONG
QUALITIES, DISPOSITIONS, AND STRATEGIES

The connection among qualities, dispositions, and specific strategies is important. All too often, a quality such as respect is discussed as a general concept without being defined in any concrete way (Barrera & Corso, 2000). Even when a quality is more concretely defined, it is too frequently defined only through specific behaviors that represent the beliefs and values of a single cultural model of agency (e.g., "Respect means not asking direct questions," "Respect means giving direct and sustained eye contact"). Whereas these behaviors do indeed express respect, they do so reliably only within particular contexts. In other contexts, they are equally likely to express disrespect. The same is true for behaviors associated with reciprocity and responsiveness.

The essence of any of the qualities is not captured by the presence of a particular behavior; rather, it is the underlying disposition that defines that quality. As stated in the Isaacs (1999, p. 132) quotation (see Chapter 3), for example, disrespect is rooted in the belief that those who are different from ourselves are somehow wrong and, therefore, need to change. In contrast, respect is rooted in the belief that differences do not make us wrong. Although some behaviors (e.g., yelling at someone to change) clearly express one or the other belief, it is possible for an identical behavior to communicate either belief, given the underlying disposition. Explaining our point of view, for example, could communicate that either we believe the other person to be wrong (e.g., if it is done repeatedly or insistently) or we believe that the other person's viewpoint can be right even though radically different from our own (e.g., if it is done without insisting or making judgmental comparisons).

Similarly, there is a direct link between establishing and sustaining reciprocity and responsiveness and the specific dispositions and qualities with which they are associated. The core essence of reciprocity is the recognition of diversity as life enhancing—that is, adding to rather than detracting from a given interaction. This recognition is reflected in how we receive another's differing perspectives. For example, are they received with curiosity and appreciation or as though they are less valuable than our own? When diverse perspectives are received with appreciation, reciprocity is established and ensures and supports interactional behaviors that reflect our desire to make sense of others' behaviors and appreciate their value. This then leads to responsiveness.

The core recognition of responsiveness is that there is always a third choice. This recognition is based on the understanding that diverse perspectives do not need to be put at opposite and contradictory ends of a continuum, but can instead be integrated into a whole that is bigger than either perspective and complementary to both. Such recognition breaks open rigid either-or as well as both-and perceptions and mindsets that maintain options as separate or side by side rather than integrated. (See discussion of both-and frameworks in Chapter 5). Responsiveness is thus reflected in behaviors that seek to discover how diverse behaviors can be complementary and to identify how each can contribute to a larger and inclusive whole.

WELCOMING AND ALLOWING

Chapter 7 discusses the critical aspects and behaviors associated with *Welcoming* and *Allowing*, which promote and sustain the quality of respect. *Welcoming* expresses the disposition of Choosing Relationship over Control, and *Allowing* expresses the disposition of Setting the Stage for Miracles. Together, these strategies are the concrete behavioral expressions of the recognition associated with respect that *differences do not make people wrong* (see discussion of respect in Chapter 3). This belief crosses dispositions as it addresses the core essence of respect. When it is reflected in the requisite characteristics and behaviors associated with *Welcoming* and *Allowing*, respect can be reliably established even across dissimilar or contradictory beliefs and perspectives.

SENSE-MAKING AND APPRECIATING

Chapter 8 follows a similar format as Chapter 7. It explores the strategies of *Sense-Making* and *Appreciating*. Once again, the first of these two strategies—*Sense-Making*—expresses the disposition of Choosing Relationship over Control and the second—*Appreciating*—expresses the disposition of Setting the Stage for Miracles. In contrast to *Welcoming* and *Allowing*, however, *Sense-Making* and *Appreciating* focus on establishing reciprocity (i.e., on honoring *all* voices involved in particular interactions, even when contradictory to our own) (see Chapter 3 for a discussion of reciprocity). The recognition that grounds these strategies is that *diversity is always life enhancing* (i.e., all differences bring something of value to a particular situation). Believing that all diversity is life enhancing supports our ability to see others as competent individuals who base their behaviors on specific experiences and evidence. In doing so, it opens us to legitimately *hear* another's perspective and, thus, seek to find the sense of his or her behaviors. This, in turn, opens the door to appreciating his or her diverse approach to particular situations, further deepening reciprocity and setting the stage for leveraging the strengths inherent in that approach through *Joining* and *Harmonizing*, which are discussed in Chapter 9.

JOINING AND HARMONIZING

The last two strategies may be less familiar to the readers than the previous ones. The previous strategies focused on creating a context of mutuality, *Joining* and *Harmonizing* focus on identifying the complementary aspects of diverse perspectives in order to develop inclusive options that can access and mine their unique strengths and resources. Each of these strategies, therefore, seeks to access all available resources, even those perceived as embedded in the behaviors that seem to be the "problem." They honor connection rather than division across differences so that options responsive to the needs of all involved can be co-crafted.

Joining and *Harmonizing* are grounded in a recognition that is critical to establishing and sustaining responsiveness: There is always a third choice. (Note: The use of the term *third choice* here refers to a third choice inclusive of the existing ones. See Chapter 5 for a discussion of 3rd Space and third choices.)

The recognition that *there is always a third choice* is critical to responsiveness for a simple reason. As long as only two choices are perceived (e.g., choice X or choice Y), choosing one must exclude the other. Under these circumstances, it is easy to believe that the choice or perspective preferred or believed to be most correct must be defended or pushed at the expense of other perspectives (e.g., "If I am responsive to X—the other's choice—then what will happen to choice Y, my choice? Who will speak to its necessity?) When only two contradictory choices seem feasible, it is not possible to be truly responsive to choices different from our own.

Joining and *Harmonizing* thus support the transformation of noncompatible and exclusive options (i.e., contradictions that indicate only one option can be chosen) into paradoxes, which affirm that two differing options can both be chosen and that they can be, in fact, complementary to one another. When contradictions are transformed into paradoxes, there is no need to defend one or to defend against another. Without the need for such defense, diverse perspectives can co-exist in ways that allow for the emergence of unexpected options (i.e., miracles) that dissolve the need for compromise and forced choice. (See Chapter 5 for further discussion of this point.) When this paradoxical perspective is achieved, dialogue becomes truly skilled!

Taken together, the three chapters in Part III illustrate the key Skilled Dialogue strategies in more detail than in previous chapters. The application of all three Skilled Dialogue components—qualities, dispositions, and strategies—is then illustrated in Part IV, which discusses specific interactions and situations, such as the one described in the following section.

ILLUSTRATION OF DIVERSE BEHAVIORAL EXPECTATIONS

The case described here is designed to provide a concrete context for further discussion of Skilled Dialogue. (Of course, it addresses only a single situation; other situations are addressed in the examples and anecdotes in the Part III chapters.) Discussion questions are provided at the end of each chapter, which revisit this case in more depth. Please note that in Part III, the primary purpose is to describe the various strategies, and the case will only be discussed in relation to the presence or absence of the given strategies. Specific examples of how each of the strategies could be applied in this case are provided in Part IV.

Mrs. Miller and Justin: Current Situation

Justin, who is 4 years old, darted across the Garfield Early Learning Center playground, straight toward the painted roadway where Emily and Sue waited in line to ride a tricycle. As Peter slowed down his tricycle to stop, Justin came up behind him grabbing at his shirt and knocking Peter to the ground. Justin is in a frenzy, screaming, "It's my turn, it's my turn!" and takes off as fast as he can, weaving in and out of the designated roadway. Emily and Sue are angry and yelling, "Justin didn't follow the rules!" Peter is crying and pulling up his pant leg to check a bloody knee.

Mrs. Miller, their preschool teacher, had been observing the children from the other side of the playground. She shouted to Justin to get off the tricycle immediately and then turned her attention to Peter and the girls. She sent Peter to the office to have his scrape bandaged and told the children to line up. Justin rode the tricycle right up next to her and refused to get off. "I don't have to," he said. Mrs. Miller told Justin again to get off the tricycle, "Your behavior caused Peter's injury."

Justin stayed on the tricycle, slowly riding it the 10 feet to the tricycle "parking lot" and walked with his head down to the end of the line. Back in the classroom, he quietly sat in the circle as Mrs. Miller spoke about the incident.

This was not the first time Justin had acted impulsively and aggressively toward his peers and the staff. It was only the first month of school, and Justin was having an average of three incidents per week. He had torn up another child's drawing because it was "stupid." He had knocked over other children's buildings in the Block Center and pretended to laugh and roll on the floor. He had taken other children's crayons and markers and broken them. Neither the children nor Mrs. Miller knew what would set off another outburst. The children no longer wanted to sit next to Justin or be paired with him for activities. A mother of one child jokingly told Mrs. Miller after class, "We hear all about Justin at our house."

Mrs. Miller and Mrs. Taylor, Justin's mother, met after the tricycle incident on the playground to discuss Justin's behavior following Mrs. Miller's suggestion over the phone that perhaps Garfield was not the best program for Justin.

Mrs. Taylor arrived about 20 minutes late for the meeting. Mrs. Miller had planned the meeting carefully, citing each of Justin's outbursts and the behaviors she was observing. By the time Mrs. Taylor arrived, she was feeling frustrated and impatient. This was another example of Mrs. Taylor's disregard for Mrs. Miller's time and the seriousness of the situation.

Mrs. Miller said, "Hello. Please have a seat. I only have a few minutes because I need to see the students before they leave for home." She then asked about Justin's behavior at home and at his prior preschool.

Mrs. Taylor assured her that he never had a problem before and probably just needed time to adjust to the new program. She went on to share that "we" had a *very* difficult time at the preschool in the former neighborhood.

"The teacher there was inexperienced and showed favoritism to other children. The teacher just didn't like Justin," Mrs. Taylor said. She went on to state that she had done her "homework" over the summer by asking everyone which preschool was the best in town. She was told by everyone she spoke with that it was the Garfield Early Learning Center. So she was sure that Justin would do just fine.

"He just needs some time to adjust to the school. There've just been so many changes with the move and all." Mrs. Taylor went on to explain that she was disappointed that Justin did not learn anything last year at the other school. "He doesn't even know the ABCs yet or how to write his name. My nephew in Dallas who is about the same age, can write his name, write his ABCs, and he's even beginning to read!" she stated. "But I am sure you will have him reading real soon. We are paying good money to send him to this school; it's supposed to be the best school in town," she concluded.

After hearing Mrs. Taylor speak, without yet having had the opportunity to present the information she had prepared, Mrs. Miller remained silent for several minutes. She then looked at her watch, saw that it was almost time to return to her class and said, "You and I see this situation very differently, Mrs. Taylor. I'm not sure that you understand the seriousness of Justin's behavior here at the Center."

Justin: Additional Information

Justin is the youngest of two sons. His older brother Jeff is in seventh grade at the local middle school. The Taylors moved to town the previous summer when Mr. Taylor was transferred unexpectedly from his previous job. He is currently a middle management executive for a large home builder and is very involved with coaching Jeff's neighborhood soccer and basketball teams. Mrs. Taylor had worked in marketing for a magazine publisher, but chose not to work after Justin was born. She recently joined a local women's charity group and is very active in planning activities.

Mrs. Taylor is often late dropping Justin off in the morning. Circle Time is already in progress, and Justin makes sure everyone knows he has arrived. About twice a week she is late picking him up before the Center closes at 5:30.

Mrs. Miller first expressed her concerns about Justin's behavior to Mrs. Taylor the day of his first outburst. Mrs. Taylor appeared surprised and maybe a little unbelieving. "The other child must have upset Justin," was her primary comment.

Mrs. Miller suggested four times in one month that they meet for a conference. Each time Mrs. Taylor promised to get back to her after she checked her schedule, but then failed to do so. Mrs. Miller also added handwritten notes to Justin's "My Day" checklist documenting behavior events and requesting a conference.

BRAINSTORMING QUESTIONS

1. What are your initial impressions after reading this case summary? Discuss these with other practitioners. Do they agree or disagree with you?

2. Review the Skilled Dialogue strategies discussion in Chapter 6. Do you believe these strategies were or could have been applied to the conversation between Mrs. Miller and Mrs. Taylor? Rate the presence of each on a scale of 1–5, with 1 being *almost or totally absent* and 5 being *fully present*. Compare your responses to ours as you read Chapters 7–9.

3. What are your thoughts about applying Skilled Dialogue strategies to interactions with Justin? Do you think his spirit and sense of self are being nurtured by this mother and Mrs. Miller? Why or why not? Read the evidence-based beliefs in Chapter 1. What are your thoughts about their application to this situation?

4. Mrs. Miller and Mrs. Taylor are apparently seeing Justin's behavior quite differently. Review the varying models of agency discussed in Chapter 2. Do you believe that they are using different models of agency? Why or why not?

Chapter 7

Differences Do Not Make People Wrong

Welcoming and *Allowing*

This chapter provides an extended discussion and illustrations of the first two Skilled Dialogue strategies: *Welcoming* and *Allowing* (see Table 7.1). The first expresses the intention of Choosing Relationship over Control and the second expresses the intention of Setting the Stage for Miracles. These two Skilled Dialogue strategies are keys to developing interactions characterized by respect.

RESPECT

In their own way, *Welcoming* and *Allowing* each acknowledge the legitimacy of diverse behaviors and perspectives as expressions of identity that have been crafted in response to particular life experiences and environments and are based on the evidence of these experiences and environments. Both strategies communicate the recognition that people choose particular behaviors as a result of their experiential and environmental data pools. Based on these pools, they make decisions as to the behavior(s) that will best achieve a desired outcome and/or eliminate an undesired outcome. The resulting behaviors thus do not reflect their level of decision-making competency but rather the total data pool from which they have been drawn. For example, choosing to pay more attention to a salient event (e.g., a telephone call) instead of to a scheduled time (e.g., an appointment) may not reflect a person's inability to make "appropriate" decisions but rather quite the opposite. It may well reflect the most efficacious choice when experiential and environmental data support the "fact" that staying connected to a significant other carries a greater payoff than meeting the expectations of someone with whom one only has peripheral involvement (e.g., a physician). Such data may, for example, indicate that "Friends always have good news; doctors always give bad news." For someone with a different experiential and environmental data pool, the exact opposite may seem the "truth" (e.g., "Doctors have critical information and are difficult to access, but friends are much more accessible and can be called back"). Both people are exercising equally competent abilities to interpret their experiences and

Table 7.1. Chapter 7 organizer

Qualities	Choosing Relationship over Control	Dispositions	Setting the Stage for Miracles
		Strategies	
Respect (Honoring identity)	**Welcoming**		**Allowing**
		Differences do not make people wrong	
Reciprocity (Honoring voice)	*Sense-Making*		*Appreciating*
		Diversity is always life enhancing	
Responsiveness (Honoring connection)	*Joining*		*Harmonizing*
		There is always a third choice	

environment, yet they each end up with dramatically different conclusions. These conclusions do not make them wrong (in light of their given data), although they may have radically different results in different contexts (e.g., the first person may be judged as inattentive or irresponsible in contrast to the second in contexts that value giving priority to scheduled appointments). The strategies of *Welcoming* and *Allowing* counteract unbalanced interpretations and judgments. Both are anchored in the recognition that differences do not make people wrong. Together these qualities are designed to promote and sustain the quality of respect.

Although quoted earlier (see Chapter 3), Isaac's statement on disrespect bears repeating here:

> The loss of respect manifests in a simple way: My assessment that what you are doing should not be happening. [This assessment] causes me to immediately look for a way to change you, to help you see the error of your ways. . . . *People on the receiving end of this attitude experience violence—the imposition of a point of view with little or no understanding* [italics added]. (1999, p. 132)

This statement should not, however, be interpreted to mean that communicating and establishing respect means discouraging change or approving of particular behaviors. It should be interpreted only to mean that respect requires the acknowledgment that one's actions are as anchored in a legitimate pool of experiential and environmental data as another person's actions.

The strategies of *Welcoming* and *Allowing* thus challenge us to understand others' diverse behaviors, values, and beliefs as legitimate and rooted in particular evidence, rather than as limited or somehow less competent than behaviors considered more normative in other environments or contexts. The goal of this perceptual shift is not to ignore the fact that some behaviors may be less affirming or less appropriate in certain contexts than others. It is, rather, to create an environment safe enough to allow for new learning.

Two types of respect must be distinguished in order to use these strategies successfully. The first is respect that is based on what someone knows or can do. It is a conditional respect based on one's own values and beliefs. The second type of respect is independent of these factors; it is unconditional, given to another simply because he or she is a person (a "Thou"; see the discussion in Chapter 1 on I–Thou), regardless of his or her level of knowledge or ability. This latter type of respect is based on the acknowledgment of another person as someone who is, like ourselves, crafting his or her life the best way he or she can given his or her experiences and situational contexts. A corollary acknowledgement is that, if we were to find ourselves in that person's situation, we may very well feel overwhelmed or perhaps led to express the same responses we are currently devaluing. After all, how many of us can imagine surviving under the conditions many families we serve must bear?

Giving another person unconditional respect does not, however, imply a denial of the consequences of their behavior or the value of alternative behaviors in contexts other than their current ones. Routinely ignoring doctor's appointments, for example, can result in life-threatening conditions. Nevertheless, unconditional respect affirms the dignity of those exhibiting the behaviors as well as affirming what they have in common with those exhibiting behaviors considered more "appropriate" or competent. *The ability to express respect, not just for those whose behavior or skills we value, but also for those whose behavior and skills we do not understand or cannot admire, is an essential ability without which we may be able to coerce new behaviors but not stimulate true learning (i.e., teach).*

The strategies of *Welcoming* and *Allowing* are designed to communicate and sustain unconditional respect. The behaviors associated with these strategies focus on ensuring that each person with whom we interact, regardless of differences or level of skill, is recognized as being worthy of our respect, not because we admire him or her or even agree with him or her, but simply because he or she, like us, is negotiating personal circumstances and experiences as best as he or she can. This is important not only for the simple fact that everyone deserves such respect. It is also important because it is only in the context of such respect that we can invite another to change and increase his or her knowledge and/or skill repertoires in ways that acknowledge and access their existing strengths and resources rather than negate or diminish them. Only then can we truly model the respect and learning we wish others to demonstrate toward us.

WELCOMING

Although *Welcoming* is most important at the initiation of an interaction, it is also necessary throughout the entire interaction. It is not enough to welcome someone initially and then switch to tactical listening (i.e., listening only to figure out how to push our own agenda). Table 7.2 adds to the previous information given for *Welcoming* in Chapter 6. This table identifies the purpose of this strategy: to connect with another as someone of equal dignity and equal capacity and learn from experience. This is a deceptively simple purpose. Nevertheless, it is an essential one in that it establishes the tone for all subsequent interactions.

Table 7.2.   Description of *Welcoming* strategy

Quality	WELCOMING (Disposition: Choosing Relationship over Control)
	Purpose: To intentionally connect with the other as someone of equal dignity
Respect (Honoring identity)	*Critical aspects of Welcoming* • Assumption that other and I are equally competent to craft a behavioral repertoire adaptive to our given contexts • Acceptance of other's diverse behavior(s) as evidence based • Willingness to communicate unconditional respect *Possible behavioral indicators* • Relaxed body language that communicates "I'm happy to be meeting with you/discussing this concern with you." • Number of affirming or neutral comments (e.g., "I see," "Tell me more," "It sounds like you're doing all that you can in this situation") • Explicit use of welcoming statements (e.g., "I'm glad we're having this meeting") • Number of general statements prior to narrowing focus to specific agenda, when culturally appropriate (e.g., "How are you? Did you have any difficulties getting here?")

Critical Aspects of *Welcoming*

Welcoming is associated with the first three critical aspects of Choosing Relationship over Control. These have been listed and discussed in Chapter 4 and are shown again in Table 7.2. The first aspect is the assumption that the person with whom we are interacting is as competent as we are in crafting a behavioral repertoire adaptive to his or her given environment. This aspect is closely tied to the second one: the acceptance of another's behavior as evidence based within a given context. Only when someone is approached with the understanding that the behavior he or she exhibits reflects the constraints and resources of his or her environment rather than limitations of ability or competence does respect become truly possible. Finally, there is a third aspect: the willingness to communicate unconditional respect, as discussed previously. Whether the presence of these aspects is visible through verbal communication or whether it is inferred from nonverbal communications, each will have a significant influence on the other's sense of being welcomed.

Behavioral Indicators Associated with *Welcoming*

Table 7.2 also lists possible behavioral indicators of *Welcoming*. One such indicator of communicating respect through *Welcoming* is the simple use of relaxed body language that expresses a willingness to be present and interested in the other person. The use of affirming or neutral comments that express interest without judgment (e.g., "I see.", "Tell me more.", "It sounds like you're doing all that you can in this situation.") can also be a strong indicator of *Welcoming*. Other possible behavioral indicators include attentive listening, explicit use of welcoming statements, and general comments that leave room for the introduction of the other's views and opinions.

Unfortunately, it is our bias toward control rather than relationship that is often most clearly communicated. "Our typical [ENC] patterns of listening in difficult situations are tactical [focused on control], not relational. We listen for what we expect to hear. We sift through others' views for what we can use to make our own points" (Kahane, 2004, p. x).

The listening associated with *Welcoming* must be relational. That is, it must be listening with a willingness to relate to something other than what we already know, something apart from our preset ideas about who the other person is and what he or she "needs." The degree to which we are focused on our own perspective or open to another's words is reflected in our postures and movements. These postures and movements can be easily, albeit unconsciously, read. For that reason, it is easier to focus on the disposition to choose relationship and let the body follow that disposition, rather than to focus on specific postures or gestures. Verbally, however, it is useful to express *Welcoming* with comments such as "I see," "Hmm, I never thought of it that way," "Tell me more," and so forth. Although subtle, welcoming phrases such as these have a significant impact on another's openness to what we wish to communicate. In fact, they model the very receptivity that we wish to engender in the other person. Other more explicit comments, such as "I am so glad you were able to come," or "I'm glad you're here even if we're a bit short of time," also help communicate an attitude of welcoming.

Examples and Nonexamples of *Welcoming*

Table 7.3 provides illustrative examples and nonexamples of *Welcoming* using excerpts from actual conversations shared with us by workshop and training participants, whom we thank for sharing their experiences with us. It should be noted that the nonexamples are not necessarily inappropriate or wrong in any way; they simply do not illustrate the indicated strategy.

These conversations are unfortunately restricted by the fact that they can only be reported in writing in this text (see also Chapters 10 and 11 for additional examples). (Readers may sign up at http://www.skilleddialogue.com to be notified of the availability of audiovisual materials as they are developed.)

The examples shown in Table 7.3 include verbal statements and nonverbal behaviors that express *Welcoming*. Two aspects of these statements and behaviors are essential. The first is the explicit acknowledgment of the person in addition to the task at hand. *Welcoming* scripts can vary greatly across cultures. Some cultures privilege more personal nontask time (e.g., greetings, general social questions); others value such time to a lesser degree. In all cultures, however, it is considered appropriate to express some degree of recognition of the other person as more than just a means to an end, especially by the person receiving such recognition.

One of the more subtle ways to communicate *Welcoming* is the use of direct responses. Direct responses (i.e., responses that are directly and explicitly tied to what the other person has said) communicate that the other person's perspective is welcomed into the conversation. These responses need not express agreement but do need to affirm the reception of the other person's message. They can be as

Table 7.3. *Welcoming examples and nonexamples*

Quality	Examples[a]	Nonexamples[b]
	Verbal statements	*Verbal statements*
Respect (Honoring identity)	"I really appreciate that you are willing to come in. I know that your schedule is really busy, but I just felt like I needed to communicate with you directly based on what your daughter, Judy, has been doing for the last 3 weeks, which we talked about on the telephone."	"Mrs. Brown, you know that we are here to talk about your daughter's inappropriate behaviors. I have a list here of the ones that have been the greatest problem these last 3 weeks."
	"I'm so happy to see you and have you come in for this parent–teacher conference. I don't know if you have been at the school very often, but I am certainly happy to have you here. I want to make sure I said your name correctly, Mrs. Gonzalez, correct? I am Mr. Brown."	"Mr. Marvis, I'm running a bit late today. You know what all the construction has done to our travel times in this neighborhood, I'm sure. So, let's get right down to business."
	Direct responses to other's comments: Parent says she believes boredom is at the root of her child's inappropriate behaviors. Teacher responds, saying something such as "I hear that you are concerned about the cause of the behaviors, not just the behaviors themselves. Is that correct?"	Indirect responses to other's comments: Parent says she believes boredom is at the root of her child's inappropriate behaviors. Teacher responds by refocusing on behaviors rather than parent's concern, saying something such as "You know, it is just really hard for her to pay attention and stay in her seat. These are the behaviors that we find the most problematic."
	Nonverbal behaviors	*Nonverbal behaviors*
	Standing up and walking toward the other person	Remaining seated as the other person walks in
	Relaxed body language (e.g., arms uncrossed, smiling)	"Tight" body language (e.g., arms crossed, raised shoulders)

[a]Both the examples and the nonexamples are taken from comments of workshop participants describing specific situations. We thank all workshop participants who gave permission for their comments to be used as part of our research data.

[b]The nonexamples are not necessarily incorrect or inappropriate; however, they do not reflect the strategy of *Welcoming*.

simple as "I see" or "That's an interesting point" or more specific to what the other person has said (e.g., "I'm sorry to hear how frustrated you feel with all this paperwork," "I can see how difficult that could be"). Indirect responses, in contrast, reiterate the speaker's view and/or agenda and only tangentially address what the other person said. In doing so, they send a clear message that the other person's perspective and/or comment is not welcomed. For example, a parent may make a comment such as "I'm not really sure why we're having this meeting," and the child care director may provide a response such as "I'm so glad you're here." Whereas the second comment may be intended to welcome the parent, it effectively ignores the parent's concern of why the meeting is taking place. A more direct response might be "I'm sorry that you're not sure why we're here, but I am very glad to see you. Let me explain a bit about this meeting before we get started." Such direct responses communicate that the speaker's view and/or agenda is not more important than the other person's perspective and/or comments.

The nonexamples shown in Table 7.3 were selected based on statements and behaviors that either do not communicate *Welcoming* or communicate it only to a weak degree. These include statements that only address a given agenda and ignore all reference to the person with whom we are interacting, except as someone necessary to achieve a desired agenda. They also include indirect responses—statements that reference back to the ongoing agenda rather than to what the other person has just said. The nonverbal behaviors also express these same messages.

It is important to note that both verbal statements and nonverbal behaviors are subject to different interpretations based on cultural, social, and personal contexts and understandings. The initiation of Skilled Dialogue with someone as yet unfamiliar, requires that *Welcoming* be approached cautiously for that reason.

Self-Reflection Questions for *Welcoming*

Three questions may be asked to reflect on the degree to which *Welcoming* is clearly and concretely communicated through the selected behaviors (see Table 7.4). The first is "What assumptions am I making about my power, ability, or knowledge as compared with the other person with whom I am interacting?" For example, is there an assumption of knowing "better than" the other person what needs to happen or change? Is one's idea of how change should occur assumed to be the only or the best way for that change to occur? If so, then the likelihood is that, no matter what behavior is shown, there is no communication of a truly welcoming stance and, therefore, neither Choosing Relationship over Control nor promoting the development of respect between oneself and the other(s) involved in the interaction will be evident.

A second question related to the welcoming of another's behavior as evidence based is "On what am I basing my assumptions about the other behaviors and/or beliefs? Am I relying on evidence-based information, inferences and interpretations common within my own cultural contexts, previous experiences with this person, or something else?" An example of this distinction comes from my (Barrera's) early experiences as a coordinator of a birth-to-3 program for infants and toddlers with moderate to severe developmental limitations. Several of the therapists and teachers involved were insistent that the parents allow their children to

Table 7.4.   Self-reflection questions for *Welcoming* strategy

WELCOMING
(Disposition: Choosing Relationship over Control)

Question 1

   What assumptions am I making about my power, ability, or knowledge as compared with the other person with whom I am interacting?

Question 2

   On what am I basing my assumptions about the other's behaviors and/or beliefs? Am I relying on evidence-based information, inferences and interpretations common within my own cultural contexts, previous experiences with this person, or something else?

Question 3

   Are my assumptions absolutely and unequivocally true?

walk into the center rather than carry them. As the parking lot was quite a few yards from the front door, this meant walking at least 10 feet or more. When asked why they believed this to be so critical, they responded that not allowing the children to walk would impede the acquisition of necessary mobility skills. They were very sure of the truth of this assumption, and, in fact, had probably even read ENC research to that effect. The reality, however, was that carrying infants and young children was a cultural practice for most of the parents, who were Mexican American. In addition, it was a practice that in the parents' experience had never impeded the development of anyone's walking skills. Their evidence base clearly showed them that they, their peers, their children, their grandparents, and, in fact, everyone they knew had been carried without the least detriment to the development of their walking.

This example moves ahead to a third question that addresses the degree to which we are willing to respect assumptions other than our own: "Are my assumptions absolutely and unequivocally true?" The purpose of this question is not to discard our assumptions but rather to soften the conviction that there are no other acceptable choices for anyone else in any other situation. *Welcoming* needs to reflect this softening. Even when the other's behaviors and/or beliefs seem patently inappropriate or wrong, it is important to communicate our recognition that they are grounded in a legitimate evidence pool given their experiences and environments.

These three self-reflection questions can serve to assess the presence or absence of the disposition toward Choosing Relationship over Control. They can also serve to guide the selection of specific behaviors that communicate welcoming of another, not merely to change or control them, but to create a respectful relationship with them as competent individuals in their own right. Additional illustrations of *Welcoming* are discussed in the case study about Mrs. Miller and Justin, which was presented in the introduction to Part III and is revisited, at the end of this chapter, as well as in other cases reviewed in Chapters 10 and 11.

ALLOWING

The strategy of *Allowing* overlaps with and reinforces *Welcoming*. Its focus, however, shifts from expressing the disposition of Choosing Relationship over Control to expressing the disposition of Setting the Stage for Miracles. Its purpose goes beyond choosing relationship to the active creation of an inclusive context within which multiple perspectives that can enhance each other can be respected. To do this, *Allowing*, along with the other strategies that express the disposition of Setting the Stage for Miracles, calls on the use of a 3rd Space mindset. A 3rd Space mindset challenges our reliance on dualistic either-or, polarized viewpoints that prohibit multiple perspectives from occupying the same space, thus limiting outcomes to existing options rather than opening possibilities to novel and inclusive options. (For further discussion of 3rd Space, see Chapter 5 in this text and Chapter 6 in Barrera et al., 2003.)

Critical Aspects of *Allowing*

Table 7.5 lists the three aspects of Setting the Stage for Miracles necessary to the strategy of *Allowing*. The first of these aspects is a willingness to "stay with the tension"—that is, to let another's perspective simply *be,* without needing to explain or defend our own. This willingness to refrain from acting to resolve or dissolve differences explicitly communicates our "allowing" of another's belief and/or perspective. Suspending judgment in this way, however, is not about not having an opinion or about sanctioning harmful behaviors. It is about not jumping to judgment and closing our mind to the possibility of alternative perspectives. It is not about qualifying our actions (e.g., not calling child protective services), but about qualifying judgments (e.g., saying "That person doesn't seem to care" rather than "That person doesn't care"). The latter, more absolute statement communicates one person's or group's perceptions and interpretations as nonnegotiable fact, whereas the former makes it clear that they are only the perceptions and/or interpretations of one person or group, based on that person's or group's data pool.

Allowing permits dichotomous, and even contradictory, opinions and/or perspectives to *be,* without forcing them into exclusive either-or frames. For example, the strategy of *Allowing* supports believing that a person's behavior reflects a lack of caring according to our own data and, simultaneously, believing that they may nevertheless care in ways that we cannot perceive or, perhaps, about a very different aspect than the one on which we are focused.

One example of this focus on different aspects of a situation was presented by a group of Head Start teachers concerned about a mother of a 5-year-old child with significantly aggressive behaviors. When they asked this mother to initiate at home the positive behavioral supports program they had found successful at school,

Table 7.5. Description of *Allowing* strategy

Quality	ALLOWING (Disposition: Setting the Stage for Miracles)
	Purpose: To create an inclusive context for subsequent integration of apparent contradictions
	Critical aspects of Allowing • Willingness to "stay with the tension" (i.e., acknowledge other's perspective without needing to explain or defend my own)
Respect (Honoring identity)	• Release of my "stories" and fixed interpretations about others' behaviors/beliefs • Perception of other's diverse perspectives as potentially complementary rather than polarized or divisive
	Possible behavioral indicators • Refrain from offering solutions or alternate behaviors prematurely • Number of words spoken by other as compared to number of words spoken by me • Content of statements: no "buts" or other signs of defensiveness; lack of either-or comparisons/choices • Lack of interruptions; short attentive silences before initiating response • Absence of proposed solutions/suggestions related to the perceived problem

her reply was "As long as he doesn't burn the house down, I'm okay with his behavior." This statement could certainly be interpreted as meaning that she did not care about her child. After being asked to brainstorm different interpretations in order to make *Allowing* more palatable to them, the teachers realized that, given this mother's experiential history of severe physical abuse, she could well be thinking, "If I touch him, I'll kill him." From that perspective, her hands-off approach actually reflected caring deeply about her child's welfare. Although extreme, and not meant to sanction the mother's choice of behavioral responses to her child, this example clearly illustrates that what might seem negative from one perspective could, in fact, have a very different meaning when seen from another. (Even though *Allowing* is discussed before *Sense-Making* in this section, there are times when being able to place a behavior within a context that makes sense to the person perceiving it makes it easier to use the strategy of *Allowing*.)

Allowing encourages tolerating diverse stories. Its second aspect requires that we release the "stories" we tell ourselves about the meaning of another person's behavior (e.g., "Running around means that this child is hyperactive," "Mrs. Jones's absence from a set meeting means that she doesn't care about her child's problem," "Without a set bedtime, this child's learning will be compromised"). These stories and others like them stem from our own idiosyncratic experience base or from what we have read or heard and believe to be credible. Seldom are they rooted in absolute and undeniable fact. We may, for example, believe that being exposed to multiple languages in early childhood can be confusing; yet, thousands, if not millions, of people in Europe and around the world grow up in multilingual homes and communities without any documented detrimental effects. Or, we may believe that assigning specific responsibilities to young children is critical to their development as responsible adults. It is possible to refer to more than one anecdote about people that supports this belief. Yet, there are many productive and responsible adults who, as children, did not have to make their beds or clean the dishes, for example. Our explanations and interpretations of other's behaviors need to be recognized as only *our* stories—perhaps true, perhaps not true, yet nevertheless real mental constructions derived from our own experiential data pools rather than from absolute reality.

When we assume that our stories reflect universal fact (i.e., they are taken as absolute and nonnegotiable), it is no longer possible to choose relationship with the other person. We end up limiting our ability to access or understand anything outside of those stories and, thus, end up interacting only with whom we believe the other to be (e.g., the uncaring mother, the hyperactive child), rather than with whom that person may truly be (e.g., a mother expressing caring in ways we do not perceive as caring, an inquisitive child with limited impulse control abilities at this point or with insufficient stimulation, a parent too fearful to release his or her need for control).

Undesirable behaviors can, of course, be stopped or changed without releasing our stories. For example, we can tell children and parents what they *must* do, or we can (and should) call protective services when necessary. What is lost, however, when behavior is stopped or changed without releasing personal stories is the opportunity of helping the *person* behind the behavior to internalize the need to change as something that goes beyond compliance or forced choice. It is one thing, for example, to call protective services while being certain that the family being reported is uncaring; it is another to call protective services while believing that the family is caring but terribly unskilled. In the first case, there can be no successful relationship following the report. In the second, a successful relationship that can help the family increase their skill level is at least potentially possible. Ultimately, this aspect of *Allowing* has to do more with *how* we do something than with *what* we do. That is, we can do something within a context of respectful relationship or we can do it from a stance of control.

It is at the intersection of our stories with those of the other person's that problems most often arise, disrupting relationships and triggering the need for control. For example, my "story" about you might tell me that you don't respect me, whereas your "story" might tell you that you are the one not being respected!

> But difficult conversations arise at precisely those points where important parts of our story collide with another person's story. We assume the collision is because of how the other person is [or what they believe]; they assume it's because of how we are [or what we believe]. But really the collision is the result of our stories simply being different (Stone, Patton, & Heen, 1999, p. 28) [*and of our believing that there is room for only one*].

Allowing focuses on the acknowledgment of another's perspective as simply that—*their* perspective—with no need to discount or devalue it or to explain and defend our own perspective. The instinctive response, however, often tends to be one of disallowing. We immediately state our disagreement, defend our viewpoint, or in some other way indicate that only one perspective and/or story (typically ours) is legitimate (i.e., worthy of respect). It is challenging to separate judgment from action—that is, to take action (e.g., call protective services) without needing to judge the other person as "bad" or uncaring or deficient. *Allowing* invites us to stay open to the strengths of another even while we may need to attend to the consequences of his or her limitations.

The third aspect associated with *Allowing* is closely related to the release of stories. It involves releasing the tendency to polarize perspectives and learning to perceive another's diverse perspective as at least potentially complementary to our own. At this point in the Skilled Dialogue process, this perception need not be based on precise knowledge of how that might be. It can simply be based on a more general understanding of human dynamics related to interpersonal relationships. These can be perceived as either symmetrical or complementary. When perceived as symmetrical, the emphasis is on similarities (i.e., on making less of the differences). When perceived as complementary, however, it is the differences between the parties that are most noticed. That is, one set of differences serves to complement another or to provide the other half of a whole (Devito, 2005). Seen from this perspective, a parent's resistance to the perspective(s) we advocate would actually complement that perspective by bringing it into balance (e.g., reminding us that play is as important as responsibility, awakening us to the fact that we have forgotten to model the respect we are expecting).

All three aspects of *Allowing* point to the fact that honoring diverse identities requires allowing them to coexist side by side in the same space, at least long enough to explore how they might make sense and be of value. It is in doing this that we create a respectful context within which reciprocity becomes possible.

Behavioral Indicators of *Allowing*

Several behaviors are helpful in creating a respectful context. These behaviors, also shown in Table 7.5, are relatively subtle yet nevertheless powerful in Setting the Stage for Miracles, quite literally. The primary one has already been alluded to: refraining from offering solutions and alternative behaviors prematurely. Until respect has been sufficiently established, these cannot adequately take another's perspective into account. Refraining from offering solutions and alternative behaviors prematurely models the receptivity to differences that we wish to engender in the other person.

Three other closely related behaviors all focus on receptive and empathic listening. The first of these addresses the amount of "voice time" (i.e., letting others talk at least as much as ourselves). Analysis of interactions shared with us has, at times, shown that the person with whom the practitioner was speaking (typically a parent or another practitioner they were supervising) spoke only one third to one fourth as much as the practitioner who initiated the interaction.

The second behavioral indicator involves the explicit communication of our desire to truly respect the other's perspective, behavior, and/or belief as evidence based, if not as desirable or acceptable. These behaviors can include 1) the exclusion of *buts* and other such words, 2) avoidance of either-or comparisons and choices, 3) a lack of interruptions, and 4) short attentive silences prior to initiating responses. These behaviors communicate openness to the other's beliefs, perspectives, and/or opinions without sacrificing adherence to our own beliefs, perspectives, and/or opinions. To create a context of reciprocity, which is discussed in the following chapter, there must first be room for all perspectives.

Examples and Nonexamples of *Allowing*

Table 7.6 provides further information on *Allowing*. It provides illustrative comments for both examples and nonexamples of *Allowing*. As shown in the examples column, the verbal statements need not communicate agreement, they simply need to communicate a willingness to listen. In contrast, statements that emphasize the perspective or beliefs of the person(s) perceived to have the most power in the interaction (e.g., caregiver, teacher, administrator) easily communicate disallowing of diverse perspectives and/or beliefs and undermine respect, which almost invariably ensures that the message we wish so deeply to communicate will not be heard.

The examples illustrate the behavioral indicators just discussed. They show direct acknowledgment of what the other person has said, clearly communicating

Table 7.6. *Allowing* examples and nonexamples

Quality	Examples[a]	Nonexamples[b]
	Verbal statements	*Verbal statements*
Respect (Honoring identity)	"You say, if I hear you right, that there have been some problems at home."	"I hear that, but here is what I'm thinking."
	"Okay, I am glad that you expressed that concern."	"I wanted to let you know about the problems Jessica is having here at school." (when said early in the conversation)
	"Ah, I could see how you might feel that way."	
	Nonverbal behaviors	*Nonverbal behaviors*
	Listening without interruption	Interrupting to present own beliefs/perspectives
	Absence of proposed solutions/suggestions related perceived problem	Number of words spoken by other as compared with the number of words spoken by me are significantly less
	Number of words spoken by other as compared with the number of words spoken by me are about equal or more	

[a]Both the examples and the nonexamples are taken from comments of workshop participants describing specific situations. We thank all workshop participants who gave permission for their comments to be used as part of our research data.

[b]The nonexamples are not necessarily incorrect or inappropriate; however, they do not reflect the strategy of *Allowing*.

openness to his or her beliefs, perspective, and opinions. The nonexamples echo those given earlier for *Welcoming* (see Table 7.3). They reveal a clear focus on the agenda of the person initiating the interaction, as well as a lack of acceptance of the other person's perspectives and views. In many ways, *Allowing* is a less visible strategy than *Welcoming*. It is, however, one that can be easily "read" by the other person. Often, past experience with a lack of *Allowing* leads to a reluctance of that person to share his or her views with those perceived as having more power or as simply being disinterested, resulting in an appearance of agreement and an absence of the expression of true concerns or questions. It may take time before respect can be sufficiently established to support the creation of either reciprocity or responsiveness.

Self-Reflection Questions

As with *Welcoming*, three self-reflection questions can be asked to assess the degree to which the strategy of *Allowing* is actively communicated (see Table 7.7). The first of these is "Am I staying with the tension of disagreement (for at least a few minutes) without trying to resolve it or focus only on solutions to the perceived problem?" That is, are we making room for the other's perceptions and beliefs and not just our own? This question is closely tied to the second: "To what degree am I allowing the other person to speak before stating my own ideas and/or concerns about the perceived problem?" Is it clear verbally or nonverbally that we are really listening and not just giving the other person time to talk without letting anything

Table 7.7.   Self-reflection questions for *Allowing* strategy

ALLOWING
(Disposition: Setting the Stage for Miracles)

Question 1

  Am I staying with the tension of disagreement without trying to resolve it or focus only on perceived solutions?

Question 2

  To what degree am I allowing the other to speak before stating my own ideas/concerns about the perceived problem?

Question 3

  Am I releasing my stories about what is and what I think should be?

new in, or, worse, letting it in only so that we can plan a rebuttal? Even with some-one with whom we vehemently disagree, we can choose to listen.

For *Allowing* to achieve its intended goal of fostering respect, it needs to be clear that we are willing to listen to views other than our own without interruption or defensiveness. This does not necessarily result in a change of mind, but it does mean an acceptance of the other person's views as legitimate given his or her data pool. it also perhaps means remaining open to changing our mind about how or when that change might happen. The final question—"Am I releasing my stories about what is and what I think should be?"—reinforces this message.

CASE REVIEW

This section of the chapter revisits the case of Mrs. Miller, Mrs. Taylor, and Justin that was presented in the introduction to Part III. Readers are encouraged to reread this case prior to continuing with the review in this chapter.

The strategies of *Welcoming* and *Allowing* can be examined from multiple perspectives (e.g., teacher–child, teacher–teacher, teacher–parent). For purposes of this chapter, these are examined in relation to Mrs. Miller's interactions with Justin at the time of the reported incident and then with Justin's mother, Mrs. Taylor, during their meeting following that incident. They could as easily be examined from Justin's or Mrs. Taylor's perspectives, but, given that Mrs. Taylor is the designated "authority voice," it is most appropriate to examine them from her perspective first. See Part IV for a discussion based on other perspectives.

Table 7.8 summarizes the discussion of *Welcoming* and *Allowing* in relation to Mrs. Miller's interactions with Justin and his mother. The first discussion is Mrs. Miller's interactions with Justin in relation to the presence or absence of *Welcoming* and *Allowing*. Following that is a discussion of Mrs. Miller's interactions with Mrs. Taylor in relation to these same strategies.

This discussion is based only on the information provided in the case. One of the results of this type of examination may well be the determination that further information needs to be gathered. (This discussion does not provide suggestions for what might have been done differently; that aspect is addressed in Part IV where alternative behaviors are discussed.)

Table 7.8. Summary of case review: *Welcoming* and *Allowing*

DISPOSITIONS	
Choosing Relationship over Control	Setting the Stage for Miracles
Welcoming	*Allowing*
Mrs. Miller and Justin	*Mrs. Miller and Justin*
1) **Welcoming statements** No evidence of welcoming statements	1) **Absence of focus only on own agenda** No evidence of focus on what agenda might underlie Justin's behavior
2) **Communication of being pleased to have this opportunity to discuss situation** No evidence of being pleased to see Justin	2) **Lack of interruptions, giving other "voice time"** Justin is given no opportunity to present his perspective
3) **Openness to other's perspective/evidence base and use of direct statements** No evidence that Mrs. Miller talked with Justin beyond telling him it was his fault that other child got injured	3) **Lack of either-or comparisons and defense of own perspective** Mrs. Miller apparently sees no need to compare or defend her perspective
Mrs. Miller and Mrs. Taylor	*Mrs. Miller and Mrs. Taylor*
1) **Welcoming statements** Not explicitly communicated; displeasure could perhaps be inferred	1) **Absence of focus only on own agenda** Even though Mrs. Miller does not get the opportunity to discuss her planned agenda, there is an implied preference given to that agenda
2) **Communication of being pleased to have this opportunity to discuss situation** Not explicitly communicated; displeasure could perhaps be inferred	2) **Lack of interruptions, giving other "voice time"** This is present; Mrs. Taylor does get time to discuss her perspective
3) **Openness to other's perspective/evidence base and use of direct statements** Mrs. Miller does invite Mrs. Taylor to share her perspective, at least as related to Justin's previous behaviors	3) **Lack of either-or comparisons and defense of own perspective** Although Mrs. Miller does not defend her perspective, her final comments do seem to place it on an either-or footing with Mrs. Taylor's
Differences do not make people wrong	

(Left margin label: BEHAVIORAL EVIDENCE)

Mrs. Miller and Justin

It seems fairly evident that Justin has been identified as a child with significant challenging behaviors and, consequently, a child whose other aspects (e.g., cognitive abilities, language development) are receiving much less attention. It is, of course, important to address these behaviors to ensure the safety of both Justin and his peers. Addressing them outside of a larger developmental context, however, may short circuit the very results being sought. In the long run, it is equally important to nurture Justin's sense of self and spirit so that he does more than merely learn to comply. It is this latter aspect and not so much what specific behavioral support plan is selected that Skilled Dialogue strategies address. These strategies are designed to support and enhance *how* such a plan is chosen and implemented (i.e., the interactions associated with identifying, developing, and implementing the plan). This is what will, ultimately, have an impact on not just the child's sense of self and spirit, but that of all people involved—teachers and parents alike.

Welcoming   There is no information as to how Justin was welcomed into Mrs. Miller's classroom prior to the tricycle incident reported in the case study. It is clear from what is described, however, that Justin is no longer welcomed by his peers or by Mrs. Miller, whose first reaction is to shout at him. However understandable, such a reaction only reduces his sense of being welcomed or respected, and, thus, it increases the potential if not probability of further negative behavior. Mrs. Miller's reaction, in fact, makes it quite clear that respect was conditional. She communicates only displeasure without distinguishing displeasure with Justin's behavior from displeasure with Justin himself. In addition, there is no information that might indicate Mrs. Miller's openness to the presence of an evidence base that might be underlying Justin's behavior. In short, there is little to no evidence of the behaviors associated with *Welcoming*. Even though Mrs. Miller intends to be respectful, the absence of explicit *Welcoming* behaviors will almost unavoidably sabotage that intention.

Allowing   Similarly, there is little evidence of behaviors associated with *Allowing*. In this case, *Allowing* would not mean permitting the negative behavior to continue. Instead, it would mean allowing for the possibility that Justin is basing his behavioral choices on a legitimate evidence base that is distinct from Mrs. Miller's, however inappropriate those choices may be in the current context. This is a subtle but significant distinction, which is discussed more fully in Part IV of this book.

There is no focus on an agenda other than Mrs. Miller's. Justin is not asked for his perspective. Mrs. Miller, in fact, does not explain her own perspective other than to say that Justin's behavior "caused Peter's injury." She seems to be making an assumption that her perspective is evident.

Although Justin's behavior is certainly inappropriate, responding to it by neither *Welcoming* nor *Allowing* would not increase the probability of Justin learning how to self-regulate his emotions and behaviors in the future. Mrs. Miller's response reflects choosing control over relationship and, consequently, not expressing unconditional respect. Choosing relationship and expressing respect, while simultaneously acting to protect both Justin and the other children, would, in contrast, increase the probability of Justin's learning from, and listening to Mrs. Miller, and would mirror choosing relationship, and expressing respect toward others. (See also the discussion in Part IV.)

Mrs. Miller and Mrs. Taylor

It is clear that Mrs. Miller and Mrs. Taylor are not quite on the same page regarding the situation with Justin. It is also clear that there is little change in their perspectives during the conversation described. A review of Skilled Dialogue strategies might help to explain why.

Welcoming   Mrs. Miller seems strongly focused on her own perspective. Although she could well intend to welcome Mrs. Taylor, the behavioral evidence related to each of the critical aspects of this strategy communicates something quite different. There is, for example, little behavioral evidence that Mrs. Miller is assuming that Mrs. Taylor is as competent as herself in assessing Justin's behavior. Although this is not explicitly stated, the tone of the interaction is not one that communicates such an assumption. There is no explicit communication of an expectation of a joint discussion between two equally competent individuals.

Neither are there any explicit welcoming statements. Instead, Mrs. Miller comes prepared with a list of Justin's negative behaviors. There is also no evidence that Mrs. Miller is pleased to be having this meeting. Although she obviously believes it to be an essential one, her previous interactions with Mrs. Taylor have been less than optimal.

Finally, although Mrs. Taylor presents her perspective, she seems to do so more on her own initiative rather than at Mrs. Miller's invitation. Mrs. Miller does ask about Justin's behavior at home and in his prior preschool but does not explore other aspects of the situation (e.g., Justin's strengths).

Allowing   *Welcoming* and *Allowing* are often highly correlated with the presence of one supporting the presence of the other. Similarly, the absence of one is also correlated with the absence of the other. Such is the case in this situation. Mrs. Miller does allow Mrs. Taylor to discuss her perspective without interruption and does not interrupt or defend her views. Depending on her nonverbal behaviors, this behavior might communicate *Allowing* or merely tolerance. The fact that Mrs. Miller's last comment seems to place their different perspectives within an either-or continuum gives the impression that it might be the latter.

Unfortunately, this case is not atypical for many teacher–parent meetings related to children exhibiting significantly challenging behaviors. It is all too easy to narrow one's focus only to the identified problem and desired solution and, thus, inadvertently decrease the degree to which parents feel welcomed and, consequently, respected. (As noted previously, an alternative scenario is discussed in Part IV.)

DISCUSSION QUESTIONS AND ACTIVITIES

1. Think back to a conversation in which you felt that your perspective was not welcomed or allowed. What specific statements and/or behaviors communicated that message to you? Did you interpret the lack of welcome as a disagreement of viewpoints or as a reflection on your own competence?

2. Although *Welcoming* and *Allowing* are, typically, co-occurring, this is not always the case. Can you think of a time that that you felt welcomed, yet your beliefs and/or perspectives were not given equal time or value? Can you think of a time when you were allowed to present your beliefs and/or perspectives, yet they were not welcomed? What specific statements and/or behaviors sent those messages?

3.   Review the behavioral indicators in Tables 7.2 and 7.5, as well as the examples and nonexamples in Tables 7.3 and 7.6. Can you think of other behavioral indicators? Can you think of other examples or nonexamples? Discuss your rationale for these with at least two other people whose cultural, geographic, or other backgrounds are diverse from yours. Do they agree or disagree with you?

4.   Think of an interaction in which you resisted welcoming or allowing another's diverse view. Why do you think that happened? What did you imagine would happen if you had welcomed and/or allowed his or her view? Now remember an interaction in which you did welcome and/or allow another's diverse view. What was different about that interaction? How were your relationships with each person similar or different?

Diversity Is Always Life Enhancing

Sense-Making and *Appreciating*

Welcoming and *Allowing* address the need to establish respect—that is, to honor identity—as a first step toward crafting skillful dialogues that access and mine the strengths of diversity. *Welcoming* does so through Choosing Relationship over Control; *Allowing* does so through Setting the Stage for Miracles. They can only accomplish that, however, in conjunction with Skilled Dialogue's next two strategies: *Sense-Making* and *Appreciating*. Table 8.1 shows the relationship of these strategies within the overall Skilled Dialogue framework.

RECIPROCITY

Sense-Making and *Appreciating* deepen and extend respect through establishing reciprocity (i.e., honoring voice, the verbal and nonverbal expressions of identity). They do so by promoting and supporting the belief that another's diverse experiences and perspectives make as much sense and have as much value within their context as do our own experiences and perspectives within our context. Both relationship and the possibility of miracles—outcomes greater than could be anticipated—are strengthened when reciprocity is added to respect.

Acknowledging the sense and value of another's experiences and resources does not, however, mean concluding that he or she is "right" or that these experiences and resources have led to the best choices for given contexts. What it does mean is an explicit recognition that, if given identical experiences, contexts, and resources, we would most likely make similar choices. This acknowledgment is critical to establishing and maintaining reciprocity because lack of such acknowledgment inevitably silences diverse voices and covertly or overtly sabotages any respect that has been established up to that point. It communicates, subtly or explicitly, that we know "better" than to behave and/or believe like the other person (i.e., that we believe that a lack of competence rather than diverse situational variables has led to their choices). The presence of such acknowledgement, in contrast, asserts our belief in another's capacity to learn and to change.

Table 8.1.   Chapter 8 organizer

Qualities	Dispositions		
	Choosing Relationship over Control		Setting the Stage for Miracles
		Strategies	
Respect (Honoring identity)	*Welcoming*		*Allowing*
		Differences do not make people wrong	
Reciprocity (Honoring voice)	**Sense-Making**		**Appreciating**
		Diversity is always life enhancing	
Responsiveness (Honoring connection)	*Joining*		*Harmonizing*
		There is always a third choice	

Gernsbacher (2006) provides precise and eloquent examples of honoring others' experiences and perspectives in her writing on the need for reciprocity in interactions with children and adults with autism. She notes that reciprocity needs to be both "mutual and reciprocal" (2006, p. 140) and anchors her discussion with an anecdote about Sarah, a child with autism. When asked what she would wish for if she had a magic wand, Sarah replied that she "wished others could see the world through her eyes" (2006, p. 141). That phrase—to see the world through another's eyes—captures the essence of *Sense-Making* and *Appreciating*. To dialogue skillfully with others, it is not enough to simply respect them; it is also critical to find ways of coming to "see the world through their eyes" (i.e., giving as much sense and value to their views as to our own).

Establishing reciprocity requires supporting the expression of diverse world-views, beliefs, and behaviors as legitimate, given the diverse contextual and experiential data of those whose identities we seek to honor through *Welcoming* and *Allowing*. It is through reciprocity that the honoring of identity is extended by placing the *expressions* (i.e., voices) of that identity on a mutual and reciprocal footing with our own. This parity is actively sought for the purpose of identifying and appreciating the inherent strengths of those diverse worldviews, beliefs, and behaviors. *These* strengths are, after all, the most accessible and powerful resources available for generating optimal responses to targeted situations. As such, they are also the strongest foundation for developing the tools necessary to implement those responses. These strengths are, in effect, the leading edge of the zone of proximal development (Vygotsky, 1978) for the individuals involved: the place where what is already known can meet what is not yet known. It is for that reason that the phrase "diversity is always life enhancing" is associated with these two strategies. Perceiving differences as adding to rather than limiting strengths and resources is a key aspect of both *Sense-Making* and *Appreciating*.

The most difficult challenge to establishing reciprocity arises not only from situations within which there is disagreement with another's behaviors and/or beliefs but also from those within which those behaviors and/or beliefs result in harm or violence (e.g., instances of child abuse or neglect). Although the scope of this book does not allow for a full discussion of these situations, they will be alluded to in the examples and discussions (see a fuller discussion of abuse and trauma vis-à-vis Skilled Dialogue in Barrera et al., 2003).

What is important to remember is that *Sense-Making* and *Appreciating* are *never* intended to minimize or ignore the seriousness of these situations or the need to protect those involved. *In fact, these strategies should not be attempted in cases where they might be misunderstood as accepting or tolerating such behaviors and/or beliefs. Neither should they be attempted in situations with identified perpetrators that might place the practitioner or others in danger.* In situations such as these, it is clear that reciprocity cannot be established even by highly trained professionals (e.g., in cases of serious mental illness or character disorders).(The work of Anna Salter, 2004, is informative regarding this point.)

Appreciating and *Sense-Making* focus on making sense of another's behavior and appreciating its strengths so that it can be accessed as a resource rather than a hindrance (e.g., making sense of and appreciating the use of Spanish as a resource rather than a hindrance to learning English; making sense of and appreciating a parent's insistence on particular behaviors and/or beliefs as a resource rather than a hindrance to learning different behaviors and/or beliefs). This does not mean believing or saying, "Hey, that's great!" when encountering a behavior perceived to be negative. Many behaviors are unfortunately life denying (i.e., decrease the quality of one's life or damage one in some way), even when legitimately anchored in an experiential data pool. For example, the belief that "If I yell at my child, she will be quiet and more compliant" may be supported by experiential evidence within a given environment—the child does in fact become more compliant more readily when yelled at than when quietly asked to do something. However, the practices associated with that belief are nevertheless life denying to both the parent and the child involved. They decrease not only the quality of the relationship between the two, but also the quality of the life each experiences by introducing anger, fear, discomfort, perhaps guilt, and other negative emotions that decrease the ability to access new learning and sabotage rather than support intended goals.

The use of *Sense-Making* and *Appreciating* does not and should not ignore that behaviors can have life denying effects. However, their use can and should focus on the life enhancing attributes of diverse behaviors, even when subtle or hidden (e.g., "What aspect of this behavior and/or belief might support learning or change?"). Depression, for example, may contain a kernel of self-protection that might support less depressed behaviors. Aggression contains a kernel of self-assertion, which could be leveraged to support asserting the choice to behave differently. Abuse might contain a kernel of caring, however obscure and twisted, that might be leveraged to turn it around in a more positive direction. (It is important to note at this point that at no time should *Sense-Making* or *Appreciating* blind practitioners to the life denying aspects of beliefs and/or behaviors, even as they lead us to search for their positive aspects.)

The positive aspects of other behaviors, such as reliance on extended family members and compliance in the face of authority or expertise, are, fortunately, more easily identified. Similarly, the positive kernels in behaviors such as not following a regular bedtime routine or carrying children instead of letting them walk, can also be identified.

The strategies of *Sense-Making* and *Appreciating,* the two main ways Skilled Dialogue addresses the development of reciprocity, are grounded in two overlapping beliefs that support this search for positive aspects of diverse behaviors.

The first belief is that all behaviors have a positive intent from the perspective of the person enacting those behaviors. Typically, that intent focuses on the projected outcome of the chosen behavior(s). Behaviors are, typically, chosen based on what we believe the behaviors can bring to us or what they can help us to avoid, given our experiential and knowledge pools.

The second belief is that every negative behavior is a positive behavior expressed to an exaggerated level. This belief is supported by the fact that all behaviors have a spectrum of intensity. Once past a certain point, for example, talking becomes yelling and potentially no longer appropriate. (e.g., whisper → speaking voice → yelling → screaming). The core behavior (e.g., communicating one's needs) remains the same throughout the spectrum except for the degree of intensity with which it is expressed.

These two beliefs challenge us to acknowledge that, however dysfunctional, unskilled, or life denying, behaviors believed to be better than others are selected from a given spectrum based on the chooser's perspective and experiential data. Not protecting one's boundaries fiercely and aggressively, for example, may be perceived as leaving oneself completely open to violation—and so being physically aggressive toward anyone perceived as transgressing those boundaries has a "positive" intent: self-protection (although exaggerated to such an extreme degree that its life enhancing potential is diminished if not erased altogether). Going to the dentist, as a contrasting example, can be perceived as inhibiting an alternative that is less desirable—pain and potential loss of teeth. In contrast, given a different experiential and perceptual context, not going to the dentist can also be perceived as an avoidance of pain. Which perception is believed to be true by an individual will be uniquely grounded in his or her life experiences, as well as general knowledge.

SENSE-MAKING

Making sense of particular behaviors and appreciating their positive intent is not about validating those behaviors or appreciating them in the usual sense in which *appreciating* is understood. Rather, it is about coming to see them from the other's perspective in order to understand and appreciate their function or choice (i.e., finding their positive intent from the other's perspective). It is that positive intent that is the thread, however slim, that leads to the possibility of meaningful change. For example, when alternative behaviors can be shown to be more effective self-protection strategies than those currently being chosen, such as ignoring a child's needs, the strength of that intent can be leveraged in the service of learning less destructive behavior.

Similar to some types of martial arts which rely on the aggressor's physical momentum to deflect an attack, the motivation and momentum already present in a person's behavioral choice can be used to shift or expand that person's available behavioral or belief repertoire (see also discussion in Chapter 9). In this fashion, the other person with whom we are interacting will not only hear us, he or she will also be willing to work with us. If, however, we approach him or her from the perspective that what he or she is doing is wrong or flawed, then he or she will not find what is said to be credible and will be less inclined to pay attention. There will, consequently, be little or no motivation for the person to change. Such a perspective can actually communicate our belief in that person's lack of the very competence we are seeking to tap!

For example, a mother with no set bedtime for her 2-year-old child will not understand the need to set one when such a "need" lies outside her pool of experiential and cultural data. She may instead have experiential data that associates set bedtimes with "being sent to bed" as punishment and loss of parental presence. In contrast, she may associate being allowed to stay up with her own early experiences of being included in adult circles as she fell asleep listening to the murmur of her parents' voices. Perhaps she associates setting a firm bedtime with the exercise of unnecessary parental control and the expenditure of more energy than she believes she has available. Whatever her own associations, her motivation to change her current behavior will only be further reduced if she perceives the practitioner's motivation to be one of "correcting" a perceived fault or inappropriate practice. Until the person suggesting the change can make sense of the mother's need not to set a consistent bedtime, he or she will not be clear as to the particular data that can be used to support change (or to discover that there is no real need for change!).

A *Sense-Making* perspective is all too often missing when working with children who present challenging behaviors. When these children and/or their families are perceived as somehow "flawed," "defective," or simply "unmanageable," the stage is set not for miracles but for frustration, failure, and the reinforcement of all too familiar scripts. Despite wanting children and families to change, we cannot credibly communicate a shared vision (i.e., "seeing the world through their eyes") from a perspective of correction, rather such a perspective merely affirms their inability to make positive choices and sabotages both reciprocity and desired outcomes.

Sense-Making helps us to meet others where they are and to communicate our perception of them as competent negotiators of their given contexts, as people trying to find the best ways to survive and thrive, given particular life experiences. Without *Sense-Making*, we are more apt to communicate only negative perceptions of them as people who are somehow less competent or willfully resisting the "best" options. *Sense-Making* allows us to approach others as peers capable of new learning, which can be a strong motivator in its own right (see Part IV for further discussion and examples).

Table 8.2.   Description of *Sense-Making* strategy

Quality	SENSE-MAKING (Disposition: Choosing Relationship over Control)
	Purpose: To discover how diverse behaviors, beliefs, and perspectives "make sense" within a given context
Reciprocity (Honoring voice)	*Critical aspects of Sense-Making* • Curiosity about other's stories and interpretations • A learner's attitude and mindset • Nonjudgmental information gathering • Perspective taking
	Possible behavioral indicators • Direct and indirect questioning • Story elicitation techniques (e.g., "Tell me more") • Checking for understanding (e.g., "I want to make sure I understood that . . . ") • Comments that communicate interest and understanding

Critical Aspects of *Sense-Making*

One of the first and most critical aspects of *Sense-Making* (see Table 8.2) is a sense of curiosity about the stories and interpretations that support and maintain another's perspective and behavioral choices. To truly make sense of behavior that initially makes no sense to the person perceiving it, it is critical to approach every situation as a novel one and not simply turn to familiar stories and interpretations. In a fascinating chapter titled "The Blindness of Knowing," Langer made the point that "the more we know the more blind we become" (2005, p. 181); that is, the more likely we are to see only what we already know or expect rather than what is actually in front of us. Curiosity counteracts this blindness.

A sense of curiosity is best sustained through a learner's attitude and mindset (i.e., the mind-set of someone open to what he or she does not already know). This type of attitude and mind-set is the second aspect of *Sense-Making*. A learner's (instead of an expert's) attitude and mind-set is particularly critical in establishing and maintaining reciprocity because, as practitioners, we are so often in "expert" roles. Shevin made the following point that is equally true for all those in helping or teaching roles:

> As facilitators, we come to our interactions . . . from a position of great personal privilege. . . . We find ourselves in initially *unequal* [i.e., nonreciprocal] relationships . . . by virtue of
>
> 1.   our fluency . . . [with whatever skills we seek to teach]
>
> 2.   our recognized status as clinicians, staff persons, teachers . . .
>
> 3.   our being in a position to help individuals engage in activities they are not currently capable of without our help. (1993, p. 5)

If we cannot shift from an expert's or teacher's attitude and mindset to a learner's attitude and mindset, we will never truly be able to make sense of the behaviors and choices of others with whom we engage. Our perceptions of them and their behaviors and choices will remain fixed by our assumptions, freezing them in the roles of receivers with nothing to contribute. As with disrespect, there is violence in this lack of reciprocity (see Isaacs's comment in Chapter 3). Such one-sided lack of reciprocity implicitly communicates a perception of others as somehow less capable and, therefore, somehow "less than" ourselves. (Note the assumption about the other person's capacity to learn without help in the third statement in the Shevin quotation in this section.)

Making sense of another's behavior and/or perspective starts with becoming open to what we might learn from him or her. This openness, in turn, leads to nonjudgmental information gathering, a third aspect that can shed light on data that might otherwise be overlooked. The Guide to Identifying Cultural Data (see Appendix C at the end of the book) is a valuable aid to such information gathering. Although designed for use in culturally linguistically diverse settings, this table can also be used to understand perspectives grounded in other sources of differences. Its questions are intended to act as guides for gathering information that is relevant to how people view the world and their behavioral choices. (More information on this table is available in Barrera et al., 2003.)

Closely related to nonjudgmental information gathering is the fourth aspect of *Sense-Making:* perspective taking. Perspective taking is the ability referred to previously in this chapter of taking on another's perspective in order to better understand it. The varying models of agency discussed in Chapter 2 can be a useful tool for cultivating the ability to view things from multiple perspectives. An understanding of these models supports the development of perspective taking by encouraging a shift in perceptions that facilitates seeing things through another's eyes. One question that can stimulate such a shift is "What would it take for me to choose that same behavior over others?" This question prompts an examination of the quality of a another's life experience and the range of choices that person perceives as viable.

Behavioral Indicators Associated with *Sense-Making*

Several behavioral indicators are associated with the *Sense-Making* strategy (see Table 8.2). The use of direct and indirect questions, when asked in a context of curiosity rather than intrusion or inquisition, is one such behavioral indicator of *Sense-Making* (e.g., "I'm really interested in how you work with Jamie. Could you describe a typical day when he's home?", "What happens when Amy has a meltdown? What have you tried?")

Story elicitation techniques (e.g., "Tell me more," "Can you tell me about a time when that happened?") also strengthen reciprocity (i.e., communicate wanting to receive as much information as we give). Equally important is checking for understanding (e.g., "I'm hearing you say that. . . . Did I get that right?", "Could you tell me a bit more; I'm not sure I'm understanding this just yet"). Never assume understanding; always check if what is understood is accurate, even when the other person's message seems quite clear, especially when there are significant cultural differences.

Finally, it is important to communicate continued interest and understanding as the other person discusses his or her perspective, beliefs, and behaviors. Neutral comments, such as "I see," "That's really interesting," or "I've never thought of it that way" can be helpful in this regard.

Examples and Nonexamples of *Sense-Making*

Table 8.3 provides some examples and nonexamples of what *Sense-Making* might sound and look like. The verbal examples focus on eliciting information and ensuring understanding of that information, whereas associated nonverbal behaviors are designed to reinforce a message of interest and curiosity. The nonexamples illustrate an emphasis on the agenda of the practitioner, as well as a lack of interest in any additional information not directly related to that agenda.

Self-Reflection Questions

In addition to behavioral indicators, several self-reflection questions (see Table 8.4) can be used to assess the degree to which our behaviors authentically communicate our interest in making sense of another's perspectives and/or beliefs. The first

Table 8.3.   *Sense-Making* examples and nonexamples

Quality	Examples[a]	Nonexamples[b]
	Verbal statements	*Verbal statements*
	"Why do you think Tony would be forging your name and not bringing it [paper] home for you to sign?"	"Okay, so let me go into the main reason I've called you here." (In response to parent comment, "I don't know why my child causes you problems.")
Reciprocity (Honoring voice)	"Could you elaborate, if you feel comfortable doing that? What do you mean by other problems?"	"Well, you know I was kind of looking through files and paperwork and it seems like he was first referred. . . . Did the psychologist go over the report with you?" (Said in response to parent comment, "It just seems to like he doesn't listen to me.")
	"Is that what I hear you saying?" (after paraphrasing other's comment)	
	Nonverbal statements	*Nonverbal statements*
	Relaxed body language	Rushed, "tight" body language that communicates disinterest and impatience
	Absence of negative facial expressions that reflect an attitude of "How could that possibly make any sense?" or, worse, "That's totally wrong or unsound" (e.g., raised eyebrows, head shakes)	Negative facial expressions that communicate judgment of others' behavior and/or perspective as wrong or unsound
	Expressions of patience and interest	

[a]Both the examples and the nonexamples are taken from comments of workshop participants describing specific situations. We thank all workshop participants who gave permission for their comments to be used as part of our research data.

[b]The nonexamples are not necessarily incorrect or inappropriate; however, they do not reflect the strategy of *Sense-Making*.

Table 8.4. Self-reflection questions for *Sense-Making* strategy

SENSE-MAKING
(Disposition: Choosing Relationship over Control)

Question 1

   To what degree do I have a genuine interest in learning how the other person understands and feels about the current situation or problem?

Question 2

   Can I honestly say, "That makes sense," when I hear what the other has to say?

Question 3

   To what degree can I believe that, given the same life experiences and/or situations, I would make the same choices and/or behave the same way as the other person?

of these is "To what degree do I have a genuine interest in learning how the other person understands and feels about the current situation or problem?" When such interest is present, it is much more likely to be communicated, whether through the behavioral indicators just described or in other ways. A second question is "Can I honestly say 'That makes sense?' If not, what additional information might I need?"

If rapport has been sufficiently established, it is perfectly acceptable to say something such as "I'm not sure how this choice seems to be best for you. My experiences have been quite different, but I'd really like to know why or how you see it as preferable to other choices. Would you be willing to tell me?" Sometimes a comment such as the following can also be helpful: "I'm thinking that you don't see what I'm describing and asking as positive from your perspective. Would you tell me what it would mean to you (or what you think would happen) if you did X (suggested behavior) instead of Y (what you're doing now)? What changes would you have to make?" The specific words would, of course, need to be adapted to particular contexts. The idea is to communicate an honest desire to understand, not to agree or diminish either our own or the other person's perspectives and/or beliefs.

Finally, there is a third question that many find truly challenging: "To what degree can I believe that, given the same life experiences and/or situations, I would make the same choices and/or behave the same way?" When the answer is "to a high degree," an explicit comment such as "Ah, now I understand; I think I'd do the same if I were in your shoes" can go a long way to establishing reciprocity. It is, however, not always an easy answer to achieve! Deep perspective-taking is required to reach that point.

These questions not only serve to assess the presence of reciprocity, they also assess the degree to which the disposition of Choosing Relationship over Control is present. They indicate the degree of priority given to truly getting to know the other as a person in his or her own right and not just as someone with a problem that needs to be fixed.

APPRECIATING

The strategy of *Appreciating* works closely with *Sense-Making*. Its focus, however, shifts to the disposition of Setting the Stage for Miracles. With *Sense-Making*, we

Table 8.5. Description of *Appreciating* strategy

Quality	*APPRECIATING* (Disposition: Setting the Stage for Miracles)
	Purpose: To identify the positive aspects of another's behavior(s) that have something to teach us
Reciprocity (Honoring voice)	*Critical aspects of Appreciating* • Willingness to identify *gold nuggets* in other's behavior/beliefs • Recognition that every negative behavior is a positive behavior exaggerated • Willingness to learn from other's behaviors/beliefs
	Possible behavioral indicators • Explicit reframing • Naming of positive intent at core of exaggerated behaviors/beliefs • Explicit comments regarding value of other's behaviors/beliefs

move away from control and toward relationship. With *Appreciating,* we open possibilities for expanded and paradoxical options (i.e., inclusive rather than polarized options). *Appreciating* asks us to perceive and appreciate the value of both our own perspective and/or behavior and that of another, even when it may contradict our own. In so doing, this strategy taps into 3rd Space thinking (see Chapter 5 for a discussion of 3rd Space).

Skilled Dialogue's use of the word *appreciating* takes time to understand. It does not just mean valuing the other person's behavior for ourselves or in some sort of absolute sense, as in "Oh, that's a great thing to do." As noted by *The American Heritage Dictionary of the English Language, Fourth Edition* (Pickett, 2000),[1] *appreciate* can also mean "to be fully aware of or sensitive to; realize: [as in] *I appreciate your problems.*" The critical aspects of *Appreciating,* all support a willingness to step outside of one's comfort zone and actively learn from another (shown in Table 8.5 and discussed in the next section), illustrates both of these meanings.

Critical Aspects of *Appreciating*

The first of the critical aspects of *Appreciating* is the identification of the positive kernels (i.e., gold nuggets) in the other's behaviors and/or perspective, even when apparently negative. For example, the gold nugget in a child's refusal to comply with parents' requests might be the capacity for self-assertion in the face of adult pressure or the self-recognition of his or her sense of power and agency. This gold nugget can actually be quite useful in many contexts, even if not optimal in this one (e.g., it can be useful in resisting peer pressure to engage in inappropriate behavior or the pressure of an unfamiliar adult to get in a car or to go look for a lost pet).

The point of finding gold nuggets is not to ignore or minimize the life denying aspects of many beliefs and behavioral choices. It is, rather, to establish reciprocity through the recognition that offering new behavioral alternatives must take existing contexts and experiential data into account. If, for example, going—rather than not going—to the dentist brings pain, no degree of persuasion will make the alternative a desired or motivated choice until the range of perceived choices and consequences is reframed and expanded.

---

[1]Copyright © 2006 by Houghton Mifflin Harcourt Publishing Company. Reproduced by permission from *The American Heritage Dictionary of the English Language, Fourth Edition.*

Similarly, for some children, compliance with adult requests may be associated with being coerced and restricted (i.e., losing personal power or agency). For others, such compliance may be associated with gaining privileges or with being nurtured and protected. Neither group will be likely to change their perceptions of what is desirable if their current choices are not appreciated as reasonable and valuable in their given contexts.

In the highly verbal ENC, it is also important to note that merely being given new verbal information (e.g., results of a recent scientific study) is not sufficient to initiate behavioral changes. Much of a person's behavior and choices are grounded in what Langer terms "premature cognitive commitments"—that is, "mindsets that we accept unconditionally without considering or being aware of alternative [choices]" (1998, p. 92). Without a shift in experiential data, such commitments are difficult to see as anything other than fact.

Collaboration that is sufficiently reciprocal to set the stage for miracles will only begin to develop when we can appreciate the context and function of diverse behaviors not just for the other but for ourselves as well. That is, we cannot truly collaborate or honor another's voice when different from our own until we can appreciate its value and function not only in the context of the other person, but also, perhaps, in our own (i.e., find the gift it may bring to our own lives). The gift of a child's insistent self-assertion, for example, may be the recognition that we are being too self-assertive, or, conversely, that we are not being self-assertive enough in particular situations. It is one thing, for example, to recognize the value of noncompliance and say, "Oh, I see that noncompliance allows that child to assert him- or herself and avoid things he or she does not want to do," yet still think " it is not really a good or useful behavior overall." It is another to find the value of noncompliance in our own lives. Although the former recognition is an authentic part of *Appreciating*, it nevertheless subtly devalues the other's choice and, thus, undermines reciprocity. To fully honor another voice (i.e., establish reciprocity and set the stage for miracles), the additional recognition of the value of a behavior for ourselves is necessary (e.g., "Oh, wow, noncompliance is useful when I'm being asked to do too much!").

One way of coming to this additional recognition is to ask ourselves when such behavior, albeit perhaps less exaggerated and more subtle, has served a purpose that we recognize as valid for ourselves (e.g., "When has standing my ground and refusing to comply served me well?"). When have we engaged in similar behavior, although perhaps in a less exaggerated fashion (e.g., refusing to comply even in the face of another's apparently reasonable request)? Authentic appreciation is always easier when we have engaged in the behavior in question.

A second critical aspect of *Appreciating* is similar to the first—the recognition that there is a positive behavior, albeit muted or distorted, at the core of every negative behavior. At the heart of aggressive behavior, for example, may be a strong need to protect, however unskilled or exaggerated. At the heart of passivity may be the recognition of our own limitations. Without understanding the behavioral intensity spectrum, discussed previously, it is all too easy to eliminate behaviors that can serve a useful purpose yet need to be balanced rather than exaggerated.

If compliance is emphasized, for example, we may end up depriving children of the ability to reject demands that should be rejected, such as a peer's demand to lie for him or her. Conversely, if self-assertion is emphasized (e.g., "Stand up for yourself"), we may inadvertently sabotage social skills such as those necessary in asking for help.

Finally, the third aspect of *Appreciating* is necessary for the success of the first two aspects: the willingness to step outside of our comfort zone and actively learn from another person. Part of reciprocity is the understanding that everyone brings something of value to the table. *Appreciating* focuses on making that "something" explicit. This is not always an easy task. It is important, however, to remember that the people with whom we interact are also competent. Even when they do not have the specific knowledge or skills we are advocating, they nevertheless have the knowledge and skills that have allowed them to survive and perhaps even thrive in their own contexts.

All three aspects of *Appreciating* support the fact that honoring diverse voices requires acknowledging their value in some respect. This acknowledgement is a key piece of transforming existing contexts that insist there is only one perspective into complementary contexts that an enhance another (see discussion in Part III).

Behavioral Indicators of *Appreciating*

In addition to these aspects, Table 8.5 identifies behavioral indicators associated with *Appreciating*. The first behavioral indicator is the use of explicit reframing. Perkins said,

> The assumptions that lock one into a particular view of a problem are mental sets or frames. Focusing on different combinations of clues and constraints, adding what was excluded, and excluding what was included may help to break one's mental set [i.e., reframe]. (2000, pp. 224–225)

Reframing is also what Fletcher and Olwyler have called "perception-shifting: Breaking open . . . narrow judgments about the positive or negative value of [particular] qualities" (1997, p. 3). The quality of "laziness," for example, can be reframed as "efficiency," (i.e., both carry the meaning of a desire to expend as little energy as possible!) Explicit reframing of other behaviors commonly perceived as negative (e.g., hyperactivity, noncompliance) can be a powerful way of acknowledging their value.

The second behavioral indicator listed in Table 8.5 is similar. It is the explicit naming of the positive intent at the core of exaggerated behaviors and/or beliefs (e.g., saying "I can see how you really care about your child" to a parent who chooses to minimize interaction with his or her child to avoid "doing it wrong"). Explicitly acknowledging a positive intent within the belief and/or practice that has been designated as a problem communicates an openness to strengths and capabilities, as well as to the limitations. It invites the other person to see him- or herself as a potential partner rather than someone who needs to defend, justify, or resist.

The aspects of reframing and identifying a positive intent both contribute to the third behavioral aspect of *Appreciating:* making specific comments regarding the value of other's behaviors and/or beliefs to the situation in question (e.g., "Your insistence on explaining your point of view is a really great skill. I can see how it helps to make sure that what you believe doesn't get lost as we discuss what else we might do."). The idea is to communicate that the proposed change or "solution" needs to be created based on mutual input.

Shevin posed a relevant question: "How do we acknowledge and then move away from our initial position of privilege [as someone who knows more or knows better], in order to act as allies?" (1993, p. 5). This is an important question to consider even when the interaction is between professional peers rather than with children or families. Making explicit comments about the value of another's behaviors and/or beliefs is one way to do this. Such comments clearly acknowledge awareness that we are not the only ones with something of value to offer.

Examples and Nonexamples of *Appreciating*

Table 8.6 provides some examples and nonexamples of what *Appreciating* may sound or look like. The nonexamples, though not necessarily inappropriate, each illustrate an absence of *Appreciating.* They reflect the lack of balance between teaching (giving information) and learning (receiving information) to which we just referred. The examples, in contrast, reflect this balance through the explicit affirmation of the value of the other person's perspectives, beliefs, and/or behaviors. Sometimes the simple acknowledgment of someone's comments may be sufficient to communicate that we value their presence and input. The clear message that we are present and following the other's lead strongly communicates appreciation.

Table 8.6.   *Appreciating* examples and nonexamples

Quality	Examples[a]	Nonexamples[b]
	Verbal statements	*Verbal statements*
	"Ah, I could see how you might feel that way."	"I have stopped suggesting that they move but have come up with other things to suggest."
	To parents: "I value everything you've both done. I can see that you are both working in the best interests of your child."	"I certainly understand where Judy was coming from."
Reciprocity (Honoring voice)	To center director: "I can see how hard you are working and how much the community appreciates your efforts."	
	"You know, I've never thought of it that way. I'll have to remember that in the future."	
	Nonverbal statements	*Nonverbal statements*
	Affirmations such as head nodding and smiling	Negative facial expressions such as frowning and head shaking

[a]Both the examples and the nonexamples are taken from comments of workshop participants describing specific situations. We thank all workshop participants who gave permission for their comments to be used as part of our research data.

[b]The nonexamples are not necessarily incorrect or inappropriate; however, they do not reflect the strategy of *Appreciating.*

Gernsbacher (2006) made a relevant distinction between trying solely to convince others to see the world through our eyes and learning to see the world through their eyes. These choices are not exclusive, of course, but, as Gernsbacher goes on to point out, if we start with the latter, we increase the chances of the former, even with children identified as having autism.

Self-Reflection Questions

Appreciating is a strategy that may need to be practiced more than some of the others. Several questions can help to guide this practice (see Table 8.7). The first of these is "What is the gift of other's behaviors and/or beliefs to my own life? What can I learn from them?" For example, is it to persevere, take risks, assert myself, recognize the importance of organization or disorganization, or accept my powerlessness and/or limitations? When we can find the value of another's behaviors and/or beliefs for ourselves it becomes easier to appreciate those behaviors and/or beliefs in another. It also provides a powerful opportunity to model learning from another, which stimulates others' willingness to learn from us.

A second question reflects the reality that the diversity, especially that which we find most troublesome, is often a mirror of behaviors and/or beliefs that remain unacknowledged or unrecognized within ourselves: "What about the other person's behaviors and/or beliefs mirrors something that I am lacking or not appreciating in myself? Perhaps it is a strength I never learned to use, or perhaps it is something that I refuse to see within myself because I never learned to see anything positive about it."

The final question is "What is positive, although perhaps exaggerated, about another person's behaviors and/or beliefs?" This question is helpful to reflect on the degree to which the strategy of *Appreciating* may be present. It is one more way of focusing on the value inherent in diverse behaviors and/or beliefs.

The self-reflection questions emphasize the need for *Appreciating* to be genuine. When we ask participants in workshops to reflect on what they can learn from families, for example, they will say, "I learned how not to approach this parent." Although this is real learning, it is learning that cannot easily lead to genuine appreciation of that parent's behaviors. Sometimes we hear "I learned that I never want to do that!" That also is real learning, yet nevertheless learning that negates *Appreciating*. Until we can honestly say, "Wow, that person really taught me some-

Table 8.7. Self-reflection questions for *Appreciating* strategy

APPRECIATING
(Disposition: Setting the Stage for Miracles)

Question 1
    What is the gift of the other's behaviors/beliefs to my own life? What can I learn from them?
Question 2
    What about the other's behaviors/beliefs mirrors something I am lacking or not appreciating in myself?
Question 3
    What is positive, though perhaps exaggerated, about the other's behaviors/beliefs?

thing of value," or "Wow, that person really taught me something about myself," reciprocity is not fully established. Our need to teach overrides the opportunity to learn, which sabotages the development of a context within which miracles can happen.

The importance of both *Sense-Making* and *Appreciating* cannot be overemphasized. Not only do these two strategies cement the respect engendered through *Welcoming* and *Allowing*, they are also critical as the foundation for the next two strategies of *Joining* and *Harmonizing*, which are discussed in the next chapter. Without them, the transition from respect to responsiveness will falter or fail to happen at all.

CASE REVIEW

The discussion in this section turns once again to the case study of Justin; his mother, Mrs. Taylor; and his teacher, Mrs. Miller, which was introduced at the end of the Part III text and revisited in Chapter 7. As previously stated, Skilled Dialogue strategies can be examined from multiple perspectives. This chapter continues the analysis of this case but with a focus on *Sense-Making* and *Appreciating* in relation to Mrs. Miller's interactions with Justin and Justin's mother, Mrs. Taylor. These strategies could as easily be examined from Justin's or Mrs. Taylor's perspectives, but, given that Mrs. Miller is the designated "authority voice," it is most appropriate to examine them from her perspective first. Table 8.8 summarizes the discussion of this case within the same framework as Table 7.8. The discussion is, of course, based only on the information provided in the case. One of the results of this type of examination may well be the determination that further information needs to be gathered. (This review, similar to the one in Chapter 7, does not provide suggestions for what might have been done differently. That aspect is addressed in Part IV, where alternative behaviors for this case and others are discussed.)

Mrs. Miller and Justin

There is no evidence that Mrs. Miller is curious about the reasons for Justin's behaviors or that she is trying to make sense of them. Following the incident in which Peter gets hurt as a result of Justin's actions, she does not ask Justin what he is feeling or whether he is aware of his intrusion and transgression of others' boundaries. Her sole focus seems to be on stopping these from occurring again. Although this is a valid focus, gathering information as to how his behavior might make sense to Justin (i.e., seem the best alternative) could be very helpful in formulating a subsequent plan of intervention and behavioral support. Given the information in the case study, *Sense-Making* is not an evident strategy.

Similarly, there is little to no evidence of *Appreciating*. Mrs. Miller seems to have reached the conclusion that this is not the appropriate placement for Justin and expresses little interest in coming to appreciate any possible positive aspects of his behavior (e.g., exercise of personal power) or of his underlying intent (e.g., the intent to become part of the group). She does not try to frame his behavior as

Table 8.8. Summary of case review: *Sense-Making* and *Appreciating*

DISPOSITIONS		
Choosing Relationship over Control		**Setting the Stage for Miracles**
Sense-Making		*Appreciating*
Mrs. Miller & Justin		Mrs. Miller & Justin
1) **Direct and indirect questioning; story elicitation** No evidence of interest in seeking to make sense of Justin's behavior as other than willfully disruptive		1) **Explicit reframing** No evidence of explicit or implicit reframing
2) **Empathic listening; communication of interest and understanding** Mrs. Miller does not speak with Justin other than to tell him he's responsible for his peer's injury		2) **Identification of positive intent at core of exaggerated behaviors/beliefs** No evidence that Mrs. Miller believes there might be any positive intent on Justin's part
3) **Checks for understanding** No evidence of any checks for understanding		3) **Comments on value of the other's behaviors/beliefs** No evidence of any such comments
Mrs. Miller & Mrs. Taylor		Mrs. Miller & Mrs. Taylor
1) **Direct and indirect questioning; story elicitation** Unclear; appears to be more about seeking confirmation of existing judgments		1) **Explicit reframing** No evidence of explicit or implicit reframing
2) **Empathic listening; communication of interest and understanding** Mrs. Miller's listening appears to be more tactical than empathic		2) **Identification of positive intent at core of exaggerated behaviors/beliefs** Mrs. Taylor is not asked about her beliefs; no evidence that Mrs. Miller is trying to identify any positive intent underlying her lateness or apparent lack of understanding about Justin's behavior
3) **Checks for understanding** No evidence of any checks for understanding		3) **Comments on value of the other's behaviors/beliefs** Mrs. Miller makes no comments on the possible value of Mrs. Taylor's behaviors (e.g., lateness)
Diversity is always life enhancing		

The left margin of the table reads vertically: **BEHAVIORAL EVIDENCE**

anything but negative. She also makes no comments on the potential value of his behavior were it to be more balanced and less extreme (e.g., clear and strong self-assertion). Even though exaggerated to an inappropriate level in this context, such assertion could be of value in other contexts.

Mrs. Miller and Mrs. Taylor

Similarly, Mrs. Miller's focus with Mrs. Taylor, Justin's mother, seems to be on solutions rather than understanding. She seems to come to the meeting more prepared to tell than to listen. She does ask Mrs. Taylor about Justin's behavior at home and at his prior preschool. It is unclear, however, if her motivation in doing this is to increase her understanding of Justin's behavior or simply to collect additional data to support her view that this is not the best program for Justin. Nevertheless, she does ask for more information, which does evidence *Sense-Making* to some degree.

Appreciating is noticeably absent in Mrs. Miller's interactions with Mrs. Taylor. Her primary goal seems to be to communicate the need to move Justin to another placement. She makes no attempt to frame the situation as anything but problematic. Neither does she communicate any acknowledgment of a possible positive intent (e.g., "Mrs. Taylor, I can see how hard you worked to find the placement that seemed best for Justin"). Comments on what Mrs. Taylor might contribute to the situation (e.g., "We can certainly benefit from the presence of a parent so dedicated to meeting her child's needs") are also noticeably absent.

Mrs. Miller seems to be focused on controlling a situation that is negatively affecting her classroom and, potentially, her relationship with other parents. She demonstrates no tendency to believe that Justin's behavior might change or to participate in stimulating such a possibility. This problem-centered perspective is often present when practitioners find themselves with little support or resources and work with children who exhibit aggressive behavior. Many have received little training or information on how to work with these children or even on how to access available professional resources. (The chapters in Part IV revisit this case and offer alternative suggestions to increase *Sense-Making* and *Appreciating*.)

DISCUSSION QUESTIONS AND ACTIVITIES

1. Think back to an interaction where you felt you had to defend your perspective because it seemed to make no sense to the other person(s) in the interaction. How did the person communicate his or her lack of understanding? What behaviors would have instead communicated that your perspective made sense to him or her?

2. Have you ever felt that, although another person understood your perspective, he or she could not appreciate it? How did you know?

3. Revisit Questions 1 and 2, but this time put yourself in the place of the person who could not make sense of or appreciate another's perspective. Why do you think this was so? What would have helped you make sense of that behavior?

4. Look at Table 4.3 in Chapter 4. Each of the listed behaviors has been reframed, such as obnoxiousness into incessant curiosity and impatience into accelerated learning capacity. Think of three behaviors that typically "drive you nuts." Can you reframe them into positive behaviors? Ask at least three other people for their ideas.

5. Read the following statement from Allen. Discuss your thoughts about it with at least two other people. How do you think it applies to the strategies of *Sense-Making* and *Appreciating?*

> It becomes increasingly imperative that we realize that there are as many varieties of human social consciousness, of community in its largest sense, as there are varieties of life in the universe. . . . For our future good depends as much on

our recognizing our vast differences as on recognizing our powerful similarities. (Allen, 1999, p. 8)

6. Review the information on varying models of agency in Chapter 2. How can knowledge of the various models help you make sense of others' behaviors? Could a single behavior make sense differently if it is understood as reflecting a conjoint relational–interpersonal model instead of a disjoint model of agency?

There Is Always a Third Choice

Joining and *Harmonizing*

The four strategies already discussed in the last two chapters, *Welcoming, Allowing, Sense-Making,* and *Appreciating,* lay the groundwork for the two culminating strategies: *Joining* and *Harmonizing.* Both of these strategies focus on developing responsiveness. That is, their goal is specifically to develop appropriate responses based on the identities and voices of all people involved (see Table 9.1).

Neither respect nor reciprocity is sufficient to generate optimum options to interactional challenges; they can only do so when there is also responsiveness. Without responsiveness, both respect and reciprocity will ultimately be undermined because individual perspectives cannot be mutually honored. Respect honors identity, and reciprocity honors "voice," the expression of that identity. It is responsiveness, however, that establishes the connection between two people's expressions of their unique perspectives and brings them into balance.

To achieve such responsiveness, the strategies of *Joining* and *Harmonizing* emphasize perceiving and understanding differences as complementary—one adding to the other—rather than as polarized or divisive—one detracting from or diminishing the other. Such complementarity is essential to accessing the diverse strengths and resources of multiple perspectives and leveraging them in order to develop response options that are equally responsive to all participants in an interaction and not merely to some. To be responsive is to entertain the possibility of connection rather than to follow the certainty of separation. It requires being able to see beyond obvious choices and remaining open to novel possibilities.

RESPONSIVENESS

Responsiveness capitalizes on the strengths of existing resources vis-à-vis desired outcomes (see also Chapter 3). It seeks to put all participants in an interaction "on the same side" (i.e., join and harmonize diverse perspectives). The idea that everyone, however diverse their perspectives, can be on the same side is relatively

Table 9.1. Chapter 9 organizer

Qualities	Dispositions		
	Choosing Relationship over Control		Setting the Stage for Miracles
	Strategies		
Respect (Honoring identity)	*Welcoming*		*Allowing*
		Differences do not make people wrong	
Reciprocity (Honoring voice)	*Sense-Making*		*Appreciating*
		Diversity is always life enhancing	
Responsiveness (Honoring connection)	**Joining**		**Harmonizing**
		There is always a third choice	

uncommon in ENC contexts, which often tend to privilege either-or perspectives that give greater value to one than another (see Chapter 2 discussion).

When differences are so perceived (i.e. dichotomous), authentic responsiveness is precluded. There is effectively a wall between them, placing them in distinct and exclusive spaces. From that dichotomous (dualistic) perspective, each person can only look over the wall into what has been designated as space outside his or her perspective. It is only when the wall is lowered, softened, or removed, that a larger and more inclusive 3rd Space can be created. Such a space integrates two previously exclusive options into one and, thereby, yields additional choices that can honor options previously seen as exclusive (see Chapter 5 for further discussion of 3rd Space, a concept developed specifically for Skilled Dialogue by the authors).

Integrative or 3rd Space perspectives are the core of responsiveness as addressed through *Joining* and *Harmonizing*. Once such perspectives are achieved, inclusive options can be more easily identified or crafted. To accomplish such an inclusive perspective, both *Joining* and *Harmonizing* require "exploiting the power of uncertainty" (Langer, 2005, p. 15) as well as coming to understand "the whole to be found in the parts" (Senge et al., 2005, p. 41).

The suspension of assumptions engendered by *Allowing* (see Chapter 7) and the recognition of the value of diverse perspectives developed through *Appreciating* (see Chapter 8) quite literally set the stage for the type of understanding that defines both *Joining* and *Harmonizing*. Suspending our fixed assumptions and judgments opens us to both see and appreciate "emerging events, contents, patterns . . . [what] first appeared as fixed or even rigid beings to appear" softer and more fluid (Senge et al., 2005, p. 43). Fixed assumptions, in contrast, freeze our ability to perceive anything other than that with which we are already familiar. They lock us into preconceptions impermeable to new or unfamiliar data. Once our original assumptions are suspended, however, the possibility of appreciating diverse assumptions emerges, promoting the possibility of harmonizing these assumptions.

Both *Joining* and *Harmonizing* engender responsiveness by honoring the unique web of connection between people sharing specific interactions. They affirm that, although others may have engaged in similar interactions, *this* interaction is unique by virtue of the fact that the people engaged in it are unique. It is difficult, if not impossible, to be responsive when connection is not recognized.

> If you feel you've got a problem to solve that is "out there" [i.e., not connected to me] and you don't . . . see or want to see any . . . relationship between [it and yourself], you may wind up not . . . see[ing] the problem accurately. . . . You . . . may [in fact contribute] to maintaining the undesired situation rather than allowing it to evolve and perhaps dissolve. (Senge et al., 2005, p. 51).

If diverse perspectives cannot be connected, authentic responses are impossible. One or more of the perspectives represented will be shortchanged. Even when we offer wonderful suggestions and detailed intervention plans, if we do so without connecting them to the other person's perspectives, they will be responsive only to *our* perception of the problem or need. *Joining* and *Harmonizing* counteract such one-sidedness by creating options that acknowledge and access all aspects of a problem, not just those perceived by certain people.

A critical aspect of responsiveness is, thus, what Senge et al. (2005) termed "seeing from the whole" (p. 42). This ability requires focusing on the "whole" reflected in those details rather than building it *from* the details (i.e., seeing how things are connected rather than how they are separate). Being able to do this results in a joint (i.e., joined) perspective and agrees with the following insight noted by Senge et al.: "if 'we' are creating the problems we have now, then we can create something different" (2005, p. 47)

It is an unfortunate tendency to place perceived problems "out there" so that they are somehow separate from us: "It's the family," we say, making it clear that we are not involved. Or, we may affirm, "The child has ADHD," implying that the child's behavior is internally generated and separate from our own actions or lack thereof. At one level, this may certainly be true. At another level, however, it ignores the fact that the behaviors we name may be absent when the family or child interacts with a different person! Even as we try to be responsive, we so often negate our power to influence and shape, to nurture and support. The strategies of *Joining* and *Harmonizing* ask us to reclaim that power, not in an aggressive or assertive way, but with sensitivity and compassion. They invite us to shift from I–It interactions to I–Thou interactions.

Goleman (2006) discussed the differences between these two types of interactions. He said, "A defining quality of I–Thou engagement is 'feeling felt'. . . . At such moments we sense that the other person knows how we feel, and so we feel known [i.e., responded to]" (2006, p. 107). I–It, however, involves "thinking *about* the other person rather than attuning to her" (2006, p. 109). It is knowledge *about* rather than knowledge *of* (see also discussion of Anchored Understanding of Diversity in Barrera et al., 2003).

The deepest challenge of responsiveness is the need to establish at least some degree of I–Thou connection while simultaneously honoring both professional and personal boundaries. As Goleman (2006) pointed out, there is no word in English to describe this *personal-but-not-personal* type of engagement, which is more common to conjoint models of agency than to disjoint models used in cultural contexts such as ENC.

This challenge was particularly salient for me (Barrera) during the time when I directed an early intervention program. The therapists in the program would come back from home visits and describe how the mothers had asked for personal information from them, such as "Do you have a boyfriend?" or "How come you're not married?" They interpreted these questions as reflections of the mothers' desire to become friends with them and tended to shift out of their professional roles in response, sometimes asking similarly personal questions in return. We talked about the challenge this presented. Many of the mothers involved were Mexican American and operated out of a relational–interpersonal conjoint model of agency. Given that I (Barrera) shared this model, I understood that the parents did not want to relate with the therapists solely in terms of their professional roles (roles that were unfamiliar to them). Neither, however, did they want a purely personal friendship with them. Rather, the parents were seeking to establish an interactional context that was familiar to them.

There is no easy answer to this challenge of contrasting models of agency (e.g., establishing I–Thou connections that simultaneously honor both professional and personal boundaries instead of more purely professional ones). Many interactions are largely superficial—interactions with sales people, bank cashiers, neighbors seen only occasionally—and do not present this challenge. These can stay relatively impersonal. Practitioner–family as well as teacher–child interactions, however, are much more complex. They typically involve families sharing realities that are quite personal with professionals trained to remain objective. It is in relation to these latter types of interactions that the strategies of *Joining* and *Harmonizing* are discussed.

JOINING

Putting perspectives and behaviors in contradiction to each other (e.g., this "vs." that) is a common ENC tendency (see Chapter 2). The strategy of *Joining* seeks to redefine such juxtapositions from "this versus that" to "this in relationship to that." It promotes a relational perspective that conceptualizes interactions as mutually created within a shared and interdependent context or field of ideas, thoughts, and expectations. It encourages acknowledging those aspects of interactions that create the *we* within a given interaction—that is, those aspects that connect individuals one with another (e.g., teacher–learner, orderly one–disorderly one). One workshop participant described *Joining* as being defined by the shifting from using a parallel play lens to using a cooperative play lens.

There is a concept in education known as the zone of proximal development (Vygotsky, 1978), which refers to the stage or place that is developmentally the most accessible "next step" or the next easiest thing to be learned or done. In a way, *Joining* is about becoming aware of the "zone of current development"—

the space within which current interactions are taking place. The zone of current development maintains and sustains the quality and nature of the current interactions and, consequently, ensures that outcomes will remain predictable. An awareness of its nature and the scripts holding it in place, therefore, identifies the current alliance between two people so that it can be examined and changed.

Critical Aspects of *Joining*

Joining's four critical aspects define the attributes necessary for joining with another in the pursuit of a selected goal (see Table 9.2). The first aspect is the recognition that all behavior is social (i.e. jointly constructed and maintained). We all bring cognitive, behavioral, and linguistic scripts to our interactions. These scripts guide our thoughts, actions, and words. For example, someone with a script of "I am a teacher" will think, act, and talk very differently from someone with a script of "I am powerless; no one pays attention to me."

No matter what behavioral scripts we bring to an interaction, however, their specific expressions are invariably influenced by others' words and actions (Goleman, 2006; Sawyer, 2007). If one person brings an "I am a teacher" script and a second person responds with an "I am a teacher, too" script, the first person's thoughts, words, and actions will be different than if the second person responded with an "I am a learner" or an "I already know all I need to know about this" script.

Table 9.2. Description of *Joining* strategy

Quality	*JOINING* (Disposition: Choosing Relationship over Control)
	Purpose: To identify connections between others' perspectives, behaviors, and beliefs and my own perspective, behaviors, and beliefs
	Critical aspects of Joining • Recognition that all behavior is social—jointly constructed and maintained • Recognition that one's own behavior is somehow contributing to and sustaining the identified problem
Responsiveness (Honoring connection)	• Willingness to examine our role in the negative as well as the positive aspects of interaction • Identification of a common context that shapes the behaviors and/or intentions of the people interacting
	Possible behavioral indicators • Verbal acknowledgment of "we-ness" (i.e., connection between one's own behavior and the other person's behavior) (e.g., "I can see that we're both concerned about this situation") • Reference to past experiences during which one has behaved similarly to how the other person is behaving now (e.g., "I remember feeling pressured and confused in a situation like this one") • Verbal acknowledgment of how one's behaviors and the other person's behaviors complement each other (e.g., "You know, what you're doing can actually support the goal I'm describing," "If you focus on supporting Tara's independence, and I focus on helping her develop collaborative skills, we can have the best of both worlds," "I just realized I'm asking you to listen to me, yet I'm not sure I'm really listening to you; could you please repeat that?")

Joining thus starts with the acknowledgment that what we wish to change is not simply an independent behavior that exists apart from us but rather one that is somehow interdependent with our own words, thoughts, and actions.

> An empowering awareness of the whole requires a fundamental shift in the relationship between "seer" and "seen" . . . [a] looking "out at the world" from the viewpoint of a detached observer to looking from the "inside" of what is observed. (Senge et al., 2005, p. 41)

This shift from "you there and me here" to "both of us in the same place" leads to *Joining*'s second critical aspect: the recognition that one's own behavior is somehow contributing to and sustaining the identified situation or problem. This does not mean being responsible for that problem: it does mean participating in its continuation. When, for example, we approach children as those needing help because "they cannot control themselves," we de facto communicate our perception (and expectations) of them as unable to control themselves. This communication occurs even when we are not aware of it and have no intention of expressing it, yet nevertheless reinforces the perceived reality, however subtly.

Joining challenges us to choose relationship with the whole child or parent or practitioner rather than with only the part(s) we identify as problematic. This aspect connects with *Joining*'s third aspect: a willingness to look at our own role in the negative as well as the positive aspects of the interaction (i.e., to ask "How am I stimulating and/or sustaining the negative as well as the positive aspects of the current situation?). It is easy to take credit for changing a child's behavior in a desired direction. It is more difficult to acknowledge that we may be contributing, however unintentionally and unconsciously, to maintaining the very behaviors we are seeking to change. Yet, we may be doing exactly this through the beliefs and expectations our behaviors communicate.

One example of this comes from a student who complained about the fact that her class of third graders was never quiet. I (Barrera) replied, "Never? Not even for a single moment?" "Well," she responded, "There was this one time when I'd been out of the room for a while and returned to find them all very quietly attending to their work." When asked what she did then, she replied, "I immediately asked them what was wrong!" It was only after a bit more discussion that she realized the embedded message she was unintentionally sending: "Something is wrong when you are quiet." Obviously, this teacher did not expect that her students could work quietly, and she saw their silence as a sign of potential problems. Although she did not communicate this expectation and perception explicitly, her message was nevertheless clear to her students, who immediately started talking again.

These first three aspects of *Joining* support a fourth aspect: identifying a common context within which one's behaviors and/or intents complement the other's behaviors and/or intents. This final aspect encapsulates the previous ones. It is the explicit acknowledgment that the current context, however problematic, is not created independently of another's behaviors (i.e., that the problem does not reside solely in any one person). Choosing Relationship over Control as expressed through *Joining* is rooted in the emerging recognition of connectedness as a per-vasive characteristic of all reality. Science's growing understanding of reality as eco-logical rather than fragmented reinforces this recognition that meaning comes from this interconnectedness rather than from isolated parts (Senge et al., 2005).

Joining focuses our attention on the "symphony" of varied behaviors per-ceived in concert instead of on single behaviors perceived in isolation. Single be-haviors, similar to single musical notes, cannot be said to be truly meaningful apart from their relationship to other behaviors. Using a different metaphor, *Joining* is akin to attending to "an impressionist painting [where] when you step back," it reveals a picture composed of the joining of seemingly unrelated spots of paint (Senge et al., 2005, p. 200).

Behavioral Indicators Associated with *Joining*

Possible behavioral indicators of *Joining* focus on drawing attention to the whole and to the relationship among the parts within that whole. They limit attention to individual behaviors in isolation through an explicit acknowledgment of connec-tion and references to past experiences. Sample comments that express this atten-tion to the whole include the following: "You know, I think I'm doing the same thing. I'm asking you to listen; yet, I'm not sure I'm really listening to you. Could you please repeat that?" or "I think I'm looking at only one part of what hap-pened. Can you tell me more about times when you have acted differently?" (See Table 9.3 for additional comments.)

Examples and Nonexamples of *Joining*

Table 9.3 extends the description of behavioral indicators by providing examples and nonexamples of what *Joining* might sound like. The examples reflect a con-scious and explicit connection with the other person. The nonexamples reflect a more objective and disengaged perspective that talks *about* the situation without expressing any awareness of its co-constructed aspects.

Self-Reflection Questions

Several questions can be asked to reflect on *Joining* within particular interactions (see Table 9.4). The first is "What am I doing or saying that promotes or sustains the current concern or interaction?" This question asks us to reflect on the implicit and embedded messages we may be sending through our words and behaviors. Are we communicating an acknowledgement of our own role or merely describing the situation as something that exists apart from us? Are we making references to a shared context (e.g., "with me," "in my classroom") or talking as if the behavior or situation is always true regardless of context?

A second question is "To what degree do I truly believe the other can change?" It is easy to say that our belief in the other's potential for and ability to change is high. But, when we (the authors) ask workshop participants this question in a

Table 9.3.   *Joining* examples and nonexamples

Quality	Examples[a]	Nonexamples[b]
	Verbal statements	*Verbal statements*
	"Oh, good. I think that we are on the same page."	"He has been showing a bit of defiance in even wanting to do what I ask and just not doing it quite as much as he used to."
	"It's clear to me that we are both very concerned about this situation."	"Here's what I think is happening."
	"Can you think of anything that I might be doing that is not helping this situation?"	"I'm surprised that you can't see the problem; it seems very evident to us here at school."
Responsiveness (Honoring connection)		"I'm kind of concerned about Thomas. I have talked with some of his teachers and they seem to think he is having a little trouble getting things completed and finishing his work."
	Nonverbal behaviors	*Nonverbal behaviors*
	Absence of statements that reflect an either-or perspective in which only one person can be right	Body language that communicates that two diverse perspectives cannot both be correct

[a]Both the examples and the nonexamples are taken from comments of workshop participants describing specific situations. We thank all workshop participants who gave permission for their comments to be used as part of our research data.

[b]The nonexamples are not necessarily incorrect or inappropriate; however, they do not reflect the strategy of *Joining*.

slightly different form, we put that response to the test. We often ask them if they can imagine actually seeing the desired change the next time they see that person (e.g., Tommy staying in his chair and raising his hand before speaking). When asked to imagine that the person with whom they are interacting has changed overnight in exactly the way they would wish (e.g., Tommy staying in his chair and raising his hand before speaking), the answers in almost all cases vary from an absolute "No" (e.g., "I can't picture Tommy sitting still for more than a minute or two," "I don't think Patrick's mother would consistently follow our suggestion regarding the use of encouragement") to "Probably not" (e.g., "Maybe, but it'd be pretty rare") to "Only as part of a miracle."

Following these responses, we ask them to entertain the possibility that this inability to envision the very change they seek is invariably communicated in some fashion during their interactions and to think about how this might be happening. We also ask them how they also, like the children and families with whom they work, pick up on other's expectations for them. In almost all cases, they can identify either verbal or nonverbal behaviors or both that directly or indirectly communicate a lack of belief in another's capacity to change.

A last question that helps reflect on *Joining* is "What *whole* might be holding each of the present perspectives?" In other words, what is the larger context within which the individual behaviors are being generated? One way to answer this question is to imagine interactions as stage plays and give them a name (e.g., "Expert and Novice," "Helping the Less Able," or perhaps "Overwhelmed Families"). Once

Table 9.4. Self-reflection questions for *Joining* strategy

JOINING (Disposition: Choosing Relationship over Control)
Question 1 What am I doing or saying that promotes or sustains the current interaction?
Question 2 To what degree do I truly believe the other can change?
Question 3 What common context do each of the present perspectives share?

named, individual roles become clearer. Experts need novices, helpers need others who need help, and overwhelmed families need guidance and resources. Neediness requires that abundant resources and neediness be polarized; experts need nonexperts; those who can need those who can not. How else could they be distinguished? We rely on the contrast between realities to recognize and understand them (e.g., I recognize and understand extended families in contrast to nuclear families; see the discussion of Anchored Understanding of Diversity in Chapter 4).

This is not to say that changing one's perceptions and scripts will automatically result in desired (although we do receive consistent anecdotal reports from practitioners of such changes). We are, after all, not the only actors on the stage. Others have data pools that extend beyond just their interactions with us. What is certain, however, is that not changing our perceptions and scripts limits our ability to be truly responsive and will almost always result in only predictable outcomes. Changing perceptions and scripts will, at the least, always increase the probability that we can, in fact, set the stage for miracles as we move on to harmonize polarities.

HARMONIZING

Harmonizing seeks to shift shared contexts to generate inclusive and creative options responsive to all participants in an interaction; it seeks to shift from polarized sharing, where each person can have only one part of the whole, to integrated sharing, where all persons contribute to and share in the whole that is ultimately created. *Harmonizing* is similar to visual depth perception. When what is seen by each eye separately is integrated into a single image, suddenly what was flat acquires dimension. (Readers can try this out for themselves: Close one eye and then throw something up and try to catch it with one hand; then try it with both eyes open.) Another metaphor for *Harmonizing* comes from Magic Eye books (referred to in Chapter 5). These delightful books contain images that, when looked at in just the right way, become 3-dimensional and reveal a deeper underlying image different from what can be seen on the surface. *Harmonizing* is similar. When dissimilar or disparate views are integrated, a deeper, richer reality emerges that is often not predictable from initial data (i.e., a miracle).

A key aspect of *Harmonizing* is this type of transforming contradictions into unifying paradoxes within which complementary aspects can be leveraged to create a more inclusive 3rd Space. Whereas *Joining* seeks to identify how one perspective energizes and fuels its opposite (e.g., how resisting is connected with compliance), *Harmonizing* seeks to integrate the complementary aspects of the identified opposites into something inclusive of both (e.g., How can resisting and compliance work together to create something greater than either one alone?).

A visual metaphor originally used in Barrera et al. (2003) is the image of the colors blue and yellow, which when integrated "harmonize" into the color green. Similarly, an auditory metaphor likens harmonizing two diverse perspectives to individual musical notes that produce one sound when played simultaneously. It is a sound distinct from that made by either note individually and yet contains both notes within it. *Harmonizing* integrates disparate behaviors and perspectives into a common whole much the same way. (Note: The reader may wish to revisit the Paderewski anecdote in Chapter 1.)

Once diverse perspectives are harmonized (i.e., put into relationship rather than being held apart), what might have previously been deemed impossible can emerge. In this way *Harmonizing* augments *Allowing*, which first allows disparate realities to exist side by side, and *Appreciating*, which helps us to find the strengths of each reality. (See Part IV for further discussion of the interplay between the two dispositions of Choosing Relationship over Control and Setting the Stage for Miracles and their various strategies.)

Harmonizing is not, however, about minimizing differences between perspectives or behaviors merely to reduce contradictions or resolve the tension of differences. It is not about compromise or compliance. Rather, it is about actively using differences to create an inclusive space within which their strengths can be accessed without the need for compromise or sacrifice. The idea of creating such space is neither to eliminate a behavior or perspective nor to correct it. It is, instead, to support the creation of creative and integrative options responsive to all involved.

Critical Aspects of *Harmonizing*

Table 9.5 summarizes the critical aspects of *Harmonizing*. The first aspect has already been mentioned: reframing contradictions (i.e., polarized alternatives) into paradoxes (i.e., complementary pairs). Fletcher and Olwyler termed this reframing *paradoxical thinking*.

> We use the term "paradox" somewhat more loosely to mean contradictory or *seemingly* impossible combinations of ideas or actions. . . . The seeming impossibility has to do with a person's own limited frame of reference. When a way is found to make both concepts real simultaneously, a deeper truth is revealed. (1997, p. 7)

Reframing starts with a focus, not on the external problem or concern, but on the limited frame of reference within which that problem or concern is currently being understood. Interestingly, Perkins (2000) makes the point that "solution mindedness"—a set vision of the nature of the desired solution—is one of the major

Table 9.5. Description of *Harmonizing* strategy

Quality	HARMONIZING (Disposition: Setting the Stage for Miracles)
Responsiveness (Honoring connection)	*Purpose:* To identify/create a larger more inclusive context within which identified contradictions can complement each other to generate a "third choice." *Critical aspects of Harmonizing* • Willingness to reframe perceptions • Openness to brainstorming • Thinking in threes (3rd Space thinking) *Possible behavioral indicators* • Lateral thinking statements (e.g., "What if we thought of this as like making a taco? What would that look like?") • Prompting for 3rd Space options (e.g., "Can you think of another option?" "Do you think there's a way that both options might be possible?") • Identification of unitive options; that is, "Looking for the elephant" (e.g., "What do you think might happen if we put your idea together with mine?")

barriers to reframing. It is always tempting to limit our vision to only our initial understanding. According to Perkins, "People have a strong tendency to generate a quick vision of the nature of a solution [based on their familiar data pools] and set off from there" (2000, p. 150).

For example, the obvious solution to the problem of the child playing "Chopsticks" on a stage meant for a master pianist is to remove him from the stage (see Chapter 1 for a description of this scenario). The obvious answer to a child who repeatedly speaks out of turn is to set up a behavioral support program designed to extinguish that response. Correct? Perhaps. Yet, perhaps not. The point is not that these solutions are inappropriate but rather that when prematurely fixed upon as the only options, they leave no room for exploration of other richer alternatives that may both remedy the situation and nurture spirit and sense of self more deeply.

Perkins gave an example of how such fixation on limited frames of reference can blind us to all other options. He said, "There's a man with a mask at home. There's a man coming home. What's going on here?" (2000, p. 29). That is the initial scenario. At this point, what is your interpretation of what might be going on? Can you think of more than one possibility? (Take a few minutes to think about this before reading on.)

A bit more information is then provided with the following questions: "Is the man with the mask a thief? No. Does the man coming home live there? No. Is the man with the mask going to hurt the man coming home? No" (Perkins, 2000, p. 29). Does this additional data change how you are thinking about (i.e., framing) this situation?

How are you framing "home?" Are you framing it as a dwelling or house? What about the man with a mask? Are you framing him as a thief? These initial interpretative frames are what exclude other interpretations. Perkins (2000) provides three possible interpretations other than the most obvious one: 1) it's a baseball game, 2) it's a surprise costume birthday party, or 3) the man is returning to a flooded home where a diver is underwater trying to retrieve some valuables!

Such varied interpretations may seem nonsensical at first. Nevertheless, developing a wide range of options, by bringing to our attention options that we may overlook, can play a valuable role in developing creative and compassionate responses that nurture children's spirits and sense of self (see Chapter 11). Behaviors are not always what they seem, especially when grounded in diverse models of agency. Is a child who fails to respond to the teacher while continuing to talk with another child inattentive? Or, is that child in fact exquisitely attentive to a classmate perceived to be experiencing a difficulty (which the teacher obviously is not). Is it the teacher who is inattentive to that child's need to take care of the other child? What if, instead of dismissing the child's behavior as inappropriate, the teacher instead acknowledged the variations in how we pay attention and to whom? What if, instead of concluding that this child did not know how to pay attention appropriately, she framed the problem as one of diversity in their understanding of roles and rules related to attention? In the first case, she is left with a perceived need to teach attention, perhaps inadvertently ending up limiting the child's understanding and skill related to paying attention. In the second, she can leverage the child's existing ability to pay attention, using it as a basis for extending the child's repertoire of "paying attention" behaviors and simultaneously teaching respect for diversity (see Part III for more examples).

This type of brainstorming sets the stage for what might be possible when both options (e.g., listening to the teacher and paying attention to the other child) are kept on the table and are not polarized as antagonistic to one another. To do otherwise (i.e., to limit alternatives to only one option), whereas perhaps more efficient in the short run, decreases both the child's and teacher's behavioral repertoires, as well as potentially negating resources and potential strengths that could support the development of the more desired behaviors in the future.

Examples and Nonexamples of *Harmonizing*

Table 9.6 illustrates the strategy of *Harmonizing*. It provides examples of how *Harmonizing* might look or sound, as well as some nonexamples of what its absence might look or sound like. The examples emphasize a perspective that allows for two views, behaviors, and/or beliefs to be integrated within a broader more inclusive framework (e.g., "What if we could do both things?"). The requisite piece of these examples is the rejection of a need for either party in an interaction to change in order for a situation to be addressed or resolved. The idea is that optimal outcomes require the integration of all existing views, beliefs, and/or behaviors if they are to be responsive and honor connection (e.g., for there to be green, blue must remain blue and yellow must remain yellow).

The nonexamples, while perhaps valid in certain contexts, emphasize forced choice (i.e., this or that) or compromise (i.e., something that requires one or both people in an interaction to change or somehow dilute their views, behaviors, or

Table 9.6. *Harmonizing* examples and nonexamples

Quality	Examples[a]	Nonexamples[b]
	Verbal statements	*Verbal statements*
	"What if we could do both things? What do you think that might look like?"	"As we just discussed, we believe that Matthew really needs one-on-one time with his therapist instead of time in group activities with his peers."
Responsiveness (Honoring connection)	"I think we can let Matthew participate in the activities with his peers as you are suggesting and also provide some of the more specialized one-on-one time with his therapist. One could actually help the other."	"I understand that you'd like something different than what we're proposing, but I don't see how that can be possible at this time."
		"How about a compromise?"
	Nonverbal behaviors	*Nonverbal behaviors*
	Absence of statements that reflect an either-or perspective where only one option can be chosen	Body language that communicates that diverse perspectives cannot both be correct
	Body language that reflects openness to choices other than those proposed by practitioner	

[a]Both the examples and the nonexamples are taken from comments of workshop participants describing specific situations. We thank all workshop participants who gave permission for their comments to be used as part of our research data.

[b]The nonexamples are not necessarily incorrect or inappropriate; however, they do not reflect the strategy of *Harmonizing*.

beliefs) (e.g., "How about some of this and some of that?" or "How about alternating behaviors?"). As long as one person has to give up or change a value, belief, behavior, or perspective in order for there to be progress or resolution, *Harmonizing* has not been accomplished. The idea is that the loss of any one perspective diminishes the richness of the eventual outcome. (See also Part IV for more concrete examples of *Harmonizing*.)

Self-Reflection Questions

Two types of self-reflection questions can be asked when thinking about *Harmonizing* (see Table 9.7). The first type explores our perspective on the possibility of transforming contradictions into paradoxes. Questions of this type can include the following: "To what degree do I believe that the other's behaviors and/or beliefs can be valuable to this situation?" "To what degree do I believe that there may be a resolution and/or option other than the one I believe is the best? In other words, to what degree am I open to releasing my either-or forced choice perspective?" This type of question explores one's perspective on the possibility of 3rd Space.

The second type of question is more specific. It actively explores how apparently opposite or contradictory perspectives and/or behaviors can complement each other: "What might X plus Y equal?" "What might happen if the respective strengths of each perspective and/or behavior are integrated rather than divided?" "What greater, more inclusive option(s) might emerge within 3rd Space rather than dualistic space?"

Table 9.7. Self-reflection questions for *Harmonizing* strategy

HARMONIZING
(Disposition: Setting the Stage for Miracles)

General questions

  To what degree do I believe the other's behaviors/beliefs can be of value to this situation?

  To what degree do I believe there may be a resolution/option other than the one I believe is best?

  To what degree am I open to releasing my either-or forced choice perspective?

Specific questions

  What might X + Y equal?

  What might happen if the respective strengths of each perspective/behavior were integrated rather than divided?

  What greater (i.e. more inclusive) options might emerge from using a 3rd Space perspective?

Both types of questions at the core of Setting the Stage for Miracles in that they support the generation of unforeseen and unanticipated outcomes responsive to the needs of all involved and not just to those with the strongest agenda.

CASE REVIEW

This portion of the chapter turns once again to the case study included at the end of the introduction to Part III. In this chapter, Mrs. Miller's, Justin's, and Mrs. Taylor's interactions are addressed in relation to the strategies of *Joining* and *Harmonizing*. This section examines Mrs. Miller's interactions with Justin at the time of the reported incident and with Justin's mother, Mrs. Taylor, during their meeting following that incident. Table 9.8 presents the summary of this discussion in a framework similar to that used in Tables 7.8 and 8.8, but in relation to *Joining* and *Harmonizing*. The following discussion is, of course, based only on the information provided in the case. One of the results of this type of examination may well be the determination that further information needs to be gathered. (As with the review in Chapters 7 and 8, this review does not provide suggestions for what might have been done differently; that aspect is addressed in Part IV, where alternative behaviors are discussed.)

Mrs. Miller and Justin

There is little evidence of *Joining* in the incident involving Justin and his teacher, Mrs. Miller, at the playground. Mrs. Miller's understanding of Justin's behavior appears to stem from the perspective of behavior as individual and relatively independent of either the early childhood environment or the surrounding behaviors—both hers and that of Justin's peers. There is no evidence that Mrs. Miller is paying attention to her role in what happened (e.g., why was Justin apparently unsupervised at that moment given his previous behaviors?). Knowing that Justin had a history of disruptive behavior, could Mrs. Miller have perhaps paid closer attention to his actions? In addition, it is clear that Justin is now expected by everyone to exhibit such negative and disruptive behavior. Has he been given any messages about his ability or lack thereof to behave differently? How consistently is he re-

Table 9.8. *Summary of case review: Joining and Harmonizing*

DISPOSITIONS	
Choosing Relationship over Control	Setting the Stage for Miracles
Joining	*Harmonizing*
Mrs. Miller & Justin	Mrs. Miller & Justin
1) **Implicit or explicit acknowledgment of connection** No evidence that Mrs. Miller is aware of a distinct perspective that might be connected with her own	1) **Lateral thinking statements** No evidence of attempts to reframe situation
2) **Reference to past experiences** No reference to her own experiences with frustration or aggression	2) **Prompting for 3rd Space options** No evidence of how Justin's underlying need or motivation might harmonize with need for more skilled social behavior
3) **Acknowledgment of how diverse behaviors/ beliefs could complement each other** No evidence evidence of such acknowledgment	3) **Identification of unitive options** None identified
Mrs. Miller & Mrs. Taylor	Mrs. Miller & Mrs. Taylor
1) **Implicit or explicit acknowledgment of connection** Seems aware that Mrs. Taylor may have a different view but seems to see it only as limiting connection	1) **Lateral thinking statements** No evidence of attempts to reframe situation
2) **Reference to past experiences** No reference to her own experiences of frustration, hope, or desperation	2) **Prompting for 3rd Space options** No evidence of awareness that Mrs. Taylor's current behavior/perspective could complement her own
3) **Acknowledgment of how diverse behaviors/ beliefs could complement each other** No evidence of such acknowledgment	3) **Identification of unitive options** None identified
There is always a third choice	

(Left margin label: BEHAVIORAL EVIDENCE)

ceiving the message that his current behavior is expected? From the information in the case, it seems likely that there is little attention given to the times when such behavior is not present. Neither the fact that there is a shared perception of Justin as a child who cannot behave appropriately nor that there might be alternative perceptions are addressed explicitly as a possible factor in that behavior.

This latter fact is important. Although the focus of *Joining* is the acknowledgement of a shared perspective, it requires the acknowledgement that there is more than one way to view a situation. *Harmonizing* requires that at least two notes be identified before they can be harmonized; otherwise there is nothing to harmonize. When one perceives that there is only one note, or perspective, no need for harmonizing can be recognized. Because there is no such acknowledgment apparent in this situation, there can be no *Harmonizing*. There is no evidence that Mrs. Miller has even thought about Justin's need to establish and enforce his own boundaries, which he is now doing at the expense of appropriate interactions, much less about how to harmonize that need with the need for more appropriate interactions with peers. The situation at this point can best be described as being responsive only to Mrs. Miller's needs.

Mrs. Miller and Mrs. Taylor

There is a similar lack of evidence for *Joining* in Mrs. Miller's interactions with Mrs. Taylor. Although Mrs. Miller does meet with Mrs. Taylor, there is no evidence that she wishes to create a joint context within which they could discuss the situation as a shared problem rather than only as Justin's problem and, consequently, Mrs. Taylor's problem as well. In fact, in suggesting that the Center is not the right place for Justin, Mrs. Miller is in effect communicating that she wants little to do with the identified problem!

As in the previous discussion, *Harmonizing* cannot be accomplished without first *Joining*. Without acknowledging that there is more than one perspective (there are, in fact, at least four—Mrs. Miller's, Mrs. Taylor's, Justin's, and Justin's peers)— the need for *Harmonizing* will not emerge. Unfortunately, without addressing the larger issue of responsiveness, it is likely that Mrs. Miller will face similar problems with other children in the future as a result of the perception and understanding of such "problems" that resides in her beliefs and behaviors. Ever wonder why some practitioners always seem to get "those" children or "those" families?

This case is all too representative of many such situations that involve children with challenging behaviors. The root "problem" is, typically, perceived as solely the child's and/or the family's with the early childhood practitioners and/or institutions perceiving themselves as only collateral participants who, in essence, are external to the problem and only have a problem because of the presence of the child or family.

Part IV discusses and illustrates how scenarios such as this case can be perceived and responded to quite differently while still acknowledging the need to expand children's behavioral repertoires beyond the current challenging behaviors.

DISCUSSION QUESTIONS AND ACTIVITIES

1. Discuss the difference between perceiving a situation as a shared problem and perceiving it as one in which the responsibility and/or need to change is primarily assigned to only one of the participants while the other is perceived as having nothing to do with the situation.

2. Look at the following dichotomies. Can you think of a way in which they can be harmonized? Remember, *Harmonizing* is not about compromise. Black and white, for example, do not harmonize into gray! Instead they harmonize into the perception of a distinct object, which could not be perceived if there was only black or white. (Without the interplay of shadow and light—i.e., black and white—we would be unable to discern that shape of any object.)

    • Order and chaos

    • Strength and weakness

- Authority and compliance

- Independence and dependence

3. Think of a recent interaction between yourself and someone who disagreed with you. Brainstorm ways in which the contrasting opinions could have been harmonized (e.g., order and chaos harmonize into creativity, which requires both).

4. Read the discussion in Chapter 5 on 3rd Space. Find a Magic Eye book and see if you can find the hidden 3-dimensional images. Discuss how this phenomenon relates to *Harmonizing*.

Skilled Dialogue Applications

Weaving Dispositions and Strategies

The final part of this book provides the more specific information necessary for crafting respectful, reciprocal, and responsive interactions using Skilled Dialogue. It reviews material previously presented in relation to case studies drawn from our (Barrera and Kramer) own experiences, as well as those of the practitioners with whom we work. The chapters that follow emphasize the use of Skilled Dialogue in situations involving social and behavioral differences, whether stemming from cultural linguistic diversity or from other sources.

It is important to note that Skilled Dialogue is not just for situations in which there is disagreement or other significant discomfort. Situations that go smoothly also reflect Skilled Dialogue elements albeit more implicitly. In these situations, it tends to happen almost without thought. We easily welcome our friends, for example, and allow them to state their perspectives, which make sense to us because we know them so well. We appreciate their views and join with them, having found ways of harmonizing our respective differences over the years. In more challenging situations, however, Skilled Dialogue needs to be thoughtfully and explicitly applied—situations in which *Welcoming* and *Allowing* may not come easily, or in which we can neither make sense of another's behavior nor appreciate it, much less join or harmonize differences that seem impossible to bridge.

In all situations, however, the primary motivation for the promotion of Skilled Dialogue as a tool for crafting respectful, reciprocal, and responsive interactions rests on the following overarching premise:

> As we engage in supporting and promoting the development of children, it is our job and responsibility to look for and find the strengths and resources that define children's capacity to learn and grow in life-enhancing ways. Only when we do so can we truly support and promote children's spirits and sense of self.

Carrying out that job and responsibility requires that we also look for and find the strengths and resources that define our own capacity to learn and grow, as well as

167

that of the families and other practitioners with whom we work. It is as simple—and as challenging—as that.

Each time we allow ourselves to meet that challenge, we quite literally set the stage for miracles, dissolving false limits that have impeded change up until that point and creating options deemed impossible by those limits. It is this limit dissolving and option creating that ultimately provides the strongest support for positive behavioral change, for it is only when children and/or adults can see and move beyond their current perspectives that previously unaccepted or unimaginable choices become possible. All too often, however, all we can see or believe possible is what needs to change (i.e., undesired or inappropriate behaviors). This focus then blinds us to the existing strengths and resources that can be found within or underlying those very behaviors. These strengths and resources, once identified and supported, inspire, fuel, and support desired change from the inside out, rather than merely imposing from the outside in.

There are, of course, multiple avenues to look for and find strengths and resources. There are other relational approaches to communication and interaction. There are also other approaches to the integration of diverse perspectives. Skilled Dialogue has much in common with many of these approaches. It is unique, however, in two respects: 1) its integration of both relational and 3rd Space perspectives, and 2) its use of six specific strategies to embody those perspectives. These aspects are discussed here from the perspective of the Skilled Dialogue process.

SKILLED DIALOGUE PROCESS

Although built on a relatively simple framework, Skilled Dialogue may, at times, appear complex due to its nonlinear nature. The interdependence of each of its elements with every other element precludes the type of linear understanding that tends to be preferred in ENC contexts. For that reason, Skilled Dialogue may present significant challenges, especially when it is first being learned. As it is practiced, however, its simplicity re-emerges.

Some key things to remember when applying Skilled Dialogue are discussed here. First, no quality is ever truly separate from another. Responsiveness, for example, both builds on and sustains respect. Reciprocity is, ultimately, as necessary for respect as for responsiveness, and so forth. The two dispositions are similarly intertwined. Setting the Stage for Miracles cannot be reliably set without the disposition of Choosing Relationship over Control and vice versa. The six strategies, although linked to individual qualities and dispositions, are also interdependent. Although *Welcoming,* for example, is an important prequel to *Allowing, Allowing* helps to reinforce *Welcoming.* One quality is never truly separate from the others, one disposition is not complete without the others, and one strategy is insufficient on its own.

Second, Skilled Dialogue is a "craft." Neither strictly science nor strictly art, it is a semistructured process. The sequence of phases described in this section is, therefore, intended to be highly flexible, especially once the total process is learned. In some cases, for example, establishing reciprocity yields information that makes

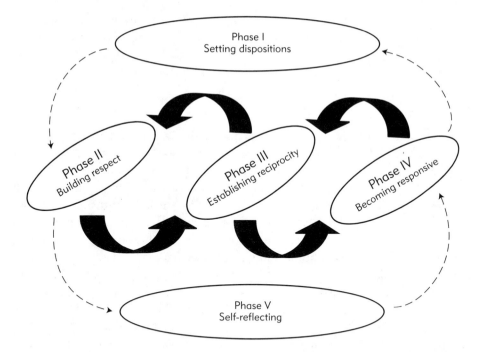

Figure IV.1. Skilled Dialogue process.

it easier for respect to be built. Only with such flexibility can Skilled Dialogue become a process that recognizes and addresses the unique aspects of particular situations. There are, therefore, no totally "right" answers to the exercises and questions provided in this section. The "answers" given in our discussions, such as those in the following chapters represent only one set of possible suggestions. Others may be equally valid. Miracles, after all, can neither be predicted nor controlled!

Figure IV.1 depicts the phases that define Skilled Dialogue. Although Phases I and V are relatively time bound (i.e., Phase I takes place prior to an interaction and Phase V after an interaction), the sequence of Phases II, III, and IV can be much more flexible. The linear fashion in which these phases are discussed, therefore, is more a function of the structure of written language than of the Skilled Dialogue process itself.

Phase I: Setting Dispositions

This first phase focuses on setting the two Skilled Dialogue dispositions: Choosing Relationship over Control and Setting the Stage for Miracles. Prior to planning a specific interaction, it is important to review the nature of each disposition and its critical aspects (see Tables 4.1, 4.2, 5.1, and 5.2). This review helps bring to light how we may be approaching an interaction. It also allows time to focus on strengthening the critical aspects that may be weak or missing. For example, asking ourselves what we believe about the competence of the person with whom we plan to interact can remind us that competence and expertise are not the same. A person can be competent (i.e., capable) and yet not have expertise in a particular area. Similarly, taking the time to reflect on whether or not we are truly curious about another's perspective can remind us to become more mindful and prevent us from acting on our presuppositions. Phase I is, in effect, a prereflection phase that helps to ensure we are disposed to both choose relationship and set the stage for miracles.

Phase II: Building Respect

Phase II starts a more active phase of Skilled Dialogue. It focuses on using the strategies associated with building respect. These strategies—*Welcoming* and *Allowing*—cross dispositions, one expressing our intent to choose relationship over control and the other to set the stage for miracles. The behavioral indicators listed for each of these strategies are important but not exhaustive. The main thrust of this phase is to decide how best to behaviorally express each disposition for the purpose of building respect (readers may want to review the parts of Chapter 3 that describe and discuss respect). It is important to select behaviors that will be most effective given the particulars of the planned interaction and the people involved. There may be individual variations as well as cultural ones (e.g., relaxed body language may not be as acceptable in some cultures or as authentic for some personalities). This is especially critical the greater the diversity that is present. (Behavioral indicators for the two strategies associated with this phase—*Welcoming* and *Allowing*—are discussed in Chapter 7).

Phase III: Establishing Reciprocity

Similarly, phase III focuses on behavioral expressions that support reciprocity (i.e., the strategies of *Sense-Making* and *Appreciating*). There are some significant cultural and personality factors here as well. In some cultures, for example, it may be deemed undesirable and inappropriate to talk as much as the person perceived to be the authority. In these cases, reciprocity cannot be measured by a comparison of how much each person speaks, but rather by how much time is given to each perspective that is present. A practitioner may need to cautiously give voice to a family's perspective when family members are not comfortable doing so themselves. Or there may be a need to consult someone outside the family who can give information on the family's perspective based on his or her familiarity with the family and/or their culture. In the same way, particular participants may be too shy or too anxious to give full voice to their own perspective. This also needs to be recognized. (The behavioral indicators for the two strategies addressed in this phase—*Sense-Making* and *Appreciating*—are discussed in Chapter 8.)

Phase IV: Becoming Responsive

Phase IV completes the active part of the Skilled Dialogue process. Similar to the two phases before it, Phase IV focuses on behavioral indicators associated with two strategies—*Joining* and *Harmonizing*—but this time for the purpose of becoming responsive to both the situation and the people involved. These strategies are discussed in Chapter 9. Readers may also want to review the definition and description of responsiveness as used in Skilled Dialogue (see Chapter 3). The thrust of this phase is to ensure that the perspectives of all involved are leveraged (i.e., mined for their strengths) so that the options that are ultimately selected reflect a unitive 3rd Space within which everyone's strengths are accessed rather than a divided dualistic space within which only certain strengths are acknowledged. Unlike the previous two phases, the behavioral indicators associated with *Joining* and *Harmonizing* are designed not just to support responsiveness, but to actually create it through the development of such options.

Phase V: Self-Reflecting

The final phase of the Skilled Dialogue process is a postinteraction reflective phase that parallels the first phase. It focuses on assessing the degree to which the Skilled Dialogue dispositions and strategies were actually present in a given interaction and identifying how the presence of these dispositions and strategies might be strengthened in subsequent interactions.

SKILLED DIALOGUE REFLECTION TOOLS

The chapters in this section provide various sample cases along with our reflections on the presence of Skilled Dialogue elements within each. More generally, several reflection tools are provided for use with actual interactions: a Skilled Dialogue Reflection Guide, provided in Appendix C and prompt questions and behavioral indicators for each strategy, provided in Part III and also in Table IV.1. Readers may want to refer to these tools. The purpose of the Guide is to identify and reflect on Skilled Dialogue elements within a particular interaction in a slightly more formal fashion that that modeled in this Part. The Guide is formatted specifically for use either prior to an interaction to set the dispositions and plan for the use of specific behavioral indicators or following an interaction as a self-reflection tool to assess the degree to which dispositions and strategies were present. The first part of this Guide asks for a description of the planned or completed interaction. This description sets the context within which Skilled Dialogue was or will be used. The second part—Overall Evaluation of Interaction—asks users to evaluate both the use of Skilled Dialogue and their overall level of satisfaction with the outcome. This part is used only when the Guide is completed as a postinteraction self-reflection. The third part—Specific Analysis of Skilled Dialogue Dispositions and Strategies—can be used either pre- or postinteraction. It first asks users to assess the degree to which they have set (preinteraction) or to which they expressed (postinteraction) the two Skilled Dialogue dispositions. Space for specific discussion is provided as well. The questions are worded for postinteraction use (e.g., "What helped or hindered my willingness to set this disposition?"). If the Guide was used as a preinteraction planning tool, these need to be reworded in the present tense (e.g., "What may be currently helping or hindering my willingness to set this disposition?"). Similarly, users are asked to rate and reflect on their planned or actual use of the Skilled Dialogue strategies. Feedback from practitioners who have used this form has confirmed its value as a preinteraction planning tool.

Table IV.1. Prompt questions and behavioral indicators for case analysis and reflection

	Choosing Relationship over Control	Setting the Stage for Miracles

Respect

Welcoming	*Allowing*
Question prompts 1. What do I believe about the other's competence? 2. To what degree can I accept the other's behaviors as evidence based (i.e., supported by direct evidence)? 3. To what degree am I willing to communicate unconditional respect? Common behavioral indicators 1. Relaxed body language 2. Affirming and/or neutral comments 3. Explicit use of welcoming comments 4. General statements prior to focusing on specific agenda	Question prompts 1. To what degree am I willing to stay with the tension? 2. To what degree am I willing to release my stories and/or interpretations? 3. To what degree am I willing to perceive the other's perspective(s) as complementary rather than divisive or polarized? Common behavioral indicators 1. Lack of words and/or statements that reflect defensiveness or disrespect 2. Lack of interruptions; attentive listening 3. Absence of proposed solutions, suggestions, or interpretations

Reciprocity

Sense-Making	*Appreciating*
Question prompts 1. To what degree was I or am I curious about the other's stories? 2. Did I or do I have a learner's attitude and mindset? 3. Was I or am I willing to collect information nonjudgmentally? 4. Was I able to or can I examine things from another's perspective?	Question prompts 1. To what degree am I willing to identify *gold nuggets* in the other's behaviors and/or beliefs? 2. To what degree am I willing to recognize exaggerated positive behavior at the core of the other's negative behavior? 3. To what degree am I willing to learn from the other's behaviors and/or beliefs?

Common behavioral indicators
1. Explicit reframing of negative into positive
2. Identification of positive intent at core of exaggerated behaviors and/or beliefs
3. Explicit comments regarding the value of the other's behaviors and/or beliefs

Harmonizing

Question prompts
1. To what degree am I willing to reframe my perceptions?
2. To what degree am I open to brainstorming?
3. To what degree am I willing to "think in threes?"

Common behavioral indicators
1. Lateral thinking statements
2. Prompts for 3rd Space options
3. Identification of unitive options (options that integrate my perspective and the other's perspective)

Responsiveness

Joining

Question prompts
1. Did I or can I recognize that all behavior is jointly constructed?
2. Was I or am I willing to change the message(s) I am sending?
3. Was I or am I willing to identify how my behaviors and the other's behaviors might be complementary?

Common behavioral indicators
1. Explicit acknowledgment of how the other's behaviors and/or beliefs connect with my own
2. References to times I have behaved and/or believed the same as the other
3. Explicit acknowledgment of how the other's behavior complements my own

The two-column case analysis format used to discuss and analyze cases in Chapters 10 and 11 is slightly different from the Skilled Dialogue Reflection Guide, yet it contains all of the same elements. This columnar format is designed only for use with this text. Because these cases are written out, it is easier to discuss them in a format that allows for parallel analysis and does not require continuous back and forth page turning. Readers are, however, encouraged to use whichever form best suits them. Both formats ask for the same information, simply in a different format.

PROMPT QUESTIONS AND BEHAVIORAL INDICATORS

In addition to the Skilled Dialogue Reflection Guide, we also provide a series of "prompt questions" useful in case analysis and self-reflection (see Table IV.1). These prompt questions address the same critical aspects of both dispositions and strategies discussed in previous chapters and can be used either for planning an upcoming interaction or for reflecting on an interaction that has already taken place. One question, for example, asks, "To what degree, for example, were you willing to believe that the other person was competent, albeit perhaps not in agreement with you?" That is, to what degree were you willing to accept that the other's behavior had a valid evidence base even if it was quite different from yours? This willingness might have been clearly expressed or not. To check for its expression, common behavioral indicators are provided below each set of questions. These behavioral indicators have been discussed in previous chapters. They are simply summarized here for convenience.

In looking at the behaviors associated with *Welcoming*, for example, were any of these present in your interaction? To what degree? Were other behaviors not listed but still indicative of *Welcoming* present? The overarching concern is the overt external expressions rather than the internal inclinations. The reflection is, thus, twofold: 1) To what degree were the critical aspects present? and 2) If present, how were they expressed behaviorally?

The following chapters illustrate the application of Skilled Dialogue. The materials just discussed are used as guides for reflecting on and analyzing the degree to which dispositions and strategies are present in any particular interaction. See also the Skilled Dialogue Self-Assessment in Appendix C.

CHAPTER ORGANIZATION

This text is written in a reiterative and spiral fashion rather than a purely linear one. Part I presents the philosophical and theoretical context within which we believe these strategies can best be implemented. Part II provides initial information on the strategies as well as on the larger framework of qualities and dispositions that support them. Part III discusses the three qualities of respect, reciprocity, and responsiveness that are the defining characteristics of Skilled Dialogue, and describes the individual strategies associated with each.

Part IV continues the discussion, focusing on the concrete application of the strategies from the perspective of specific situations (see Table IV.2 for an overview of Part IV). Each case in Chapters 10 and 11 is discussed in relation to the dispo-

Table IV.2. Chapters 10–12 organization

Chapter	Cases
10 Challenging Adult–Adult Interactions	1. Supervisor and practitioner (Mary and Susan)
	2. Practitioner and parent (Karen and Mrs. Cooper)
	3. Two practitioners (preschool) (Marilyn and Debra)
	4. Practitioner and family (Mr. James and Mrs. Faria)
11 Challenging Adult–Child Interactions	1. Practitioner, child, and parent (Mrs. Miller revisited)
	2. Teacher and child (Mrs. Bailey and Carmen)
	3. Teacher and child with autism (BJ and Miss Anne)
	4. Reflective teacher (Miss Sheri)
12 Practice Cases	Shorter case studies illustrating various strategies with discussion questions

sitions and their associated strategies. Choosing Relationship over Control, for example, taps into our socioemotional abilities and strengths. Our analysis of its presence focuses, therefore, on the degree to which there is evidence that participants were disposed to create a *relational* space where disparate identities could be welcomed, disparate voices could be placed into contexts that make sense, and the connections between disparate perspectives could be acknowledged.

Being disposed to choose relationship over control calls on us to give priority to establishing rapport with others, rather than primarily on "fixing" a given situation (i.e., to relate with them as more than just someone who needs to change or carry out our predetermined agenda). The rationale for the disposition for Choosing Relationship over Control is grounded in the evidence-based belief discussed in Chapter 1, especially the belief that "I–thou trumps I–it every time." It is a core disposition toward nurturing children's spirits and sense of self.

The disposition of Setting the Stage for Miracles is similarly discussed. This disposition taps into our capacity for cognitive creativity. It focuses on creating a *cognitive* space within which disparate identities can be mutually allowed, disparate voices can be simultaneously appreciated, and disparate perspectives can be harmonized. Particular attention is paid to the idea and practice of 3rd Space thinking. It is, after all, the use of 3rd Space thinking that quite literally "sets the stage" for "miracles" (i.e., outcomes that lie outside the narrow limits of dualistic thinking and that leverage and integrate the strengths of contradictions into inclusive and unanticipated mutually generated options).

Also examined in relation to each case is the explicit use of Skilled Dialogue strategies as these define the relational space where disparate identities can be welcomed, disparate voices can be placed into contexts that make sense, and the connections between disparate perspectives can be acknowledged. Each strategy is discussed and illustrated in relation to the concrete aspects of the cases presented. In some cases, most of the strategies may be clearly present. In others, few or none of the strategies may be present to any significant degree. In these latter cases, we discuss how they might have been introduced into the interaction.

The material in both Chapters 9 and 10 is rooted in the assumption that the strengths and resources most relevant to any particular behavioral change or learning are best accessed and mined through establishing relationship and dissolving the limits of existing perceptions and conceptions. It is in this way that Skilled Dialogue strategies can be tools for crafting authentic behavioral supports that can, in turn, ensure the outcomes of the more specific and external positive behavioral supports more commonly addressed in the literature. Chapter 11 illustrates how this might be as it focuses on interactions between adults and children. It presents an array of case studies and vignettes of varying length and detail.

The cases examine Skilled Dialogue applications from different perspectives. In Mrs. Miller's case, which was introduced in Chapter 7 and is revisited at the beginning of Chapter 10, Skilled Dialogue is discussed from the perspective of the practitioner. This is not its sole application, however. It could also be discussed from other perspectives, such as those of family members, fellow EC practitioners, and even the perspective of the child involved. Although these latter perspectives do not allow for conscious and explicit self-reflection as do adult perspectives, they can be used by adults to teach children about Choosing Relationship over Control and Setting the Stage for Miracles. All four types of perspectives—family members, practitioners, colleagues, and children—are represented in this part of the book.

Challenging Adult–Adult Interactions

This chapter presents four cases involving interactions among adults (e.g., practitioners, colleagues, family members, supervisors). Background information is presented for each case, followed by an analysis of the degree to which Skilled Dialogue dispositions and strategies are in evidence. (This analysis follows Part II of the Skilled Dialogue Reflection Guide in Appendix C). The first case is that of Mary and Susan, a lead teacher and a director at an early childhood center. This case involves contrasting perceptions of Mary's behaviors with families. The next two cases—Mrs. Cooper and Karen (a practitioner and a parent) and Marilyn and Debra (two teachers)—involve similar contrasting views. In the first of these, the contrast occurs in how to respond to children's achievements. In the second case, there are contrasting views of how to respond to children's behaviors. The final case, Mr. James, focuses on a practitioner's decision to focus on his own behavior rather than on another's behavior.

It is our intent with these cases to illustrate what Skilled Dialogue might look like, as well as how to think about its application to particular situations. As a dynamic process, however, such illustration is significantly limited by a written format. Readers are encouraged to send their questions directly to the authors via our web site if they wish additional information or explanation (http://www.skilleddialogue .com).

A two-column format is used to analyze each of the cases. (For each case, the numbers in parentheses in the case description column refer to the numbers by particular statements in the analysis column.) This format is used within the text in place of the Skilled Dialogue Reflection Guide that is normally used (see Appendix C). Given that these cases are written out, the use of this format reduces the need for turning pages back and forth between the case and the analysis. All of the items addressed in Part III of the Skilled Dialogue Reflection Guide are contained in this format as well.

CASE ANALYSIS

The analysis of each case study targets particular sections of the interaction specific to either dispositions or strategies, following the five-phase process shown in

Figure IV.1 of the introduction to Part IV. Each case starts with setting the Skilled Dialogue dispositions. The judgment as to the presence of the dispositions is based on the prompts for *all* critical aspects associated with relevant disposition (see Tables 7.8, 8.8, and 9.8), as well as on the presence or absence of the behavioral indicators shown in Table IV.1. Then each analysis moves through building respect, establishing reciprocity, and becoming responsive. Here, the focus of the analysis is on the strategies associated with building respect, establishing reciprocity, and becoming responsive. These are identified as they come up in the scenario, rather than in the strict horizontal sequencing discussed previously. The last phase shown in Figure IV.1—self-reflecting—is not discussed as it is represented by the analysis itself.

MARY AND SUSAN

Background Information   The Dalton City Preschool and Child Care Center is located about 10 miles from the city center and serves a diverse population of young children, including Hispanic, Middle Eastern, African American, Puerto Rican, and ENC. The majority of the families qualify for food stamps, although most have at least one parent working full or part time. The center is located on the edge of a historically African American neighborhood. Mary Hinds, who was just promoted to the position of lead teacher at Dalton City Preschool and Child Care Center, told a colleague, Sonya, her good news. "I have been hoping for a position like this for years. I can still teach 2 days a week and do home visits 3 days a week."

When she saw Sonya again a few weeks later, however, her enthusiasm was glaringly absent. "What happened?" Sonya asked. "You'll never believe me," Mary responded. "Susan called me in for a meeting this morning because she was concerned about my performance." She proceeded to describe who Susan was and what had happened.

Susan Matthews was the director of Dalton and served on the selection committee that the board of directors formed to fill the new position of lead teacher. Susan, a person of ENC, was also once a teacher at Dalton and moved into administration about 7 years ago. The position of lead teacher had been created when the board suggested Susan create the position of lead teacher in order for the program to meet accreditation demands for parent involvement and parent education as required by city and state grants. During our meeting she told me that I had great energy and was doing a wonderful job, *but* I was spending too much time with the African American families. On top of that, she said I was too informal with them."

"'I have gotten reports that you seem to get off track, lose sight of the reason for your visits, and end up just chatting and visiting. That is not what we hired you for,' was what she said. I was shocked. I didn't know what to say and just listened and then left. But I have to meet with her again. Not only do I not want her to evaluate me negatively, I have to say something if I'm to keep being responsive to the needs of these families. What can I do?"

"I've just been to this training session on Skilled Dialogue," Sonya said. "This sounds like the perfect case to use it. Let me tell you all about it." Mary and Sonya talked for several more hours over the course of the next few days. As they reviewed the Skilled Dialogue notes, Mary reflected back on her conversation with Susan. Susan was basically telling her she was favoring the African American families by spending too much time and being too friendly with them because she (Mary) was also African American. Mary became more frustrated just thinking about it! She promptly e-mailed Susan for a meeting on Thursday.

Case description	Analysis
	Phase I: Setting dispositions
	Choosing Relationship over Control: Mary had worked hard to set this disposition. She reminded herself that she could not control Susan's perspective or opinions, nor should it be necessary.
	Setting the Stage for Miracles: Rather than telling herself that there wasn't much probability of a positive interaction, given the last one, Mary reminded herself that outcomes can never really be predicted and that, often, what seems inevitable never happens.
	Phases II–IV: Respect (*Welcoming* and *Allowing*), reciprocity (*Sense-Making* and *Appreciating*), and responsiveness (*Joining* and *Harmonizing*)
Mary greeted Susan cheerfully, "Hi, I am so glad you are able to see me today." (1)	(1) *Welcoming:* Mary first greeted Susan and expressed her anticipation of the coming meeting. Susan, however, remained focused on the previous conversation and did not greet Mary in a similar fashion. In fact, she does not really greet Mary at all.
"Looks like the children were baking today," was Susan's comment in reply.	
"They had great fun making cookies—we used those giant fall leaf cookie cutters. Of course the use of frosting was very creative. Give me a minute, I just want to wash my hands and take off this apron. I don't want to leave a trail of flour! Grab some coffee if you like." (2)	(2) *Allowing:* Mary consciously refrained from immediately taking the floor and used *Allowing* to give Susan the opportunity to lead the discussion if she wished to, thus reinforcing the dispositions of

(continued)

Case description	Analysis

"Okay, Mary, how can I help you?" Susan asked as she sat down at the table with a fresh cup of coffee.

Choosing Relationship over Control and Setting the Stage for Miracles.

"Well, Susan, it is not so much needing help as wanting to better understand your concerns about my interactions with our African American families. I thought really carefully about what you said, and I guess I am just a little confused. Can you tell me about what you want me to do or what I am not doing correctly?"(3)

(3) *Sense-Making:* Mary used the strategy of *Sense-Making* by asking for further clarification of Susan's concerns.

"Mary, it is simple, you are spending too much time at their houses, and it seems like you feel you have to be their best friend, and that is not the point of the program. All the families should have the same time with you. Maybe if you were a little more formal you would get better outcomes. That's it." (4)

(4) *Allowing:* Mary listened to Susan without interrupting, allowing her to express her perspective fully.

Mary responded, "Yes, I understand. I know it is critical to the program that I gather the information and complete the forms for each family. And I really admire how you have increased the accountability of the program, especially your concern that every family is visited in a timely manner so that no one is forgotten. Your dedication to the families is so important. That is why this position was created—to build relationships with our families. (5)

(5) *Appreciating:* Mary was careful to express her recognition of the value of Susan's work and perspective.

"Susan, has it been your experience that each family has its own needs?" Mary went on to say. (6)

"Yes," Susan responded.

(6 and 7) *Joining:* Mary then began to connect her perspective with that of

(continued)

Case description	Analysis
"That each family has its own family dynamics?" Mary continued. "Like grandmothers, aunts, or others besides the immediate families living at home? Who may be ill? Who have lost their jobs?" (7)	Susan's so that Susan could see that they are not in opposition.
"Yes," said Susan. "Those things are critically important; they certainly have an impact on the children. But you can find out that information in a more efficient way. You just need to make better use of your time, Mary."	
"I'm glad to hear you put it that way. My concern is with collecting the information effectively, and I believe that part of that is paying attention to *how* information is gathered in a sensitive and culturally appropriate way. (8) So, to be respectful and culturally responsive, I interact somewhat differently with each family. In the case of our African American families, I spend more time talking *with* them rather than *to* them. I need to hear their stories of what is going on in their lives. To serve them best, I need to build trust and bonds and share language and experience. And you know what Susan? That takes time—that is how the African American culture works, that is why I am so successful with them, and that is why our enrollment in the community has increased." (9)	(8) *Harmonizing:* Once she could see that Susan had joined with her, Mary moved on to further frame their perspectives into a single perspective, showing how one could complement the other.

(9) *Joining:* Mary returned to *Joining* by restating Susan's administrative priority. |
| Susan responded, "I had not really thought of it that way, Mary. You have really made a difference for our families, especially the involvement of the African American families in the program. But I am still concerned about the time spent." | |

(continued)

Case description	Analysis

"We have the same goals, Susan—every family is visited every month, *and* we want to build respectful relationships and be culturally responsive. That often will take additional time at each visit. So how can we do both?" (10)

(10) *Harmonizing:* Having strengthened the connection between their two perspectives, Mary then addressed *Harmonizing* more explicitly by clearly identifying their two positions and explicitly communicating that one is not in opposition with the other.

"Mary, I need to have you visit each family every month. I cannot change that. I also agree you need to individualize your interactions with each family as needed and that may take additional time per visit. I am not sure how we can do both."

"Susan, maybe we could arrange the schedule differently? Maybe let the parents select the time for their visit. Or, I could even meet with two families together when they live in the same building. I could extend my home visit times on Tuesdays and Thursdays and schedule the African American families on those days." (11)

(11) *Harmonizing:* Mary then identified some possible third choices to further illustrate how her perspective could work together with Susan's without forcing a choice between the two.

"Mary, all of those ideas are great! You work out a schedule so you will still visit every family once a month while taking that time you need or that each family needs, and I will review it."

"Thank you, Susan. I think this will work out to meet both our needs. I will e-mail you the revised schedule tonight."

KAREN AND MRS. COOPER

Background Information   Karen, Anna's mother, has brought Anna to Lakewood Day Center since she was 8 weeks old. She always dropped her off at 6:45 a.m. and picked her up at 5:30 p.m. Mrs. Cooper, the caregiver, considered Karen a typical working mother. Anna was always clean, happy, and rarely missed a day. Karen has always appeared pleased with the staff at the center and often lingered to chat when picking up Anna in the evening. In a 3-week span following the last holiday, however, something changed. Karen requested that Mrs. Cooper keep Anna at the center until 6 p.m., the latest time possible, and she seemed short and irritated with the staff.

Thirteen-month-old Anna just started to take her first steps at Lakewood. She had been making progress each day, becoming steadier and gradually taking a step or two before she dropped to a crawl and sped off. Mrs. Cooper, and the rest of the staff were so excited and happily encouraged her to walk to them, congratulating her with hugs and smiles. Everyone at Lakewood celebrated when one of their little ones started to walk! Today Anna walked across the room by herself! Everyone clapped and encouraged her to try again. Mrs. Cooper was thrilled and took a photo to give to Anna's mother that evening when she came by to pick Anna up.

Case description	Analysis
"Karen, you will never guess what happened today!" Anna walked all the way across the room all by herself. She was so proud of herself; I just had to take a picture for you!" Karen barely looked at the photo as she grabbed it out of Mrs. Cooper's hand and said a very stern "Thank you" as she picked up Anna and quickly left. Mrs. Cooper is confused, hurt, and angry by Karen's behavior. She simply wanted to share the special day with her. She was still angry that evening when she got home. What was wrong with Karen? She was just trying to help her. Why had Karen changed so much? Why had she changed Anna's hours without explanation? Why was she so angry with her?	
Then Mrs. Cooper remembered a 2-day Skilled Dialogue workshop she attended last summer. She had used some of the strategies now and then. This situation was perfect to try them again. She reviewed the handouts and training materials from the workshop. She would be a good listener and let Karen tell her why she was so angry.	**Phase I: Setting dispositions** *Choosing Relationship over Control:* Mrs. Cooper believed that she had chosen relationship when she had decided to share her excitement about Anna's progress. Realizing that had not been confirmed by Karen, she revisits the scenario and decides to try again.

(continued)

Case description	Analysis

Setting the Stage for Miracles: By not "freezing" her state of anger and confusion, Mrs. Cooper opened the door for a changed outcome, thus resetting her disposition to set the stage for miracles.

"Karen, it's Mrs. Cooper at Lakewood, I would really like to meet with you when you have time. When is a good time for you? We can meet on a Saturday if you like. Let me know what works best for you. I am looking forward to hearing from you!" (1) Karen and Mrs. Cooper decided to meet on a Saturday morning at a park nearby so Anna and her older sister could play.

Phases II–IV: Respect (*Welcoming* and *Allowing*), reciprocity (*Sense-Making* and *Appreciating*), and responsiveness (*Joining* and *Harmonizing*)

(1) *Welcoming* and *Allowing:* Mrs. Cooper both welcomed Karen ("I'd really like to meet with you" and "I'm looking forward to hearing from you") and allowed her to voice her agreement or disagreement as to the proposed time.

"Hi Karen! Hi girls! I am so glad we could get together. I know your weekends are valuable time, so thank you for taking the time to meet." (2) The girls went off to play on the preschool playground equipment, and Karen and Mrs. Cooper found a bench nearby to watch them play.

(2) *Welcoming:* Mrs. Cooper continued to communicate *Welcoming* as they started their meeting.

"Karen, this was the perfect place to meet, you are such a good mom, always thinking about your girls. (3) How have you been doing lately?" (4)

(3) *Appreciating:* Mrs. Cooper shifted into *Appreciating* as she acknowledged Karen's choice of meeting place.

(4) *Sense-Making:* Mrs. Cooper initiated *Sense-Making* by asking a general question about how Karen is.

Karen explained that she was tired. Her supervisor had laid off other employees and those left, if they wanted to keep their job, had to pick up their work. "That is why Anna has to stay late every day. I am so tired when I get home. All I do is feed and bathe the girls and put them to bed, and then we get up and do it again the next day—over and over. This is not what I had planned." (5)

(5 and 6) *Allowing:* Mrs. Cooper listened without interrupting or interjecting any

(continued)

Case description	Analysis

Mrs. Cooper listened attentively and encouraged Karen to talk. (6) Karen shared that she was very tired and knew that she was missing all the important parts of Anna's life. She was sad that she was missing everything Anna was doing.

comments, allowing Karen ample time to state her perspective on the current situations in her life.

"Well, you know, I know lots of mothers who work, so let's figure out what you can do! Could you ask your supervisor for different hours? Maybe you could work longer on some days and leave earlier on others? Hmm, maybe have a sitter at your home after the center closes on some days? You could arrange for another parent to take Anna to your house at 6:00, and then you could work later a few days a week and have some early days, too! I know somebody that may be able to drive Anna home a few days a week. What do you think?" (7)

(7) Stopped using strategies: At this point Mrs. Cooper stopped using any Skilled Dialogue strategies and instead shifted into a problem-solving mode, offering multiple suggestions without really waiting for Karen's input. While useful, a problem-solving mode can often be only one sided, excluding the input of the person with the identified problem. The appropriate Skilled Dialogue strategies to use here would have been *Sense-Making* and *Appreciating* so that Karen could feel that her perspective was both acknowledged and valued. The facile offering of solutions can all too often communicate that "This is easy to figure out—see how many ways I can come up with?", which implies that all the other person had to do was think!

"I really don't think that would work. My supervisor is not going to let me change my hours, and I really am so tired and worn out as it is. I don't think I can stand longer days, and I look forward to taking Anna home at 6:00. We really need to go now; we have errands to run today." (8)

(8) At Karen's abrupt decision to leave, Mrs. Cooper realized that she was no longer really communicating respectfully or reciprocally with her, much less responsively. She silently reminded herself that Karen's situation was one that both makes sense and is valid given the context within which Karen is operating

(continued)

Case description	Analysis

(i.e., she returned to *Sense-Making* and *Appreciating*, albeit nonverbally, as she realized that Karen was running on "fumes," as well as that her reaction earlier had been based on her missing out on the event rather than on the staff sharing it with her).

"I can see how frustrated you must be and how difficult it must seem to change things. It seems like you can choose to work and keep your job or spend time with Anna, but never both." (9)

(9) *Joining:* Mrs. Cooper needed to reconnect, so she chose the strategy of *Joining* to do that. In so doing, she reestablished connection and communicated that she can see the situation from Karen's perspective.

"That's it exactly. My heart wants me to spend time with Anna, but my mind tells me I have to work in order to pay the rent, buy groceries, and provide for her." (10)

(10) Karen acknowledged that she then felt that her perspective was both heard and valued.

"I'm so impressed with how you are dealing with the pressure, Karen. I know it may seem you're not doing it well, but I can see that you do spend time with Anna, like we're doing here today. And you always bring her to school well dressed and fed; that says you really do pay attention to her. I'm sure your supervisor is aware of how conscientious you are about work also. Maybe the problem is not about doing both things, but about recognizing how well you are already doing it." (11)

(11) Mrs. Cooper used *Appreciating* more explicitly to strengthen the renewed connection and simultaneously open the door to seeing the situation from a different perspective, a prerequisite for *Harmonizing*. Though suggestions are made at this point, they differ from the original problem-solving solutions that were offered in that these take into account Karen's perspective.

"I never thought of it that way," Karen said thoughtfully.

Mrs. Cooper said, "You know, one of the things you said bothered you was missing Anna's triumphs. And I know it's not the same as being there, but maybe, if you talked with your supervisor, she'd let you take a short call from us when

(continued)

Case description	Analysis
she's doing something really significant, and we can record it for you to view on your cell phone as it's happening. I realize you couldn't always take the call, but do you think that would help?" (12)	(12) *Harmonizing:* Having stated the two things that seem at odds with each other, Mrs. Cooper illustrates how they might be harmonized into a third option, one that would meet both the need to work and the need to spend time with Anna. (Although it is best to brainstorm jointly with the other person to arrive at this point, in this case, Mrs. Cooper could see that Karen was at a point where she would have had great difficulty generating creative options. By providing one herself, Mrs. Cooper modeled how this could be done in the future.)

MARILYN AND DEBRA

Background Information   Marilyn is an experienced preschool teacher in an urban school district. She has a degree in child development, a prekindergarten to primary teaching credential, and a master's degree in education. She has been teaching for 25 years, the last 10 years of which have been at Wilson Elementary School. Marilyn helped develop and revise the first public school preschool curriculum in the city schools. She is now teaching the children of her former students. She is well respected at the school and in the community, and was chosen Teacher of the Year. Every year parents sign up to have their child in Miss Marilyn's class.

Debra recently transferred to Wilson from a kindergarten—first grade classroom in the district. It is her first year teaching preschool. She had been waiting for an opening and is excited to be co-teaching with Marilyn. Debra is taking graduate courses in early childhood education and is looking forward to applying the theories she is learning to their preschool classroom.

Marilyn and Debra worked closely the week before school, preparing the room and learning centers for the children. Debra thought they were a great team and shared the same philosophy and beliefs about young children and learning. The first day of school Marilyn changed. She spoke to the children in short, distinct, and direct sentences, constantly correcting or redirecting them. Nothing missed her darting eyes; she could detect "misbehavior" before it occurred. Debra thought the children sitting on the rug appeared almost frightened, fearing a move would make them a target of Marilyn's sharp voice. Debra could not possibly ignore this "teaching style." She knew Marilyn loved children, so why this assertive interaction with the children? Debra decided to compensate for Marilyn's harshness and became particularly warm and supportive of the children when she was teaching.

Case description	Analysis

Phase I: Setting dispositions

Choosing Relationship over Control: It is obvious that Marilyn's initiation of this interaction is more focused on control than on relationship! She was ready to "tell" Debra what should be and how it should be. It was only toward the end of the interaction that she began to refocus her intentions.

Setting the Stage for Miracles: In the beginning all that Marilyn was setting the stage for was a classroom run as she would like it to be run. This disposition is not evident, although as she refocused on relationship, its presence may be implied.

"We have to talk," Marilyn said when the last child was gone. "Debra, your soft nicey, nicey attitude is not going to work with these children. They need structure; they need the security of knowing who is in charge. They don't get that from a teacher who is always fixing things for them or ignoring their problem behavior. We have to guide them early and nip the bad behavior in the bud. Most of these children are not getting any direction at home, it is up to me to make sure they learn how to act in school and are ready for kindergarten. The kids and their parents will appreciate and love you by the end of the year. You have got to be tough the first few months. No more coddling. I have been

Phases II–IV: Respect (*Welcoming* and *Allowing*), reciprocity (*Sense-Making* and *Appreciating*), and responsiveness (*Joining* and *Harmonizing*)

(continued)

Case description	Analysis

doing this for years, so I know that the kids are going to be confused, and we won't have any control in here." (1)

(1) *Welcoming, Allowing, Sense-Making, Appreciating:* Not present at all. Marilyn believed that she already understood Debra, and that none of what she saw was good!

"Marilyn, I just didn't expect such a structured classroom, I mean the way you talk to the children. I believe children need to express themselves, not just know how to follow directions. I think I can get the same results by being more nurturing, listening to them." (2)

(2) *Sense-Making:* Although Debra also did not use *Welcoming* or *Allowing,* she did attempt to explain her views so that Marilyn might be able to make sense of them as positive rather than negative.

"So tell me why you think your way will work better?" (3)

(3) *Sense-Making:* This might sound like the initiation of *Sense-Making,* but Marilyn's tone made it clear that she was already convinced that Debra's views made no sense and had no value.

(4) *Sense-Making:* Debra took Marilyn's comment literally and started to discuss her perspective in greater depth, again with the hope that it would make better sense to Marilyn.

Debra spoke for some time about her beliefs about classroom management, community building in the classroom, and classroom meetings from readings in her coursework. (4) Marilyn listened without interrupting. (5)

(5) *Allowing:* Marilyn did allow Debra to state her perspective without interruption. If, however, she was only doing this to shoot it down more effectively, it would not be truly *Allowing.* If she was doing it sincerely in order to better understand, then it would be *Allowing.*

Suddenly, it was as if she could hear herself as she had sounded in her first years as a teacher. She remembered being that idealistic, and she remembered the teacher who had told her exactly what she was telling Debra. She never wanted to work with that teacher again after that. Maybe she was being too harsh with Debra. (6)

(6) *Appreciating:* Whether intentionally or not, Marilyn's listening led her to remember her own stance once upon a time and, thus, she started to appreciate Debra's perspective (i.e., to appreciate where she might be coming from). It

(continued)

Case description	Analysis
	also led her to appreciate the impact of her own behavior toward Debra.
"Debra, maybe I'm coming on a bit too strong. I do believe in a high degree of structure, but I can hear how deeply you believe in a different approach. (7) Maybe we can keep talking over the next few days and see if we can come to understand each other better?" (8)	(7) *Appreciating:* Marilyn then expressed her appreciation of Debra's perspective somewhat more explicitly.
	(8) *Welcoming:* Somewhat belatedly, Marilyn welcomed the opportunity for further discussion and, thus, indirectly welcomed Debra.
"That is a great idea," Debra replied, grateful for the opportunity to improve both their communication and their relationship as co-teachers.	

MR. JAMES AND MRS. FARIA

Background Information   Mr. James is in charge of the Middle Town Primary School's After-School Academic and Learning Support Program, which runs right after school until 5 p.m. The program is designed to provide young children from prekindergarten to fifth grade with academic and learning support. It also, of course, provides a place for children to stay until their parents have completed their workday, but that is not its primary purpose. This is carefully explained to all of the parents when they sign up their children for the program. One mother, Mrs. Faria, still seems to not understand this purpose, and Mr. James has grown increasingly frustrated with her. She always comes at 4 p.m. instead of 5 p.m. to pick up Jackie, her 6-year-old son. When asked why she came so early, she explained that she has to pick up her 3-year-old daughter at that time from a nearby child care center and she does not want to have to make two trips. Mr. James explained to her that pulling Jackie out an hour early prevents him from getting the full support he needs with his schoolwork and learning assignments. This is particularly important because Jackie was recently diagnosed with a learning disability. Mr. James was also concerned because the granting agency that funds the program must show evidence of student growth and, with children being pulled out early, the level of that growth is placed at risk. Three months passed, however, and Mrs. Faria did not change her behavior. Mr. James's interactions with her were becoming more and more negative as his frustration grew. After all, she only lived two blocks from the school! He decided that he must meet with her once again. Before that happened, however, he ran into a colleague that told him about Skilled Dialogue, and he decided to give it a try.

Case description	Analysis
Prior to calling Mrs. Faria to schedule another meeting with her, Mr. James focused on Skilled Dialogue's two dispositions. He decided that he would focus on establishing a positive relationship with Mrs. Faria, rather than try to control her—that had not worked anyway! He also reminded himself that everyone can change, sometimes in the most unexpected ways and stopped thinking negatively of Mrs. Faria's potential for change.	**Phase I: Setting dispositions** *Choosing Relationship over Control:* Mr. James clearly set this disposition as he got ready to schedule the meeting with Mrs. Faria. He realized that he may need to suspend his agenda in order to develop a more positive relationship with this parent. *Setting the Stage for Miracles:* This disposition was clear as Mr. James reminded himself to stop thinking negatively and remain open to unexpected outcomes.
	Phases II–IV: Respect (*Welcoming* and *Allowing*), reciprocity (*Sense-Making* and *Appreciating*), and responsiveness (*Joining* and *Harmonizing*)
"Hello, Mrs. Faria. I'm so glad you were able to make time for us to meet again. How are you doing?" (1)	(1) *Welcoming:* Mr. James expressed pleasure at seeing Mrs. Faria and placed the focus on her first by asking how she was.
"I'm okay. Is this about picking Jackie up early again?"	
Mr. James replied, "Actually it's not. It's about getting to know you better and seeing how we can better meet your needs as well as Jackie's." (2)	(2) *Sense-Making:* Sometimes, it is important that others make sense of our behavior before we try to make sense of theirs. That way, they are more likely to be open to our request for more information.
Mrs. Faria replied, "Well, you know I'm doing the best I can. I simply can't make two trips, one to pick up each child."	
"I do know that," said Mr. James, "but I'm not sure I understand. Are you willing to share with me what making more than one trip would mean to you? I'm	

(continued)

Case description	Analysis

sure it's the best decision for you right now; I just want to understand it better." (3)

Mrs. Faria replied, "You know, I didn't think you wanted to know. I really appreciate your asking. I work two jobs and just have a few hours between my day job and my evening job. I like to pick up my kids, take them home, and still have time to spend with them before I have to leave. It's also the only time I have to grocery shop, cook, or get dinner ready. Even the few more minutes it would take to make a second trip mean a lot to me. Also, I take care of my mother-in-law, and I have to go see her on my way to my evening job, so that takes more of my time. Some days I feel like I have no time at all for the kids or for myself. My husband and I barely see each other during the week. He's usually just getting home as I'm leaving."

"Wow, I never realized you had such a hectic schedule," said Mr. James. "It sounds like you are handling it quite well, though, all things considered." (4)

"I do the best I can. But you can see why I have to pick Jackie up early."

"Yes, I certainly can understand your decision to do that. You know, I don't want you to have to add one more trip. (5) At the same time, I also really want Jackie to get the full benefits of this program so that he can stay on grade level, especially now, with the identification of his learning disability. Can we look at how we might be able to do both things—keep your trips down to just

(3) *Sense-Making:* Mr. James probed for additional information, making it clear that it was his lack of understanding, rather than Mrs. Faria's behavior, that was his concern.

(4) *Appreciating:* Mr. James explicitly expressed his recognition of Mrs. Faria's pressures and his appreciation of her skill in dealing with them.

(5) *Joining:* Mr. James expressed his understanding of Mrs. Faria's decision, as well as his support of her need not to make two trips. He agreed with her, but did not stop there. He returned to his need, giving each equal time and value.

(continued)

Case description	Analysis
one and at the same time allow Jackie to stay here until 5 p.m.?" (6)	(6) *Harmonizing:* The two "sides" of the situation were made explicit, but they were not put at odds with each other. Rather, Mr. James emphasized how they might both be addressed.
"I just don't see how," replied Mrs. Faria.	
"Right now, I can't either. Let's meet again in a few days after we've had some time to think. Talk with your husband and friends, maybe they'll have some ideas. In the meantime, I'll see what I can do here, and you keep picking Jackie up at the same time. How does that sound?" (7)	(7) *Harmonizing* cannot and should not be forced. In some cases, such as with Mary and Susan or Karen and Mrs. Cooper, possible third choices can be suggested because it is clear that they will be perceived as helpful rather than directive. Because Mr. James had previously been highly directive, however, it was probable that suggested third choices would be perceived as a continuation of that pattern. For that reason, providing time is the most helpful. Mrs. Faria may return with some choices of her own, or she may be more willing to listen to possible choices from Mr. James in subsequent meetings.
"Well, okay. As long as I don't have to make two trips."	
"I understand. Thanks again for making the time for this conversation." (8)	(8) *Joining:* Seeing that Mrs. Faria still felt the need to state her boundaries, Mr. James reinforced their connection by using statements of *Joining* again.

CONCLUSION

Skilled Dialogue is a dynamic process that is unique to each situation and/or interaction. Whereas the dispositions and strategies remain the same across situations and interactions, they are embodied and expressed differently in every case, depending on the individual participants. The four cases described in this chapter are intended only as initial illustrations of Skilled Dialogue's use across a variety of situations. They are based on scenarios derived from stories shared with us by various Skilled Dialogue learners. However "unreal" they may seem, neither the original interactions nor those following the application of Skilled Dialogue have been exaggerated. It is our intent that these cases, along with the cases in Chapter 11 and the vignettes in Chapter 12, provide sufficient material to allow readers to begin to generalize both dispositions and strategies to other scenarios in a realistic fashion.

Challenging Adult–Child Interactions

This chapter presents four case studies involving practitioners and children. Background information is presented for each case, followed by an analysis of the degree to which Skilled Dialogue dispositions and strategies are in evidence. (This analysis parallels Part II of the Skilled Dialogue Reflection Guide in Appendix C). The first case is that of Mrs. Miller, who was introduced in the chapters in Part III. Few of the Skilled Dialogue strategies were in evidence in Mrs. Miller's interactions with Justin and his mother (see Tables 7.8, 8.8, and 9.8). In this chapter, the case has been revised to illustrate how these strategies might have been applied if Mrs. Miller had an opportunity to redo her interactions. The next two cases—concerning Mrs. Bailey and Miss Anne—involve similar interactions with children displaying behavioral difficulties. The final case, Miss Sheri, is somewhat different. It focuses on a practitioner's reflections rather than on a child's behavior in order to illustrate what Skilled Dialogue might look like when used outside of an interaction as well as how to think about its application to particular situations prior to engaging in those situations. As a dynamic process, however, such illustration is significantly limited by a written format. Readers are encouraged to send questions directly to the authors via our web site (http://www.skilleddialogue.com).

MRS. MILLER REVISITED

As discussed in Part III, Mrs. Miller's interactions with both Justin, her student, and Mrs. Taylor, his mother, do not adequately reflect the dispositions of Choosing Relationship over Control and Setting the Stage for Miracles, nor is there much evidence of the strategies associated with these dispositions. This chapter revisits this case, but this time as it might have happened if Mrs. Miller opted for a "do-over" after reflecting on the Skilled Dialogue questions associated with each strategy. This is, of course, only one possible revision of the actions. The original version is shown parallel to the first to facilitate identifying exactly what has been changed. The entire case is included, even though it includes both adult–child (i.e., Mrs. Miller and Justin) and adult–adult interactions (i.e., Mrs. Miller and Justin's mother).

Mrs. Miller's "Do Over"

Original version	"Do-over" version
	Mrs. Miller went home and thought about the situation with Justin and his mother. She did not feel good about either her latest interactions with Justin or with Mrs. Taylor. She sat down to review the Skilled Dialogue reflections questions and strategies she had picked up at a training earlier in the year. The next day she began to plan a do-over that she hoped would turn out better for all concerned. She knew that if she did not change something, she would no longer be able to work with Justin.
	Mrs. Miller imagined the events as if she were witnessing Justin's behavior all over again.
Justin, who is 4 years old, darted across the preschool playground, straight toward the painted roadway where Emily and Sue waited in line to ride a tricycle. As Peter slowed down his tricycle to stop, Justin came up behind him and grabbed his shirt, which knocked Peter to the ground. Justin was in a frenzy, screaming, "It's my turn, it's my turn!" and taking off as fast as he could on the tricycle, weaving in and out of the designated roadway. Emily and Sue were angry, yelling that Justin did not follow the rules. Peter was crying and pulling up his pant leg to check a bloody knee.	Justin, who is 4 years old, darted across the preschool playground, straight toward the painted roadway where Emily and Sue waited in line to ride a tricycle. As Peter slowed down his tricycle to stop, Justin came up behind him and grabbed his shirt, knocking Peter to the ground. Justin was in a frenzy, screaming, "It's my turn, it's my turn!" and taking off as fast as he could on the tricycle, weaving in and out of the designated roadway. Emily and Sue were angry, yelling that Justin did not follow the rules. Peter was crying and pulling up his pant leg to check a bloody knee.
Mrs. Miller, the preschool teacher, had been observing the children from the other side of the playground. She shouted to Justin to get off the tricycle immediately and then turned her attention to Peter and the girls. She sent Peter to the office to have his scrape bandaged and told the children to line	*Mrs. Miller imagined recruiting student volunteers from the local university to make observations targeted at identifying a pattern(s) to Justin's outbursts so that they could be more effectively predicted.*

(continued)

Original version	**"Do-over" version**

up. Justin rode the tricycle right up next to her and refused to get off. "I don't have to," he said. Mrs. Miller told Justin again to get off the tricycle, "Your behavior caused Peter's injury." Justin stayed on the tricycle and slowly rode it the 10 feet to the tricycle "parking lot" and then walked head down to the end of the line. After returning to the classroom he quietly sat in the circle as Mrs. Miller spoke about the incident.

This was not the first time Justin had acted impulsively and aggressively toward his peers and staff. It was only the first month of school, and Justin was having an average of three incidents per week. He had torn up another child's drawing because it was "stupid." He had knocked over other children's buildings in the block center and pretended to laugh and roll on the floor. He had taken other children's crayons and markers and broken them. Neither the children nor Mrs. Miller knew what would set off another outburst. The children no longer wanted to sit next to Justin or be paired with him for activities. A mother of one child jokingly told Mrs. Miller after class, "We hear all about Justin at our house."

She also imagined responding differently to Justin.

Mrs. Miller rushed over, made sure that Justin was stopped and not about to do anything else, and then looked at Peter carefully. She sent him to the office to have his scrape bandaged before turning her attention to Justin. When he rode the tricycle over to her, she got down on his eye level and gently said, "Would you put the tricycle away so that we can talk about what happened?"

Justin was slow to comply, but she allowed him several minutes to go over to the tricycle "parking lot." "Thank you, Justin. I really appreciate your listening," she said as soon as he had done that. Justin walked head down to the back of the line, and Mrs. Miller made sure to smile her approval. Once they were back in the classroom, she involved the other children in various activities and walked over to Justin.

"Can we talk about what happened?" she asked. "I really want to understand because when you pull other children away from what they are doing, I feel sad because I believe that it's important to be kind and gentle with everyone. I also feel confused because I believe that we can all be kind and gentle." Justin listened, but did not respond. Mrs. Miller waited without saying anything else. Finally, Justin whispered, "I was angry."

(continued)

Original version	"Do-over" version
	"Why were you angry?" Mrs. Miller replied.

"Why were you angry?" Mrs. Miller replied.

"I'd been waiting and waiting for my turn," he said.

Mrs. Miller answered, "Yes, I know that. I watched you, and you did a good job of waiting until you went over to Peter."

"Well, it was time for me," Justin said.

"I can see why you thought that," answered Mrs. Miller. "Can you think of other ways to tell someone it's your turn? Kind and gentle ways?"

Justin replied, "No one listens. I tried."

Mrs. Miller said, "Oh, I see. You know other ways, but they're not working. Is that right?"

"Yes," answered Justin.

"Well, let's see," said Mrs. Miller. "It's important to tell others it's your turn, right?"

"Uh-huh," he answered.

"And you know I believe in kind and gentle behavior. Right?"

"Uh-huh," he said again.

"So, let's see. How can we do both things?"

Mrs. Miller then went on to help Justin brainstorm alternative ways of asking for his turn, repeatedly emphasizing that being kind and gentle *and* asking for one's turn could happen at the same time.

She could not be sure that Justin's behavior would change if she responded in this way, but she was willing to give it a try. She planned several practice opportunities over the next few days, during which she could role play her response with another teacher. She also planned opportunities for Justin to role play asking for his turn in kind and gen-

(continued)

Original version	**"Do-over" version**
	tle ways after she had tried her alternative response.
Mrs. Miller and Mrs. Taylor met yesterday after the latest incident on the playground to discuss Justin's behavior. Mrs. Miller had already suggested over the phone to Mrs. Taylor when requesting a meeting that perhaps Garfield Center was not the best program for Justin.	*Mrs. Miller also imagined making changes in her interaction with Justin's mother.* Mrs. Miller felt frustrated and challenged with the situation. It seemed that all she could remember was Justin's negative behavior. That seemed to be the only thing she and Mrs. Taylor talked about. Granted the negatives seemed to outweigh the positives, at least in intensity, but there *were* positives. For example, Justin had reminded another child that he had left his ball on the playground, he had missed his turn on the tricycle yesterday without incident, he always seemed regretful after behaving inappropriately, and he had stood up for a smaller child whose toy had been taken by an older student. She planned to keep index cards handy so that she could write these down and share them with Mrs. Taylor.
Mrs. Taylor arrived about 20 minutes late for the meeting. Mrs. Miller had planned the meeting carefully, citing each of Justin's outbursts and the behaviors she was observing. By the time Mrs. Taylor arrived, she was feeling frustrated and impatient. This was another instance of Mrs. Taylor's disregard for her time and the seriousness of the situation.	When Mrs. Miller met with Mrs. Taylor the next time, she would tell Mrs. Taylor that there was an urgent need to meet so that they could evaluate how Garfield Center could best serve Justin's needs. In this way, she hoped to communicate more of a collaborative focus.
Mrs. Miller had suggested four times in the last month that they meet for a conference. Mrs. Taylor always promised to get back to her after she checked her schedule, but then failed to do so. Mrs. Miller had also added handwritten notes to Justin's "My Day" checklist documenting behavior events and requesting a conference.	She remembered to tune into her relief that Mrs. Taylor had actually come, even if she was 20 minutes late as she had been in the past. She would keep a small note to remind herself to release her previous judgments about Mrs. Taylor and to instead focus on the potential for a more productive relationship with her. After all, if she could not establish such
Mrs. Miller said, "Hello. Please have a seat. I only have a few minutes because I will need to see the students before they leave for home." She then asked about Justin's behavior at home and at his prior preschool.	

(continued)

Original version	"Do-over" version

a relationship with her, there was not much hope of working together to help Justin.

Mrs. Taylor assured her that he never had a problem before and probably just needed time to adjust to the new program. She went on to share that "we" had a *very* difficult time at the preschool in the former neighborhood. "The teacher there was inexperienced and showed favoritism to other children. The teacher just didn't like Justin." Mrs. Taylor stated that she had done her "homework" over the summer by asking several people which preschool was the best in town. It was the Garfield Early Learning Center, was the reply. So she was sure that Justin would do just fine. "He just needs some time to adjust to the school. There have been so many changes with the move and all."

Mrs. Miller imagined how their conversation might go once Mrs. Taylor arrived.
"I'm so glad to see you. I know that you have had some trouble making our last two meetings, and I was worried that you might not be able to make this one. We have some really important things to discuss, and your thoughts would be very helpful. Let's make the most of the time we have remaining before I need to see the students before they leave for home. Would you like anything to drink before we get started?"
Mrs. Taylor shook her head. "No, I just want to get started. What has Justin done now?"

Mrs. Taylor went on to explain that she was disappointed that Justin did not learn anything last year at the other school. "He doesn't even know the ABCs yet or how to write his name. My nephew in Dallas, who is about the same age, can write his name, write his ABCs, and he is even beginning to read!" she stated. "But I am sure you will have him reading real soon. We are paying good money to send him to this school; it's supposed to be the best school in town," she concluded.

"Well, he's done a lot of things," Mrs. Miller commented and began to list some of Justin's more appropriate behaviors. "Unfortunately, this morning was not one of his better times." She went on to describe the previous day's incident as neutrally as she could. "Have you seen any behavior like this at home or at his previous preschool?"

After hearing all this without yet having had the opportunity to present the information she had prepared, Mrs. Miller remained silent for several minutes. She then looked at her watch, saw that it was almost time to return to her class,

She remembered what Mrs. Taylor had said in their last conversation about Justin never having had a problem before and probably just needing time to adjust to the new program. She had shared that "we" had a *very* difficult time at the preschool in the former neighborhood. "The teacher there was inexperienced and showed favoritism to other children. The teacher just didn't like Justin." She had pointed out that

(continued)

Original version	"Do-over" version

and said, "You and I see this situation very differently, Mrs. Taylor. I'm not sure that you understand the seriousness of Justin's behavior here at the Center."

she had done her "homework" over the summer, asking several people which preschool was the best in town. It was the Garfield Early Learning Center, they said. She had reiterated that she was sure that Justin would do just fine. "He just needs some time to adjust to the school. There have been so many changes with the move and all."

"This time," Mrs. Miller thought, "I will listen without interruption and nod my head to communicate that I am following the conversation. When Mrs. Taylor pauses, I won't rush her; I will remain silent and wait to see if there is more she wants to say. Even though we will probably be running out of time by this point in the meeting, I will remind myself that these initial opportunities to establish rapport are critical.

Mrs. Miller remembered that Mrs. Taylor had explained how disappointed she was that Justin "didn't learn anything last year at that other school." "He doesn't even know the ABCs yet or how to write his name. My nephew in Dallas, who is about the same age, can write his name, write his ABCs, and he is even beginning to read!" she had stated. "But I am sure you will have him reading real soon. We are paying good money to send him to this school; it's supposed to be the best school in town," she concluded.

This time, Mrs. Miller thought, she would remember to acknowledge what Mrs. Taylor said. She decided to capitalize on her interest in Justin learning to read and say something such as, "Well,

(continued)

Original version	"Do-over" version
	I can see that you've had a trying time. It's also clear that you've worked very hard to find this placement for him. I'm glad to hear that. I can also hear that you really want Justin to start learning to read. Is that correct?"

Mrs. Taylor might then respond by saying, "Well, reading is very important, isn't it? But all everyone talks about is his behavior. Maybe if he could read or at least name the letters, he would feel more like the other kids and not be so frustrated!"

"You might have a point there, Mrs. Taylor. There are many parts to learning to read, of course. As you pointed out, social behavior and reading can go hand in hand. That can happen because reading has to do with understanding what someone else—the writer—has to tell us. This kind of understanding has to start orally and socially before it can be transferred to written language. It's based on understanding of what others are saying or want to say. This requires paying attention to them. Does that make sense to you?"

She would then go on to talk about how improving Justin's ability to communicate with other children could support his learning to read and conclude by saying, "I'm sorry we can't finish our discussion today, Mrs. Taylor. Is there another time this week when we could get together again?" |

What changes did Mrs. Miller wish to make in her do-over? What dispositions and strategies would these changes reflect? Readers may wish to review the prompts and behavioral indicators in Table IV.1 in the Part IV introduction to see if they can identify examples or nonexamples of Skilled Dialogue dispositions and strategies prior to reading the following analysis.

CASE ANALYSIS FORMAT

The case analysis targets particular sections of the interaction specific to either dispositions or strategies, which follows the five-phase process shown in Figure IV.1 in Part IV, starting with setting dispositions, then moving through building respect, establishing reciprocity, and becoming responsive. The last phase—self-reflecting— is not discussed as it is represented by the analysis itself.

Phase I: Setting Dispositions

The judgment as to the presence of the dispositions is based on the prompts for *all* critical aspects associated with relevant disposition (see Tables 7.8, 8.8, and 9.8), as well as on the presence or absence of the behavioral indicators shown in Table IV.1 in Part IV.

Phases II–IV: Building Respect, Establishing Reciprocity, and Becoming Responsive

The next focus of the analysis is on the strategies associated with building respect, establishing reciprocity, and becoming responsive. These are identified as they come up in the scenario, rather than in the strict horizontal sequencing discussed earlier.

Analysis of Mrs. Miller's Do-Over

A two-column format is used to analyze Mrs. Miller's do-over. (The numbers in parentheses in the case description column refer to the numbers by particular statements in the analysis column.) This format is used in place of the Skilled Dialogue Reflection Guide format (see Appendix C). Given that these cases are written out, the use of this format reduces the need for turning pages back and forth between the case and the analysis. All of the items addressed in Part II of the Skilled Dialogue Reflection Guide are contained in this format as well.

Background Information Mrs. Miller went home and thought about the situation with Justin and his mother. She did not feel good about either her latest interactions with Justin or with Mrs. Taylor. She sat down to review the Skilled Dialogue reflection questions and strategies she had picked up at a training earlier in the year. The next day she began to plan a do-over that she hoped would turn out better for all concerned. She knew that if she did not change something, she would no longer be able to work with Justin or his mother.

Case description   **Analysis**

Phase I: Setting dispositions

In imagining a different response to Justin, Mrs. Miller set her intentions directly.

Choosing Relationship over Control: During the first interaction, Mrs. Miller was primarily disposed to correct (i.e., *control*) the situation that had arisen in her classroom. In her do-over, she took the time to revisit the situation from a more open and relational perspective as evidenced by a new willingness to make sense of what happened and somehow join with Justin rather than merely change his behavior.

Setting the Stage for Miracles: This disposition is somewhat less evident at the beginning of Mrs. Miller's do-over. Her willingness to imagine a different scenario (i.e., to reframe her perceptions), however, signals a beginning to setting this disposition.

Mrs. Miller and Justin

Mrs. Miller imagined the events as if she were witnessing Justin's behavior all over again. Justin, who is 4 years old, darted across the preschool playground, straight toward the painted roadway where Emily and Sue waited in line to ride a tricycle. As Peter slowed down his tricycle to stop, Justin came up behind him and grabbed his shirt, which knocked Peter to the ground. Justin was in a frenzy, screaming, "It's my turn, it's my turn!" and taking off as fast as he could on the tricycle, weaving in and out of the designated roadway. Emily and Sue were angry, yelling that Justin did not follow the rules. Peter was crying and pulling up his pant leg to check a bloody knee.

Phases II–IV: Respect *(Welcoming* and *Allowing)*, Reciprocity *(Sense-Making* and *Appreciating)*, and responsiveness *(Joining* and *Harmonizing)*

(continued)

Case description	Analysis

She imagined recruiting student volunteers from the local university to make observations targeted at identifying a pattern(s) to Justin's outbursts so that they could be more effectively predicted. (1)

She also imagined responding differently to Justin

She rushed over, made sure that Justin was stopped and not about to do anything else, and then she examined Peter for possible injuries. She sent him to the office to have his scrape bandaged before turning her attention to Justin. When he rode the tricycle over to her, she got down to his eye level and gently said, "Would you put the tricycle away so that we can talk about what happened?" (2)

Justin was slow to comply, but she allowed him several minutes to go over to the tricycle "parking lot." (3) "Thank you, Justin. I really appreciate your listening," she said as soon as he had done that. (4) Justin walked with his head down to the back of the line, and Mrs. Miller made sure to smile her approval. (5) Once they were back in the classroom, she involved the other children in various activities and walked over to Justin.

"Can we talk about what happened?" she asked. "I really want to understand because when you pull other children away from what they are doing, I feel sad because I believe that it's important to be kind and gentle with everyone. I also feel confused because I believe that we can all be kind and gentle." Justin listened, but did not respond. Mrs. Miller

(1) *Sense-Making:* This illustrates Mrs. Miller's awareness of needing to achieve a better understanding of what is happening with Justin so that she can better understand it from his perspective.

(2) *Welcoming* and *Allowing:* In contrast to her initial response, this new response illustrates a clear attention to Justin rather than just to his behavior (i.e., one aspect of *Welcoming* is Mrs. Miller's getting down to Justin's eye level and her use of a gentle tone). In not immediately bringing up the incident, there is also an element of *Allowing* (i.e., Justin's perspective is not immediately challenged).

(3) *Allowing:* Mrs. Miller allowed Justin time to comply, thus evidencing her respect for him as a child who can also be respectful. She did not treat him as a child who needs to be controlled or who cannot be trusted.

(4) *Appreciating:* Mrs. Miller clearly expressed her appreciation for Justin's listening and compliance, thus reinforcing her message that they can enter into a reciprocal relationship within which each one's voice can be heard.

(5) *Appreciating:* Were it not preceded by (3) and (4), this smile could be interpreted as a "reward" designed to control Justin's behavior in the future. Given the context of the previous two behaviors, however, it can be seen as merely an extension of her appreciation of Justin as someone with whom she can have a reciprocal relationship.

(continued)

Case description	Analysis

waited without saying anything else. Finally, Justin whispered, "I was angry." (6) (7)

(6) *Sense-Making:* Rather than immediately judging Justin's behavior as she did initially, Mrs. Miller started asking what happened, thus honoring Justin's voice. (This does not mean that she will allow the behavior to continue or that she will communicate it was acceptable. It is not a matter of outcome as much as one of timing.)

(7) *Allowing:* Mrs. Miller accepted Justin's statement "I was angry" without judgment or contradiction.

"Why were you angry?" Mrs. Miller replied. (8)
"I'd been waiting and waiting for my turn," he said.
"Yes, I know that. I watched you, and you did a good job of waiting until you went over to Peter," Mrs. Miller replied. (9)

(8) *Sense-Making:* Mrs. Miller continued to gently probe for information. It is typical during *Sense-Making* to return to *Allowing* as well as to interject *Appreciating* (see 5 and 9).

(9) *Appreciating:* As Mrs. Miller gathered more information, she was quick to recognize and affirm positive aspects of Justin's behavior, which built a base of reciprocity to subsequently strengthen *Joining* and *Harmonizing.* (Without first having in place the strategies that build respect and establish reciprocity, the dispositions become less evident or disappear altogether, and the strategies become difficult to apply. When the first four strategies are in place, however, the dispositions remain strong and *Joining* and *Harmonizing* happen almost automatically.)

"Well, it was time for me," Justin said.
"I can see why you thought that," answered Mrs. Miller. (10) (11)

(10) *Allowing:* Mrs. Miller did not contradict or try to correct Justin. Rather, she allowed him to state his perspective and affirmed her understanding of it.

(11) *Joining:* Mrs. Miller seemed to be able to take Justin's perspective, which is a significant part of *Joining.* She did

(continued)

Case description	Analysis
	not seem to connect her behavior with Justin's in any way, which is the other part of this strategy. She failed to ask herself how she might have contributed to the initial situation (e.g., perhaps by ignoring Justin's growing frustration, which in its own way mirrored Justin's lack of attention to Peter). A statement, such as "I'm sorry I didn't notice your frustration," would have been a powerful example of modeling self-responsibility.
"Can you think of other ways to tell someone it's your turn? Kind and gentle ways?" Mrs. Miller asked. "No one listens. I tried." "Oh, I see. You know other ways, but they're not working. Is that right?" (12). "Yes," Justin answered "Well, let's see. It's important to tell others it's your turn, right?" Mrs. Miller asked. "Uh-huh." "And you know I believe in kind and gentle behavior. Right?" "Uh-huh." "So, let's see. How can we do both things?" (13)	(12) *Harmonizing:* Mrs. Miller started to move into *Harmonizing* by suggesting that there are multiple ways to achieve desired outcomes. There was some implicit *Joining* when she also suggested that Justin already knew this (i.e., "I'm with you on this, and I believe you're with me also."). (13) *Harmonizing:* Mrs. Miller moved into *Harmonizing* more directly by asking Justin how they might do both things (state his desire to ride the tricycle—have his way—and be kind and gentle—be respectful of others). She continued with this by initiating brainstorming of alternative ways.
Mrs. Miller then went on to help Justin brainstorm alternative ways of asking for his turn, repeatedly emphasizing that being kind and gentle *and* asking for one's turn could both happen at the same time. She could not be sure that Justin's behavior would change if she responded in this way, but she was willing to give it a try. She planned several practice opportunities during the next few days during which she could role play her response with another teacher. She also	

(continued)

Case description	Analysis

planned opportunities for Justin to role play asking for his turn in kind and gentle ways after she had tried her alternative response.

Mrs. Miller and Mrs. Taylor

Mrs. Miller also imagined making changes in her interaction with Justin's mother.

Mrs. Miller felt frustrated and challenged with the situation. It seemed that all she could remember was Justin's negative behavior. That seemed to be the only thing she and Mrs. Taylor talked about. Granted the negatives seemed to outweigh the positives, at least in intensity, but there *were* positives. For example, Justin had reminded another child that he had left his ball on the playground, he had missed his turn on the tricycle yesterday without incident, he always seemed regretful after behaving inappropriately, and he had stood up for a smaller child whose toy had been taken by an older student. She planned to keep index cards handy so that she could write these down and share them with Mrs. Taylor.

Phase I: Setting dispositions
In imagining her "re-do," Mrs. Miller actually set her intentions quite consciously.

Choosing Relationship over Control: During the first interaction, Mrs. Miller was primarily disposed to state her discomfort and need for change (i.e., *control*) regarding Justin. Now, she is taking the time to revisit the situation from a more open and relational perspective as evidenced by a new willingness to also look at the positives (i.e., to relate with Mrs. Taylor rather than just state all that was wrong).

Setting the Stage for Miracles: This disposition is evident in Mrs. Miller's willingness to imagine a scenario in which she and Justin's mother work together to meet Justin's needs, not just her own.

Phases II–IV: Respect (*Welcoming* and *Allowing*), reciprocity (*Sense-Making* and *Appreciating*), and responsiveness (*Joining* and *Harmonizing*)

When Mrs. Miller met with Mrs. Taylor the next time, she would tell Mrs. Taylor that there was an urgent need to meet so that they could evaluate how Garfield Center could best serve Justin's needs.

(continued)

Case description	Analysis

In this way, she hoped to communicate more of a collaborative focus. (1)

(1) *Welcoming:* Mrs. Miller has now set a clear intent to welcome Mrs. Taylor as someone with whom she can work collaboratively.

She remembered to tune into her relief that Mrs. Taylor came, even if she was 20 minutes late as she had been in the past. (2) She would keep a small note to remind herself to release her previous judgments about Mrs. Taylor and to instead focus on the potential for a more productive relationship with her. After all, if she could not establish such a relationship with her, there was not much hope of working together to help Justin.

(2) *Allowing:* The strategy of *Allowing* is evident in Mrs. Miller's willingness to tune into her relief rather than into her frustration regarding Mrs. Taylor's "late" arrival.

Mrs. Miller imagined how their conversation might go once Mrs. Taylor arrived.
"I'm so glad to see you. I know that you have had some trouble making our last two meetings, and I was worried that you might not be able to make this one. We have some really important things to discuss and your thoughts would be very helpful. Let's make the most of the time we have remaining before I need to see the students before they leave for home. Would you like anything to drink before we get started?" (3) Mrs. Taylor shook her head.

(3) *Welcoming: Welcoming* is once more in evidence in both the words and tone of Mrs. Miller's initial words with Mrs. Taylor.

"No, I just want to get started. What has Justin done now?"
"Well, he's done a lot of things," Mrs. Miller commented and began to list some of Justin's more appropriate behaviors. (4)
"Unfortunately, this morning was not one of his better times." She went on to describe the previous day's incident as neutrally as she could. "Have you seen

(4) *Appreciating:* In listing Justin's positive behaviors, Mrs. Miller indirectly expressed appreciation for Mrs. Taylor's work with him as these behaviors reflect on her role as a parent.

(continued)

Case description	Analysis

any behavior like this at home or at his previous preschool?" (5)

She remembered what Mrs. Taylor had said in their last conversation about Justin never having had a problem before and probably just needing time to adjust to the new program. She had shared that "we" had a *very* difficult time at the preschool in the former neighborhood. "The teacher there was inexperienced and showed favoritism to other children. The teacher just didn't like Justin."

She had pointed out that she had done her "homework" over the summer, asking several people which preschool was the best in town. It was the Garfield Early Learning Center, they said. She had reiterated that she was sure that Justin would do just fine. "He just needs some time to adjust to the school. There have been so many changes with the move and all." (6)

"This time," Mrs. Miller thought, "I will listen without interruption and nod my head to communicate that I am following the conversation. I will remember to acknowledge all her hard work in trying to find the best placement for her son." (7)

"When Mrs. Taylor pauses, I won't rush her; I will remain silent and wait to see if there is more she wants to say. Even though we will probably be running out of time by this point in the meeting, I will remind myself that these initial

(5) *Sense-Making:* Mrs. Miller now eases into *Sense-Making* as she starts to probe for more information on what may be happening in Justin's world at home.

(6) *Allowing:* As she listened to Mrs. Taylor's perspective, Mrs. Miller did not contradict her or try to change her opinion about what happened. (*Allowing* is an important aspect of *Sense-Making*. It communicates a willingness to listen and opens up trust rather than distrust, thus making it more likely that information will be shared more fully.)

(7) *Appreciating:* Mrs. Miller reminded herself to express her appreciation of Mrs. Taylor's work in searching for a good school.

(continued)

Case description	Analysis
opportunities to establish rapport are critical." (8)	(8) *Allowing:* Mrs. Miller returned to *Allowing* to gather more information and strengthen her rapport with Mrs. Taylor.

Mrs. Miller remembered that Mrs. Taylor had explained how disappointed she was that Justin "didn't learn anything last year at that other school." "He doesn't even know the ABCs yet or how to write his name. My nephew in Dallas, who is about the same age, can write his name, write his ABCs, and he is even beginning to read!" she had stated. "But I am sure you will have him reading real soon. We are paying good money to send him to this school; it's supposed to be the best school in town," she concluded.

This time, Mrs. Miller thought, she would remember to acknowledge what Mrs. Taylor said. (9) She decided to capitalize on her interest in Justin learning to read and maybe say something such as,
"Well, I can see that you have had a trying time. It's also clear that you have worked very hard to find this placement for him. I'm glad to hear that. I can also hear that you really want Justin to start learning to read. Is that correct?" (10)

(9) *Joining:* In acknowledging what Mrs. Taylor said, Mrs. Miller communicated an "I'm with you" message. She also implicitly acknowledged that behavior is co-constructed and that, by changing her behavior, she promoted change in the overall interaction.

(10) *Appreciating:* In using *Appreciating* at this point, Mrs. Miller strengthened her "I'm with you message." She then quickly reinforced this message by restating Mrs. Taylor's previous messages.

Mrs. Taylor might then respond by saying, "Well, reading is very important, isn't it? But all everyone talks about is his behavior. Maybe if he could read or at least name the letters, he would feel more like the other kids and not be so frustrated!"

"You might have a point there, Mrs. Taylor. There are many parts to learn-

(continued)

Case description	Analysis

ing to read, of course, as you pointed out. Social behavior and reading can go hand in hand. That can happen because reading has to do with understanding what someone else—the writer—has to tell us. This kind of understanding has to start orally and socially before it can be transferred to written language. It's based on understanding of what others are saying or want to say. This requires paying attention to them. Does that make sense to you?" (11)

She would then go on to talk about how improving Justin's ability to communicate with other children could support his learning to read and conclude by saying, "I'm sorry we can't finish our discussion today, Mrs. Taylor. Is there another time this week when we could get together again?" (12)

(11) *Harmonizing:* Mrs. Miller once again supported Mrs. Taylor's perspective (i.e., joined their perspectives with the statement "You might have a point there."). She then moved on to suggest that there might be no need for an either-or choice between development of social behavior and reading skills. (12)

Note: Frequently, diverse perspectives cannot be quickly harmonized. It is important to allow time for people to mull over the idea of third choices that integrate what seem to be opposites. For that reason, Mrs. Miller decided that she had made enough progress for one day and decided to continue the discussion at a later date.

MRS. BAILEY AND CARMEN

Background Information   Mrs. Bailey looked across the room as the students were sorting through magazines for colorful pictures of objects that begin with the /th/ sound. Mrs. Bailey is the faculty team leader for three kindergarten classrooms. She has been teaching kindergarten for more than 20 years and takes pride in the positive learning environment and academic curriculum the team has developed. Mrs. Bailey is active at the district and county level in supporting the education of young children. She conducts workshops for colleagues, particularly in the area of classroom management. She believes that the goal of the kindergarten program is getting the children off to a good start.

Until her behavioral changes, Carmen had been one of the most outgoing and friendly children in Mrs. Bailey's current class. The other children followed her lead and chose her as a "buddy" for activities. She started kindergarten reading at a 1.3 grade level and was fluent in Spanish and English. Carmen's mother, Linda, is an attractive, pleasant woman who walks Carmen to school every morning and home again at 2 p.m. She is expecting her second child and runs an internet business from her home. Carmen's father is the owner of a successful import business and travels out of town quite often. Carmen frequently shares the gifts her father brings back from his trips during Sharing Time.

The situation described here was Carmen's third outburst in one week. What was going on? It was so unlike her. Mrs. Bailey had intended to discuss Carmen's sudden change in behavior with her mother, but had been interrupted by another parent on one occasion and distracted by a sick child the day of the second occurrence. At lunch, Mrs. Bailey left a voicemail for Linda asking her to stop by when she picked up Carmen as she wanted to discuss a matter with her.

The prompts and behavioral indicators in Table IV.1 of Part IV provide a summary for examining the degree to which Skilled Dialogue is applied in this case. Readers are may wish to review these before proceeding.

Analysis of Mrs. Bailey's Case

Case description	Analysis
	Phase I: Setting dispositions There are times when things happen suddenly and our dispositions may not be well set. This seems to be the case with Mrs. Bailey, who is reacting to an immediate situation.
Mrs. Bailey and Carmen Mrs. Bailey looked across the room as the students were sorting through magazines for colorful pictures of objects that begin with the /th/ sound. Unexpectedly, Carmen let out a screech and grabbed a magazine from David's hand, holding it tightly to her chest. "I want it. It is my picture. I saw it first. It's mine." David backed away and took another magazine from the pile in front of him.	*Choosing Relationship over Control:* There is only minimal evidence of the critical aspects associated with Choosing Relationship over Control as Mrs. Bailey reacts to the sudden crisis in her classroom. Mrs. Bailey directs Carmen to return the magazine without first really connecting with her or waiting to hear her perspective. This behavior reflects an assumption that Carmen's actions are not evidence based, as well as a lack of curiosity about what happened. Even though Mrs. Bailey does

(continued)

Case description	Analysis
Mrs. Bailey quickly went over to Carmen and asked her what happened and told her to return the magazine to David. Carmen refused and clutched the magazine to her chest. She sat on a chair and refused to make eye contact with Mrs. Bailey or verbally respond. She just shook her head no back and forth, tightly holding the magazine.	ask what happened, she does not wait for a reply.

Setting the Stage for Miracles: When relationship is not chosen, the disposition of Setting the Stage for Miracles is almost always also absent. This appears to be the case in this scenario.

Phases II–IV: Respect *(Welcoming* **and** *Allowing)*, **reciprocity** *(Sense-Making* **and** *Appreciating)*, **and responsiveness** *(Joining* **and** *Harmonizing)*

Mrs. Bailey tried to redirect her, but she refused. (1) This was Carmen's third outburst in the last week. On the first occasion the children were lined up to go outside when Carmen suddenly pulled on Kelly's shirt, pushing her out of the line and yelling, "I was here first, you cut in line, I'm here, you can't do that, get out, get out!" (2)	(1) *Welcoming:* There is no evidence of behavioral indicators associated with *Welcoming* (i.e., no affirming or neutral comments and no preliminary general statements, such as "Hello Carmen. You look unhappy about this. Would you like to tell me what happened?").

(2) *Allowing:* Remembering the previous incidents at this time indicates that Mrs. Bailey did not use the *Allowing* strategy, which requires the release of existing stories and interpretations. She instead placed this incident into the context of those stories and interpretations, assuming that it had the same meaning and function.

After some questioning, Mrs. Bailey determined that Kelly had briefly taken one step out of the line and quickly got back in line, which enraged Carmen. (3)	(3) *Sense-Making:* Mrs. Bailey took the time to gather additional information about what happened, although she did not do so very thoroughly.

Carmen held on to her anger the rest of the afternoon. The second occurrence was during lunch. Carmen wanted to

(continued)

Case description	Analysis
trade her fruit and none of the children want to trade with her, so she took Cory's canned fruit and dumped it out on the table. What was going on? It was so unlike her. (4)	(4) *Sense-Making:* Mrs. Bailey paid attention to the patterns of Carmen's behaviors and realized that her behavior on this day was not typical.

Mrs. Bailey and Linda, Carmen's Mother

Phase I: Setting dispositions

Choosing Relationship over Control: Mrs. Bailey seemed disposed to choose relationship with Carmen's mother. Leaving only a voicemail, however, is less personal and therefore reduces the strength of this disposition.

Setting the Stage for Miracles: It is difficult to determine the degree to which this disposition was present in this interaction. Mrs. Bailey did not tell Linda the purpose of her request for a meeting, which might express this disposition to at least a slight degree.

Mrs. Bailey had intended to discuss Carmen's sudden change in behavior with her mother, but had been interrupted by another parent on one occasion and distracted by a sick child the day of the second occurrence. At lunch, Mrs. Bailey left a voice mail for Linda, asking her to stop by when she picked up Carmen as she wanted to discuss a matter with her. (1)

Phases II–IV: Respect (*Welcoming* and *Allowing*), reciprocity (*Sense-Making* and *Appreciating*), and responsiveness (*Joining* and *Harmonizing*)

(1) *Welcoming:* Phone messages are not as welcoming as in-person contacts. Mrs. Bailey did not wait to actually talk with Linda and only left a voice mail message. *Welcoming* would have been much stronger if she had communicated in person.

Linda arrived on time as usual to pick up Carmen. She hugged Carmen and told her to play on the swings in view of the classroom. Carmen handed her mother her backpack and happily headed to the swings.

Mrs. Bailey and Linda sat down at the little tables in front of the door. "Carmen's

(continued)

Case description	Analysis
behavior in the last 2 weeks has been very unusual for her. She has sudden outbursts with other children, usually about something she wants or something she wants to do. This is a really new behavior for her." (2)	(2) *Welcoming* and *Allowing:* Mrs. Bailey started into her topic immediately, without first greeting Linda. She also did not allow time for Linda to say hello or to express how she is feeling. Both of these behaviors decrease *Welcoming* and *Allowing,* making the interaction more task focused and less relational.
Linda took a deep breath and explained she had seen the same behavior at home. "Carmen suddenly becomes very selfish; she wants something and she demands it immediately or she gets very angry and yells and makes a scene in stores or at her grandmother's house. It seems to be getting worse and happening more often. I don't know what to do. She can't act this way when her new brother comes. She had a doctor's appointment on Tuesday, and he says there is nothing wrong with her physically. I don't know what to do. You understand kids this age; what do we do?" (3)	(3) *Allowing:* Mrs. Bailey did allow Linda to express her perspective and concern at this point. (Note: This brief interaction seems to be on the right track for gradually using all of the strategies, but its outcome will depend on Mrs. Bailey's response to Linda. How would you respond to Linda's question about what to do? See the following discussion.)

This case illustrates that it is not necessary that all six strategies be used in a single interaction. The analysis of Mrs. Bailey's interactions with Carmen and Linda, her mother, show that the initial strategies of *Welcoming, Allowing,* and *Sense-Making* were present, at least to some degree. It is not uncommon for people to use only these strategies initially. The addition of *Appreciating* prior to ending the interaction would, however, have strengthened it and paved the ground for the use of the remaining strategies in subsequent interactions with Linda. Review the strategies and discuss how they might have been strengthened in short interactions such as this one.

BJ AND MISS ANNE

Background Information   BJ is a delightful 3-year-old boy with moderate autism who attends the Evergreen Elementary preschool program for children with special needs. His mother, Carolina, walks him to school every morning with his 3-month-old brother. When they arrive at school, BJ is often upset and frustrated. Or they arrive late or do not come at all. His mother stated that it is so difficult to get him up and ready for school. It is such a struggle that sometimes she gives up and decides it is better that he stays home. Carolina is a caring and loving mother. BJ always wears freshly ironed shirts and pants, with his hair neatly combed and smoothed into a shiny black cap. She speaks to him with patience and understanding while he hugs her leg. Miss Anne, the preschool teacher, has noted soft-spoken Carolina's unlimited patience when speaking in Spanish or English to BJ, even during his most challenging behavior.

BJ has a limited vocabulary of both Spanish and English. Since September he has had great success using a daily schedule to transition through daily classroom activities. Every week another item has been added to his personal schedule. He has become more confident using the schedule and is beginning to attach language to the day's activities and schedule. Miss Anne has noticed a significant decrease in BJ's frustration-related outbursts. She observed his independent use of the visual schedule as a way for him to communicate with others and control his environment. She is looking forward to the upcoming individualized education program (IEP) meeting where she will share his significant progress in four of his annual goals!

Yet, Miss Anne is disappointed in BJ's lack of progress at home. She has been encouraging Carolina to implement a daily schedule to make his transition to and from school easier, as well as daily living activities in the home. She provided Carolina articles to read about the benefits of a visual schedule for children with autism. She even made Carolina a simple daily schedule that could be modified to meet BJ's and his family's needs. Miss Anne invited her to observe BJ's use of a schedule in the classroom for making choices, transitioning activities, and decreasing problem behavior. Still Carolina refuses to use a schedule and BJ continues to arrive at school upset, late, or not at all. One afternoon Miss Anne arranged a conference to discuss the problem with Carolina. She also arranged for supervision for BJ and care for the baby. Her goal is to convince Carolina that it is in BJ's best interest that she begin to use a visual schedule at home, at least as a tool to get him to school on time.

Case	Analysis
	Phase I: Setting dispositions
	Choosing Relationship over Control: This disposition seems weak in light of Miss

(continued)

Case	Analysis
	Anne's expressed goal to *convince* Carolina to use a visual schedule. As the conversation progresses, however, her focus seems to shift and more of this disposition is evident.
	Setting the Stage for Miracles: This disposition is also initially absent and only becomes evident as Miss Anne begins to explore Carolina's perspective.
	Phase II: Building respect *(Welcoming* and *Allowing)*
"Carolina, I am so glad we were able to meet today. Come on in, have a seat. Can I get you coffee or water?" (1)	(1) *Welcoming:* Miss Anne welcomes BJ's mother cordially, clearly expressing her pleasure at their meeting.
"No thank you, I'm fine."	
"BJ had a great day today. He chose the water table this afternoon and really had a good time pouring the water into all the different containers with Michael and Jeff. You know it is so great to see him be able to choose what he wants to do during the day." Miss Anne closed the door and sat down across the table from Carolina.	
"Tell me about how things are going at home with the new baby? How is the sleeping going?" (2)	(2) *Welcoming:* Miss Anne extended her welcoming by asking about the new baby, which communicated "I'm really interested in you."
"We are doing pretty well. You forget how tired you are with a new baby. It was much easier with one child. We are still trying to get on a routine, but it seems like either the baby needs something or BJ is acting up and time gets away from me. But I just love having two children; it is what I always wanted, so we are doing just fine. This is just	

(continued)

Case	Analysis
how it is with two little ones! These are the best years, I don't want to rush them. We will just move along at BJ's pace, and the baby will sleep through the night at some point! You know, my mother raised six of us, and I never remember her getting upset. Things got done when they got done," Carolina said. "That is how I want to raise my sons, doing daily things together. We do laundry together, work in the flower bed together, have story time every night. It doesn't make any difference what time it is, just that everyone is happy. You know what happens when I do push BJ! You see it sometimes in the morning when he gets here a little crabby or he throws a tantrum before we get here because he doesn't want to get ready to come to school. Sometimes it is just better to let children be who they are and not push them." (3)	(3) *Allowing:* Miss Anne listened without interruption, allowing Carolina to express herself as much as she feels necessary.
"I can see your focus is really on the children and not the clock. Carolina, that is a wonderful attitude, and it seems to really work for BJ. (4) I am curious, what is a typical day like at your house?" (5)	(4) *Appreciating:* Miss Anne interjected a note of appreciation to communicate her recognition of what Carolina is saying.
Carolina told Miss Anne about their mornings, breakfast, getting ready for school, and some of the struggles she often faces with BJ. Then she shared their after-school activities through bedtime.	(5) *Sense-Making:* She then quickly returned to *Sense-Making,* asking for more information that might help her understand the current situation from Carolina's perspective.
"Carolina, so what is the hardest part of the day for you? What would you like to see go more smoothly?" (6)	(6) *Sense-Making:* With this question, Miss Anne deepened her use of *Sense-*

(continued)

Case	Analysis
"I guess getting BJ to decide what he wants for breakfast and eating it. I tell him his choices, and then I usually make the choice for him. Then, if he doesn't like it, he refuses to eat it, and he has to eat before I can dress him, so, as you know, we are late. Then, if he is having a really bad day, we just stay home, and he eats when he wants. I don't like to push him. He is only 3 years old. If it were not for his autism, he would be home with me all day, and we wouldn't even have to deal with the mornings." (7)	*Making,* making her curiosity and desire to understand more evident.
	(7) *Allowing:* She returned to *Allowing* as she listened once again without interruption.
Miss Anne replied, "I can see why you don't want to upset BJ by pushing him in the morning. I know that mornings when things don't go well for me, stress me, too. " (8)	(8) *Joining:* Miss Anne acknowledged Carolina's concern and "joined" her in the understanding of how stressful mornings can be when they don't go as planned. *Joining* thus extends both *Sense-Making* and *Appreciating* by moving participants into common ground.
Carolina replied, "I know. I just want him to have what I had growing up and it didn't turn out that way."	
"Carolina, I can see how much you want to have a much more peaceful start to the day with BJ, just as when you were a child. It sounds like we need to find a way to make your mornings more peaceful with BJ. That way the two of you can spend some quality time in the morning rather than the frustration of him refusing to eat what you have selected. What do you think? Can you think of an idea? What did your mother do in the morning with six children to feed? Maybe we can use some of her ideas." (9)	(9) *Harmonizing:* Miss Anne began to introduce the idea of *Harmonizing* Carolina's desire for a peaceful morning with BJ's refusal to eat anything other than what he wants. She communicated that one need not necessarily be at odds with the other and prompted for concrete suggestions.

(continued)

Case	Analysis

Carolina answered, "Well, she would call us to get up, and we would all go downstairs and eat together. She served us breakfast. Whatever she fixed, we ate."

Miss Anne asked, "What happened if one of the kids didn't like what she fixed?"

"Well, they usually ate a little of it, and then they had to wait for lunch." (10)

(10) *Allowing:* Miss Anne allowed Carolina to express her ideas without interjecting her own.

Miss Anne said, "I know that many parents use that approach. I have another idea that may help with breakfast. Let's take photos of the three favorite things you say BJ likes to eat for breakfast. Here, you can borrow my camera. I will blow the photos up on the computer and laminate them, and you can put them on the lower half of the refrigerator so that BJ can choose from the three items. Do you think that might work? Other than this option, can you think of anything else?" (11)

(11) *Harmonizing:* Miss Anne continued to harmonize by introducing an idea of her own. Her first statement, "I know that many parents use that approach" made it clear that her idea is not contradictory to the one given by Carolina.

"Well, I guess he doesn't *have* to eat a lot of breakfast. He is not going to starve. You always feed him a healthy lunch here, and lunch is not such a problem at home, just breakfast. So I could try the photos so he can select what he wants, and then if he doesn't want to eat it, I will just move on to getting him dressed for school. I guess it was good enough for me and my brothers and sisters!" (12)

(12) *Harmonizing:* Miss Anne gently led Carolina to the integration of both ideas.

Miss Anne replied, "I'm excited Carolina, let's try it and see how it goes a few times. If it doesn't work, we will try something else. I know how important

(13) *Appreciating:* Miss Anne expressed her appreciation of Carolina's new per-

(continued)

Case	Analysis
it is to you to really be there for your children, and this may be a way you can really have more quality and more peaceful time in the morning." (13)	spective and left the door open for what might happen, affirming her disposition to set the stage for miracles!

MISS SHERI REFLECTS ON HER INTERACTIONS WITH MARIA

This case illustrates how Skilled Dialogue can be used to increase the respect, reciprocity, and responsiveness present in certain interactions with children without having to involve them directly in its use. Based on their age and/or exceptionalities, many children may not be able to understand the dispositions or begin to use the strategies. They can, however, learn them through a conscious modeling process. In addition, they will definitely benefit from the adults' changed behavior.

Background Information   Sheri is a new childcare provider at the Kerry Day Care Center. She loves her job and feels she gets so much positive feedback from the children. At lunch one day, Sheri was sharing with a co-worker how much she was enjoying her job when she was asked about Maria. "How do you like being with Maria? Poor Maria, she is such a mess." Sheri was silent; she was stunned by the recognition that she was not really paying attention to Maria. Why did she "never seem to get around" to interacting and being playful with her? Why did she enjoy all of her other children except Maria?

Maria is a 4-year-old child with long, drab, unkempt hair and a broken front tooth. She is often dressed wearing the same clothes 3 or 4 days in a row. Her clothes are two sizes too small or too large. Her fingernails are bitten down and dirty. She always looks sad, even when she smiles. She plays by herself and fades into the activity of a noisy group, as she makes no requests of peers or staff.

At the end of the day, Sheri reflected on the day's activity. She found that all the other children demand so much of her attention and energy that she never "gets" to Maria. The next morning, Sheri made a commitment to really observe Maria during the day and to note whom she spoke to and which children she played with. By naptime, Sheri was disappointed to have observed that Maria had only spoken to one staff member and two children all day. How long has this been going on?

That afternoon, Sheri requested to review Maria's enrollment and progress file. She had been at the child care center since she was 18 months old. There was nothing negative in the notes, just that she appeared to be a shy child. Maria's mother worked in the city, and a neighbor dropped her off and picked her up at the center when she took her own son to school. Sheri decided that she needed to re-examine her judgments of and interactions with Maria. (Although Skilled Dialogue is not a strictly linear process in its application, the phase sequence followed in this case is usually most helpful in either preparing for an interaction or in reflecting on one, as Sheri is doing. Readers will note that in this case the columns are reversed: the Skilled Dialogue elements on the left and the thought content on the right. When using Skilled Dialogue for self-reflection rather than in relation to a specific interaction, it is important to first start with the elements, considering the implications of each one for the situation on which one is reflecting. The orientation of the columns reflects this sequence. As with the case columns, the parenthetical numbers in the right column match the reflections in the left column.)

Skilled Dialogue elements	Sheri's reflections
Phase I: Setting dispositions	*Sheri starts by reflecting on the two Skilled Dialogue dispositions: Choosing Relationship over Control and Setting the Stage for Miracles.* I really need to think about this situation with Maria. It seems like every day I am more and more reluctant to work with Maria. I remember learning this approach called Skilled Dialogue—maybe it can help.
(1) *Choosing Relationship over Control:* Sheri first focused on this disposition because it is the one that paves the way for Setting the Stage for Miracles.	(1) First they talked about choosing relationship. That's a hard one, but I really want to get close to Maria so that I can really help her to learn. Right now, I have been choosing relationship only with my own thoughts, not with her. So, starting tomorrow, I will remind myself to really pay attention to her.
(2) *Setting the Stage for Miracles:* Sheri then shifted her focus to this second disposition.	(2) The other thing they talked about was Setting the Stage for Miracles. You know, I really haven't expected much from Maria. I've stereotyped her as a child who is a "mess." What if there's a very different child underneath that stereotype? I'll keep an open mind.
Only after setting both dispositions did she begin to look at the strategies.	
(3) **Phase II: Building respect** (*Welcoming* and *Allowing)*	(3) Oh yeah, and then there were these six strategies. Let me see how I might be able to use them in this case. It starts with building respect by using the strategies of *Welcoming* and *Allowing.* I haven't

(continued)

Skilled Dialogue elements	Sheri's reflections
	welcomed Maria; I'm sure I never look happy to work with her, and I'm never as excited around her as I am around the other children. Maybe I can start there. What about *Allowing?* Hmmm— I've certainly allowed her to be alone and quiet, haven't I? But I guess that's not really *Allowing.* I definitely haven't withheld my judgments of her, and I tell myself all sorts of stories about who and how she is, don't I? Perhaps I can suspend my judgments and stories and simply observe and listen to her. I'll try that.
(4) Phase III: Establishing reciprocity *(Sense-Making and Appreciating)*	(4) There was also something about reciprocity that involved *Sense-Making* and *Appreciating.* Well, I've started trying to make sense of why Maria is so unkempt and stays so quiet by reviewing her files. Maybe I could also arrange a meeting with her grandmother, with whom she spends quite a bit of time, and see what she can tell me. In the meantime, I can at least appreciate that even when I pay little attention to her, she pays attention to what is happening, and being quiet can be a real strength at times. She's good at that. Let's see what else I can find out about her that is positive. I'll ask my co-teacher, who seems to spend more time with her than I do.
(5) Phase IV: Becoming responsive *(Joining and Harmonizing)* Finding that she is not yet ready to use these strategies with Maria, Sheri explored them in relation to herself. This can be a very useful strategy and can set the stage for miracles on its own at times (i.e., it can bring about unexpected outcomes).	(5) Finally, they said that we needed to become responsive, not just reactive. That's where the strategies of *Joining* and *Harmonizing* came in. I'm not sure how those might work. I'll have to wait until I get to know her better. In the meantime, however, what I can try to harmonize is my inattention to her with my belief that all children

(continued)

Skilled Dialogue elements	Sheri's reflections
	deserve loving attention. Maybe if I did that I'd learn something about myself as well as her!
	Hmmm. Let's see. What would I tell someone who faced this same situation? How could I tell them to *join?* Well, I do know what it's like to feel that I don't quite measure up. I remember my early student teaching days. Also, I can remember not feeling that anyone would listen to me if I spoke up, even if I said the right thing.
	What is it that really needs to be harmonized? Is it Maria's appearance with my expectations? I'd suggest that maybe the core issues are attention and inattention—attention to Maria's external appearance and inattention to her needs and who she truly is. Too little attention to her strengths and too much attention to her limitations.
	I think I'd tell them to reframe their inattention, to become inattentive not to Maria herself, but to what they see as negative. I'd also ask them to shift the attention they are already using to pay attention not to Maria's external appearance, but to her inner strength and inner beauty!
	Oh, I'm beginning to get it. Seen from this perspective, it's not my inattention that's bad, it's what I'm not attending to that is the problem. Inattention can actually be a necessary part of learning to see and appreciate Maria as a whole child, with both strengths and flaws, if I use it to help me overlook some of what I find so negative! Okay, I will start following my own advice!

CONCLUSION

Using Skilled Dialogue in situations involving practitioners, children, and families can be quite challenging, yet exciting and valuable at the same time. We hope that the case studies we have described in this chapter, along with those in Chapters 10 and 12, provide some insight into both the challenges and the benefits. Readers are encouraged to contact us via our web site (http://www.skilleddialogue.com) with questions and/or comments. Information on additional opportunities to learn about the use of Skilled Dialogue will also be posted on that web site.

Chapter 12

Practice Cases

This chapter contains additional cases with discussion questions. These cases may be analyzed in the same format as those discussed in Chapters 10 and 11, or they may simply be used for further discussions of Skilled Dialogue dispositions and strategies. Readers who have questions and/or who seek additional information regarding Skilled Dialogue applications to these cases may contact the authors via their web site (http://www.skilleddialogue.com).

ROBERT

Robert is a 5-year-old child in Nancy's inclusive preschool classroom. He has moderate language and motor skill delays. Robert is a happy child who engages in play with all of his peers and especially likes to build forts with cardboard and wooden blocks. Nancy believes that Robert's mother, Susan, is too protective of him. On the first day of school, Susan provided Nancy with a list of what Robert should and should not do at school. She explained, "We spent years trying to conceive Robert. We did not plan on having only one child, but that is the case, so we don't want to take any chances of anything happening to him."

Robert did not participate in several field trips because Susan thought that it was too cold, the drive was too far, or he could get ill being near the animals. One day in the classroom a wooden block fort that Robert was building with two other boys fell over, and one of the blocks hit him on the forehead, leaving a bright red mark. When Robert's mother noticed the mark, she was extremely agitated and accused Nancy in front of other parents of not protecting her son. Robert's mother threatened to take her concerns about Nancy's lack of supervision to the school board. Although Nancy believes that she was unfairly judged, she wants to engage Robert's mother in a positive conversation that will result in the best outcomes for Robert. Therefore, Nancy set up an appointment to talk to Susan the following afternoon.

"Susan, I am so glad you were able to come!" Nancy said. "We have not had a chance to really sit down and chat about Robert. Have a seat; I am just going to clean a few things off my desk so that I can see you." Nancy sat down behind her desk facing Susan.

"Okay, now, let's talk about Robert's problem. The way I see it, Robert is a very capable young child who needs an opportunity to interact more freely with the other children. He needs to explore his environment. I am sure you would agree.

You know, he shouldn't be so fearful of every little thing. The purpose of our program is to guide a child's development. I know you have seen all the other children doing all sorts of exciting activities, which are so critical for their development. I hate to see Robert not participate. I am really afraid that he will fall behind the other children. You know how quickly they grow at this age. They learn something new every day! I mean the skills they develop now make a real difference in how well they do in first and second grade.

"Okay, now let's talk about what Robert likes to do at home. Can you tell me about who Robert plays with at home? Neighbors? Other family members?"

"I am not concerned about *who* Robert plays with or *how* he plays at home. I am concerned about what is going on in this classroom," Susan replied. "I am concerned about the lack of safety in your classroom!"

Discussion Questions

Complete the Skilled Dialogue Reflection Guide (see Appendix C) for this short scenario.

1. Is there evidence of both dispositions—Choosing Relationship over Control and Setting the Stage for Miracles?

2. Which Skilled Dialogue strategies seem most evident in this case study—*Welcoming* and *Allowing, Sense-Making* and *Appreciating,* or *Joining* and *Harmonizing?*

3. Which strategies are less evident or missing altogether?

4. What possible options for collaboration between Susan and Nancy might be discovered using the strategies of *Joining* and *Harmonizing* to create 3rd Space? What is currently hampering the development of such options?

KAREN AND LISA

Karen and Lisa are co-teachers at the Cook Early Childhood Center and Parent Education Program. The center provides a preschool curriculum, and offers parent education on personal well-being for parents as a way of caring for their children. Families and staff members plan weekend community activities to develop support networks. Lisa has not attended any of the weekend activities for the last 4 weeks. She always has an excuse—either she is ill or her children have some last minute need. As a result, Karen is angry with Lisa because she knows that Lisa accepted the job knowing it included participation in weekend activities. Whenever Karen and Lisa join the program team in planning upcoming activities, Lisa is always very enthusiastic and volunteers for several tasks. Karen is frustrated picking up Lisa's responsibilities as well as her own.

Discussion Questions

Answer the following questions from Karen's perspective.

1. How might Karen best prepare for her next meeting with Lisa?

2. Which disposition do you believe Karen needs to focus on most strongly for the next meeting?

3. Which strategies might be most in need of being strengthened? (Hint: Pay particular attention to the strategies of *Sense-Making* and *Appreciating*.)

JUAN, GRACE, AND DENISE

Four-year-old Juan was placed in an inclusive preschool classroom for "at-risk" children that is staffed by Grace, a general education teacher, and Denise, an early childhood special education teacher. Juan is bilingual and has a language delay in both Spanish and English. Grace and Denise disagree as to how to best approach Juan's use of Spanish in the classroom. Because he speaks English, Grace wants him to use only English in the classroom when communicating with staff and peers. Denise does not want Juan to be corrected and asked to constantly repeat himself in English. She believes the goal is language development, no matter what language he speaks. Grace and Denise have brought this escalating instructional dispute to their program director.

Discussion Questions

1. If you were the program director, describe how you would use Skilled Dialogue to address this instructional dispute between two highly valued teachers.

2. Develop a scripted dialogue that the program director might use to demonstrate *Welcoming* and *Allowing* to both teachers. Discuss this dialogue with colleagues and then extend it to include the remaining four strategies: *Sense-Making, Appreciating, Joining,* and *Harmonizing.*

CONNIE AND MARILYN

Connie is frustrated with her supervisor at the early childhood center where she teaches. She has been a head teacher for 15 years, and the parents love her and even bring her gifts throughout the year. It is like her second home. She is nice to everyone, regardless of the situation. Her supervisor, Marilyn, was hired 4 months ago and has yet to learn all of the children's names. Marilyn told Connie that she would like her to attend a 2-day professional development training on building partnerships with parents and families. Connie does not want to go to the training and leave the children. In addition, she believes that she knows all about working with parents because she has done it successfully for 15 years. Training is a waste of time in her mind. She told Marilyn that she does not need or want to go. Marilyn has observed that, although Connie is a caring and outgoing staff member, she lacks appropriate boundaries in working effectively with parents and families and, for that reason, insists that she go to the training.

Discussion Questions

1. Discuss how Marilyn could use Skilled Dialogue to address Connie's refusal to attend training. Specifically, describe how Marilyn can demonstrate responsiveness to Connie's perspective through *Joining* and *Harmonizing.*

2. Discuss how Marilyn could support the development of 3rd Space options.

JOSE

Jose is 3 years old and is enrolled in Miss Katy's preschool class. Jose has cried and clung to his mother, Mrs. Ortega, every morning since school started 3 weeks ago. Miss Katy is not worried about his behavior. She understands it is typical at this age and believes that it is part of Jose's development of independence. In fact, within 10 minutes of his mother leaving, he is fine and joins in classroom activities. Miss Katy invited Mrs. Ortega to observe his behavior after she leaves through the one-way observation window. However, Mrs. Ortega is embarrassed by Jose's behavior and apologizes repeatedly to Miss Katy.

Mrs. Ortega has started to bring Miss Katy homemade baked goods "because working with Jose is so hard." Miss Katy explained to Mrs. Ortega on several occasions that Jose's behavior is typical and she is not concerned.

On one occasion, Jose had a particularly difficult separation. He was crying, throwing himself on the floor, refusing to let go of his mother's coat, and begging his mother not to leave. Miss Katy's efforts to distract Jose were unsuccessful. Mrs. Ortega apologized profusely and was on the verge of tears. She said that if Jose did not stop his "horrible behavior" she would not let him come to school any more. Miss Katy decided to schedule a meeting with Mrs. Ortega to discuss the situation.

Discussion Questions

1. What role could different cultural values and beliefs play in this situation?

2. Describe how differing cultural values and beliefs can be addressed through the use of Skilled Dialogue.

3. How could Miss Katy use the strategies of *Sense-Making* and *Appreciating* in this case, and how might they lead to *Joining* and *Harmonizing?*

TOMMIE AND MISS KATHY

Tommie is a 6-year-old child with significant developmental delays in language and social skills. His teacher, Miss Kathy, has been encouraging his mother to implement a daily routine to make his transition to and from school easier, as well as to ease daily living activities at home. She provided Tommie's mother with articles to read on the benefits of such routines for children with developmental delays. She even made her a sample daily schedule to use as a model. Miss Kathy invited her to observe Tommie's use of a schedule in the classroom for making choices, transitioning activities, and decreasing problem behavior. Even with this explicit support, however, Tommie's mother refuses to use a schedule, and Tommie continues to arrive at school upset, late, or not at all. Miss Kathy believes Tommie's mom is uncooperative and is not interested in her son's success at school.

Discussion Questions

1. How might the use of Skilled Dialogue assist Miss Kathy in building a collaborative relationship with Tommie's mother?

2. Which disposition might Miss Kathy focus on first—Choosing Relationship over Control or Setting the Stage for Miracles?

3. Discuss how Miss Kathy can work with Tommie's mother by honoring her identity voice and the connection that exists between them.

4. Using the Skilled Dialogue Reflection Guide (Appendix C) as a pre-interaction planning tool, plan the next meeting between Miss Kathy and Tommie's mother. What might each of the strategies look like in this case?

ANGIE AND ARTURO

Angie has been teaching kindergarten for 15 years. Each year her students come from three different preschool programs in town. One of her students, Arturo, is 5 years old and has no previous school experience. His family just moved from a nearby town where he had not attended any childcare or pre-kindergarten program. Arturo, thus, has not had the opportunity to learn the behavioral expectations of a classroom, such as how to walk in the hall, line up, keep his hands and feet to himself, or when and how to listen to directions. As a result, he is often both literally and figuratively out of step with the other children. Angie is frustrated that Arturo is disrupting instruction and taking time away from the other children. Angie knows she needs to teach Arturo specific behaviors, but she never seems to have the time.

Discussion Questions

1. Discuss how Angie could use the Skilled Dialogue disposition of Choosing Relationship over Control to begin to address Arturo's behavior. How might she start to think of it in a new way? What might she start to say and do when Arturo does not behave in expected ways?

2. Which critical aspects and behaviors associated with *Welcoming* and *Allowing* might be used to demonstrate respect for Arturo?

JACOB AND MISS PAT

Jacob has a smile on his face every morning when he arrives at Miss Pat's special education preschool classroom. He is also demanding and intense, and everyone knows when he is happy, angry, or sad. He likes to control the other children and the classroom materials. He gives Miss Pat and the other children directions, such as "Miss Pat, that is not the way it goes," "Miss Pat, that is the wrong color, use red," and "Amy, you are wrong; you are stupid." He is not physically aggressive, but he is verbally aggressive, and the other children refuse to play with him. He is unable to read other's social cues and charges into other children's play inappropriately. Miss Pat is beginning to feel that it is a good day when Jacob does not come to school!

Discussion Questions

1. What Skilled Dialogue strategies could Miss Pat use to understand the reasons behind Jacob's behavior? Describe her first steps in using the selected strategy(ies).

2. Discuss what *Sense-Making* and *Appreciating* might look like in this case.

3. Discuss what *Joining* and *Harmonizing* might look like in this case.

CHARLES, GRANDMOTHER SIMONE, AND MRS. PETERSON

Charles is a 5-year-old boy who was sent to live with his Grandmother Simone when his mother was incarcerated 2 years ago for drug abuse and neglect. The whereabouts of his father are unknown. His mother is now attempting to regain custody and has a scheduled weekly visit at the grandmother's house. However, she did not show up the last two Sundays. Grandmother Simone reported to Mrs. Peterson, Charles's kindergarten teacher, that Charles gets very angry when she does not arrive, destroys everything in sight, yells at his grandmother that he hates her, throws himself on the floor, and cries until he is exhausted. On Monday mornings following those weekends, Charles does not want to go to school and refuses to get in the car. Grandmother Simone is tired of fighting with Charles and has not brought him to school for the last 6 days. She called Mrs. Peterson and explained why she could not bring him to school. She said that she is tired of fighting with him and that "he can go next year." Mrs. Peterson wants to use Skilled Dialogue to address Charles's attendance.

Discussion Questions

1. Discuss why it is critical that Mrs. Peterson first make a commitment to choose relationship over control?

2. Role-play Grandmother Simone and Mrs. Peterson using the strategies of *Welcoming* and *Allowing*. Relate the behavior expressions of these strategies to the following statement: "Differences do not make people wrong."

3. Continue to role-play using the remaining four strategies (*Sense-Making*, *Appreciating*, *Joining*, and *Harmonizing*). What might be a third choice that is inclusive of the existing choices (i.e., responding to Charles's need to attend a learning environment or responding to his need to stay home)?

CODY AND MRS. MILLER

Mrs. Miller teaches a kindergarten–1st grade inclusive classroom. At the end of the first month of school, Mrs. Miller feels she has made a terrible mistake accepting her first teaching job in an inclusive classroom of 14 children and one aide. Cody, a student in her classroom, likes to run out of the classroom and away from adults. He runs out two to three times a day. He laughs and smiles as he makes his escape. Either Mrs. Miller or the aide has to leave the classroom to search for him, and they always find him in a different location. The classroom door has a push bar, so she cannot lock the door, and there is a school policy against locking classroom doors even if she could. Mrs. Miller is always fearful that he will "escape" and make it to the busy street in front of the school. Mrs. Miller has not received any support from her principal or the school psychologist. Cody's behavior is not considered severe enough for a referral for special education services, and she has been told to maintain better control of her classroom. Mrs. Miller has used timeouts and rewards with Cody, but nothing has worked. She wants to use Skilled Dialogue with Cody.

Discussion Questions

1. Discuss how Mrs. Miller could begin to work with Cody using Skilled Dialogue. How would she demonstrate respect, reciprocity, and responsiveness at his developmental level? What might be some of the words and/or phrases she could use?

2. What new understandings of his escapes might she develop through *Sense-Making* and *Appreciating?*

3. Using these new understandings, what complementary aspects of their diverse perspectives (i.e., Cody's need to leave the classroom and Mrs. Miller's need to ensure his safety and have him stay in the classroom) might she identify and leverage (i.e., use to develop inclusive behavioral options that access Cody's strengths and resources)?

MISS ALEX AND MISS AMY

Miss Alex has been teaching the toddler program at Lakeview Preschool for 10 years, and she is proud of her program and her behavior management skills. Her children are "preschool ready" when they leave her program. Miss Amy, a colleague, taught 1 year and is new to Lakeview Preschool. Miss Alex and Miss Amy teach in joining classrooms, and their children share in many activities throughout the day.

They each have very different ideas about time-out as a positive behavioral support strategy. Miss Alex believes that time-out should be used as an alternative to scolding and punishment. Children should be placed in the Thinking Chair after demonstrating inappropriate behavior. While children are in the Thinking Chair, they are not allowed to participate in classroom activities and interactions with other children and staff. When they are done "thinking" about what they did, they may rejoin the group.

Miss Amy believes that use of the Thinking Chair is inappropriate because it does not teach a child how to correct his or her behavior. It does not provide an opportunity for the child to develop internal control over his or her behavior and it decreases self-confidence. She firmly believes that time-out is a punishment, not a positive guidance strategy. Miss Amy is feeling very stressed about Miss Alex's criticism of her classroom management skills and her opposition to the time-out chair. Miss Amy has casually shared her feelings about time-out with Miss Alex, but she feels she is not getting her point across and needs to have a more serious conversation with Miss Alex without offending her.

Discussion Questions

1. Discuss what examples Miss Amy could use to demonstrate the dispositions and six strategies of Skilled Dialogue as these are used with children?

2. What strategy do you think might be the most challenging for Miss Amy to implement? Why? What specific behavioral language could she use to address this challenge?

References

Albert, L. (1996). *Cooperative discipline.* Shoreview, MN: AGS Publishers.

Albert, L. (2003). *Cooperative discipline: A teacher's handbook.* Shoreview, MN: AGS Publishers.

Allen, P.G. (1999). *Off the reservation: Reflections on boundary-busting, border-crossing loose cannons.* Boston: Beacon Press.

Anderson, P.P., & Fenichel, E.S. (1989). *Serving culturally diverse families of infants and toddlers with disabilities.* Washington, DC: National Center for Clinical Infant Programs.

Anthony, E.J., & Cohler, B.J. (Eds.). (1987). *The invulnerable child.* New York: Guildford Press.

Aquilino, W.S., & Supple A.J., (2001). Long-term effects of parenting practices during adolescence on well-being outcomes in young adulthood. *Journal of Family Issues, 22*(3), 289–308.

Association for Supervision and Curriculum Development. (2007). *The learning compact redefined: A call to action. A report of the Commission on the Whole Child.* Alexandria, VA: Author.

Barrera & Corso. (2000). [Cultural diversity and early childhood: A critical review of literature with implication for ECSE research, evaluation and practice.] Unpublished research.

Barrera, I., Corso, R.M., & Macpherson, D. (2003). *Skilled Dialogue: Strategies for responding to cultural diversity in early childhood.* Baltimore: Paul H. Brookes Publishing Co.

Battistich, V. (1999, October). *Assessing implementation of the Child Development Project.* Paper presented at the Meeting on Implementation Research in School-Based Models of Prevention and Promotion, Pennsylvania State University, State College.

Baumrind, D. (1991) The influence of parenting style on adolescent competence and substance use. *Journal of Early Adolescence, 11*(1), 56–95.

Beaty, J.J. (1999). *Prosocial guidance for the preschool child.* Upper Saddle River, NJ: Merrill.

Bell, S.H., Carr, V., Denno, D., Johnson, L.J., & Phillips, L.R. (2004). *Challenging behaviors in early childhood settings: Creating a place for all children.* Baltimore: Paul H. Brookes Publishing Co.

Bilmes, J. (2004). *Beyond behavior management: Six life skills children need to thrive in today's world.* St. Paul: Redleaf Press.

Block, P. (2002). *The answer to how is yes: Acting on what matters.* San Francisco: Berrett-Koehler.

Bowers, C.A., & Flinders, D.J. (1990). *Responsive teaching: An ecological approach to classroom patterns of language, culture, and thought.* New York: Teachers College Press.

Bowman, B.T. (1994). The challenge of diversity. *Phi Delta Kappan, 76,* 218–224.

Bowman, B.T. (1999). *Kindergarten practices with children from low-income families.* In R.C. Pianta & M.J. Cox. (Eds.), *The transition to kindergarten* (pp. 281–301). Baltimore: Paul H. Brookes Publishing Co.

Bryner, A., & Markova, D. (1996). *An unused intelligence: Physical thinking for 21st century leadership.* San Francisco: Conari Press.

Canter, L., & Canter, M. (1992). *Assertive discipline: Positive behavior management for today's classroom.* Santa Monica, CA: Canter and Associates.

235

Childre, D., & Rozman, D. (2005). *Transforming stress: The Heartmath solution for relieving worry, fatigue, and tension.* Oakland: New Harbinger Publications.

Childs, C. (1998). *The spirit's terrain.* Boston: Beacon Press.

Chivian, E. & Berstein, A. (Eds.). (2008). *Sustaining life.* New York: Oxford University Press.

control. (2008). Retrieved December 11, 2008, http://www.merriam-webster.com/dictionary/control

controlling. (2008). Retrieved December 11, 2008, http://www.merriam-webster.com/dictionary/controlling

Copenhaver-Johnson, J.F. (2006). Talking to children about race: The importance of inviting difficult conversations. *Childhood Education, 83,* 12–22.

Crimmins, D., Farrell, A.F. Smith, P.W., & Bailey, A. (2007). *Positive behavioral strategies for students with behavior problems.* Baltimore: Paul H. Brookes Publishing Co.

Cummins, J. (1984). *Bilingualism and special education: Issues in assessment and pedagogy.* Philadelphia: Multilingual Matters.

Cummins, J. (1989). A theoretical framework for bilingual special education. *Exceptional Children, 56*(2), 111–119.

Curwin, R.L., & Mendler, A.N. (1990). *Am I in trouble? Using discipline to teach young children responsibility.* Santa Cruz, CA: Network Publications.

Curwin, R., & Mendler, L. (2008). *Discipline with dignity: New challenges, new solutions.* Alexandria, VA: ASCD Publications.

Devito, J.A. (2005). *The interpersonal communication book.* Boston: Allyn & Bacon.

Dobson, T., & Miller, V. (1993). *Aikido in everyday life: Giving in to get your way* (2nd ed.). Berkeley, CA: North Atlantic Books.

Dunst, C., Trivette, C., & Deal, A. (1988). *Enabling and empowering families.* Cambridge, MA: Brookline Books.

Essa, E. (2008). *What to do when, practical guidance strategies for challenging behavior in preschool.* Florence, KY :Thomas Delmar Learning.

Foster, G.M. (1970). Character and personal relationships seen through proverbs in Tzintzuntzan, Mexico. *The Journal of American Folklore, 83*(329), 304–317.

Freedman, J., & Combs, G. (1996). *Narrative therapy: The social construction of preferred realities.* New York: W.W. Norton.

Fritz, R. (1989). *The path of least resistance: Learning to become the creative force in your own life.* New York: Fawcett Columbine.

Fritz, R. (1991). *Creating: A practical guide to the creative process and how to use it to create anything—a work of art, a relationship, a career or a better life.* New York: Fawcett Columbine.

Fletcher, J.L., & Olwyler, K. (1997). *Paradoxical thinking: How to profit from your contradictions.* San Francisco: Berrett-Koehler.

Gardner, H. (1993). *Frames of mind: The theory of multiple intelligences.* New York: Basic Books.

Gartrell, D. (2003). *The power of guidance: Teaching social-emotional skills in early childhood classrooms.* Florence, KY: Thomson Delmar Learning.

Gernsbacher, M.A. (2006). Toward a behavior of reciprocity. *Journal of Developmental Processes, 1,* 139–152.

Goldstein, S., & Brooks, R. (2002). *Raising resilient children: A curriculum to foster strength, hope, and optimism in children.* Baltimore: Paul H. Brookes Publishing Co.

Goleman, D. (1995). *Emotional intelligence.* New York: Bantam.

Goleman, D. (2006). *Social intelligence: The new science of human relationships.* New York: Bantam.

Gordon, A., & Browne, K. (1996). *Guiding young children in a diverse society.* Boston: Allyn & Bacon.

Groome, T. (1980). *Christian religious education.* New York: Harper & Row.

Gurian, M. (2007). *Nurture the nature: Understanding and supporting your child's unique core personality.* San Francisco: Jossey-Bass.

Hall, E.T., & Hall, M.R. (1990). *Understanding cultural differences.* Boston: Intercultural Press.

Hanson, M.J., & Lynch, E.W. (2003). *Understanding families: Approaches to diversity, disability, and risk.* Baltimore: Paul H. Brookes Publishing Co.

Hatfield, E., Cacioppo, J.T., & Rapson, R.T. (1993). *Emotional contagion.* New York: Cambridge University Press.

Howes, C., & Ritchie, S. (2002). *Matter of trust: Connecting teachers and learners in the early childhood classroom.* New York: Teachers College Press.

Isaacs, W. (1999). *Dialogue and the art of thinking together.* New York: Doubleday.

Jackson, C., Henriksen, L., & Foshee, V.A. (1998) The Authoritative Parenting Index: Predicting health risk behaviors among children and adolescents. *Health Education & Behavior, 25*(3), 321–339.

Jackson, N., Robinson, H., & Dale, P. (1977). *Cognitive development in young children.* Pacific Grove, CA: Brooks/Cole Publishing Company.

Jaffe, E. (2007). Mirror neurons: How we reflect on behavior. *APS Observer, 20*(5).

Jaworski, J. (1996). *Synchronicity: The inner path of leadership.* San Francisco: Berrett-Koehler.

Josselson, R. (1996). *The space between us.* Thousand Oaks, CA: Sage

Kahane, A. (2004). *Solving tough problems: An open way of talking, listening, and creating new realities.* San Francisco: Berrett-Koehler.

Kaiser, B., & Rasminsky, J.S. (2007). *Challenging behavior in young children: Understanding, preventing, and responding effectively* (2nd ed.). Boston: Allyn & Bacon.

Katie, B., & Mitchell, S. (2002). *Loving what is: Four questions that can change your life.* New York: Three Rivers Press.

Kellam, S.G., Mayer, L.S., Rebok, G.W., & Hawkins, W.E. (1998). The effects of improving achievement on aggressive behavior and of improving aggressive behavior on achievement through two prevention interventions: An investigation of causal paths. In B. Dohrenwend (Ed.), *Adversity, stress, and psychopathology* (pp. 486–505). Oxford, United Kingdom: Oxford University Press.

King, S., & Browitt, J. (Eds.). (2004). *The space of culture: Critical readings in Hispanic studies.* Newark: University of Delaware Press.

Kohn, A. (2006). *Unconditional parenting: Moving from rewards and punishments to love and reason.* New York: Atria Books.

Koplow, L. (Ed.). (2007). *Unsmiling faces: How preschools can heal* (2nd ed.). New York: Teachers College Press.

Kopp, C.B. (1982). *Child: Developing in a social context.* Reading, MA: Addison-Wesley

Kostelnik, M.J., & Stein L.C. (1993). *Guiding children's social development* (2nd ed.). Albany, NY: Delmar.

Kostelnik, M., Whiren, A., Soderman, A.K., Gregory, K., & Stein, L.L. (2008). *Guiding children's social development: Theory to practice* (6th ed.). Albany, NY: Delmar.

Lahiri, J. (2006, March 6). My two lives. *Newsweek, 147*(10).

Landy, S. (2002). *Pathways to competence: Encouraging healthy social and emotional development in young children.* Baltimore: Paul H. Brookes Publishing Co.

Langer, E.J. (1997). *The power of mindful learning.* New York: Perseus Books.

Langer, E.J. (2005). *On becoming an artist: Reinventing yourself through mindful creativity.* New York: Ballantine Books.

Mah, R. (2006). *Difficult behavior in early childhood: Positive discipline for pre-K-3 classrooms and beyond.* Thousand Oaks, CA: Corwin Press.

Marcum, D., & Smith, S. (2007). *Egonomics: What makes ego our greatest asset (or most expensive liability).* New York: Simon & Shuster.

Markus, H.R., & Kitayama, S. (1991). Culture and the self: Implications for cognition, emotion, and motivation. *Psychological Review, 98*(2). 224–253.

Markus, H.R., & Kitayama, S. (2003). Models of agency: Sociocultural diversity in the construction of action. In V. Murphy-Berman & J.J. Berman (Eds.), *Cross-cultural perspectives on the self: Nebraska Symposium on Motivation, vol. 49* (pp. 2–57). Lincoln: University of Nebraska Press.

Moll, L.C., Amanti, C., Neff, D., & Gonzalez, N. (1992). Funds of knowledge for teaching: Using a qualitative approach to connect homes and classrooms. *Theory into Practice 31*(2) 132–141.

Murray, D.E. (1992). Unlimited resources: Tapping into learners' language, culture, and thought. In Murray, D.E. (Ed.), *Diversity as resource: Redefining cultural literacy* (pp. 259–274). Alexandria, VA: TESOL.

Nakkula, M.J., & Ravitch, S. (1998). *Matters of interpretation.* San Francisco: Jossey-Bass.

Nelsen, J. (2006). *Positive discipline.* New York: Ballantine Books.

Noddings, N. (2005). *The challenge to care in schools.* New York: Teachers College Press.

Palmer, P.J. (1997). *The courage to teach: Exploring the inner landscape of a teacher's life.* San Francisco: Jossey-Bass.

Payne, R. (2005). *A framework for understanding poverty.* Highlands, TX: aha! Process, Inc.

Perkins, D. (2000). *The eureka effect: The art and logic of breakthrough thinking.* New York: W.W. Norton.

Pickett, J.P. (Ed.). (2000). *The American Heritage dictionary of the English language* (4th ed.). Boston: Houghton Mifflin.

Pieper, M.H., & Pieper, W.J. (1999). *Smart love.* Boston: The Harvard Common Press.

Pink, D.H. (2006). *A whole new mind.* New York: Riverhead Books.

Porter, A. (1990). *Young children's behavior: Practical approach for caregivers and teachers* (2nd ed.). Baltimore: Paul H. Brookes Publishing Co.

Radziszewska, B., Richardson, J.L., Dent, C.W., & Flay, B.R. (1996) Parenting style and adolescent depressive symptoms, smoking, and academic achievement: Ethnic, gender, and SES differences. *Journal of Behavioral Medicine, 19*(3), 289–305.

related. (2008). In *Merriam-Webster Online Dictionary.* Retrieved December 11, 2008, from http://www.merriam-webster.com/dictionary/related

relation. (2008). In *Merriam-Webster Online Dictionary.* Retrieved December 11, 2008, from http://www.merriam-webster.com/dictionary/relation

relationship. (2008). In *Merriam-Webster Online Dictionary.* Retrieved December 11, 2008, from http://www.merriam-webster.com/dictionary/relationship

Remen, R.N. (2000). *My grandfather's blessings.* New York: Riverhead Books.

Resnick, M.D., Bearman, P.S., Blum, R.W., Bauman, K.E., Harris, K.M., Jones, J., et al. (1997). Protecting adolescents from harm: Findings from the National Longitudinal Study on Adolescent Health. *Journal of the American Medical Association, 278,* 823–832.

Reynolds, E. (1990). *Guiding young children: A child centered approach.* Mountain View, CA: Mayfield Publishing.

Rizzolatti, G., Fogassi, L., & Gallese, V. (2006, November). Mirrors in the mind. *Scientific American, 295*(5), 54-61.

Roberts, M. (2001). *Horse sense for people: Using the gentle wisdom of the join-up technique to enrich our relationships at home and at work.* New York: Viking Press.

Rodd, J. (1996). *Understanding young children's behavior.* New York: Teachers College Press.

Rosenberg, M.B. (1999). *Nonviolent communication: A language of compassion.* Encinitas, CA: PuddleDancer Press.

Rosinski, P. (2003). *Coaching across cultures: New tools for leveraging national, corporate, and professional differences.* Yarmouth, ME: Nicholas Brealey.

Saifer, S. (2003). *Practical solutions to practically every problem: The early childhood teacher's manual.* St. Paul, MN: Redleaf Press.

Sawyer, K. (2007). *Group genius: The creative power of collaboration.* New York: Basic Books.

Salter, A. (2004). *Predators: Pedophiles, rapists, and other sex offenders.* New York: Basic Books.

Schulte, L.E., Edick, N., Edwards, S., & Mackiel, D. (2004). The development and validation of the Teacher Dispositions Index. *Essays In Education, 12.*

Seelye, H.N., & Wasilewski, J.H. (1996). *Between cultures: Developing self-identity in a world of diversity.* New York: McGraw-Hill.

Senge, P.M., Scharmer, C.O., Jaworski, J., & Flowers, B.S. (2005). *Presence: Human purpose and the field of the future.* New York: Currency/Doubleday.

Sewall, L. (1999). *Sight and sensibility: The ecopsychology of perception.* New York: Tarcher.

Shafir, R.Z. (2000). *The Zen of listening: Mindful communication in the age of distraction.* Wheaton, IL: Quest Books.

Shelton, C. (1999). *Quantum leaps.* Woburn, MA: Butterworth-Heinemann.

Shevin, M. (1993). Establishing reciprocity in facilitated communication interactions. *Facilitated Communication Digest, 1*(4), 5–7.

Simons-Morton, B., Haynie, D.L., Crump, A.D., Eitel, S.P., Saylor, K.E. (2001). Peer and parent influences on smoking and drinking among early adolescents. *Health & Education Behavior, 28*(1), 95–107.

Slaby, R.G., & Parke, R.D. (1968). The effect on resistance-to-deviation of observing a model's affective reactions to response consequences. *Developmental Psychology, 5,* 40–47.

Slocumb, P.D., & Payne, R.K. (2000). Removing the mask: Giftedness in poverty, from *Slocumb-Payne Teacher Perception Inventory: A Rating Scale for Students from Diverse Backgrounds;* Highlands, TX: aha! Process.

Stewart, E.C., & Bennett, M.J. (1991). *American cultural patterns: A cross-cultural perspective.* Yarmouth, ME: Intercultural Press.

Stone, D., Patton, B., & Heen, S.(1999). *Difficult conversations.* New York: Viking.

Thomas, R.R. (1996). *Redefining diversity.* New York: AMACON.

Tishman, S., Jay, E., & Perkins, D.N. (1992). Teaching thinking dispositions: From transmission to enculturation. *Theory into Practice, 32*(3), 147–153.

Tortora, S. (2005). *The dancing dialogue: Using the communicative power of movement with young children.* Baltimore: Paul H. Brookes Publishing Co.

Vygotsky, L. (1978). *Mind in society.* Cambridge, MA: Harvard University Press.

Watson, M. (2003*). Learning to trust.* San Francisco: Jossey-Bass.

Wheatley, M.J. (1992). *Leadership and the new science: Learning about organization from an orderly universe.* San Francisco: Berrett-Kohler.

Wheatley, M.J. (2005). *Finding our way: Leadership for an uncertain time.* San Francisco: Berrett-Koehler.

Wind, Y., & Cook, C. (2004). *The power of impossible thinking: Transform the business of your life and the life of your business.* Philadelphia: Wharton School Publishing.

Winslade, J., & Monk, G. (2000). *Narrative mediation: A new approach to conflict resolution.* San Francisco: Jossey-Bass.

Wood, P. (2005). *Secrets of the people whisperer: A horse whisperer's techniques for enhancing communication and building relationships.* Berkeley, CA: Ulysses Press.

Yaconelli, M. (1998). *Dangerous wonder: The adventure of childlike faith.* Grand Rapids, MI: Zondervan Publishing Company.

Yankelovich, D. (1999). *The magic of dialogue: Transforming conflict into cooperation.* New York: Simon & Schuster.

Zaiss, C. (2002). *True partnership: Revolutionary thinking about relating to others.* San Francisco: Berrett-Koehler.

Zander, R.S., & Zander, B. (2000). *The art of possibility: Transforming professional and personal life.* Boston: Harvard Business School Publishing.

Overview of Behavioral Approaches to Challenging Behavior

There are various contemporary approaches and models of positive behavior management. There is no "perfect" behavioral approach. Good teaching occurs when teachers care and respect their students. In this appendix, the authors describe some of the most frequently used positive behavioral approaches used by classroom teachers. The approaches reflect varying degrees of respect, reciprocity, and responsiveness. It is the primary focus and implementation of each approach that is unique.

POSITIVE BEHAVIORAL INTERVENTIONS AND SUPPORTS

The Positive Behavioral Interventions and Supports (PBIS) approach was originally developed for children with severe disabilities as an alternative to more traditional behavioral methods. PBIS currently is used by educators and parents to achieve long-term positive social behavior in all children through the assessment and modification of the learning environment. It is based on research that examines the environment of where the problematic behavior occurs. Behavior is addressed through effective environmental and culturally appropriate interventions that result in the problem behavior being less effective and relevant and the desired behavior more functional for the student. PBIS is the application of research-validated practices to create school environments that improve lifestyle results, including personal, health, social, family, work, and recreation, by shaping each child's behavior.

PBIS differs from traditional behavioral approaches in that it focuses on changing the environment. It can be used for individual students with persistent behavior problems, as well as implemented as a schoolwide program. The first goal is to identify the problem behavior, extinguish the behavior, and teach a more appropriate replacement behavior. Functional Behavioral Assessment (FBA) is a critical component of PBIS. The FBA provides input from several individuals who observe the student with the challenging behavior. The FBA outcomes clearly identify and define the problem behavior, the frequency and duration of the behavior, and actions and occurrences that precede the behavior and occur after the behavior. The PBIS plan is developed based on the FBA and will provide strategies to avoid the problem behavior and encourage positive social behavior by creating a new "environment." The adaptations to the environment may include student grouping, an inclusive classroom, and modifications of classroom activities and materials. The PBIS approach is based on research that concludes that thoughtful arrangement of the physical environment significantly increases the frequency and duration of positive behavior for a student with behavioral challenges.

Student grouping in PBIS is understood as the inclusion of students with good social skills interacting and participating in shared activities with students with less developed social skills. Student grouping may also include the placement of children in circle time or specific activities so that a child has the opportunity to observe and model the appropriate behavior of peers without direct adult intervention. Organizing the classroom environment and the prudent selection of materials and toys also discourages the problem behavior and teaches the child replacement behavior. For example, selecting materials and activities may include the replacement of tricycles with a wagon to encourage children to spontaneously give each other rides, and limiting and cycling learning center materials increases the opportunities for peer interactions and provides "new" experiences when rotated. The introduction of new toys and rotation of toys are natural motivators and encourage positive peer interaction. Toys and materials that require sharing—rocking boats, wagons, mural paintings, and large toys that require two or more children to move —reduce problem behavior and provide positive role models for the child with less developed social skills and behavioral challenges.

PBIS has evolved from an individual child-based approach to a popular highly structured continuum of schoolwide behavioral support. School administrators, faculty, staff, and student family members participate in planning teams and learn how to teach students the importance of schoolwide expectations at home and in the community.

If you would like to read more about positive discipline, visit http://www .pbis.org for schoolwide programs and http://www.nasponline.org/publications for information about individual child applications.

CHILD SELF-MANAGEMENT THROUGH PERSONAL MESSAGE

Child self-management is the ability of the child to regulate his or her actions to match personal values and societal expectations rather than depend on others to enforce compliance (Kopp, 1982). Characteristics of child self-management include impulse control, delayed gratification, initiation and implementation of plans of action (e.g., sharing a toy with another child), and the ability to initiate positive interactions with others without adult or peer oversight. The development of a child's self-management skills increases with his or her maturity and is based on positive interactions with parents and the significant adults in his or her life. Toddlers and young children respond to rewards and punishments from adults they care about to determine if their behavior is successful.

This approach uses a personal message to increase the development of a child's self-management skills, resulting in increased positive behavior (Kostelnik, Whiren, Soderman, Gregory, & Stein, 2008). Before constructing a personal message, the adult must determine the intent of the child's behavior. When the intent of the child's behavior is clearly identified then alternative behaviors agreeable to the child and the adult are suggested. Step one of the personal message is to reflect on the behavior and acknowledge the child's perspective. Reflection provides time for the adult to process the event, consider the uniqueness of the child, and show respect for the child by seeing the behavior from the child's perspective. For example, "You can really ride your bike fast," "It is really crowded out here today; I am afraid we might have an accident and someone could get hurt," and "Slow down and the other children will slow down behind you."

The second step in the personal message attaches the adult's emotions to the child's behavior and then provides a reason why the behavior causes the emotion. For example, "I am worried when you throw those big wooden blocks. Someone could really get hurt. I would feel so sad if any of you got injured." Sharing the adult's emotions allows the child to develop empathy, a closer honest relationship with an adult, and observe the linking of words to feelings. Providing the child a reason why his or her behavior is a concern for the adult is critical as the child must be very clear what specific behavior needs to be changed. The adult's reasons provide causality and link the behavior to the adult's reaction. Children who experience adults modeling reasoning to address problem solving demonstrate increased self-management skills and less aggression than children not exposed to the adult reasoning (Slaby & Parker, 1968).

The third step of the personal message tells the child the replacement behavior or what he or she needs to do. For example, "Put the blocks down, don't throw them" and "Slow down and the other children will slow down behind you." The child now has an understanding of the rule and why the rule is important to the adult. Good rules specify the exact behavior that adults value and find acceptable (Jackson, Robinson, & Dale, 1977). Young children respond more quickly to being told *what* to do, rather than *what not* to do, as they often do not attend to each word that is spoken.

Another use of the personal message is to reinforce a child's positive behavior. The positive personal message identifies the adult's positive reactions and/or feelings and clearly states the child's positive behavior. For example, "Thank you for waiting at the door. I'm so pleased. You did a good job waiting quietly." In this example, the child knows specifically what behavior was rewarded—waiting quietly at the door. Positive personal message provides a direct reinforcement of a young child's behavior and helps the child internalize the positive behavior to support developing self-management skills.

If you would like to know more about positive personal messages read *Guiding Children's Social Development and Learning, Sixth Edition* (Kostelnik et al., 2008).

POSITIVE DISCIPLINE

The Positive Discipline approach (Nelsen, 2006) suggests strategies students, teachers, and members of the community can use to develop interpersonal relationships in which each individual child is respected, valued, and expected to act in a positive manner. Positive Discipline is based on research that reports children increase their positive behavior when they experience both firmness and kindness from their parents. Children who rate their parents as authoritative demonstrate less socially risky behaviors (Aquilino & Supple, 2001; Baumrind, 1991; Jackson et al., 1998; Radziszewska et al., 1996; Simons-Morton et al., 2001). Older children's connectedness to home and school decreases socially inappropriate behavior and increases academic performance (Resnick et al., 1997). Behavioral interventions that teach children skills for positive social interactions and a sense of belonging in the elementary grades have long-term positive effects (Battistich, 1999; Kellam et al., 1998).

This approach suggests strategies for teachers and parents that demonstrate kindness and firmness in teaching children social skills that encourage the development of self-discipline, self-respect, cooperation, appropriate behavior, and problem-solving skills. The foundational understanding to Positive Discipline is that children must feel they are part of a larger group and be provided opportunities to make positive contributions to that group: family, classroom, school, or community. As members of the larger group, they learn that acting responsibly and demonstrating appropriate behavior is directly linked to the privileges they earn. The child learns to be an active member in an environment of kindness, firmness, dignity, and respect. When children are not provided opportunities to make a contribution to the group to feel successful or earn privileges based on meeting their responsibilities and positive behavior, they often feel incapable, which results in inappropriate and avoidance behaviors.

Teachers and parents must provide opportunities for children to make meaningful contributions to the classroom and family. In contemporary society, children frequently do not have natural opportunities to feel needed or to be a valuable contributor. Positive Discipline's basic tenet is that most problem behavior is eliminated when a teacher or parent uses effective strategies to help a child develop the Significant Seven Perceptions and Skills (Nelsen, 2006).

1. Strong perceptions of personal capabilities: "I am capable."

2. Strong perceptions of significance in primary relationships: "I contribute in meaningful ways and I am genuinely needed."

3. Strong perceptions of personal power or influence over life: "I can influence what happens to me."

4. Strong intrapersonal skills: the ability to understand personal emotions and to use that understanding to develop self-discipline and self-control

5. Strong interpersonal skills: the ability to work with others and develop friendships through communicating, cooperating, negotiating, sharing, empathizing, and listening

6. Strong systemic skills: the ability to respond to the limits and consequences of everyday life with responsibility, adaptability, flexibility, and integrity

7. Strong judgmental skills: the ability to use wisdom and to evaluate situations according to appropriate values

When children have the opportunity to develop these understandings and skills through contribution, they gain feelings of belonging and increased self-significance. Discipline is the direct relationship of the child's level of reasonability to the level of privileges they earn. Positive behavior results in earned privileges. A child's occurrence of misbehavior or lack of responsibility is addressed by not earning privileges, which is followed by a teacher or parent providing future opportunities of responsibility and rebuilding feelings of success and capability. Children who develop feelings of success and capability through responsible behavior are less likely to misbehave or demonstrate avoidance behaviors.

If you would like to read more about Positive Discipline, visit http://www .positivediscipline.com.

COOPERATIVE DISCIPLINE

Cooperative Discipline (Albert, 2003) is based on two understandings. First, a classroom must provide a safe orderly environment in which children can learn. Second, teachers must build students' self-esteem, which results in more responsible behavior and increased academic achievement. Cooperative Discipline is a positive behavioral approach that promotes self-discipline by increasing a child's self-esteem, which results in better decision making and self-discipline.

Teachers are encouraged to replace an authoritative, directive attitude with one of cooperation and collaboration, and to move from student criticism to encouragement. Children with healthy self-esteem feel valued, which results in behavior that is cooperative and responsible. Children are instructed and reminded that they are individually responsible for their appropriate behavior. Positive behavior is expected at all times, not just when an adult is present to enforce the rules. Cooperative Discipline suggests that inappropriate behavior can be prevented by building a child's self-esteem while disciplining them through a positive approach.

Cooperative Discipline is based on three beliefs. Children should feel *capable, connected,* and able to make a *contribution* in the classroom (Albert, 1996). Students need to feel capable of being academically successful, as well as socially successful with others. Teachers help students to feel capable by providing a safe environment where mistakes are accepted and learning objectives are attainable for all students. In this environment, everyone has an opportunity to experience success.

The teacher's role in Cooperative Discipline is to understand why a child is misbehaving and the goals of the inappropriate behavior. Then the teacher must intervene immediately, build the child's self-esteem, and provide a positive outcome for a positive behavioral change in the future. The teacher is responsible for guiding the child to choose positive behavior.

Cooperative Discipline suggests the Five As—acceptance, attention, appreciation, affirmation, and affection—as teacher strategies in developing a caring relationship with a child that results in the child being accepting of behavioral guidance. Acceptance is understood as accepting the child as a person, not his or her misbehavior. Attention is demonstrated by greeting each child every day, showing a sincere interest in him or her as an individual and in his or her activities, and encouraging him or her to appropriately ask for attention when he or she needs support. The teacher models very specific appreciation of a child's positive behavior by clearly stating why the behavior is positive for the child and others. The teacher provides affirmation and encouragement through consistent reminders of the child's strengths and previously successful efforts in learning new skills and subject content. Affection is demonstrated by the teacher by always separating the child from his or her behavior. The teacher is steadfast in his or her caring, although he or she may be disappointed in the inappropriate behavior.

Children should be provided opportunities to contribute to the class to feel they are part of the classroom community and that their input makes a difference. A child's class contribution increases self-esteem, increases a feeling of being capable, and forms connections with others in a safe learning environment (Albert, 1996).

Cooperative Discipline provides very specific skills and techniques for dealing with inappropriate student behavior and classroom management. The concept of cooperation extends to administrators, teachers, staff, and parents who all share a common understanding of school and classroom discipline and work collaboratively. Parents play an active role in this approach, receiving guidelines in Cooperative Discipline to use at home and being expected to assist their child in generalizing his or her skills schoolwide, at home, and in the larger community. Parents approve of this behavior approach as they know their child's misbehavior will be addressed in a positive caring manner, and they will be a partner in addressing their child's behavior.

If you would like to read more about Cooperative Discipline visit http://www.montville.net/woodmont/cas/cd/goals.html.

ASSERTIVE DISCIPLINE

The concept of Assertive Discipline was developed to increase the classroom management skills of teachers in gaining appropriate behavior from their students (Canter & Canter, 1992). This popular approach is based on assertiveness training and applied behavior analysis and provides practical classroom strategies for developing logical and consistent consequences for inappropriate behavior. Teachers are asked to take control of their classroom by exercising their authority, insisting on cooperation, and administering a system of behavioral consequences. Whereas this approach acknowledges it is crucial to catch a child being "good" and for the teacher to recognize their positive behavior choices, it is based on the notion that students behave because they know the consequences of breaking the rules.

The teacher is the ultimate authority in the classroom who clearly articulates his or her expectations, sets consistent behavioral limits, and develops a schedule of consequence for inappropriate behavior. At the start of the school year, both students and parents are informed of expected appropriate behaviors and rewards, consequences for inappropriate behavior, and the system for implementing the consequences.

Canter suggests a three-step cycle of behavior management to establish an Assertive Discipline system in the classroom. First, the teacher must directly teach the specific student behaviors expected and not assume the students know what to do. Teachers clearly articulate to the students the specific instructions for each activity during the day—floor time, learning centers, transitions between activities, and so forth before the behavior is required.

Teachers may want students to raise their hands, line up a certain way, clear their desks, put their backpacks on a hook, close their books when they are done, or stay in their seats until their name is called. After the specific behavior is taught, the teacher must teach the students how to follow the directions. First, directions are stated orally, written down (on a board or flip paper), and modeled by the teacher or a student. A student then restates the directions, the students are asked if there are any questions, and then they immediately engage in the activity.

Second, teachers use positive repetition to reinforce students when they follow the directions. Rather than focusing attention on the students who did not follow directions, teachers should focus on those students who did follow the directions, rephrasing the original directions as a positive comment. For example, "David got his lunch bag and quietly got right in line."

Third, when a student continues to engage in inappropriate behavior after a teacher has taught specific directions and has used positive repetition, then the teacher uses the consequences outlined in the classroom Assertive Discipline plan. Canter suggests a teacher should not use a negative consequence until he or she has reinforced at least two students for the appropriate behavior. It is best for the teacher to stress the positive first rather than the negative to avoid reinforcing a student's negative behavior or creating a negative classroom environment.

When implementing an Assertive Discipline plan students should be told in advance the expected classroom behavior, what will happen if they behave, and what will happen if they choose not to behave. Students learn appropriate behavior by being given clear choices. They learn that they are responsible for their choices and that their choices have consequences. It is the teacher's responsibility to directly teach students to behave appropriately because they cannot be held responsible for something they have not been taught.

To maintain a positive environment for teaching and learning, the teacher must determine the appropriate behavioral expectations for the students and require compliance. The behavior of one student should not have an impact on the learning of another student. In the Assertive Discipline approach, teachers act assertively, quickly, and consistently in addressing each incident of challenging behavior. Students are not understood as adversaries, but as individuals who need structure and who benefit from instruction. It is in the best interest of the students if the teacher provides a safe, teacher-in-charge environment. From this perspective, the teacher builds a positive caring relationship with the students while preparing them for increased academic performance and respectful interactions with those in the larger community.

If you would like to read more about Assertive Discipline visit http://maxweber
.hunter.cuny.edu/pub/eres/EDSPC715_MCINTYRE/AssertiveDiscipline.html

DISCIPLINE WITH DIGNITY

The Discipline with Dignity (Curwin & Mendler, 2008) approach was developed to
provide teachers the structure and skills to effectively manage a variety of challenging behaviors. It is based on a 3-dimensional method for addressing behavior
management: prevention, action, and resolution. Strategies are provided for each
dimension.

The three steps of Discipline with Dignity are as follows:

1. Prevention: Teaching is predictable. You can prevent most disruptions with
    the right mind set!

2. Action: What do we do when a problem occurs? We use both short- and long-
    range strategies.

3. Resolution: How do we deal with the most difficult situations? We often use
    creative and unconventional strategies to apply to these most difficult instances.

Teachers learn techniques to prevent challenging behaviors, to successfully
deal with "button-pressing" behaviors of individual students or groups of students
and maintain their professional dignity, and to effectively address the needs of students with chronic behavior problems.

Discipline with Dignity teaches students responsible thinking, cooperation,
mutual respect, and shared decision making and can be used in a single classroom
or inform a schoolwide disciple program. This program allows students to develop
their self-esteem by giving them the tools and encouragement to make responsible
decisions about their behavior. The student's dignity is the foundation of the program. Positive behavioral change can only take place when the student's dignity
is respected, preserved, and enhanced.

The goals of Discipline with Dignity include asking the following questions:

•   Does a desired behavior improve when no one is watching?

•   Does the strategy used promote motivation to learn?

•   Does the strategy used increase the dignity of the child and teacher?

•   Does the strategy work in the long run as well as the short run?

•   Does it make sense?

There are three unique features of this approach. Classroom rules are succinct, clear, and developed by the teacher and the students to reflect the values of
the classroom and the school, thereby creating a connectedness to the group and
the larger school community.

Consequences are not viewed as punishments, and all of them have an educational element. Students are allowed to "have the last word," which eliminates the
majority of power struggles.

If you would like to read more about Discipline with Dignity visit http://www
.educationworld.com/a_admin/admin/admin534.shtml

Frequently
Asked Questions

1. What is Skilled Dialogue?

Skilled Dialogue is an approach to interactions and communication that focuses on establishing and strengthening respect, reciprocity and responsiveness in order to honor diverse identities, voices and connections. It is anchored by two dispositions: Choosing Relationship over Control and Setting the Stage for Miracles. These dispositions are concretely expressed through six distinct strategies: *Welcoming, Allowing, Sense-Making, Appreciating, Joining,* and *Harmonizing.* Skilled Dialogue is NOT a problem-solving approach; rather, it is an approach designed to create a cognitive and social-emotional context within which optimum solutions may be identified and chosen.

2. For what types of interactions is Skilled Dialogue best suited?

Skilled Dialogue is best suited for interactions that are not proceeding as anticipated due to the presence of some degree of challenge, frustration or disagreement. Such challenge, frustration or disagreement may stem from cultural linguistic diversity or from other sources of differences in behaviors, values, beliefs, and perspectives. It is equally well suited for interactions where respect, reciprocity, and responsiveness are already established and practitioners wish to sustain and deepen them.

3. Is Skilled Dialogue only for situations/ interactions where there is disagreement?

Although it is particularly well suited for interactions where disagreement is present, Skilled Dialogue can enhance any interaction by ensuring that all aspects of the diverse perspectives present can be honored and leveraged to create optimum responses.

4. What are the steps in Skilled Dialogue?

Skilled Dialogue is not a linear process and thus does not necessarily follow set steps. It does, however, include five phases, which may be visited repeatedly as needed. The first phase focuses on setting the dispositions that undergird the Skilled Dialogue strategies, and the final or fifth phase addresses self-reflection. The three middle phases address each of the key outcomes: respect, reciprocity, and responsiveness. Each phase supports and is supported by the other four. For more information, read Part IV in the book. The phases are as follows:

Phase I: Setting Dispositions

Phase II: Building Respect

Phase III: Establishing Reciprocity

Phase IV: Becoming Responsive

Phase V: Self-Reflecting

5. Must all the strategies be used in a given situation/interaction? Must they be used in order?

Typically, the strategies will be used in "clusters;" that is, *Welcoming* and *Allowing* will be used to build respect, *Sense-Making* and *Appreciating* will be used to establish reciprocity, and *Joining* and *Harmonizing* will be used to generate responsive options. However, not all may be present in a single interaction. One may, for example, focus on building respect in an initial interaction and not move on to the other strategies until a second or third interaction. The last two in particular take time and may not be fully achieved until a third or fourth interaction. In other situations, the first strategies may already be in place (e.g., one knows the other person quite well) and only need to be reinforced. In that case, the focus may primarily be on the latter strategies.

Most often the strategies are used in order, especially when learning to use them. This order, however, need not be followed rigidly in all cases. It may be necessary to return to some strategies several times before proceeding to others, for example. The order, though, is one that tends to flow naturally (e.g., *Welcoming* is strengthened by *Allowing*, which opens to the door to curiosity, the mainstay of *Sense-Making*, and so forth.)

6. Does the other person in the interaction need to know Skilled Dialogue?

No, any other person in the interaction does not need to know Skilled Dialogue. It is not, for example, about whether families use Skilled Dialogue; it is about whether practitioners use Skilled Dialogue. One person's use of the Skilled Dialogue dispositions and strategies is sufficient to increase the respect, reciprocity, and responsiveness present in any interaction. At the very least, the use of Skilled Dialogue, even if by only one person, will make it easier to interact with others. At most, the interaction will become truly collaborative and result in outcomes that are satisfactory to everyone involved.

7. How can I find out more about Skilled Dialogue?

Readers are invited to visit the authors' web site (http://www.skilleddialogue.com). They are also welcome to e-mail the authors with specific comments or questions. In addition, they may contact Paul H. Brookes Publishing Co. for information about other materials and/or events related to this book.

Blank Forms

Guide to Identifying Cultural Data
Skilled Dialogue Self-Assessment
Skilled Dialogue Reflection Guide

Guide to Identifying Cultural Data

Child's name: _____   Date completed: _____   Completed by: _____

Note: The questions in the second column tend to arise frequently. There may be others that are not identified on this form. Feel free to add any other questions that need to be answered.

Developmental/curricular area	Questions to answer
Communicative-Linguistic Language(s) of child's primary caregiving environment(s)	1. What language(s) are spoken in the child's primary caregiving environment(s)? 2. Which caregivers speak which language(s) with the child?
Child's relative language proficiency (proficiency in English and other language[s] used)	1. How proficient is the child in understanding and using the language(s) other than English for communicating? 2. How proficient is the child in understanding and using English for communicating? 3. Would the child be considered monolingual? Partial bilingual (speaks and understands one language, only understands another)? Bilingual, dominant in one language (speaks and understands both languages but is significantly more proficient in one)? "Balanced" bilingual (similar levels of proficiency in both languages—may not be strong in either, or may be equally strong in both)?
Patterns of language usage in child's primary caregiving environment(s)	1. With what situations and topics does each language tend to be associated? 2. Which varieties of each language are spoken (e.g., if English is spoken, in which ways is it similar to or different from what is considered the "standard" variety of English?) 3. If two or more languages are used, what seems to govern which language is used when?

From Barrera, I., Corso, R.M., & Macpherson, D. (2003). *Skilled Dialogue: Strategies for Responding to Cultural Diversity in Early Childhood* (pp. 232–236). Baltimore: Paul H. Brookes Publishing Co.; adapted by permission.
In *Using Skilled Dialogue to Transform Challenging Interactions: Honoring Identity, Voice, and Connection* by Isaura Barrera and Lucinda Kramer

Guide to Identifying Cultural Data (cont.)

Developmental/curricular area	Questions to answer
Relative value placed on verbal and nonverbal communication	1. To what degree is communication in the home verbal? To what degree is it nonverbal?
	2. What is the relative value placed on nonverbal communication as compared with verbal communication? Is this true in all situations, or only in some?
Relative status associated with languages other than English and with bilingualism	1. What is the social status accorded in the community to the language(s) other than English spoken in the child's home (e.g., is the accent associated with it considered a mark of distinction or of low education)?
	2. What is the social status accorded in the community to persons who are bilingual? Is being bilingual considered a desirable goal?
Personal-Social	
Degree of acculturation into EuroAmerican Normative Culture (ENC)	1. How familiar is the child/family with ENC?
	2. How much experience does the child/family have participating in this culture?
	3. How skilled is the child/family at negotiating within this culture (e.g., accomplishing desired activities/goals)?
Degree of acculturation into U.S. early intervention/early childhood special education culture	1. How familiar is the child/family with early intervention/early childhood special education culture (e.g., rules and expectations)?
	2. How much experience does the child/family have participating in this culture?
	3. How skilled is the child/family at negotiating within this culture (e.g., accomplishing desired activities/goals)?

From Barrera, I., Corso, R.M., & Macpherson, D. (2003). *Skilled Dialogue: Strategies for Responding to Cultural Diversity in Early Childhood* (pp. 232–236). Baltimore: Paul H. Brookes Publishing Co.; adapted by permission.
In *Using Skilled Dialogue to Transform Challenging Interactions: Honoring Identity, Voice, and Connection* by Isaura Barrera and Lucinda Kramer

Guide to Identifying Cultural Data (cont.)

Developmental/curricular area	Questions to answer
Sense of self (e.g., relative weight on independence, dependence, and interdependence)	1. How does the family define autonomy? To what degree is it valued?
	2. To what degree is cooperation and group interaction/support valued?
	3. What are the characteristics of persons with high credibility in the family's culture? Which characteristics/behaviors seem to be most highly valued?
Perceptions of identity and competence	1. How do family members define themselves; (e.g., by ethnic, professional, or other labels; by personal attributes)?
	2. Which characteristics denote competence?
Roles and rules associated with parenting and child rearing	1. How would family members describe "good" parenting?
	2. What skills/attributes do they consider desirable in a "well-brought-up" child?
	3. What roles do different family members play in child rearing? Who is responsible for what?
Knowledge and experience regarding power and social positioning	1. What is the family's experience regarding social and personal power? In what situations, if any, would family members describe themselves as powerless or "at a disadvantage"?
	2. Does the family belong to and identify with a group with "minority" status?

From Barrera, I., Corso, R.M., & Macpherson, D. (2003). *Skilled Dialogue: Strategies for Responding to Cultural Diversity in Early Childhood* (pp. 232–236). Baltimore: Paul H. Brookes Publishing Co.; adapted by permission.
In *Using Skilled Dialogue to Transform Challenging Interactions: Honoring Identity, Voice, and Connection*
by Isaura Barrera and Lucinda Kramer

Guide to Identifying Cultural Data (cont.)

Developmental/curricular area	Questions to answer
Values/beliefs/skills associated with instrumental and emotional support (e.g., gaining access to external resources and getting personal support)	1. How does the family obtain support? What sources are valued?
	2. When does the family believe that it is acceptable to seek instrumental support? Emotional support?
Sensory-Cognitive Funds of knowledge: what type of knowledge is valued; concept structures and definitions (e.g., how *family* is defined)	1. What areas of knowledge are valued and supported by the family?
	2. About what are the family members very knowledgeable?
	3. Are funds of knowledge primarily personal, communal, or institutionalized?
	4. To what degree are funds of knowledge oral? To what degree are they written?
	5. What role does the family's cultural identity (or identities) play in its funds of knowledge?
Preferred strategies for acquiring new learning	1. What are the child's/family's preferred strategies for learning (e.g., modeling, questioning)?
	2. To what degree are the strategies explicit and direct? To what degree are they implicit and indirect?
	3. To what degree are the strategies oral? To what degree are they nonverbal?
	4. How do different family members teach the child something that they consider important?
	5. Which of Gardner's (1993) seven intelligences tends to be favored?

From Barrera, I., Corso, R.M., & Macpherson, D. (2003). *Skilled Dialogue: Strategies for Responding to Cultural Diversity in Early Childhood* (pp. 232–236). Baltimore: Paul H. Brookes Publishing Co.; adapted by permission.
In *Using Skilled Dialogue to Transform Challenging Interactions: Honoring Identity, Voice, and Connection* by Isaura Barrera and Lucinda Kramer

Guide to Identifying Cultural Data (cont.)

Developmental/curricular area	Questions to answer
Preferred strategies for problem solving and decision making	1. What are the child's/family's preferred strategies for problem solving and decision making? Do these differ according to certain characteristics of the problem or situation? If so, how?
	2. To what degree is problem solving or decision making independent? To what degree is problem solving or decision making a cooperative activity? If viewed as cooperative, who gets involved in the process?
	3. To what degree the are strategies linear? To what degree are they circular or global?
	4. To what degree is problem solving deductive? To what degree is it inductive?
Worldview (i.e., assumptions about how the world works and about what is "right" and what is "wrong")	1. How does the family tend to explain events such as their child's developmental challenges?
	2. What assumptions does the family hold about how the world works (e.g., mechanistic, organic-ecological)?
	3. What views do family members express about cultural and other differences? Do they favor the view that there is only one "right" way, or do they accept that multiple realities can exist?

From Barrera, I., Corso, R.M., & Macpherson, D. (2003). *Skilled Dialogue: Strategies for Responding to Cultural Diversity in Early Childhood* (pp. 232–236). Baltimore: Paul H. Brookes Publishing Co.; adapted by permission.
In *Using Skilled Dialogue to Transform Challenging Interactions: Honoring Identity, Voice, and Connection* by Isaura Barrera and Lucinda Kramer

Skilled Dialogue Self-Assessment

Choosing Relationship over Control

PRE Skill Level: 1 2 3 4   **POST Skill Level: 1 2 3 4**
(Circle the number that best describes your skill level; see descriptions below.)

LEVELS

1. **BASIC AWARENESS:** I have conceptual understanding of this disposition. Given scenarios, I can distinguish between choosing relationship and choosing control.

2. **BEGINNING APPLICATIONS:** I can give examples and nonexamples to illustrate this disposition.

3. **INTERMEDIATE APPLICATIONS:** I can suspend my agenda in favor of relationship in at least some situations where there is no disagreement or only mild disagreement.

4. **SKILLED APPLICATIONS:** I can suspend my agenda in all or almost all situations even when there is significant disagreement or diversity of perspectives.

Welcoming

PRE Skill Level: 1 2 3 4   **POST Skill Level: 1 2 3 4**
(Circle the number that best describes your skill level; see descriptions below.)

LEVELS

1. **BASIC AWARENESS:** I can describe this strategy and recognize it if given a specific scenario.

2. **BEGINNING APPLICATIONS:** I can give examples and nonexamples to illustrate this strategy.

3. **INTERMEDIATE APPLICATIONS:** I can greet the other with interest and warmth and believe that his or her behaviors/ perspectives are as evidence based as my own (in at least some situations).

4. **SKILLED APPLICATIONS:** I consistently greet the other with interest and warmth and believe that his or her behaviors/perspectives are as evidence based as my own even when I disagree strongly with him or her or do not value his or her perspectives.

Setting the Stage for Miracles

PRE Skill Level: 1 2 3 4   **POST Skill Level: 1 2 3 4**
(Circle the number that best describes your skill level; see descriptions below.)

LEVELS

1. **BASIC AWARENESS:** I have conceptual understanding of this disposition. Given scenarios, I can distinguish between setting the stage for miracles and not doing so.

2. **BEGINNING APPLICATIONS:** I can generate examples and nonexamples to illustrate this disposition.

3. **INTERMEDIATE APPLICATIONS:** I can remain open to outcomes and/or conclusions other than those I believe best or can predict based on existing data in at least some situations.

4. **SKILLED APPLICATIONS:** I can remain open to outcomes other than those I believe are best or can predict based on existing data in most if not all situations AND actively seek outcomes responsive to the other's needs/ perspectives as well as my own.

Allowing

PRE Skill Level: 1 2 3 4   **POST Skill Level: 1 2 3 4**
(Circle the number that best describes your skill level; see descriptions below.)

LEVELS

1. **BASIC AWARENESS:** I can describe this strategy and recognize it if given a specific scenario.

2. **BEGINNING APPLICATIONS:** I can give examples and nonexamples to illustrate this strategy.

3. **INTERMEDIATE APPLICATIONS:** I can release my judgments and interpretations of the other's behaviors or perspectives in at least some situations; that is, I can allow the other to act/believe as he or she does without imposing my judgments or trying to correct him or her.

4. **SKILLED APPLICATIONS:** I consistently refrain from defending/privileging my perspective and allow the other to act/believe as he or she does without imposing my own judgments or interpretations.

Skilled Dialogue Self-Assessment (cont.)

Sense-Making

PRE Skill Level: 1 2 3 4 POST Skill Level: 1 2 3 4
(Circle the number that best describes your skill level; see descriptions below.)

LEVELS	
1	BASIC AWARENESS: I can describe this strategy and recognize it if given a specific scenario.
2	BEGINNING APPLICATIONS: I can give examples and nonexamples to illustrate this strategy.
3	INTERMEDIATE APPLICATIONS: I can usually establish reciprocal contexts and elicit the other's stories and perspectives.
4	SKILLED APPLICATIONS: I can truthfully say and believe most if not all of the time that if I was in the other's shoes I would probably do/believe as he or she does.

Joining

PRE Skill Level: 1 2 3 4 POST Skill Level: 1 2 3 4
(Circle the number that best describes your skill level; see descriptions below.)

LEVELS	
1	BASIC AWARENESS: I can describe this strategy and recognize it if given a specific scenario.
2	BEGINNING APPLICATIONS: I can give examples and nonexamples to illustrate this strategy.
3	INTERMEDIATE APPLICATIONS: I can usually identify with the other's feelings, beliefs, and/or behaviors and remember when I have felt, thought, and/or behaved in a similar fashion.
4	SKILLED APPLICATIONS: I can consistently perceive how the other and I are each reflecting similar or complementary aspects of the same perspective or behavior.

Appreciating

PRE Skill Level: 1 2 3 4 POST Skill Level: 1 2 3 4
(Circle the number that best describes your skill level; see descriptions below.)

LEVELS	
1	BASIC AWARENESS: I can describe this strategy and recognize it if given a specific scenario.
2	BEGINNING APPLICATIONS: I can give examples and nonexamples to illustrate this strategy.
3	INTERMEDIATE APPLICATIONS: I can identify *gold nuggets* (i.e., what is of value in the other's perspective/behavior) at least some of the time.
4	SKILLED APPLICATIONS: I can really believe and say that I have learned something of value from the other in all or almost all situations.

Harmonizing

PRE Skill Level: 1 2 3 4 POST Skill Level: 1 2 3 4
(Circle the number that best describes your skill level; see descriptions below.)

LEVELS	
1	BASIC AWARENESS: I can describe this strategy and recognize it if given a specific scenario.
2	BEGINNING APPLICATIONS: I can give examples and nonexamples to illustrate this strategy.
3	INTERMEDIATE APPLICATIONS: I can usually come up with at least one "third choice" that capitalizes on both my strengths and those of the other.
4	SKILLED APPLICATIONS: I can consistently facilitate brainstorming and identify 3rd Space options that meet the other's stated need(s) as well as my own.

Using Skilled Dialogue to Transform Challenging Interactions: Honoring Identity, Voice, and Connection
by Isaura Barrera and Lucinda Kramer

Skilled Dialogue Reflection Guide

I Description of Interaction

Participants:

Setting:

Purpose/Problem:

History (e.g., Was this a first meeting? Had there been previous meetings?):

II Overall Evaluation of Interaction

Use of Skilled Dialogue:

1 (Limited/weak)	2	**3** (Okay)	4	**5** (Strong)

Level of Satisfaction with Outcome(s):

1 (Low)	2	**3** (Okay)	4	**5** (High)

Comments:

III   Specific Analysis of Skilled Dialogue Dispositions and Strategies

Choosing Relationship over Control	Setting the Stage for Miracles
To what degree was I willing to choose relationship over control? **1** (Low)　2　**3** (Some)　4　**5** (High) Examples: What helped or hindered my willingness to set this disposition?	To what degree was I willing to set the stage for miracles? **1** (Low)　2　**3** (Some)　4　**5** (High) Examples: What helped or hindered my willingness to set this disposition?

Strategies

To what degree was **Welcoming** present? **1** (Low)　2　**3** (Some)　4　**5** (High) Examples: What helped or hindered my willingness to welcome the other person?	To what degree was **Allowing** present? **1** (Low)　2　**3** (Some)　4　**5** (High) Examples: What helped or hindered my willingness to allow the other person to hold and express his or her perspective?
To what degree was **Sense-Making** present? **1** (Low)　2　**3** (Some)　4　**5** (High) Examples: What helped or hindered my ability to make sense of the other person's behaviors, beliefs, and/or perspectives?	To what degree was **Appreciating** present? **1** (Low)　2　**3** (Some)　4　**5** (High) Examples: What helped or hindered my ability to appreciate the other person's behaviors, beliefs, and/or perspectives?
To what degree was **Joining** present? **1** (Low)　2　**3** (Some)　4　**5** (High) Examples: What helped or hindered my willingness to join with the other person and see how our diverse behaviors, beliefs, and/or perspectives were connected?	To what degree was **Harmonizing** present? **1** (Low)　2　**3** (Some)　4　**5** (High) Examples: What helped or hindered my ability to harmonize diverse behaviors, beliefs, and/or perspectives with the other person's?

Use the back of this sheet for additional comments if necessary.

Index

Page numbers followed by *f* indicate figures; those followed by *t* indicate tables.

Acculturation, 11
  see also Cultural diversity
Actions, *see* Agency, models of
Adult–adult interactions, case examples
  practitioner, child, and parent, 110–112,
    195–212
  practitioner/teacher and parent,
    182–187, 190–193
  supervisor and practitioner, 178–182
  two practitioners, 187–190
Adult–child interactions, case examples
  practitioner, child, and parent, 110–112,
    195–212
  teacher and child, 212–217
  teacher and child with autism,
    217–222
Agency, models of
  behavioral repertoires and, 22, 22*f*
  contrasting models, 152
  types of, 23–27, 23*t*, 25*t*, 27*t*
  worksheet for exploring, 32*t*
Allowing strategy
  behavioral indicators, 121*t*, 124, 172*t*
  case examples, 101, 126–129, 127*t*
  critical aspects, 121–124, 121*t*
  examples and nonexamples, 124–125,
    125*t*
  overview, 97–98, 109, 120, 121*t*
  self-reflection questions, 125–126, 126*t*,
    172*t*
Anchored Understanding of Diversity, 35,
  52–57
Appreciating strategy
  behavioral indicators, 140*t*, 142–143,
    173*t*
  case examples, 102, 145–147, 146*t*
  critical aspects, 140–142, 140*t*
  examples and nonexamples, 143–144,
    143*t*
  overview, 98–100, 109, 139–140, 140*t*
  self-reflection questions, 144–145, 144*t*,
    172*t*
Assertive Discipline behavioral approach,
  246–248
Attachment theory
  Choosing Relationship over Control, 17
  developmental discipline, 10
Autism, individuals with
  need for reciprocity, 132
  teacher and child case example,
    217–222

Behavioral approaches
  Assertive Discipline, 246–248
  child self-management, 242–243
  Cooperative Discipline, 245–246
  Discipline with Dignity, 248
  limitations of, 7–8
  Positive Behavioral Interventions and
    Supports (PBIS), 241–242
  Positive Discipline, 244–245
Behavioral indicators
  Allowing strategy, 121*t*, 124, 172*t*
  Appreciating strategy, 140*t*, 142–143, 173*t*
  Harmonizing strategy, 159*t*, 173*t*
  Joining strategy, 153*t*, 155, 173*t*
  Sense-Making strategy, 136*t*, 137–138,
    173*t*
  Welcoming strategy, 116–117, 116*t*, 172*t*
Behavioral literacy, cultural context and,
  11–12, 12*f*
Behavioral scripts, 117, 153
Behaviors
  behavioral languages, 28–31
  behavioral repertoires, 22, 22*f*, 135
  contrasting behavioral perceptions, 67*t*
  cultural context of, 15–16
  envisioning change, 156
  making sense of, 61–62
  negative behavior as exaggerated posi-
    tive behavior, 82, 100, 134, 141–142
  perceived differences in, 16–17
  viewed as rocks or diamonds, 18, 21
  worksheet for exploring diverse
    perspectives, 29*t*, 32*t*
  see also Challenging behavior; Differences
    in behavior
Belief systems, perceptions of behavior
  and, 17
Bilingualism, 20, 75
Body language, *see* Nonverbal messages
Boundaries
  awareness and acknowledgment of, 41–43
  perception of differences as, 20–21
  in 3rd Space, 76, 77

Case analysis
  behavioral indicators, 172*t*–173*t*, 174
  practice cases, 227–234
  prompt questions, 172*t*–173*t*, 174
  Skilled Dialogue Reflection Guide, 171,
    177, 195, 261–262

Case examples
    Allowing strategy, 101, 127*t*, 128, 129
    Appreciating strategy, 102, 145–146, 146*t*
    Choosing Relationship over Control,
        64–65
    Harmonizing strategy, 103, 162–164, 163*t*
    Joining strategy, 102–103, 162–164, 163*t*
    practice cases, 227–234
    practitioner, child, and parent inter-
        actions, 110–112, 195–212
    practitioner–practitioner interactions,
        187–190
    practitioner/teacher and parent inter-
        actions, 182–187, 190–193
    reciprocity, 38–39, 44–45
    respect, 38–39, 41–43
    responsiveness, 38–39, 48–49
    Sense-Making strategy, 101–102, 145–146,
        146*t*
    Setting the Stage for Miracles, 84–86
    supervisor and practitioner interactions,
        178–182
    teacher and child interactions, 195–208,
        212–217
    teacher and child with autism, 217–222
    Welcoming strategy, 101, 127*t*, 128, 129
Challenging behavior
    Choosing Relationship over Control,
        57–58
    example of diverse perspectives, 28, 29*t*,
        30
    perceived differences in, 15–16
    as request for recognition, 2
    responses to, 7
    Sense-Making perspective, 135
    viewed as rocks or diamonds, 18, 21
    see also Behavioral approaches
Child self-management, 242–243
Choosing Relationship over Control
    Anchored Understanding of Diversity
        and, 52–57
    critical aspects, 59–64, 60*t*
    definitions and overview, 13, 34*t*, 35,
        51–52, 53*t*
    diverse behavioral contexts, 57–59
    examples, 53*t*, 64–65
    purposes of, 52, 53*t*
    resources, 68–70
    respect and, 60–61, 65–66
    strategies associated with, 94–97, 94*t*
Classroom management skills of teachers,
    246–248
Cognitive anchoring of relationships, 52–57
Cognitive/linguistic development, vulner-
    ability of, 5
Collaboration
    Appreciating strategy, 141
    emphasis of in Skilled Dialogue, 7

Colleagues, interactions among, *see*
        Adult–adult interactions, case
        examples
Communication
    direct and indirect responses, 117–118
    messages, explicit recognition of, 62–63
    willingness to change messages, 64
Complementary nature of diversity, 63–64,
    79–80, 123–124, 149
Conjoint models of agency
    example of challenging behavior, 29*t*, 30
    overview, 23, 23*t*, 25–27, 25*t*, 27*t*
    worksheet for exploring, 32*t*
Connection, honoring, *see* Responsiveness
Contractual–structural conjoint model of
        agency
    example of challenging behavior, 29*t*, 30
    overview, 23, 23*t*, 25–26, 25*t*
    worksheet for exploring, 32*t*
Contradictions
    Allowing strategy and, 121–122
    complementary nature of, 63–64, 79–80,
        123–124
    paradoxes, 87, 100, 110, 140, 158–160
    perceptions of differences as, 19–20, 21
    reframing, 158–160
Control
    contrasted with relationships, 8, 17
    definition, 51
Cooperative Discipline behavioral
        approach, 245–246
Creativity, *see* Setting the Stage for
        Miracles
Cultural diversity
    as basis for perception of differences,
        15–16, 57
    behavioral literacy in cultural contexts,
        11–12, 12*f*
    EuroAmerican Normative Culture (ENC)
        perceptions of, 18–21
    finding value in, 82
    Guide to Identifying Cultural Data, 58,
        137, 254–258
    layers of culture, 12*f*
    welcoming scripts, 117
    see also EuroAmerican Normative Culture
        (ENC)
Curiosity, sense of, 61, 136–137

Delayed gratification, *see* Child self-
        management
Dialogue, definitions of, 33, 37
Dichotomies, *see* Dualistic space
        perspective
Differences in behavior
    Choosing Relationship over Control,
        57–59

complementary nature of, 63–64, 79–80,
    123–124, 149
contrasting behavioral perceptions, 67t
culture as basis for, 15–16
EuroAmerican Normative Culture (ENC)
    perceptions of, 18–21
gold nuggets, identifying, 67t, 81–82, 99,
    133–134, 140–141
perceptions of, 16–17
reciprocity and, 43–46
respect and, 39–43
responsiveness and, 46–49
welcoming behavior, 72–73
willingness to stay with tension of,
    78–79, 98, 121
Discipline with Dignity behavioral
    approach, 248
Disjoint model of agency
    example of challenging behavior, 28,
        29t, 30
    overview, 23, 23t, 24–25, 25t
    worksheet for exploring, 32t
Dispositions
    definition, 34
    interactions with qualities and strategies,
        93, 104–105, 108, 168
    overview, 34t, 35
    sequencing by, 103, 104–105
    setting, 169–170
    see also Choosing Relationship over
        Control; Setting the Stage for Miracles
Disrespect, 38, 40, 41, 114
    see also Respect
Diversity
    life-enhancing nature of, 43, 132
    see also Differences in behavior
Dualistic space perspective, 75, 76–77, 80

ENC, see EuroAmerican Normative
    Culture
Equal competency, assumption of, 60, 116
EuroAmerican Normative Culture (ENC)
    common perceptions of differences,
        18–21
    definition, 15
    disjoint model of agency and, 24
    dualistic space perspective, 75
Evidence-based beliefs
    acceptance of diverse behaviors, 60, 116
    as basis for Skilled Dialogue, 2, 8–12

Face-to-face interactions, 55–57
Families, case examples, 110–112,
    182–187, 190–193, 195–212
Functional Behavioral Assessment (FBA),
    241–242

Goals
    discerning intentions of others, 37, 134,
        142
    setting for children, 2
Gold nuggets
    Appreciating strategy and, 99, 140–141
    examples, 67t
    reciprocity and, 133–134
    willingness to identify, 81–82
Guide to Identifying Cultural Data, 58,
    137, 254–258

Harmonizing strategy
    behavioral indicators, 159t, 173t
    case examples, 103, 162–164, 163t
    critical aspects, 158–160, 159t
    examples and nonexamples, 160–161,
        161t
    overview, 100, 109–110, 157–158, 159t
    self-reflection questions, 161–162, 162t,
        173t
Horizontal sequencing of strategies, 103,
    104

Identity, honoring, see Respect
Impulse control, see Child self-
    management
Inspiration, compared to motivation, 10–11
Intentions, discerning, 37, 134, 142
Interpretations, release of, 79
I–Thou versus I–It relationships, 2, 8, 9–10,
    13, 151–152, 175

Joining strategy
    behavioral indicators, 153t, 155, 173t
    case examples, 102–103, 162–164,
        163t
    critical aspects, 153–155, 153t
    examples and nonexamples, 155, 156t
    overview, 95–97, 109–110, 152–153, 153t
    self-reflection questions, 155–157, 157t,
        173t

Language
    behavior as, 28–31
    see also Communication
Learner's attitude and mindset, developing,
    61, 136–137
Learning from others' behaviors, 82–83,
    100, 142, 144–145
Learning theory, 6, 17
Listening
    Allowing strategy, 124
    Welcoming strategy, 117

Messages
    explicit recognition of, 62–63
    personal message for development of
        self-management skills, 243
    willingness to change, 64
Mindfulness, children's self-esteem and,
    37–38
Miracles
    definition, 71
    see also Setting the Stage for Miracles
Models of agency, see Agency, models of
Motivation
    compared to inspiration, 10–11
    primary happiness and, 10

Negative behavior as exaggerated positive
    behavior, 82, 100, 134, 141–142
Negative/null thinking, 18–19
Nonjudgmental information gathering,
    61–62, 137
Nonverbal messages
    Allowing strategy, 125t
    Appreciating strategy, 143t
    Harmonizing strategy, 161t
    Joining strategy, 156t
    Sense-Making strategy, 138t
    Welcoming strategy, 116, 116t, 118t
    willingness to change, 64
Nurturing children's spirits and sense of
    self, 1, 2, 5–7, 8, 12, 13, 16, 17, 21,
    31, 107, 127, 159, 160, 167, 175

Paradoxical thinking, 87, 89, 100, 110,
    140, 158–160
    see also Setting the Stage for Miracles
Parents, case examples involving, 110–112,
    182–187, 190–193, 195–212
PBIS, see Positive Behavioral Interventions
    and Supports
Perceptions
    reframing, 83, 142, 158–160
    see also Differences in behavior
Perspective taking, 62, 137
Phases, in Skilled Dialogue, 168–171,
    169f
Positive Behavioral Interventions and
    Supports (PBIS), 241–242
Positive Discipline behavioral approach,
    244–245
Possibility, see Setting the Stage for Miracles
Practitioners
    practitioner and parent interactions,
        182–187, 190–193
    practitioner, child, and parent inter-
        actions, 110–112, 195–212
    reflections of, 222–225

supervisor and practitioner interactions,
    178–182
teacher and child interactions, 195–208,
    212–217
teacher and child with autism, 217–222
two practitioners case example, 187–190
see also specific strategies

Qualities
    interactions with dispositions and
        strategies, 93, 104–105, 108, 168
    sequencing by, 103, 104
    see also Reciprocity; Respect;
        Responsiveness
Questions
    direct and indirect, 137
    see also Self-reflection

Reciprocity
    Appreciating strategy, 98–100, 102, 109,
        139–145, 140t
    effect on self-esteem, 37–38
    establishing (Phase III of the Skilled
        Dialogue process), 170
    examples and nonexamples, 43t, 138t,
        143t
    interaction with dispositions and
        strategies, 104, 108, 168
    overview, 34t, 43–46, 131–134
    Sense-Making strategy, 95, 101–102, 109,
        134–139, 136t
    vignette, 38–39, 44–45
Reflection, see Self-reflection
Reframing perceptions, 83, 142, 158–160
Relational–interpersonal conjoint model
    of agency
    examples, 29t, 30, 152
    overview, 23, 23t, 26–27, 27t
    worksheet for exploring, 32t
Relationships
    Anchored Understanding of Diversity,
        35, 52–57
    contrasted with control, 8, 9, 17
    definition, 51
    development of trust and acceptance
        with adults, 6
    emphasis of in Skilled Dialogue, 7
    I–Thou versus I–It, 2, 8, 9–10, 13,
        151–152, 175
    symmetrical relationships, 123
    see also Choosing Relationship over
        Control
Respect
    Allowing strategy, 97–98, 109, 120–126,
        121t
    boundaries and, 41–43

building (Phase II of the Skilled Dialogue process), 170
Choosing Relationship over Control and, 60–61, 65–66
effect on self-esteem, 37–38
examples and nonexamples, 40*t*, 118*t*, 125*t*
interaction with dispositions and strategies, 104, 108, 168
overview, 34*t*, 39–43, 113–115
unconditional respect, 61, 115, 116
vignette, 38–39, 41–43
Welcoming strategy, 94–95, 109, 115–120, 116*t*
Responsiveness
developing (Phase IV of the Skilled Dialogue process), 170–171
effect on self-esteem, 37–38
examples and nonexamples, 47*t*, 156*t*, 161*t*
Harmonizing strategy, 100, 109–110, 157–162, 159*t*
interaction with dispositions and strategies, 104, 108, 168
Joining strategy, 95–97, 109–110, 152–157, 153*t*
overview, 34*t*, 46–49, 149–152
vignette, 38–39, 48–49

Schoolwide behavioral support, 242
Self, sense of, 5–7, 107, 167
Self-esteem
Cooperative Discipline approach and, 145–146
Discipline with Dignity approach and, 248
effect of adult mindfulness on, 37–38
Self-management of children, 242–243
Self-reflection
Allowing strategy, 125–126, 126*t*, 172*t*
Appreciating strategy, 144–145, 144*t*, 172*t*
case example, 222–225
Harmonizing strategy, 161–162, 162*t*, 173*t*
Joining strategy, 155–157, 157*t*, 173*t*
as Phase V of the Skilled Dialogue process, 171
prompt questions for case analysis, 172*t*–173*t*, 174
Sense-Making strategy, 138–139, 139*t*, 172*t*
Skilled Dialogue Reflection Guide, 171, 177, 195, 261–262
Welcoming strategy, 119–120, 119*t*, 172*t*
Sense-Making strategy
behavioral indicators, 136*t*, 137–138, 173*t*

case examples, 101–102, 145–147, 146*t*
critical aspects, 136–137, 136*t*
examples and nonexamples, 138, 138*t*
overview, 95, 109, 134–135, 136*t*
self-reflection questions, 138–139, 139*t*, 172*t*
Sequencing
of Skilled Dialogue phases, 168–171, 249–250
of Skilled Dialogue strategies, 103–105
Setting the Stage for Miracles
contrasted with prescriptive outcomes, 8
critical aspects, 77–84, 78*t*
definitions and overview, 13, 71–74, 72*t*
examples, 72*t*, 84–86
overview, 34*t*, 35, 168
resources, 88–92
strategies associated with, 94*t*, 97–101
3rd Space, 35, 74–77, 91–92
Singular space perspective, 76
Skilled Dialogue approach
evidence-based beliefs, 2, 8–12
framework for, 33–35, 34*t*
frequently asked questions, 249–251
overview, 12–13, 21, 167–171, 249
process and phases, 168–171, 169*f*, 249–250
Reflection Guide for, 171, 177, 195, 260–261
Self-Assessment form for, 258–259
sequencing, 103–105, 168–171, 249–250
web site, 177, 195, 251
see also specific strategies
Skilled Dialogue Self-Assessment form, 174, 259–260
Skills, *see* Dispositions
Social contexts
behaviors and, 57–59, 62–64
recognizing behavior as social, 153–155
Social/emotional development
focus on as contradictory to nurturing and sense of self, 6
Positive Discipline approach, 244–245
vulnerability of, 5
Stories
elicitation techniques, 137
release of, 79, 101, 122–123
Strategies
interactions with qualities and dispositions, 93, 103–105, 108, 168
overview, 93–101, 94*t*
sequencing, 103–105
see also Case examples; *specific strategies*
Supervisor and practitioner case example, 178–182

Teachers
  classroom management skills, 246–248
  reflections of, 222–225
  teacher and child interactions, 195–208,
    212–217
  teacher and child with autism, 217–222
  see also Practitioners; *specific strategies*
Third choices, 100, 109–110
3rd Space
  Allowing strategy and, 120
  overview, 35, 74–77
  resources, 91–92
  responsiveness and, 150
  see also Setting the Stage for Miracles
Threes, thinking in, 83
Trust Bridge Exercise, 91–92

Unanchored perspective of relationships,
    53–54
Unconditional respect, 61, 115, 116

Vertical sequencing of strategies, 103,
    104–105
Vignettes, *see* Case examples
Voice, honoring, *see* Reciprocity

Walls, in 3rd space, 77, 150
Welcoming strategy
  behavioral indicators, 116–117, 116*t*,
    172*t*
  case examples, 101, 126–129, 127*t*
  critical aspects, 116, 116*t*
  examples and nonexamples, 117–119,
    118*t*
  overview, 94–95, 109, 115, 116*t*
  self-reflection questions, 119–120, 119*t*,
    172*t*

Zone of proximal development, 132,
    152–153